MERTON PUBL

MORDEN LIBRARY,
MORDEN ROAD,
LONDON, SW19 3DA
Telephone No: 01-542 1701
01-542 2842

PL22 (rev)

Membership Cards:	Readers are given a membership card which entitles them to borrow four books at any one time. A reader must present his membership card at the issue desk each time a book is borrowed. Readers are responsible for all books borrowed on their membership cards, the loss of which must be notified as soon as possible. A charge of 5p. will be made for the replacement of a lost membership card. Membership cards are not transferable.
Issue of Books:	A date card is placed in the pocket of every book when issued to show the date on which the book is due for return. The card also bears the serial number of the loan. THIS CARD MUST ALWAYS BE KEPT IN THE POCKET.
Period of Loan:	Books are issued for a period of 21 days. Fines will be charged on books retained beyond the period allowed.
Renewals:	Provided they are not reserved by another reader, books may be renewed by post or telephone, or in person, by giving the serial number on the date cards, the dates due and the author and title of each book.
Return of Books:	Service at the counter would be greatly assisted if readers would kindly open their books at the front when returning them.
Exchange of Tickets:	Readers desiring to transfer to a library where photo-charging or computer charging is not used, are asked to exchange their membership card for conventional tickets.
Infection:	If this book has been in contact with any notifiable disease, it should NOT be returned to the Library but handed to the Public Health Inspector.

RELATIVE DEPRIVATION
AND
SOCIAL JUSTICE

Reports of
The Institute of Community Studies

RELATIVE DEPRIVATION AND SOCIAL JUSTICE

A Study of Attitudes to Social Inequality in Twentieth-Century England

by

W. G. Runciman

LONDON
ROUTLEDGE & KEGAN PAUL

First published 1966
by Routledge & Kegan Paul Ltd.
Broadway House, 68–74 Carter Lane
London, E.C.4V 5EL

Printed in Great Britain by
Redwood Press Limited
Trowbridge, Wiltshire

© *W. G. Runciman* 1966

Second impression 1967
Third impression 1972

ISBN 0 7100 3923 9

TO
MY FATHER

CONTENTS

vii

Contents

TABLES

ix

Tables

x

Jede sinnvolle Wertung fremden Wollens kann nur Kritik aus einer eigenen 'Weltanschauung' heraus, Bekämpfung des fremden Ideals von Boden eines eigenen Ideals aus sein.

WEBER

(Any meaningful assessment of someone else's aspirations can only be a criticism of them in the light of one's personal view of the world, a struggle against alien ideals from the standpoint of one's own.)

PREFACE

THIS study would not have been possible without the support of the Institute of Community Studies and its Director, Dr. Michael Young, to whom my chief thanks are due. The Institute both financed the pilot survey carried out in 1961 and also sponsored the application for a grant from the Elmgrant Trust which covered the greater part of the costs of the main survey described in Part Three of this book. I am much indebted also to the Fellows' Research Fund of Trinity College, Cambridge and a private donor for the funds which made it possible to cover the remaining costs of the survey.

The interviewing in the pilot survey was done with the help of Mrs. Dorothy Losey, Mrs. Norma Phillips and most of all Miss M. L. Doughty. In the main survey, Mr. Donald Monk of Research Services Ltd. gave generously of his help. Most of the analysis of the survey was carried out in the academic year 1962–3 when I was a visitor at the Survey Research Center of the University of California at Berkeley. I am grateful to Professor Charles Y. Glock for allowing me to use the facilities of the Center and to Professor Kingsley Davis for extending to me the hospitality of the Department of Sociology. In addition, I am grateful to many individual members of the Survey Research Center for their helpfulness.

Professors Asa Briggs, Robert K. Merton and John Rawls very kindly read one or more chapters of an earlier draft and gave me a number of valuable criticisms. The whole draft was also read by Dr. Michael Young and Mr. Peter Willmott, whose suggestions did much to remedy my failings of presentation and style. The deficiencies which remain are my own responsibility entirely.

My greatest debt is to my wife, whose assistance was invaluable throughout the project, and who in particular did much of the work which lies behind Parts Two and Three of the book.

Any book which ventures at the same time into the three separate fields of social history, social psychology and political theory runs the risk not only of deterring the general reader but of failing to satisfy the specialist in any one of the three. Historians of twentieth-century Britain will not need to be reminded of the attitude of the General Council of the T.U.C. to the General Strike; but they may want a fuller treatment of the slender evidence for the political attitudes of the mass of urban workers in the inter-war period. Social psychologists will not need a summary of the results of the best-known experiments on reference groups; but they may want to see more of the details of the tables run in the analysis of the sample survey. Political theorists will not need to be given a definition of Pareto optimality; but they may want an expanded discussion of the objections which can be raised against a contractual theory of justice. I have tried to write in such a way that non-specialists will not find the argument too impenetrable or specialists find it too greatly oversimplified. But such an attempt can never be entirely successful, and I venture only to hope that it may succeed in illustrating how far all three fields on which I have drawn are necessary ingredients of any useful discussion of social inequality.

For the same reason, I have not appended a bibliography which could only be too long for the general reader and too short for the specialist. I have given a list of references, but in no part of the book do these furnish more than a limited and intermittent guide to the relevant literature. In particular, Part Two is not an attempt to summarize, let alone to rewrite, the social history of twentieth-century Britain. Such a résumé as I have given is based entirely on secondary works or on such well-known sources as Hansard, the newspapers and the annual reports of the T.U.C. A full account of the changes in the social structure since 1918 has still to be written; this book is no more than a preliminary exploration of one viewpoint from which they can be described and assessed.

W. G. R.

PART ONE
INTRODUCTION

I

THE STUDY AND
ITS METHODS

A LL societies are inegalitarian. But what is the relation between the inequalities in a society and the feelings of acquiescence or resentment to which they give rise? People's attitudes to social inequalities seldom correlate strictly with the facts of their own position. It might be thought plausible to assume that a person's feelings about the structure of his society should vary with his own location; whatever the system of stratification, should we not expect those at the top to be pleased with it and those at the bottom dissatisfied? But this is not what happens. Dissatisfaction with the system of privileges and rewards in a society is never felt in an even proportion to the degree of inequality to which its various members are subject. Many people at the bottom of society are less resentful of the system, and many nearer to the top are more so, than their actual position appears to warrant. The reactionary peasantry, the affluent radicals, the respectful poor are familiar from the histories of many places and times, and they all have in common that there is a discrepancy between their position of inequality and their acceptance or rejection of it. This discrepancy, moreover, has prompted very different conclusions among political theorists of opposing persuasions. If inequality is bad, then there is a multitude of social differences which those who are the victims of them ought to perceive and resent; if they do not, they must be guilty of 'false consciousness'. But if inequality is inevitable and even good, then those in a subordinate position who willingly accept their place are not only sensible but also virtuous. Once the structure of a society has been examined and its pattern of inequalities mapped out, two questions at once arise, either of which leads in turn to the other: first, what is the relation between institutionalized inequalities and the awareness or resentment of them? And second,

3

which, if any, of these inequalities ought to be perceived and re-sented—whether they are or not—by the standards of social justice?

This book is concerned with both these questions as they apply to twentieth-century Britain. They are large questions, and any dis-cussion of them raises issues of a wider application than one single place and time. But they have a particular and obvious relevance when applied to Britain. Britain is the country where the Industrial Revolution began, and although subsequently overtaken in the lead it is still one of the few which has passed into what it is currently proverbial to describe as 'affluence'. Yet it retains a social structure which in many ways can be described as the most traditional of any industrialized country in the world. Its Socialist government gave the world the phrase 'Welfare State', but its hereditary monarchy has survived with undiminished prestige. Its working class led Marx to predict that advanced capitalism must bring the proletariat to supremacy through revolution, yet the British Labour movement is notorious for its gradualism. Its trade unions staged a General Strike in 1926, but its working-class electorate has repeatedly failed to maintain in power the political party founded to represent its interests. These contradictions have long been familiar to observers of British society and have been variously admired or deplored according to the observer's political taste. But what has in fact deter-mined the actual relation between inequality and the acceptance or resentment of it?

A common assumption is that the radicalism of the under-privi-leged has been steadily assuaged by rising prosperity and the shrewd, if reluctant, reformism of the English governing class. But the relation between inequality and grievance is a great deal subtler than this. As industrialization advanced, it brought with it not only a heightening of prosperity but a heightening of grievance. The expanding proletariat came gradually to share in many of the bene-fits which industrialization yielded; but its members became at the same time increasingly aware that many other benefits, or even rights, were being denied to them. The question to be asked at the outset is whether the resentment of inequalities may not be exacer-bated as often as assuaged by social and economic progress. It is, moreover, a question as hard to answer for the twentieth century as the nineteenth. By the 1950's it had begun to be widely assumed in England both that social inequality had markedly diminished and that this was one of the principal reasons for the seeming decline of working-class radicalism. But both of these assumptions could be called in question. On one side were the arguments that manual workers had caught up with non-manual workers in their level of reward, that careers had increasingly opened to talent, that the ideological issues of the 1930's were dead. But on the other were the arguments that there remained resentments as deeply felt, although of a different kind, that educational and social privilege still persisted, that obsolescent hierarchical institutions were preserved and that the distribution of wealth was not yet as egalitarian as was generally assumed. There were inequalities still visible in the social structure which, however they might compare in degree with those of earlier generations, were sufficient to make the issue of 'false consciousness' as relevant as ever. It is just as difficult for the period after the Second World War as for the 1840's or the 1930's to establish what has in fact been the relation between inequality and grievance and how far this relation has been such as would accord with the requirements of social justice.

The evidence which I shall present on the first of these questions is of two kinds: a résumé of some aspects of the social history of England since 1918 in the light of the relation between inequality and grievance, and the results of a national sample survey carried out in the spring of 1962. The second question obviously requires a different sort of argument; but in the concluding chapters of the book I shall try to show how a modified version of the contractual theory of justice enables it to be answered. At the same time, I shall try to show that not only the relation between inequality and grievance but also the requirements of social justice are different for each of the three kinds, or dimensions, of social inequality generally labelled class, status and power. It follows from this that the relation between actual inequalities and such resentment of them as could be vindicated by appeal to social justice will be different in each case. Only when the distinction is consistently adhered to can we talk clearly about either what is, or what should be, the structure of inequalities in the English (or any other) social system and the attitudes of its members towards them.

This book, therefore, may be described as a work at once of sociology and political philosophy, provided that the term 'sociology' is understood in a qualified sense. It may be that the empirical relationships which I shall suggest between grievance and inequality hold true more widely than for twentieth-century Britain. But it is not my purpose to argue to what extent this might be so. The use of a sample survey might seem to suggest an excursion from social history into social 'science'; but the survey should rather be regarded as a continuation of the historical discussion which precedes it. Indeed, the dependence of the two kinds of evidence is reciprocal: only a survey can furnish quantified evidence for the stated attitudes of a class or nation as a whole; but a survey has little or no meaning

5

except by reference to the events which have shaped the social context in which it was carried out. It can be 'scientific' only to the extent that history itself is a science.

It might also be thought that my borrowing of the term 'relative deprivation' from social psychology suggests an attempt to formulate more rigorous or more generalized conclusions than those of the conventional political theorist or social historian. But 'relative deprivation' and the connected term 'reference group' are used only because they make the discussion of social inequality, whether historical or philosophical, more compact and unambiguous than it would be without them. What I shall say could, perhaps, be rephrased in other terms. But it would have to be much more loosely and circuitously put, and the idea of 'relative deprivation', obvious though it is, provides the key to the complex and fluctuating relation between inequality and grievance.

To emphasize that this study is social 'science' only in a limited sense is not to deny many of the claims made for sample surveys by their practitioners. It is merely to say that the techniques of the sample survey are useful only if they are the servants and not the masters of historical interpretation. Indeed, the value of sample surveys is if anything better demonstrable from the viewpoint of the social historian than of the experimental psychologist. Surveys furnish at best only a weak imitation of controlled experiments; but as source material for the social historian they are uniquely rewarding. Without the evidence of a survey, any account of how a class or a people felt about the social structure in which they lived is very largely conjectural. There are, of course, a whole number of other sources—letters, newspapers, diaries of eyewitnesses and the rest. But not only is there no guarantee of how far the opinions recorded are representative; there is also no means of obtaining the sort of detailed and specific information which is yielded by the cross-tabulation of a sample survey. Such questions as how many people changed their votes between given elections, and for what stated reasons; how far the spokesmen for a class or region typified the grievances of those they claimed to represent; what social characteristics were shared by the supporters of a religious or political movement; whether in times of overt calm the voiceless majority was contented or only apathetic; just how many of the young, or the educated, or the rich, or the churchgoing held given attitudes on the issues of the day—all these questions can be answered from survey data with far greater confidence and precision than could be otherwise attained. From the social historian's viewpoint, therefore, a sample survey is a rich source of evidence about opinions and feelings hitherto beyond his reach.

But just because the survey must be treated as historical and not experimental evidence, it can be very differently interpreted by different historians. It may, like any primary source, rule out a number of rival assertions, provided always that the information which it provides is held to be reliable. But even if interviewers are reliable and informants truthful—which, like chroniclers or diarists or newspaper correspondents, they may not be—a survey cannot yield a definitive explanation or proof. Indeed, it is likely to raise as many questions as it answers. Each of the questions which I have listed as being answerable by a survey only raises in its turn the question 'why?'. And the question 'why?' cannot be settled by simple reference to the pattern of statistical correlation disclosed within the survey material. It can only be settled in the same way and to the same extent as any other question where the historical explanation of human conduct is involved. Nor can the survey validate by itself the psychological assumptions of cause and effect on which historical explanations must rest. By itself, a survey is no more than a snap-shot of the social landscape at one place and time. It may, like an aerial photograph, enable us for the first time to see clearly the outline of the woods and fields; but this only increases our curiosity to look under the trees.

It would therefore be misleading to think of the survey to be described here as testing general hypotheses, whether formulated on the strength of the historical evidence or of some broad social-psychological theory. Language of this kind is commonly used by survey analysts, and it is easy enough to see what is meant by it. But it risks obscuring the fact that the explanations called for cannot be made strictly analogous to those of natural science. To talk of 'hypotheses' suggests both some general validity such that confirmed hypotheses become 'laws' and a procedure of prediction and verification according to the canons of 'scientific method'. But talk of scientific method needs careful definition. In the first place, the facts which a survey discloses are historically unique. Secondly, a consistent correlation, even if predicted in advance, is neither a historical explanation nor even a definitive demonstration that such an explanation is correct. Thirdly, it is immaterial to the validity of an explanation or correlation whether it was predicted beforehand or not. It is true that under certain conditions a falsified prediction might demonstrate an explanation to be incorrect. But a correct explanation, or a correct account of a correlation, will be no less correct if it is arrived at after the event. My purpose, therefore, should merely be described as an attempt to depict some aspects of the relationship between inequality and grievance in England between 1918 and 1962 and to suggest what some of the reasons may have been for this relation. The survey is only a 'test' of the historical evidence in the sense that any fresh primary material affords the historian the chance of rejecting or improving on his previous ideas.

It would likewise be a mistake to regard the survey as furnishing anthropological, as opposed to historical, evidence by which I mean the sort of account of a society or an institution which is given by a 'participant-observer' on the basis of systematic fieldwork. The anthropologist has been able over a period to talk to perhaps every member of a small society, to observe every one of its institutions, and to test the accounts of it which he is given against further observation and hearsay. The survey researcher cannot do this. His material has the advantage that it makes quantitative comparisons possible between the different kinds of people whose opinions or characteristics he wishes to study. But he can neither enlarge upon what his interviewers report to him nor test it in the sense that the anthropologist can. He remains in the situation of the historian presented with a hitherto unknown document. The new source enlarges his possibilities of description to the extent that he believes it can be trusted, and it contributes to the explanations for which he is looking to the extent that it contradicts or fits in with such theories as he has provisionally formulated. But it is not a substitute for fieldwork any more than for an experiment. A sample survey can, like all historical evidence, help theorists of behaviour in their attempts to arrive at general truths about human conduct. But it must be interpreted as historical evidence no less than the sort of material used by social historians for periods before surveys were known. Parts Two and Three of this book, therefore, should be seen as the connected parts of a single argument; the difference between them is one of style, not of kind.

Only Part Four rests on an argument wholly different in kind. But here again, there is a reciprocal link with what precedes it. It is impossible to talk about attitudes to social inequality without raising, if only by implication, the question of social justice. It is likewise impossible to talk about social justice in isolation from any actual system of institutionalized inequalities. Just as there can be alternative interpretations of the empirical relation between inequality and grievance, so there can be alternative views of how it should be assessed by the standard of justice. But if the argument which I shall put forward is correct, then it is possible not only to suggest how grievance has been related to inequality in twentieth-century England but also to show the extent to which grievances have been felt which could be vindicated in principle by appeal to social justice.

II

RELATIVE DEPRIVATION AND THE CONCEPT OF REFERENCE GROUPS

THE related notions of 'relative deprivation' and 'reference group' both derive from a familiar truism: that people's attitudes, aspirations and grievances largely depend on the frame of reference within which they are conceived. Examples readily suggest themselves from everyday experience. A person's satisfactions, even at the most trivial level, are conditioned by his expectations, and the proverbial way to make oneself conscious of one's advantages is to contrast one's situation with that of others worse off than oneself. The frame of reference can work in either of two ways. On the one hand, a man who has been led to expect, shall we say, promotion in his job will be more aggrieved if he fails to achieve it than a man whose ambitions have not been similarly heightened. On the other hand, a man taken to hospital after some minor mishap will feel a good deal less sorry for himself if he is put in a bed next to the victim of a serious accident who has been permanently maimed. The same applies at the level of classes or even nations. Although at first sight a paradox, it has become a commonplace that steady poverty is the best guarantee of conservatism: if people have no reason to expect or hope for more than they can achieve, they will be less discontented with what they have, or even grateful simply to be able to hold on to it. But if, on the other hand, they have been led to see as a possible goal the relative prosperity of some more fortunate community with which they can directly compare themselves, then they will remain discontented with their lot until they have succeeded in catching up. It is this natural reaction which underlies the so-called 'revolution of rising expectations'. The usefulness of the terms 'relative deprivation' and 'reference group' is that they can help both to describe and to explain when and how these familiar psychological effects occur.

9

The term 'relative deprivation' was originally coined by the authors of *The American Soldier*, the large-scale social-psychological study of the American army which was carried out during the Second World War. The authors of *The American Soldier* do not give any rigorous definition of relative deprivation,[1] but its general sense is immediately apparent. If A, who does not have something but wants it, compares himself to B, who does have it, then A is 'relatively deprived' with reference to B. Similarly, if A's expectations are higher than B's, or if he was better off than B in the past, he may when similarly placed to B feel relatively deprived by comparison with him. A strict definition is difficult. But we can roughly say that A is relatively deprived of X when (i) he does not have X, (ii) he sees some other person or persons, which may include himself at some previous or expected time, as having X (whether or not this is or will be in fact the case), (iii) he wants X, and (iv) he sees it as feasible that he should have X. Possession of X may, of course, mean avoidance of or exemption from Y.

The qualification of 'feasibility' is obviously imprecise, but it is necessary in order to exclude fantasy wishes. A man may say with perfect truth that he wants to be as rich as the Aga Khan, or a woman that she wants to be as beautiful as a reigning film star; but to include these under the heading of relative deprivation would rob the term of its value. Despite this restriction, however, relative deprivation retains the merit of being value-neutral as between a feeling of envy and a perception of injustice. To establish what resentment of inequality can be vindicated by an appeal to social justice will require that this distinction should somehow be made. But in determining first of all what is the empirical relation between inequality and grievance, it is important to use a term which in no way begs the distinction between 'legitimate' and 'illegitimate' grievances.

Relative deprivation may vary in magnitude, frequency or degree. The magnitude of a relative deprivation is the extent of the difference between the desired situation and that of the person desiring it (as he sees it). The frequency of a relative deprivation is the proportion of a group who feel it. The degree of a relative deprivation is the intensity with which it is felt. It is obvious that the three need not coincide. The proportion of a group feeling relatively deprived may be quite independent of either the magnitude or the intensity of the relative deprivation, and relative deprivation may be just as keenly felt when its magnitude is small as when it is large. Relative deprivation should always be understood to mean a *sense* of deprivation; a person who is 'relatively deprived' need not be 'objectively'

[1] Samuel A. Stouffer *et al.*, *The American Soldier, I: Adjustment During Army Life* (Princeton, 1949), p. 125.

deprived in the more usual sense that he is demonstrably lacking something. In addition, relative deprivation means that the sense of deprivation is such as to involve a comparison with the imagined situation of some other person or group. This other person or group is the 'reference group', or more accurately the 'comparative reference group'. The addition of 'comparative' is made necessary because 'reference group' can be used in two other senses which will not necessarily overlap with the comparative sense. It can not only mean the group with which a person compares himself; it can also be used to mean either the group from which he derives his standards of comparison or the group from which the comparison is extended and to which he feels that he belongs.

The term itself was first coined by Herbert Hyman in 1942,[2] but the idea behind it can be traced a good deal further back in the literature of social psychology. Like the idea behind relative deprivation, it is simple enough, but to make it more precise it is necessary to deal with a number of difficulties. Quite apart from its different possible senses, the reference 'group' need not be a group at all; it may be a single person or even an abstract idea. This initial disadvantage of the term has been recognized by Hyman himself.[3] But the use of it is now so well established that it does not seem worthwhile to try to replace it with a more general term. We must simply remember that 'reference group behaviour' can be applied to a son whose driving impulse is to emulate his father, or a lapsed Catholic blaspheming in order to emphasize his rejection of the Church, just as much as to a *bourgeois gentilhomme* imitating the habits and attitudes of the aristocracy. It is groups, and particularly classes, with which the present study is mainly concerned; but it is important to emphasize that this by no means exhausts the scope of reference 'group' behaviour.

The major difficulty, however, is that reference groups may carry one or all of the three different senses, and these have not always been adequately distinguished by the writers who have adopted the term. Two of the three senses have been distinguished[4] in terms of

[2] H. H. Hyman, 'The Psychology of Status', *Archives of Psychology* No. 269 (New York, 1942).

[3] *Ibid.*, pp. 25–29; and in 'Reflections on Reference Groups', *Public Opinion Quarterly* XXIV (1960), p. 390. For the same point made by other users of the term, cf. S. M. Eisenstadt, 'Studies in Reference Group Behavior, I: Norms and the Social Structure', *Human Relations* VII (1954), p. 213; T. Shibutani, 'Reference Groups as Perspectives', *American Journal of Sociology* LX (1955), p. 565; and Ralph H. Turner, 'Role-taking, Role Standpoint and Reference Group Behavior', *ibid.* LXI (1956), p. 329.

[4] H. H. Kelley, 'Two Functions of Reference Groups', in G. H. Swanson *et al., Readings in Social Psychology* (2nd edn.; New York, 1952), pp. 410–414.

the 'comparative' and 'normative' function of the reference group. A 'comparative' reference group is the group whose situation or attributes a person contrasts with his own. A 'normative' reference group is the group from which a person takes his standards. Examples of the first might be a prosperous entrepreneur emulating the fortune of his rival, or a clerical worker trying to distinguish his manner of speech from that of manual workers, or a revolutionist trying to secure for his fellow-proletarians the goods and prerogatives of the bourgeoisie. Examples of the second might be a schoolboy imitating his classmates, or a convert to Communism adopting the political attitudes of those whom he regards as the 'true' working class.

The two may overlap, and often do. For example, a manual worker might at the same time envy the wealth of middle-class people and try to act like them, and there would be no inconsistency in this. But an important difference appears when these two functions of reference groups are connected to the idea of relative deprivation. Where a comparative reference group is 'positive' (in the sense that a person wants to share the situation of another group, not to dissociate himself from it), a relative deprivation is necessarily engendered. Where the reference group is a normative one, it may or may not be. Consider the same example of a manual worker who is very conscious of the situation of the 'middle class' (whatever he means by this). If he wants what he sees the middle class as having then he is by definition relatively deprived, and one can speak of the relative deprivation as generated by his choice of reference group. But as his normative reference group, the 'middle class' carries no necessary implications for his sense of relative deprivation. If it leads him to see that he is, say, poorer than most of the normative group, then at the same time as he tries to imitate its standards of consumption a comparison may be generated which makes him feel relatively deprived of a middle-class income. But if it leads him to share the conservative politics of the middle class, it may inhibit those comparisons which a radical political viewpoint might have encouraged him to feel. Only comparative reference groups are bound up by definition with relative deprivation. A normative reference group will generate a relative deprivation only if it embodies an unfavourable comparison at the same time as it sets a standard or imposes an outlook.

The third sense of 'reference group' is the particular role a person has in mind in the context of the inequality which he feels—a proletarian, a corporal, a Negro, a student and so on. This group may or may not be the source of his norms; but whether or not it fulfils the additional function of the normative reference group, it is the basis of the comparison which he makes. Everyone is, of course, in some sense a member of an almost infinite multiplicity of groups, for every attribute which a person shares with others makes him by definition the joint member, with them, of at least this one group. But most of these are irrelevant to any feelings of inequality. The 'membership reference group' is, as it were, the starting-line for the inequality with the comparative reference group by which a feeling of relative deprivation is engendered.

The membership reference group does, however, have to be further distinguished from the common attribute which is shared by both the membership and comparative reference groups and which thereby furnishes the basis for the claim that the inequality should be redressed. A man who says, 'As a skilled worker I am entitled to better pay' may mean either that as a skilled worker he should have the pay to which all skilled workers are entitled, or that as a skilled worker he shares the attribute of better-paid workers which entitles them to their better pay. In the first case, skilled workers are not his membership reference group but the justifying criterion for his feeling of relative deprivation; his membership reference group is only the set of underpaid skilled workers. These may share some further attribute—for example, the lack of an apprenticeship qualification—which gives rise to the inequality between one skilled worker and another; but they may equally well have nothing else in common beyond their occupation, and be paid less than other skilled workers for a variety of separate and extraneous reasons. In the second case, on the other hand, the man believes that as a skilled worker he either is or does something —for example, exercises an uncommon talent or contributes to national productivity—to the same degree as those who are better paid. His membership reference group, therefore, is the class of skilled workers, of whom he feels that some or perhaps all are underpaid, and his justifying criterion is talent or productivity.

There may still appear to be some ambiguity in the notion of the membership reference group, since some inequalities are such that for a person to move to a position of equality with his comparative reference group means ceasing to be what he was, while others are such that he cannot cease to be what he was. A bricklayer who becomes the equal in income of an executive may well do so by ceasing to be a bricklayer; but a Negro bricklayer who becomes the equal in status of white bricklayers does not do so by ceasing to be a Negro. Once again, however, the confusion only arises if the membership group, comparative group and what one could call the justifying group or category are not sufficiently clearly distinguished. The distinction between inequality within and inequality between groups is purely a matter of definition; any inequality can be described as either, according to how one chooses to delimit the boundaries between groups. If relative deprivation is to be precisely described, all inequalities which give rise to feelings of relative deprivation must be treated as inequalities between and only between the membership reference group and comparative reference group. The Negro bricklayer who becomes the equal of white bricklayers and the bricklayer who becomes the equal of executives both do so by leaving their membership reference groups of disrespected Negroes and ill-paid bricklayers respectively. The attributes of being a bricklayer or being a Negro are merely the correlates (for the moment) of the position of inequality which is resented. There is, to be sure, an important difference between rising with and rising independently of the membership reference group, to which I shall return later on. But this is not to be confused with distinctions arbitrarily drawn between rising within groups or classes and rising between them. The questions to ask are first, to what group is a comparison being made? second, what is the allegedly less well-placed group to which the person feels that he belongs? and third, by virtue of what further attribute does he feel that the inequality should be redressed?

The comparative group is thus in one sense a 'membership group', since without at least one common attribute there could be no comparison. But this is a different sort of membership. A woman claiming equal pay for equal work does not, of course, think she is a man, but only a fellow-worker who is, as such, entitled to an equal reward with men. The point is made by Merton and Rossi in their discussion of reference group theory when they say that 'some similarity in status attributes between the individual and the reference group must be perceived or imagined for the comparison to occur at all'.[5] It is also familiar to writers on justice: justice cannot be applied except between people who have some relevant attribute in common.[6] Indeed, the validity of a claim to justice will depend on whether or not the petitioner does share the crucial attribute with his comparative reference group. But this group, by definition, is never the same as what I have called the 'membership reference group'. The 'membership reference group' is rather the membership

[5] R. K. Merton and Alice S. Rossi, 'Contributions to the Theory of Reference Group Behavior', in R. K. Merton, *Social Theory and Social Structure* (rev. edn.; Glencoe, Ill., 1957), p. 242.

[6] See e.g. P. Tisset, 'Les Notions de Droit et de Justice', *Revue de Métaphysique et de Morale* XXXVII (1930), p. 66, quoted Ch. Perelman, *The Idea of Justice and the Problem of Argument* (London, 1963), pp. 14–15: 'Where there is no common measure, and therefore no identity, the question of realising justice does not even arise'.

14

group by whose unequal position a sense of relative deprivation is engendered.

Any one person will have a multiplicity of reference groups, membership, comparative and normative. These may vary not only from topic to topic, but even on a single topic they could in theory change from one moment to the next. But on broad issues of social equality, the relative deprivations common to a group or class will be fairly consistent. Hyman, in his original paper, makes the point that despite the enormous multiplicity of possible reference groups, the number habitually used by any one person is small, and particular reference groups are likely to be specified in the context of particular problems.[7] It is true that the same people will give different answers when the questions 'what sort of people are you thinking of as "people like yourself"?' or 'who do you compare yourself with?' are asked in different contexts. But on topics where social inequalities are at issue—as opposed to topics where purely individual differences are involved, such as intelligence or physical strength—the answers given are likely to follow a fairly stable pattern.

The most difficult question of all, however, is how far a person's reference group should be seen as the cause or the effect of his other aspirations and attitudes. This is particularly difficult with comparative as opposed to normative groups. In the language of survey research, should they be treated as a dependent or an independent variable? There are two ways of looking at the problem. On the one hand, we could say that a person who sees his opportunities as limited will choose a comparative reference group not too far from his present situation, so that his magnitude of relative deprivation is accordingly kept low. On the other hand, we could say that because he only compares himself with groups close to his own position his goals are limited, and his magnitude of relative deprivation is by this means kept low. Which description is correct in any given case?

There is an obvious risk of tautology, since a limited reference group entails by definition that the magnitude (although not necessarily the degree) of a person's relative deprivation is low. Neither one, therefore, can be cited as evidence for the other. In addition, it will be a tautology to speak of a low level of aspiration as being either a cause or an effect of the choice of reference group, since a low level of aspiration precludes by definition a claim derived from a comparison with some much more fortunate set of people. The two are only not synonymous if the person either sees others as much more fortunate than himself but does not want whatever it is that they have, or chooses a 'negative' reference group in the sense that

[7] Hyman, 'The Psychology of Status', p. 47.

15

he is satisfied precisely because he is different from it. But a reference group can nonetheless be either a cause or an effect of a person's other attitudes or grievances. A conversion to Marxism may change someone's comparative reference groups, or a change of his comparative reference groups help to convert him to Marxism. In the event, it will almost always be safe to say that the influence is reciprocal; but there may be no certain means of distinguishing between cause and effect, or of detecting which of several possible reference groups is the influence acting on a particular attitude.[8]

The question must, therefore, always be asked in two separate parts: first, what determines a person's choice of reference group? second, what results from the choice? There may be a spiral effect in the direction of either a higher or a lower magnitude of relative deprivation. A comparison with someone much better off may produce consequences which will encourage a further comparison with someone better off still, or a comparison with someone worse off may be conducive to a relative contentment in which no comparisons leading to a sense of grievance will be likely to obtrude. But the particular comparison chosen is the crux of the relation between inequality and grievance. An explanation of the relation between inequality and grievance requires, therefore, some notion both of what causes changes of reference groups and what results from them.

On the effects of reference groups as an independent variable, there is even some experimental evidence, which may be briefly cited. Hyman's original study included an experiment designed to show how subjective judgments of status could be altered by experimental alteration of reference groups. Hyman found that depending on the category of people with whom the experimental subjects were asked to compare themselves, they rated their status on a variety of topics differently. This is not a surprising result, but it demonstrates under laboratory conditions how the alteration of reference groups leads to a change in subjective estimations of status. In an earlier study, Chapman and Volkmann had already demonstrated how levels of aspiration can be related not only to determinants resulting from individual success or failure, but also to determinants in the social environment.[9] In an intelligence test

---

[8] On the way that this problem can prove insuperable in the absence of experimental evidence, see the abstract of Norman Kaplan, *Reference Group Theory and Voting Behavior* (Ph.D. thesis, Columbia University, 1955), in *Dissertation Abstracts* XV (1955), p. 1458. Whether the influence is that of a comparative or a normative reference group, it may be impossible to establish which of several possible choices is a determinant of attitudes.

[9] Dwight W. Chapman and John Volkmann, 'A Social Determinant of the Level of Aspiration', in Eleanor E. Maccoby *et al.*, eds., *Readings in Social Psychology* (3rd edn.; London, 1959), pp. 281–290.

16

administered by the experimenters, the level of aspiration of the subjects was altered when they were told the performance of other groups before they had taken the test themselves. When, however, they were not told of the performance of other groups until after they had taken the test themselves, then their level of aspiration remained the same. Once again, the result is what common sense would lead one to expect. But, as we shall see, the assumptions of common sense may turn out to be misleading, and the results of the Chapman and Volkmann experiment have obvious analogies on a larger scale. As they themselves put it, 'Whatever change in aspiration-level is induced by a change in the frame of reference may have enormous social consequences: the new judgment may serve as a catalyst for major social changes in which whole groups abruptly revise their ambitions and perhaps their status.'[10]

The influence of a 'normative' reference group may be illustrated from an experiment conducted by Charters and Newcomb. The Catholic students in a large class were assigned to three equal and randomly selected groups. The first group attended class with the non-Catholics. The second group met together in a small room but were told nothing not told to the main class. The third group also met in a separate room but were told that their help was needed as Catholics in perfecting an attitude scale designed to be relevant to Catholics. This third group gave answers to an identical set of attitude questions which were far more closely in accordance with orthodox Catholic norms than those of the others.[11] The experiment accordingly shows not only the effect of reference groups on attitudes, but also the importance of what the investigators call the 'salience' of reference groups—that is, the extent to which a particular group is uppermost in a person's mind. Once again, the result accords with common sense. But since the relation of reference groups to attitudes in a wider social context raises chicken-and-egg problems of considerable difficulty, it is worth remembering that the effect of reference groups as an independent variable is capable of experimental demonstration.

The most famous finding, however, in the literature on reference groups comes from the evidence of a survey rather than an experiment. It is one of the findings reported in *The American Soldier*, and the relevance of reference groups to it has been well brought out in the subsequent paper by Merton and Rossi to which I have al-

[10] *Ibid.*, p. 282.
[11] W. W. Charters, Jr., and Theodore M. Newcomb, 'Some Attitudinal Effects of Experimentally Increased Salience of a Membership Group', in Maccoby, *op. cit.*, pp. 276–281. Cf. Newcomb, *Social Psychology* (New York. 1950), pp. 227–8.

ready referred. In the Military Police, where opportunities for promotion were very poor, satisfaction with opportunities for promotion was found to be higher than in the Air Corps, where opportunities for promotion were conspicuously good.[12] Although, on reflection, this result may be explicable enough, it is certainly not what common sense would initially lead one to expect. If the finding had been that the better the chances of promotion, the more likely people were to be satisfied about it, this would have appeared an unnecessary demonstration of the obvious. But it is only when the notion of reference groups is introduced that the actual finding can be readily explained.

This is, in effect, the explanation given by the investigators. They do not use the term reference group, but they comment that what is needed is 'the theory that such opinions by soldiers represent a relationship between their expectations and their achievements relative to others *in the same boat with them*'.[13] The implications of this idiomatic but imprecise phrase are more fully brought out by Merton and Rossi. Those who were not promoted in the Military Police tended to compare themselves with the large number of their fellows who were also not promoted, while those few who had been promoted were likely to appear to themselves to have done relatively better. In the Air Corps, by contrast, the man who was not promoted would be likely to compare himself with the large number of his fellows who *had* been promoted, while these, though successful, would appear to themselves to have done relatively less well. This explanation, once put forward, is intuitively as well as statistically convincing. It does not have the certainty of an experimental result since we cannot be sure that, for example, entrants to the Air Corps did not share traits of character which might incline them to different attitudes from those of the Military Police. But the finding is quite striking enough to lead us to look at the general relation between inequality and grievance in terms of reference group choices.

There is an initial caveat to be entered, for the authors of *The American Soldier* are careful to stress that men who are dissatisfied with their opportunities for promotion would not necessarily like to change to other jobs. In other words, satisfaction with one aspect of social or occupational situation need not correlate with satisfaction with others. But even so, it is obvious that the promotion finding has wider implications. If the rate of satisfaction with mobility varies with the number of comparable people seen to be better off, then this conclusion will, in the phrase of Merton and Rossi, 'bear upon

[12] Stouffer, *op. cit.*, pp. 250–53.
[13] *Ibid.*, p. 251.

some of the more strategic areas of study in the larger social system'.[14]

If we turn from the effects of the choice of reference group to its possible cause, the choice seems in this instance to be numerically determined. The more people a man sees promoted when he is not promoted himself, the more people he may compare himself with in a situation where the comparison will make him feel relatively deprived. This arithmetical determinant of satisfaction is emphasized in *The American Soldier* and, given the appropriate assumptions, can be extended and formalized. On a pure model of this kind, assuming random comparisons, there will be definable points where the frequency of relative deprivation and thereby the likelihood of dissatisfaction with promotion will reach their maximum and minimum.[15] But the actual extension of opportunities for promotion need not be the only determinant of this sort of effect. In the first place, it may be some other influence which causes those who have been promoted to be taken as a comparative referent. In the second, some other group may be taken as a referent because of a belief that its opportunities are better (whether in fact they are or not). A numerical determinant may be the most important influence, and where it can be shown that this is so, the relation between inequality and grievance (or rather, frequency of grievance) becomes not only explicable but quantifiable. This, however, is a special case; only in rare circumstances will the frequency of relative deprivation be directly related to actual inequality. The larger question is to what extent the inverse correlation found in Stouffer's study might hold true in other situations and on other topics: what might it imply for the reactions of a group or class whose members are denied access to the higher positions in their society?

On the 'pure' numerical model, the frequency of relative deprivation will be at a minimum when either everybody or nobody is promoted; in between, it will rise and fall as actual mobility rates rise. But the assumption that relative deprivation will be least frequent where promotion opportunities are worst is not intuitively very convincing. Unless people literally cannot conceive of a society in which social mobility is possible, it is plausible to suppose that some, at least, of the members of a subordinate class will feel relatively deprived in relation to their superiors. They will not, of course, be taking as a reference group members of their own class who have risen from it, as in the example of the Military Police; their sense of grievance will rather stem from their comparing the

---

[14] *Op. cit.*, p. 240.
[15] See James A. Davis, 'A Formal Interpretation of the Theory of Relative Deprivation', *Sociometry* XXII (1959), pp. 280–296.

classes as such. But the effect is the same—they will be tempted to compare themselves with people placed above them. Under what circumstances, therefore, will the correlation hold between a higher rate of mobility and a lower rate of satisfaction with the system of social inequality? In the words of Merton and Rossi,

> '. . . it is scarcely probable that this relationship between actual mobility rates and individual satisfaction with mobility chances holds throughout the entire range of variation. If promotion rates were reduced to practically zero in some of these groups, would one then find an even more "favourable opinion" of promotion chances? Presumably, the relationship is curvilinear, and this requires the sociologist to work out toward the conditions under which the observed linear relationship fails to obtain.'[16]

Suppose we assume a society in which the rate of upward mobility increases progressively and evenly over time. Assume also that the unpleasantness of subordination, and therefore the intensity of grievance among those who feel it, is constant throughout. If it is true that a little mobility produces less frequent dissatisfaction than does more mobility, and also that zero mobility produces more frequent dissatisfaction than does a little mobility, then the relation between the mobility rate and the frequency of relative deprivation in any given population might look something like this:

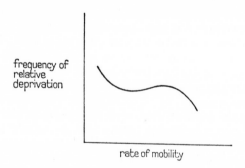

Fig. 1

I must emphasise as strongly as I can that this use of a graph is purely illustrative. It might seem tempting to label the four points on the curve slavery, feudalism, industrialization and democracy; but this could never be properly quantified and tested, even if these terms could be satisfactorily defined. In a later chapter, I shall give some figures which suggest that this curvilinear relationship does hold good on one topic relevant to equality of status. But the use

[16] *Op. cit.*, p. 236, n. 7.

20

of the graph is rather that it directs our attention to particular points along the progress of a society towards greater equality for the members of its subordinate strata. If the assumption represented in the graph is correct, and if it can be applied outside of occupational mobility rates to other topics relevant to social equality in general, then there are some points between which satisfaction rises as equality spreads, but others between which an improving situation leads to a higher, not lower, incidence of relative deprivation.

The readiest illustration of an advance towards equality leading to an increase in relative deprivation is the common observation that revolutions are apt to occur at times of rising prosperity. Although no one would suggest that this is more than a part of the explanation of any particular revolution, historians of various times and places, including eighteenth-century France and twentieth-century Russia, have noticed the tendency for overt discontent to be relatively rare in stable hardship and to rise alike in frequency, magnitude and intensity as opportunity is seen to increase. The argument is stated at its most succinct by Tocqueville in discussing the French Revolution: 'Thus it was precisely in those parts of France where there had been most improvement that popular discontent ran highest . . . Patiently endured so long as it seemed beyond redress, a grievance comes to appear intolerable once the possibility of removing it crosses men's minds . . . At the height of its power feudalism did not inspire so much hatred as it did on the eve of its eclipse.'[17] To take an example closer to the present study, it has been emphasized by Henry Pelling in his account of the origins of the Labour Party that in late nineteenth-century Britain 'the immediate onset of what economic historians now call the "Great Depression", so far from encouraging Socialism and the break-up of the Liberal Party, actually discouraged working class militancy and destroyed the "advanced" elements then in existence'.[18] Furthermore, 'The period of [the workers'] greatest political and industrial advance (1888 to 1891) was a period of comparative prosperity'.[19] Such a tendency can perhaps be explained by the cautious pessimism which hardship inevitably breeds. But this, in effect, is to say that in hard times comparative reference groups will be more restricted than in good, which is a part of the generalization being put forward. The same point that is made by Pelling was made in more general terms by Masterman in 1909.

[17] A. de Tocqueville, *The Old Regime and the French Revolution* (Garden City, N.Y., 1955), pp. 176–7.
[18] H. Pelling, *The Origins of the Labour Party 1880–1900* (London, 1953), p. 6.
[19] *Ibid.*, p. 8.

'Socialism amongst the working peoples propagates and triumphs in times of plenty, withers up and vanishes in times of depression. This is exactly the reverse of the accepted belief, which thought that the poor are stung into Socialism by suffering, as poets are stung into poetry by wrong.'[20]

This does not mean, however, that if times get sharply worse the frequency and intensity of relative deprivation may not be heightened. It is only poverty which seems irremediable that is likely to keep relative deprivation low. Marx and Engels were not foolish to hope for economic crises as the catalysts of revolution, for when a stable expectation is suddenly disappointed this is at least as likely to promote relative deprivation as when an expectation is suddenly heightened. What is common to both situations is that people are made aware of not having what they have been brought to think it feasible or proper or necessary that they should have. The upsetting of expectations provokes the sense of relative deprivation which may in turn provide the impetus for drastic change. Where apparently stable expectations are disappointed, the comparative reference group is likely to be the previous situation of the membership reference group. But when expectations are rising faster than the likelihood of their fulfilment, it is both more interesting and also more difficult to ascertain what has determined the choice of reference group by which the feeling of relative deprivation has been engendered.

Very violent changes can produce what since Durkheim we speak of as 'anomie'—the vacuum of standards which results from the dislocation of a stable social context. Where this occurs, there is danger of confusion and violence precisely because people do not know where to look for their reference groups, whether comparative or normative, and thereby become prone to exaggerated hopes or fears. But it is not always a sudden change by which reference groups are upset. If the poor begin to compare themselves directly to the rich, it may be a result of the storming of the Bastille or of a century of ideological change. Nor need the curvilinear relationship between inequality and grievance suggested by *The American Soldier* finding be progressive over time. All that we should expect is that under certain conditions the relative deprivation of a subordinate group will be augmented rather than diminished in both magnitude and frequency by an advance towards greater equality, whether of opportunity or of condition.

The likelihood of a rise in dissatisfaction accompanying an advance towards equality will of course vary greatly from one topic

[20] C. F. G. Masterman, *The Condition of England* (London, 1909), pp. 150-151.

to another. My own argument, indeed, will be that for British manual workers and their families during the present century it has operated very differently in the different dimensions of social inequality. But the important conclusion which follows from the discussion so far is that there is no stronger initial reason to expect the resentment of inequality to correlate with relative hardship than with relative good fortune. Apart from historical examples which suggest themselves, a particularly striking example of a curvilinear relationship between inequality and grievance is furnished by a piece of recent research carried out in the United States. In a study of the effects of a tornado on a community wholly unprepared for it, it was found that

'the feeling of being relatively better off than others *increases* with objective loss up to the highest loss category . . . The highest proportion feeling less deprived than others is among those with medium personal loss—some injury to a household member, or death to a non-household member or a close friend. Among those without serious personal losses, those with only medium property damage were subjectively worse off and less active than those with high property damage.'[21]

As is shown in the discussion from which this quotation is taken, these apparently paradoxical results can at once be explained by bringing in the notion of reference groups. Those hardest hit correspond to those at the left of the graph in Figure 1. But those only a little way from where the disaster struck most severely are likely to contrast themselves with those hardest hit, and by this standard they are likely to feel fortunate to have escaped as lightly as they did. Those at the edge of the disaster area, by contrast, are less likely to be aware of the situation of the severest sufferers and more likely therefore to feel relatively deprived by comparison with those who suffered little or no loss of any kind. Finally, those outside the scope of the study altogether will, we may safely assume, have no occasion to feel relatively deprived at all. This is a remarkably apt illustration of just the sort of curvilinear relationship which the promotion example suggested.

Consider the first low po'nt on the curve. In the Military Police, or among the Arkansas households where only medium loss has been suffered, the low frequency of relative deprivation is plausibly explained by saying that for these people things are visibly not as bad as they could be; at the same time, the situation of a number of comparable people who are very much better off is not readily

---

[21] Allen H. Barton, *Social Organization Under Stress: A Sociological Review of Disaster Studies* (National Academy of Sciences—National Research Council; Washington, D. C., 1963), p. 63. The particular study was carried out in Arkansas by the National Opinion Research Center.

brought home to them. Relative deprivation, therefore, is likely to be low in magnitude and intensity as well as in frequency. The same seems often to be true of a subordinate class in a larger social system. In the absence of an external stimulus, the limited reference groups by which relative deprivation is kept low (in any or all of the three senses) tend to be self-perpetuating. This feedback effect generated by modest comparisons underlies many familiar generalizations about the hold of habit, the correlation between poverty and conservatism, or the unambitiousness of the underprivileged. Once the vicious circle has been broken, this may set off a rising spiral of expectations and comparisons which will continue until a new equilibrium is reached. But some external influence is needed. The interesting question, therefore, will always be what first broke the equilibrium at the lower level and so gave rise to the change of reference groups.

One of the most obvious of such external influences is war. It is often said that war is the most effective impetus behind social change, and although it is not always clear what is meant by this, a part of the process supposed to occur is the dislocation of familiar standards of reference. Expectations are first of all heightened by the feeling that some tangible rewards will result from victory. But as well as this, new comparisons are generated in two different ways. First, the underprivileged strata who are seen to have shared the exertions and sufferings of war in equal measure with their social superiors are encouraged to feel a common aspiration with their superiors for a joint share in a better world. Second, the purely physical disturbances of war bring the members of different classes into more immediate contact with each other than is ever likely to occur in peacetime. The result is that the magnitude, frequency and intensity of relative deprivation are all markedly heightened among people whose previous reference groups had been much closer to their own immediate situation.

War, however, is not the only disturbance by which reference groups may be upset. It is one of the biggest; but disturbances can often be brought about simply by the receipt of news. Orwell, in *The Road to Wigan Pier,* describes a man saying to him that there was no housing problem until people were told about it; or in other words, a sense of relative deprivation was aroused as soon as a different standard was introduced from outside. For people to be told that their economic or social situation is bad may be enough to convince them that it is, even if they had not been thinking so before. The proverbial stirring-up of discontent performed by revolutionaries and agitators depends precisely on their persuading people to judge their situation in terms of comparisons which it had not previously occurred to them to make. In the same way, education can upset traditional reference groups and heighten the general level of aspiration; better close the schools, as Ernest Bevin said in 1920, than create aspirations and then deny them. Conversely, religion can sometimes restrict aspirations; if it teaches that the existing order is just, it can inhibit those comparisons between one stratum and the next which might lead to the system's overthrow. The subversive potentialities of knowledge derive from its capacity to act as an independent influence on reference groups and thereby create relative deprivations where they did not exist before.

A third disrupter of reference groups is economic change. Prosperity can break the vicious circle between poverty and conservatism by making people aware of the possibility of a higher standard than it would previously have occurred to them to hope for. Conversely, a decline in prosperity, if not too violent, can restrict the sense of relative deprivation by inhibiting comparisons with more fortunate groups. There may at the same time be an influence the other way round—prosperity may, for example, result in turn from the urge to realize higher aspirations, as in Schumpeter's theory of the entrepreneur. But for the mass of the population, war, or education, or economic change are external influences by which their attitudes and expectations are altered. If it is true that the sense of inequality in society depends on the choice of reference groups, then the influences behind reference group choices will be the determinants of the relation between grievance and inequality. In particular, they will explain this relation when it is most discrepant—that is, when those at the bottom seem least discontented with the system which places them there.

Political theorists of many different persuasions have wondered at the acquiescence of the underprivileged in the inequalities to which they are subjected, and have explained this acquiescence in terms of ignorance, or habit, or traditionally restricted expectations. If the least fortunate strata of society—Saint-Simon's 'classe la plus nombreuse et la plus pauvre'—were fully aware of how unequally they were being treated, would not all societies break out into revolution? 'What is needed', said Durkheim, 'if social order is to reign is that the mass of men be content with their lot. But what is needed for them to be content, is not that they have more or less but that they be convinced that they have no right to more.'[22] In stable societies with a long and unbroken history of customary inequalities, it is not difficult to see how the aspirations of the underprivileged could be kept low enough for the pattern to remain

[22] E. Durkheim, *Socialism and Saint-Simon* (ed. Gouldner; London, 1959), p. 200.

undisturbed. But once the possibility of improvement has been disclosed, it becomes more remarkable that inequalities should continue to be passively accepted by the great majority of those at the lower levels of society. We must beware of confusing acquiescence with contentment: the impossibility of remedy can inhibit action without inhibiting the sense of grievance. But even in societies which are no longer 'traditional', it is only rarely that egalitarian resentments are as militant or as widespread as the actual structure of inequalities would suggest to be plausible. The United States affords the most striking example. Indeed, there is a twofold interest in contrasting it with Britain, since the United States has always appeared to European observers to foreshadow the changes which their own societies would in due course undergo. In the United States, the belief in equality is more strongly entrenched and more widely held than in any other country in the world, yet this belief is not borne out by the actual structure and workings of the American system. How is it, therefore, that inequality can be so disproportionate to grievance even where equality is believed to be feasible?

One suggested answer is that the social discontents of Americans are kept low because they continue to believe, however erroneously, that the rags-to-riches myth is true.[23] A man who believes that he is shortly to rise to great heights will not resent a brief position of inferiority. The captain who knows he will succeed the colonel does not mind saluting him, for he looks forward to being saluted in his turn. The foreman who expects to become a manager is unlikely to be a militant trade unionist. But this is not a sufficient explanation of the American case. Many manual workers in the United States may hope to rise into management or to establish a business of their own, but they are more realistic when directly asked about their expectations. An altogether different answer to the question is suggested by Hyman,[24] who has shown in a reanalysis of opinion poll results how the aspirations of less fortunate Americans are modified in accordance with their position. On Hyman's analysis, the aims of the less fortunate are channelled towards positions which are likely to be feasible for them rather than positions which will only be attained by those whose starting-point was much higher. This same conclusion is suggested by a similar study which was carried out in France in 1951 and is, as far as I know, the only other survey evidence published on this topic. In this study, by

[23] See e.g., S. M. Lipset and R. Bendix, *Social Mobility in Industrial Society* (Berkeley, Calif., 1959), p. 81.
[24] Hyman, 'The Value Systems of Different Classes', in R. Bendix and S. M. Lipset, eds., *Class, Status and Power* (Glencoe, Ill., 1953), pp. 426–42.

Stern and Keller,[25] the respondents in a small national sample were asked what they would consider a satisfactory standard of living for 'people like themselves'. When the investigators analyzed the spontaneous reference groups given, they found little comparison with 'out-groups' and little evidence of class resentment. Their results therefore bear out Hyman's. Although the United States has a much more egalitarian ideology than France, the magnitude and frequency of relative deprivation seem to be similar: in both countries, although people may be anxious to improve their position in terms of where they actually stand, they seldom feel relatively deprived by reference to members of more fortunate groups with whom they have no reason to compare themselves.

It is dangerous to generalize too freely from this into talking about the 'unambitiousness' of the underprivileged, since the distance between a person's situation and his reference group may be equally large whether he is a labourer's son who wants to be a craftsman or a solicitor's son who wants to be a high court judge.[26] It may well be that the magnitude of the relative deprivations which are felt by the underprivileged is no greater than the magnitude of those felt by the very prosperous. The point is rather that whatever the relative magnitudes of relative deprivation, those near the bottom are likely, even in a society with an egalitarian ideology, to choose reference groups nearer the bottom than self-conscious egalitarianism would imply. Or to phrase it more carefully, they are likely to modify their reference groups in such a way that their aspirations are diverted from those goals which the rags-to-riches myth misleadingly holds out for them.

This more circumspect phrasing is made necessary by the alternative implication suggested by Merton. In a paper entitled 'Social Structure and Anomie',[27] Merton has argued that those who find themselves denied the positions which the egalitarian myth has led them to believe are open to them may be driven to adopt high but 'deviant' ambitions. In the American culture, success is mandatory; those to whom conventional success is denied because of their inferior position will therefore tend to seek success of a less conventional or even legitimate kind. Merton advances this argument

[25] Eric Stern and Suzanne Keller, 'Spontaneous Group References in France', *Public Opinion Quarterly* XVII (1953), pp. 208–17.

[26] See L. T. Empey, 'Social Class and Occupational Aspiration: A Comparison of Absolute and Relative Measurement', *American Sociological Review* XXI (1956), p. 704; and cf. Suzanne Keller and M. Zavalloni, 'Classe Sociale, Ambition et Réussite', *Sociologie du Travail* IV (1962), p. 2.

[27] Reprinted in *Social Theory and Social Structure,* Chapter IV.

without recourse to the notion of reference groups—which is surprising, in view of their relevance to it and Merton's own discussion of reference group theory. But if we translate his argument into these terms, it can be summarized by saying that the American ideology encourages the underprivileged to make extravagant reference group comparisons; but since the relative deprivations to which these give rise are demonstrably unlikely to be satisfied, the original reference groups may be modified by the adoption as goals of more feasible but less respectable positions of wealth and influence. The result is that 'deviant' ambitions are chosen by members of the underprivileged strata more frequently than would occur in the absence of the cultural norm of success for all. The ideology of egalitarianism influences reference group choices which in turn help to promote 'deviant' behavior.

This argument might seem to be incompatible with Hyman's. Merton suggests that an egalitarian ideology promotes large ambitions among the underprivileged, while Hyman emphasizes rather their adjustment to the depressing realities of inequality. If, however, we keep in mind the caveat about 'unambitiousness', it is clear that the two amount to the same. Even in a society where the ideology of egalitarianism is most powerful, those at the bottom modify their ambitions in accordance with the facts of their situation. They may, it is true, continue to feel relatively deprived of wealth and success to a greater extent than they would in a society where equality was held neither desirable nor possible. But their reference groups will not be those implied by a literal adoption of the belief that there is a place at the top for everyone. Even where equality is an article of faith, the facts of inequality tend to restrict those feelings of relative deprivation which they might be thought to stimulate. The 'normal' situation, where inequality is not seen to be markedly diminishing, is for reference groups to be close to home.

The choice of reference groups has in fact been studied by several American writers. Reissmann found in Evanston, Illinois that policemen were behind the other groups which he studied in both achievement and status but that they were also low in aspiration, and as far as his evidence went, satisfied with their position.[28] Their comparative reference group was simply the other members of a not prosperous family. This not only affords a good example of a discrepancy between relative deprivation and objective situation, but shows how a close and visible reference group can serve to accommodate aspirations to actual position. Reissmann also makes the point that age makes a difference to aspiration: those whose

[28] Leonard Reissmann, 'Levels of Aspiration and Social Class', *American Sociological Review* XVIII (1953), pp. 233–242.

achievement was low had had higher aspirations when young, but those who had in fact been successful seemed to have had their aspirations heightened by success. Success, therefore, can itself provide the external stimulus by which comparisons are heightened, whereas those who are forced to adjust themselves to lesser achievement will reduce their aspirations in accordance with their experience.

A similar conclusion is suggested by Chinoy's analysis of interviews conducted between 1946 and 1951 with sixty-two automobile workers in 'Autotown' (the alias given to Lansing, Michigan). Chinoy set out to discover in some depth how the aspirations of his sample were related by them to the traditional myth of opportunity and advancement for all. I do not want to discuss his findings in any detail, but only to draw attention to one of the ways which he documents whereby workers choose reference groups in terms of which they appear to themselves to have done well. Chinoy quotes from two respondents who clearly interpreted 'getting ahead' neither in terms of successfully out-distancing their fellows nor in terms of attaining the standards of a superior class, but simply in terms of improvement relative to their own previous situation. No reference group is chosen which would show up the disparity between situation and aspiration; advancement is taken to mean simply, in Chinoy's words, 'the progressive accumulation of things'.[29]

It has even been suggested that manual workers would rather not be confronted with the reality of equal opportunity. Lane concludes from detailed interviews with a small sample of workers in New Haven[30] that 'people tend to care less about *equality* of opportunity than about the availability of *some* opportunity.' Provided, therefore, that the myth of equal opportunity is being successfully rationalized away, relative deprivation may, as the previous argument implies, be heightened, not reduced, by greater opportunities. The studies of Reissman, Chinoy and Lane all show that even in the United States, where the goal of success is felt as mandatory, people often choose reference groups closer to their actual circumstances than those which might be forced on them if their opportunities were better than they are.

There is, however, one difficulty involved in generalizing about reference group choices which is largely concealed by the sort of examples which I have cited. In talking about soldiers in the Military Police, or auto workers in Michigan, we are talking about men

[29] Ely Chinoy, *Automobile Workers and the American Dream* (Garden City, N.Y., 1955), p. 126.
[30] Robert E. Lane, 'The Fear of Equality', *American Political Science Review* LIII (1959), pp. 35–51.

in a situation where only limited kinds of comparison are relevant. When Chinoy talks to auto workers about their occupational aspirations, it is safe to assume that they are answering as self-conscious auto workers; if they cite a reference group outside of their occupation, it is by contrast with their occupation that it should be interpreted. Similarly, when an interviewer talks to soldiers about promotion opportunities, the framework of the discussion is necessarily delimited, since a small and clearly definable population includes all the relevant candidates for reference group comparisons. But if we move from this to talking about resentments of inequality in the context of a total society, then the scope of reference group choices, both comparative and membership, becomes enormously enlarged. What happens when people make comparisons in more than one of their various capacities, and these capacities have different rankings in the hierarchy of the society to which they belong? Suppose, for example, that we are talking to a Negro businessman in the United States about equality of opportunity. As a Negro comparing himself with white businessmen, he is likely to feel relatively deprived; as a businessman comparing himself with unskilled Negroes, he is likely to feel relatively gratified. In his answers to questions about social equality he may feel aware of either or both comparisons with equal intensity. How, therefore, should his attitude be described?

The problem has received some attention among American social psychologists under the headings of 'status-consistency' and 'status-crystallization'.[31] Given people who belong at the same time to social categories which are differently ranked, the problem is to discover how far their attitudes or behaviour are influenced by their awareness of the discrepancies in the status of their differently ranked roles. It has been suggested, for example, that such people are likelier than others to adopt liberal political attitudes. But attempts to generalize along these lines have been subjected to some effective criticism, and no very illuminating conclusions have emerged from the studies so far carried out. It seems agreed that it is a mistake to look at status as though it were unidimensional, and that 'all forms of status inconsistency are psychologically disturbing';[32] but this hardly needs saying. The significance of status inconsistency for the relation between inequality and grievance is intuitively obvious. A person who occupies two different roles or categories may well be driven by his awareness of the discrepancy

[31] See initially Gerhard E. Lenski, 'Status Crystallisation: a Non-Vertical Dimension of Social Status', *American Sociological Review* XIX (1954), pp. 405–413.

[32] Elton F. Jackson, 'Status Inconsistency and Symptoms of Stress', *American Sociological Review* XXVII (1962), p. 469.

between them into a resentment of the status accorded to him in his lower-ranked role. A university graduate who works under a man who is much better paid but has no formal qualifications may well feel that his qualifications are insufficiently rewarded; the Negro businessman may well feel more keenly aware of discrimination against Negroes than the Negro labourer. Such discrepancies will not always have the same effect. But they furnish another possible influence on the nature and frequency of feelings of relative deprivation. When, for example, manual workers achieve a greater equality of reward, but not of status, with workers who used to be above them in both, then it is probable that their frequency of relative deprivation of status will rise in proportion as their relative deprivation of income is appeased.

There is, however, yet another possible difference in the nature of the relative deprivation which they will feel. This is the difference which I briefly mentioned earlier. The manual worker whose prosperity has heightened his relative deprivation of status may have come to feel that his occupation as a whole is insufficiently esteemed.[33] But suppose that his prosperity rather leads him to identify with those in other occupations whose level of reward is the same. If his disparate statuses (in the sense of high reward but low esteem) influence his attitudes in this rather different way, then he will not so much wish to rise in social prestige with his membership reference group as out of it.

This is the one final distinction in types of relative deprivation which is relevant to the relation between inequality and grievance. A person's sense of relative deprivation will be affected not only by which of several membership reference groups is the basis for his chosen comparison; it will also be affected by what he feels about its relation to his comparative group. The two will, of course, share at least the common attribute without which a sense of relative deprivation could not be engendered at all. But suppose a person succeeds in reaching a position of equality with his comparative group. Did he want to rise out of his membership group, or with it? If the first, then he was dissatisfied with his position as a member of what he saw as his group; if the second, then he was dissatisfied with the position of what he saw as his group relative to other groups in the larger system. The difference between the two is obvious, but important. It is also closely bound up with the person's choice of normative reference group.

The distinction can easily be illustrated by hypothetical examples.

[33] For example, the effect of higher wages on miners as described by N. Dennis *et al.*, *Coal is Our Life* (London, 1956), p. 76 could be rephrased in these terms.

A junior business executive balked of promotion is continuously and resentfully aware of the senior directors of his firm; he compares his position with theirs, he aspires to become one of them, and he sees this prospect as a perfectly feasible one in terms of his expectations or demands. He has no feeling that the social categories either of junior executives or of businessmen in general are lower in rewards, or esteem, or influence than they should be, nor does he feel himself a member of any other group which is ill-treated by his society as a whole. But he feels intensely deprived relative to the position of other people whom he regards as deserving no greater recognition than himself. He is, therefore, relatively deprived only in terms of his personal situation; there may be others in the same situation with whom he shares some kind of fellow-feeling, but his achievement of what would assuage his feeling of relative deprivation is in no way bound up with theirs.

Consider, by contrast, a factory worker who feels that he is grossly underpaid. He is conscious, and even militantly conscious, of belonging to the working class. He has no ambition to rise above his fellows. But he feels that he and all those like him are insufficiently rewarded both in money and status by the society to whose welfare they are contributing by their work. He feels relatively deprived as one of a class whose members all share the same conditions of life and employment. His comparative reference group might even be the same as that of the junior executive who feels he should have a higher salary; both may feel relatively deprived by reference to what they picture as the unjustified perquisites of the chairman's nephew who holds an executive position. But there is an important difference between them when it comes to their own half, as it were, of the comparison which they are making. The factory worker comparing himself with those whom he sees as better rewarded feels relatively deprived as a factory worker—the chairman's nephew, he feels, should be no better rewarded than 'people like us'. The junior executive balked of promotion feels relatively deprived because he thinks he is more talented than other junior executives—the chairman's nephew, he feels, should be no better rewarded than 'people like me'.

The distinction can be conveniently represented in the form of a fourfold table.

	Relatively deprived because of own position as member of group.	
	Satisfied	Dissatisfied
Satisfied	A	B
Dissatisfied	C	D

Relatively deprived because of group's position in society.

Fig. 2

It would, of course, be unwarrantable to assume that any single person, who may occupy a variety of roles and hold a variety of attitudes to them, can arbitrarily be assigned to one or another of these four categories. If nothing else, a consistent distinction must be made between relative deprivation in the three different dimensions of social inequality which are discussed in the following chapter. But as long as it is clear that the four categories are no more than ideal types, then it may be useful to describe them in a little more detail.

Type A could perhaps be labelled 'orthodox', since it covers anyone who is neither ambitious within his group nor resentful on its behalf. It is, however, perfectly possible for a person to be anxious to change the structure of his society without himself feeling relatively deprived. Type A, therefore, will not only include the studious conformist or the successful social climber; it will also include the prosperous altruist who is not himself relatively deprived, but is at the same time driven by guilt or conviction into radical attitudes. In addition, Type A will include those who are low in the social hierarchy but who, for whatever reasons, are not in fact resentful of their position. It is the members of Type A who show how Durkheim's problem comes to be solved—how, that is, people who do not have very much become comfortably convinced that they have no right to more—and who exemplify all the most glaring disparities between inequality and grievance.

Type B, by contrast, covers the sort of 'striver' who is dissatisfied with his present situation, but not in a way that gives him common cause with others like him. A hypothetical example of Type B has been described already in the junior executive balked of promotion. He can be presented in such a way that he appears a rather greedy and unpleasant sort of person, but this may be unfair. He might, for example, be a poor but talented artist who feels that his merits are unrecognized, or an intelligent adolescent denied a university scholarship, or an unemployed man refused the scale of benefit to which he is entitled under the regulations in force.

Type C also has been described already. It includes all the exemplars of the strong lateral solidarity traditionally found within the working class. But members of Type C need not belong only to a group which resents the inequalities to which it is subjected in the hierarchy of economic class. The member of a religious movement or a minority race may equally feel only a collective relative deprivation, and have no wish to improve his personal position in relation to any of the social categories to which he feels that he belongs. In general, the relative deprivations of Type C are those which play the largest part in the transformation of an existing structure of social inequalities.

Type D, finally, consists of those most relatively deprived of all, who are dissatisfied both with the position of their group and also with their membership of it. Their ideal type will be the tribune of the plebs—the man who not only feels the deprivations and injustices imposed on his class but who explicitly aspires to lead or even ultimately to rule his class in the course of securing redress on their behalf. Individual examples of Type D have had striking effects on the course of history. But for the purposes of the present study the two most interesting types are B and C. In order to refer to them, and to the two types of relative deprivation which they exemplify, I shall use the terms 'egoist' (for Type B) and 'fraternalist' (for Type C).

Neither term is entirely satisfactory, but it is better to use existing words in a specialized sense than to have recourse to neologisms. Although 'fraternalistic' relative deprivations are more naturally suggestive of a working-class person and 'egoistic' of a middle-class person, this need not be so by definition. There is nothing to prevent a working-class person feeling relatively deprived within but not on behalf of his class, and, as we shall see, middle-class people are very capable of fraternalistic relative deprivation. There is, however, a significance in the fact that 'fraternalism' is traditionally characteristic of the working, and 'egoism' of the middle class; and a part of the answer to the relation between inequality and grievance might lie in the circumstances by which the working class has been influenced in the direction of egoistic rather than fraternalistic relative deprivations. The difference between the two, indeed, can be redefined in terms of normative reference groups. Consider once again the example of a working-class person whose comparative reference group is the middle class, or a section of it. If his normative reference group is the working class, then his relative deprivations will in principle be fraternalistic; if it is the middle class, they will be egoistic.

The distinction cannot in practice be applied quite as easily as this suggests. Not only can the notion of a normative reference group not be rigorously defined, but it need never imply any one particular comparison out of the range of relevant inequalities. A manual worker may well think of himself as belonging to the 'middle class' (whatever this means to him), and whether or not he feels relatively deprived will depend on the comparisons which he makes as a self-styled middle-class person. Furthermore, his assessment of others in what he sees as his class will in turn affect whether his relative deprivation, if he feels one, is of a fraternalistic or an egoistic kind. But once the answers to these more detailed questions can be ascertained, or at least inferred, then the relative deprivation which he feels—with whatever intensity—can in principle be fully described.

It will be clear from the account I have given that none of these terms lend themselves to completely strict definition; but they do provide a framework within which the relation of inequality to grievance can be discussed with reasonable precision. Whatever term is used for it, relative deprivation lies at the heart of this relation. The way in which comparative reference groups are chosen, the membership reference group which gives the comparison its basis and the normative reference group which either exacerbates or mitigates the perception of inequality contain between them the answer to why inequalities are or are not regarded with a resentment proportionate to their magnitude. The only term which has been left altogether undefined is inequality itself, and it is to this that we must now turn.

III

THE THREE DIMENSIONS
OF SOCIAL INEQUALITY

WHAT exactly should be meant by 'social inequality'? Few of the many writers about it have been greatly concerned with niceties of terminology, for the various differences which can exist between groups or classes in wealth, or rank, or privilege have been readily visible and easy to describe since Aristotle and before. In post-industrial Europe, the obvious question has been how far the proletariat (whether or not referred to by this term) could or ought to advance towards a condition of equality with the strata of society above it. Some writers, like Tocqueville or J. S. Mill or Alfred Marshall, have thought that European society was without doubt advancing towards a greater equality: 'Eight centuries ago', wrote Mill in 1830, 'society was divided into barons and serfs . . . At every succeeding epoch, this inequality of condition is found to have somewhat abated; every century has done something considerable towards lowering the powerful and raising the low.'[1] Others, and most notably Marx, have argued that inequality was steadily widening. But whatever disagreement there might be about the consequences of industrialization, the question itself has always been obvious enough. Few observers of the evident differences between the rich and the poor have felt the need to define a rigorous and comprehensive theoretical framework within which the various kinds of social inequality should be classified. But social inequalities are diverse and intricate and some sort of categorization is a necessary prerequisite to any clear discussion of them. If social inequalities of any kind are to be either evaluated or explained they must be first of all distinguished by reference to the number of separate dimensions in which the members of societies are collectively ranked above or below one another—that is, the meaning to be given to 'social stratification' as such.

[1] J. S. Mill, 'Tocqueville on Democracy in America (vol. I)' in *Essays on Politics and Culture* (ed. Gertrude Himmelfarb; New York, 1963), p. 175.

The Three Dimensions of Social Inequality

The classification which results from putting the question in this form is not a new one. Sometimes it is phrased as the distinction between 'economic', 'social' and 'political' equality. Alternatively, it can be phrased as the distinction between equality of 'class', 'status' and 'power'. But although it is a familiar distinction, it is almost always obscured or overridden by others. It is seldom, if ever, used to provide the fundamental classification under which all the others[2] ought at the outset to be subsumed. Any classification, of course, is legitimate if it answers to the purpose at hand. But if there are three, and only three, basic dimensions in which societies are stratified—class, status and power—then it necessarily follows that all social inequalities (in the sense opposed to individual inequalities such as height or weight) are inequalities of one or other of these three, and only three, kinds. It is, perhaps, self-evident that inequalities of class, status and power need not always coincide. But surprising as it seems, there is as far as I know no major writer on social inequality who has explicitly formulated and consistently retained the tripartite distinction. Indeed, I would go so far as to say that every one of the best-known discussions of inequality, from Aristotle to Rousseau to Tocqueville to Tawney, has been confused by the neglect of it.

It does, however, raise difficulties of both terminology and substance. The terms class, status and power, as used in this sense, are generally credited to Max Weber. But it is not entirely clear what he meant by them, and even if a three-dimensional model is correct, the three are not terms of the same logical kind. It will, therefore, be convenient to recapitulate the distinction in approximately Weber's terms.[3] How far this represents a view with which Weber himself would have agreed does not matter very much. What does matter is that the distinction should be sufficiently well drawn to make clear what it means to argue that both the relation between inequality and relative deprivation and the implications of social justice for this relation are different in each of the three dimensions of social inequality.

A person's 'class'-situation, in Weber's sense, is the location which he shares with those who are similarly placed in the processes of

---

[2] For example, the useful distinction between 'civil', 'political', and 'social' equality drawn by T. H. Marshall, *Citizenship and Social Class* (Cambridge, 1950); or the five-fold distinction made by Lord Bryce, *The American Commonwealth* (2nd edn.; New York, 1910), II, Chapter CXIII; or the different five-fold distinction made by Giovanni Sartori, *Democratic Theory* (Detroit, 1962), p. 340.

[3] This account derives chiefly from the relevant passages translated in H. H. Gerth and C. Wright Mills, eds., *From Max Weber* (New York, 1947).

production, distribution and exchange. This is close to the Marxist definition of class, and should be taken to cover not merely the possession or lack of capital, but also opportunities for any accretion of economic advantage under the conditions of the commodity and labour markets. Under the heading, therefore, of inequality of class we must consider not only differences of income between workers in different occupations, but also such differences as opportunities for upward mobility, advantages in kind, provisions for retirement and security of employment. In addition, there falls under the heading of class-situation what David Lockwood has called 'work-situation'. 'Work-situation', as distinct from 'market-situation', is defined as 'the set of social relationships in which the individual is involved by virtue of his position in the division of labour'.[4] What this means is that manual workers, as a distinct stratum in the economic system, need to be seen not only as vendors of their labour-power, on the Marxist model, but also as persons whose location in the processes of the market habitually separates them, as workers, from those engaged in clerical or managerial tasks. Class-situation, therefore, is itself a complex phenomenon which embraces aspects of a person's economic situation in society which need not be in strict correlation with each other. They all, however, reflect inequalities directly derived from the productive system, so that to speak of a person's 'class' is to speak of his approximate, shared location in the economic hierarchy as opposed to the hierarchies of prestige or of power.

'Status', by contrast, is concerned with social estimation and prestige, and although it is closely related to class it is not synonymous with it. Whether people recognize each other as social, as opposed to economic, equals is apt to depend on whether they share the same class-situation. But this is not necessarily so, as can be easily demonstrated by comparing, for instance, a curate and a bookmaker, or (an example of Orwell's) a naval commander and his grocer. Distinctions of status separate from class are visible among both non-manual and manual workers and their families. Within the same profession and therefore class, doctors or lawyers will belong in different status-groups according to social origin or secondary education or manner of speech. Among manual workers who are all operatives in the same factory, some will assume superior status in the neighbourhood where they live on the basis of a greater exclusiveness or respectability in social contacts and mode of life.[5] Just as habits and norms divide the middle from the

---

[4] David Lockwood, *The Blackcoated Worker* (London, 1958), p. 15.

[5] If documentation is thought necessary, see the description given in the study of a Liverpool housing estate in *Neighbourhood and Community* (Liverpool, 1954), pp. 42 ff.

upper-middle status-groups, so they divide the 'respectable' working-class status-groups from the 'rough'; even such apparently random factors as family size may be a determinant.[6] There is always some sort of relation between the hierarchies of class and status, but status derives from a different aspect of economic behaviour from that which determines class location itself. As Weber emphasizes, status is generally determined by style of consumption rather than source or amount of income. The *nouveau riche* is the most familiar example. He may well be better placed in the economic hierarchy than the impoverished aristocrats whose social recognition he solicits; but until he has successfully modelled his manners and style of life upon theirs, they do not accept him as their equal. Status, like class, can be exceedingly complex. In different societies a man's status may depend not merely on his style of life but on such factors as his race or his age or his religious beliefs, and the problem of 'status-crystallization', which was referred to in the last chapter, depends precisely on this fact. In addition, there may not be complete agreement in any society as to what entitles a person to high or low status. Surveys have shown that there is a remarkable unanimity among industrialized countries on the prestige ranking of different occupations;[7] but there may well be groups within all societies who do not share the commonly accepted gradings and by whom some attributes are quite differently ranked.[8] Thus several qualifications may have to be made in assigning to either a group or a single person a place in the prestige hierarchy of his society. But such placings must be subsumed under the general heading of status, as distinct from class, however much overlap or discrepancy may appear.

Inequality of status, therefore, covers those differences in social attributes and styles of life which are accorded higher or lower prestige. It is in this sense, not the sense of economic class, that the United States is sometimes spoken of as 'classless' or 'egalitarian'; inequalities of class are as wide as in Europe, but, as every European visitor to America has noticed, people in an inferior class-situation feel far less unequal in status. 'There is no rank in America,' wrote Bryce in 1893; 'that is to say, no external and recognized stamp, marking one man as entitled to any social privileges or to deference and respect from others'.[9] In Britain, by

[6] See L. Kuper, ed., *Living in Towns* (London, 1953), p. 78.
[7] See particularly A. Inkeles and Peter H. Rossi, 'National Comparisons of Occupational Prestige', *American Journal of Sociology* LXI (1956), p. 329–39.
[8] As found by Michael Young and Peter Willmott, 'Social Grading by Manual Workers', *British Journal of Sociology* VII (1956), pp. 337–45.
[9] *Op. cit.* II, p. 813.

contrast, distinctions of status are deep-rooted, pervasive and readily visible. Status is manifested in such attributes as education, accent, style of dress and (sometimes independently of class-situation) type of job. Inequality of status, not class, is at issue when a clerical worker looks down on an artisan because he works with his hands or a middle-class father does not want his son to marry a working-class girl. Very often, relative deprivation of status rather than of class lies at the root of what is termed 'class-consciousness'. Although inequalities of all three kinds are complementary aspects of the same situation, this does not make them identical with each other.

It is, therefore, perfectly possible to claim or desire a greater equality of class but not of status, or of status but not of class. The difference can be readily illustrated by taking the two to their extremes. It is possible to envisage two kinds of egalitarian utopias (leaving aside, for the moment, egalitarianism of power). In the first, all economic differentials are abolished, so that a university professor or a minister of state is no more highly rewarded than a labourer; but there still exist graded status-groups whose members rate each other as social equals in a recognized hierarchy of esteem. In the second kind of utopia, every man treats every other as a social equal, whatever individual differences in character and aptitude may remain; but economic differentials are still permitted, and rewards, although not determining status, are themselves determined by criteria which yield considerable variations. Perhaps neither utopia could in practice be realized. But they serve to illustrate that the demands for equality of class and of status need not be synonymous. Such loosely-used phrases as 'social equality' or 'a classless society' may cover either or both of them.

In the same way, inequality of power need not be coterminous with inequality of status or even of class, although the connection between class-situation and power-situation is usually demonstrable enough. Just as it is possible to want to equalize rewards without equalizing status, or vice versa, so it is possible to want to increase or diminish inequality of power independently of either status or class. The holders of power in a society need not be the most highly rewarded of its citizens, or even the most highly esteemed, and the demands of the relatively powerless may be independent of grievances of either class or status. It is true that trade unions, which are the most obvious example of a power-group or stratum, are normally concerned with the attainment of power in order to redress economic inequalities. It is also true that the demand for political equality in the sense of the franchise has almost always been tied both to economic interests and to the demand for social recognition for an underprivileged class. But it is possible to demand universal suffrage or equality before the law or workers' control of industry irrespective of demanding equality of class or status. The wish for a greater say in the decisions to which one's group will be required to submit may be an entirely independent motive. To the extent that power is a separate dimension of stratification from class and status, it must be a separate dimension of social inequality.

Political-cum-legal equality—what the Greeks called *isonomia*—is often distinguished from other kinds; but power is seldom explicitly treated as a dimension of stratification analogous to status and class. There is no equivalent terminology for power. We speak of a 'low-status' occupation, but not of a 'low-power' one; we speak of the 'middle class', but never of the 'middle power-stratum'. Weber himself does not use an equivalent word to *Klassen* and *Stände* when he talks about power: indeed, he is usually concerned with the relative power of classes and status-strata more than with the power hierarchy on its own. He does sometimes speak of 'politically oriented corporate groups', but, even if the phrase is accurate, it is much too cumbrous for ordinary use. In any case, when discussing stratification and inequality we need a word with the overtones of 'stratum' rather than 'group' or 'faction'. It must cover not only 'parties' in the usual sense but also pressure-groups, or trade unions, or any other collectivity whose potential for coercion enables us to place its members at a common level in the hierarchy of power. It might be argued that there is a second good reason for the deficiency of vocabulary since power may be of many different kinds and those who hold it in varying degrees may not feel the least common identity as a social group. But this problem arises equally in the analysis of class and status: Marx's discussion of the French peasantry is the most celebrated of many statements of it. Social inequalities and the attitudes to them must as far as possible be equivalently analyzed in each of the three dimensions of social stratification irrespective of the separate issue of how far the members of a particular category are conscious of their common location.[10]

But although the tripartite distinction may not have been as clearly followed in discussion of inequality as one might expect, this does not mean that the importance of power in the social hierarchy has gone unrecognized. It has even been suggested, for instance, that in advanced industrial societies 'class' should be taken to mean 'conflict groups that are generated by the differential distribution of

[10] To a few writers, however, 'classes' are by definition self-conscious 'action-groups', and on this view it presumably follows that social inequalities are not necessarily differences of 'class' (or status or power).

authority in imperatively coordinated associations'.[11] It might be preferable, for the sake of clarity, to rephrase this as the suggestion that stratification by power is more important that stratification by class, rather than as a redefinition of 'class'. But a strong case can be made for saying that in advanced industrial societies the genesis of 'class conflict' is to be looked for in the distribution of authority rather than of economic benefits. The inequality of power inherent in industrial relations is similarly brought out by G. D. H. Cole in his comment that 'employers and workmen may be, in the eyes of the law, equal parties to a civil contract; but they are never equal parties in fact. The worker, under contract, is bound to serve his employer; the employer is entitled to order the workman about. The relation between them is thus essentially unequal.'[12] A wide variety of writers have argued that equality is unattainable precisely because whatever form a society takes there will have to be some men who are giving orders and others who are following them. To choose only a trivial example, some cogent remarks to this effect can be found in the mouth of Dick Deadeye in Gilbert and Sullivan's *H.M.S. Pinafore*. There is nothing very novel in the emphasis on either status or power as against economic class. What is difficult is to retain the tripartite distinction throughout all discussion of social stratification and the feelings of relative deprivation to which it gives rise.

The problem of terminology can be met only by laying down a chosen procedure and following it as consistently as possible. The lack of a generally accepted practice is largely due to the variety of overtones which the term 'class' has acquired in English. We speak of a 'middle-class' house, or education, or way of speaking, when status rather than class is meant. We use the term 'ruling class' to talk about the holders of power. The phrase 'social class' may cover either or both of class and status. Furthermore, both 'class' and 'status' often carry a still broader sense: 'class' can be a virtual synonym for 'category' and 'status' for 'role'. Nor has the situation been helped by the diversity of jargon among academic writers; the sociological literature contains every kind of possible phrase, including both 'class status' and 'status class'. The practice which I shall accordingly follow is this: I shall use 'class' and 'status' in the sense which I have roughly defined and which derives

[11] Ralf Dahrendorf, *Class and Class Conflict in an Industrial Society* (Stanford, 1959), p. 204.

[12] G. D. H. Cole, *British Trade Unionism Today* (London, 1939), p. 86; cf. e.g., R. H. Tawney, *Equality* (rev. edn.; London, 1952), pp. 65–66, or Allan Flanders, *The Fawley Productivity Agreements* (London, 1964), p. 235: 'To use a political analogy, management represents the government of industry, and the unions, at their most effective, never more than a permanent opposition'.

from Weber; I shall use 'stratum' as the general term for a group or category of people who can be collectively ranked in any one, or all, of the three dimensions of social inequality; and I shall use 'stratification' as the corresponding abstract noun. I shall, however, use the phrases 'working class' and 'middle class' as synonyms for the manual and non-manual strata respectively (postponing for the moment the further difficulties of the manual/non-manual distinction). I shall also use 'working-class' and 'middle-class' as the corresponding adjectives, without in either case tying the meaning to class, status or power except to such extent as is made clear by the context.

This procedure is neither very elegant nor wholly unambiguous, but it is the best that can be done. The matter is further complicated by the use of survey material in which people are asked questions about 'class' which are neither phrased nor answered in terms of Weber's distinction. As a result, what people say has to be translated out of their own words and into the words of the investigator. There is, however, no objection in principle to this. It is true that whatever theoretical or terminological framework is used by the academic investigator, his subjects will not necessarily think in terms of it; but the framework will not be right or wrong solely for that reason.

At the same time, this is not to say that people's own views of the question can be disregarded by the investigator. In the first place, people's own pictures of how their society is stratified plays an important part in their feelings, or lack of feelings, of relative deprivation. In the second, stratification by status depends by definition on the prestige which people assign to their own and other groups; people may be wrong about 'subjective' status in the sense that their own prestige is not what they think it is, but the status-structure of their society is in fact determined solely by the feelings of its members. It is, therefore, just as important to know how stratification is seen by people themselves as to establish an 'objective' framework for assessing their views in terms of the relation between inequality and grievance.

There is some useful material on 'subjective' stratification from Britain,[13] as well as some from the United States,[14] Germany,[15]

[13] F. M. Martin, 'Some Subjective Aspects of Social Stratification', in D. V. Glass, ed., *Social Mobility in Britain* (London, 1954), Chapter III; Elizabeth Bott, *Family and Social Network* (London, 1957), Chapter VI.

[14] In particular, R. Centers, *The Psychology of Social Class* (Princeton, 1949); but see also e.g., J. G. Manis and B. N. Meltzer, 'Attitudes of Textile Workers to Class Structure', *American Journal of Sociology* LX (1954), pp. 30–35.

[15] H. Popitz *et al.*, *Das Gesellschaftsbild des Arbeiters* (2nd edn.; Tübingen, 1961).

French Switzerland,[16] and Australia.[17] On the basis of these studies, the pictures of Western industrial society which its inhabitants have can in principle be classified in terms of class, status and power models (or mixed models incorporating elements of all three). Although different terminologies have been used by the different investigators as well as by the different respondents whom they have interviewed, the distinction still holds good. A pure power model is not found very often; it is the type of model used by people who see society in terms of 'us' and 'them', where 'them' means those seen to be in authority, such as the government and the bosses, rather than the rich or the socially esteemed. A status model is the type where society is seen as arranged in a graded hierarchy of prestige; users of status models tend to see the social hierarchy as composed of more numerous and overlapping 'classes' (that is, status-strata) than the users of power or class models. A class model, finally, is a model based on distinctions of job or income, and particularly on the economic aspects of a person's job. In a status model also, occupation may play an important role. But in a status model, the social aspect is more significant than the economic. The prestige of a job, or the style of life that goes with it, or the educational qualifications which it requires, are what matter for the hierarchy of status. In a power model, by contrast, the authority invested in certain occupational positions is their most important feature; and in a class model, the significance of occupations is the wealth or security of tenure which will accrue from them. In either a pure model or a combination of the three society may in principle be seen as divided into any number of separate strata. But in practice, the users of class models seem seldom to envisage more than two or at most three strata; only the users of status models may be aware of a slightly more complex multiplicity of levels.

It is obvious that many people will operate with a mixture of these models. Moreover, they may apply a different model in a different context or they may have no explicit views on the matter at all. But not the least interesting result of these studies is to show how rarely this is so. There are bound to be a few respondents whose pictures of society are so anomalous or unclear that any categorization would be illegitimate. In addition, there are always a few who resolutely refuse to avow any acceptance of the term 'class' at all. But in general, the studies carried out afford strong evidence that in advanced industrial societies the majority of people do have an explicit picture of their social hierarchy and that most

[16] A. Willener, *Images de la Société et Classes Sociales* (Berne, 1957).
[17] O. A. Oeser and S. B. Hammond, *Social Structure and Personality in a City* (London, 1954), Chapters XXI and XXII.

of these pictures fall into one or other of a relatively few distinguishable categories.[18] The 'subjective' evidence cannot by itself show how systems of stratification ought best to be classified; but it does provide further support for the validity of the tripartite distinction between class, status and power.

The most difficult question, however, is not how many dimensions of stratification there are, but where the dividing-line should be drawn within each. The dividing-line around which this study is organized is that between the manual and non-manual strata, defined in terms of occupation or, in the case of married women, husband's occupation. But this division, although widely used, could be argued to be no more significant for social inequality than others, and it is in any case difficult to define exactly. The Registrar-General uses it but he does not give a criterion for it, and he deliberately conflates class and status: his two classifications by 'social class' and 'socio-economic group' are explicitly based on considerations of 'standing within the community' and on the correlation of occupational position with similarities of 'social, cultural and re-creational standards and behaviour'[19]. No single criterion is satisfactory; and whatever definition is used, there will be some difficult borderline cases. But despite the difficulty of precise demarcation, the manual/non-manual division can be defined and applied in such a way that the number of borderline cases is small. I have therefore relegated the problem of applying it to an appendix,[20] where it is discussed with detailed reference to the analysis of the survey. It is, however, necessary to give some justification for adopting it in the first place as the principal line of demarcation, however widely it may be recognized and used.

It can, indeed, be attacked from either of two opposite viewpoints. On one view, deriving from Marx, the dichotomy is not between manual and non-manual workers but between the capitalists and the propertyless; on the opposite view, deriving from the alleged *embourgeoisement* of the working class, the line is, if anywhere, between skilled and unskilled, since many manual workers have become so prosperous as not to be ranked as proletarians but rather as members of a newly emergent 'middle class'. Either of these two criticisms can be supported by the observation that many manual workers now earn as much as or more than many white-collar workers. On either argument, some manual and some non-manual

[18] See particularly the tables shown in Willener, *op. cit.*, p. 161 and Popitz, *op. cit.*, p. 233.
[19] *Classification of Occupations 1960* (H.M.S.O.), pp. x–xi.
[20] See Appendix 3, 'The Manual/Non-manual Distinction.'

workers, even if they should still be assigned to different status-strata, nevertheless belong to the same economic class: to the Marxist, all clerical workers are below the proletarian line; to the anti-Marxist, many manual workers are above it. Both these arguments, however, are outweighed by other aspects of the structure of inequalities which still divide the manual from the non-manual worker in class as well as status. To argue that this remains the fundamental distinction is not to deny that a partial breakdown of it may be taking place. But the breakdown, if that is what it is, cannot be claimed to have gone so far that the two categories have merged, whether on one side of the line or the other. It is therefore necessary to look at the changes which are taking place initially in terms of the manual/non-manual distinction, even if the conclusion to which this leads is that the distinction is not as significant as it once was.

This is not to say that the divisions to be drawn within the two strata are not for some purposes as significant as those between them. In the hierarchy of class, there is obviously a difference between craftsmen and labourers, just as there is between the lowest-paid clerical workers and the possessors of land or capital or highly marketable professional skills. In the hierarchy of status, the difference between the middle and the upper strata may be as wide or wider than that between the artisan and the clerk: the members of the upper stratum may no more often treat as equals those differently brought up from themselves than the lower stratum of white-collar workers will treat the skilled manual workers with whom they might have shared a common schooling. In the hierarchy of power, indeed, it is hardest to show that the manual/non-manual division is fundamental. The lower-paid white-collar worker is in general as much the recipient of orders as the manual worker, and may have no more influence than the member of a strong trade union on the processes of decision by which his working life is governed; it is only the tendency of the non-manual stratum not to form trade unions and to identify its political interests with the strata opposed to labour which shows the division to be important in the dimension of power as well as status and class. If, however, one looks in broad terms at the social structure of an advanced industrial society such as Britain, it is difficult not to see the biggest single division as that between the two out of three people the head of whose household works with his hands, and the one out of three the head of whose household does not.

Of the reasons why manual and non-manual workers should still be assigned to separate strata, one of the most important is 'work-situation' in Lockwood's sense. Although manual and clerical workers can be described with equal truth as virtually propertyless, and although their level of wages and salaries overlaps to an increasing extent, they are nevertheless engaged, as a result of their different location in the processes of production, in fundamentally different work. It is not only different in its externals—the white collar as against the calloused hands, or the desk instead of the machine. It is different in terms of the relation between employer and employee. The clerical worker may be less one of 'them' than the manual worker thinks him, but he is still closer to 'them', both literally and metaphorically, than the manual worker is. This may not have been so in the days when a 'factory' consisted of a handful of craftsmen who were all on personal terms with the head of the firm; and it may not be so in the future when both manual and clerical work have become completely automated. But in the mid-twentieth century, the division between 'works' and 'staff' is basic to large-scale industry, and it is this division which places the clerical worker on one side and the manual worker on the other. Moreover, the non-manual worker's work-situation is a determinant of his place in the status hierarchy also; he is associated with the employers by being associated with that part of the productive process where authority is exercised and decisions taken. This still does not make his own location in the power hierarchy of society any higher than that of the manual worker; this is always a function of unionization more than of location in the productive process. But in conditions of work the white-collar worker is on the other side of a distinctive line from the manual worker, and this is both a significant aspect of his class-situation and also one of the determinants of his status.

The class-situation of the non-manual worker is different in other respects also. Even if his salary, particularly at the early stages of his career, is below what is earned by many manual workers, he has the prospect of both a greater security of tenure and a greater increment in reward. By and large, the non-manual worker's income can be expected to rise steadily with length of service and experience, whereas a manual worker may well reach his maximum earning power in his 20's. There are exceptions to this, notably in the steel industry, where a manual worker's earnings will increase markedly as a result of promotion within the range of manual work. But this is rare. The great majority of manual jobs are such that there is no premium on experience, and increasing age, particularly if coupled with ill-health, will be a greater disadvantage than it will ever be in non-manual work. The premium on experience may become a disadvantage when unemployment is severe, because a man whose job in one firm has been taken away will find his experience no recommendation to any prospective employer except the one who has just declared him redundant. But as we shall see in the following chapter, even when unemployment in Britain has been widespread its incidence has been a good deal lower among non-manual than manual workers. Moreover, greater economic advantages are enjoyed by non-manual workers in such things as holidays, allowances and provisions for retirement, and apart from all these the manual worker is likely to have to work considerably longer hours than the clerical worker in order to equal him in income. Thus neither the partial equivalence of earnings between the manual and non-manual class, nor their common propertylessness, should be allowed to outweigh the distinction in class-situation between them.

The argument for continuing to treat the manual/non-manual division as basic is further supported by the evidence on subjective attitudes to stratification, even though, as I have said, this does not make it necessarily correct. In spite of the additional divisions or sub-divisions also cited by respondents, the relevant studies seem to bear out the significance in most people's minds of this central division. Willener, though explicitly more cautious than Centers about placing too much emphasis on a manual/non-manual dichotomy,[21] still notes how often responses are given in terms of either 'middle class' or 'working class'. There are many people who will place themselves in either the 'middle' or 'working' class without exactly meaning by this the manual or non-manual stratum; but this is still the commonest criterion given. Martin found that among a sample drawn in Greenwich and Hertford in 1950 four out of five respondents explicitly assigned themselves to the 'working' or 'middle' class when asked first 'How many social classes would you say there are in this country?', second 'Can you name them?', and then 'Which of these classes do you belong to?'[22] Popitz suggests that the manual/non-manual distinction may be considerably reinforced by the belief of manual workers that it is only they who really 'work';[23] in other words, what they see clerical workers doing seems to them not only easier (in the English term, 'cushier') than what they do themselves, but it is also harder for them to see its relation to the actual production of goods. Zweig, writing about London in 1946–7, called the difference in mentality, attitude and behaviour between the two 'perhaps the most outstanding single fact' brought to light by his enquiry.[24] In England, further evidence may be adduced from the popular image of the two major political parties, particularly the Labour Party. To most Englishmen, the Labour

[21] *Op. cit.*, p. 216.
[22] *Op. cit.*, pp. 54–5.
[23] *Op. cit.*, pp. 237 ff.
[24] F. Zweig, *Labour, Life and Poverty* (London, 1948), p. 88.

Party is the party of the working class; and the working class means those who work with their hands.

In the same way, the evidence for subjective attitudes to stratification reinforces the argument for treating the manual/non-manual line as fundamental in the hierarchy of status. Evidence about self-rated 'class' is likely to be relevant here precisely because the distinction between class and status is explicit in very few people's minds; attitudes about status expressed in terms of 'class' can preserve the manual/non-manual distinction even when rewards are more or less equal. There is not yet sufficient evidence to dispute Lockwood's assertion, in his discussion of the status-situation of the clerical worker, that 'there are many indications that the division between manual and non-manual work is still a factor of enduring significance in the determination of class-consciousness, despite changes in the relative economic position of the two groups'.[25] This seems, moreover, to be true on both sides of the line. Not only do manual workers often seem contemptuous of the lower-middle class,[26] but it is often the members of the lower-middle class who are most anxious to distinguish themselves in prestige and social contacts from manual workers. Willmott and Young, studying the London suburb of Woodford in 1959, concluded that a greater equivalence of incomes, houses and styles of life had the effect of reinforcing the endeavours of the middle class to preserve the status barrier between themselves and manual workers.[27] The equivalence of incomes makes it possible in principle for working-class families to adopt a style of life similar to that of middle-class families whose earnings are the same; the assimilation in style of dress which has to some extent taken place since the Second World War is one manifestation of this.[28] But the visible differences in manners, education and leisure are still there; and the division at places of work between 'staff' and 'works' still continues to reinforce the disincentive for those on either side of the line to treat each other as status equals.

If manual and clerical workers were all to treat each other as equals, ask each other with equal frequency into each others'

[25] *The Blackcoated Worker*, p. 131.

[26] Martin, *op. cit.*, p. 61; and cf. e.g., Zweig, *The British Worker* (London, 1952), p. 206.

[27] Peter Willmott and Michael Young, *Family and Class in a London Suburb* (London, 1960), p. 122.

[28] See e.g. the remark of a middle-aged East End workman that 'In my days, you could tell a workman by his dress, even on a Sunday, but you can't now', quoted by Zweig, *The British Worker*, p. 164; and cf. Mark Abrams, *The Changing Pattern of Consumer Spending* (London, 1959) for evidence on the assimilation of styles of life.

houses as friends, and so on, then differences in styles of dress or speech or leisure, however visible, would cease to constitute barriers of status. But no one can seriously suppose that this has yet happened in Britain; and therefore the differences which remain in styles of dress and the rest can be legitimately described as 'objective' status differences. It is also true that gradations of status may be so subtle that it becomes impossible to draw a line between one subdivision and the next. There have always been intricate subdivisions within the manual as well as the non-manual stratum: the 'aristocrats of labour' of the Victorian period were aristocrats of status as well as of class, and some middle-class differentiations of status in terms of schooling, or accent, or family are particularly difficult to pin down. No hard and fast line can be drawn within the hierarchy of status to distinguish the 'respectable' working class from the 'rough', or the 'U' middle class from the 'non-U', although both these distinctions have a meaning. But one of the strongest arguments for drawing the principal line between manual and non-manual workers is the well-attested difference in the traditional values and ethos of the two strata—a difference which at once derives from and helps to preserve the other differences of which I have been speaking.

This difference can be put in one way by saying that working-class norms are 'collectivist' and middle-class norms 'individualist';[29] this is one reason why the relative deprivations felt by working-class people are more likely to be what I have called 'fraternalistic' and those felt by middle-class people 'egoistic'. The 'collectivistic' norms extend over a wide area of attitudes and behaviour, including not merely attitudes to the social structure. For Britain, they are vividly described in Hoggart's *Uses of Literacy*.[30] They embody a whole different attitude to life from that in which the middle-class child is reared, and they are reinforced throughout adult life by the differences in both work-situation and market-situation which separate the manual from the non-manual stratum. They are not, of course, universally shared by manual workers and their families. But they are sufficiently strong and widespread to reinforce very considerably the barriers of status which divide the two strata. Even where a manual and a non-manual family may be earning as much as each other the difference in outlook is likely to be enough to sustain the mutual distrust described in Woodford by Willmott and Young. Quite apart, moreover, from the wish of the middle class not to accept manual workers as social equals, the 'collectivist' attitudes of

[29] J. H. Goldthorpe and David Lockwood, 'Affluence and the British Class Structure', *Sociological Review* n.s. XI (1963), pp. 146–8.
[30] Richard Hoggart, *The Uses of Literacy* (London, 1957).

the working class may lead its members not to have any wish to be so treated. Some convincing evidence for this is provided by investigations carried out in the United States.[31] Even in a country where manual incomes are higher and status-differences less than in Britain, it seems that prosperity need not assimilate manual workers to non-manual in either personal contacts or social norms.

The claim that the working and middle class were becoming steadily fused was quite often made in the 1930's, and increasingly so during the 1940's and '50s. But it must for all the reasons which I have given be heavily qualified. It has, indeed, come under effective attack, notably in the work of Lockwood.[32] It is unquestionable that the difference between the manual and non-manual strata was in many respects wider in 1918 than 1962; the changes which occurred between these two dates will in part be documented in the following chapters. But they are not such as to shift the most important dividing-line in the British social structure, whether considered in the light of inequalities of status or of class. The principal question, therefore, in examining the relation between inequality and grievance, is how far the relative deprivations felt by the members of the manual stratum are proportionate to its position of inequality by comparison with the non-manual.

This is true also in the dimension of power. Power raises difficulties of its own, and I shall say less about it than the other two. But any discussion of the relation between inequality and grievance would be incomplete without some reference to it. Not only are the implications of social justice different for power as against class and status. In addition, it is impossible to understand the radicalism, or lack of it, of the British working class without understanding something of how both its power-situation and its members' own view of its power-situation have altered since 1918. I shall not explore this in any detail, since it leads almost at once into the separate and specialized field of industrial sociology. In a country where universal suffrage and equality before the law are established and where there

---

[31] See particularly A. Kornhauser *et al.*, *How Labour Votes* (New York. 1956), Chapter VII and Bennett M. Berger, *Working-class Suburb* (Berkeley, Calif., 1960); and cf. e.g., R. A. Dahl, *Who Governs?* (New Haven, 1961), pp 232–3.

[32] As well as *The Blackcoated Worker*, see 'The New Working Class' *Archives Européennes de Sociologie* I (1960), pp. 248–259, and Goldthorpe and Lockwood, *op. cit.* For an attempt to relate some of the evidence of the present study to Goldthorpe and Lockwood's model of *embourgeoisement*, see W. G. Runciman, '*Embourgeoisement*, Self-rated Class and Party Preference', *Sociological Review* n.s. XII (1964), pp. 137–154. For references to statements of the *embourgeoisement* thesis, see the footnotes to the papers by Goldthorpe and Lockwood and by myself.

is a strong left-wing party explicitly formed to represent the working-class interest, inequalities of power are perceived and resented mainly in the relations between employer and employee. This complex topic lies outside the scope of this book, and the sample survey does not attempt to deal with it. I shall, however, suggest that the relation between inequality and grievance is different in this dimension of inequality also. In each dimension, the relation between inequality and grievance can only be settled by asking separately what are the inequalities to which manual workers and their families are subject, and whether the relative deprivations which they feel are proportionate to them. Only then can the further question be asked whether the relative deprivations felt in each dimension accord with the demands of social justice.

PART TWO
THE HISTORICAL BACKGROUND
1918-1962

IV

CHANGING COMPARISONS
OF CLASS

INEQUALITIES of class, and the feelings of relative deprivation to which they give rise, can generally be described in monetary and therefore quantitative terms. Provided that account is taken not only of income but of fringe benefits, hours worked, chances for mobility and provisions for retirement, the class-situations of the manual and non-manual strata can be approximately compared. Evidence for the relative deprivation felt by either stratum is, unfortunately, less reliable and harder to find. But there is enough indirect evidence for the period since 1918 to suggest what results might be expected from a survey in 1962, and why. The period between 1918 and 1962—between Lloyd George's 'homes fit for heroes' and Harold Macmillan's 'never had it so good'—saw many changes in all three dimensions of social inequality. In none did grievance correlate with actual inequality. If class is considered first, it is readily demonstrable that relative deprivation was only intermittently felt in proportion to the facts of the distribution of wealth. Three main influences in fact determined the pattern of reference group choices: first, the effects of war; second, the speed and impact of economic advance or recession; and third, changes in the visibility of economic inequalities. The outcome of these was that the non-manual stratum, although in general better off than the manual, was no less likely to feel relatively deprived. The manual stratum, by contrast, was largely inhibited from the choice of non-manual reference groups by which its sense of relative deprivation would have been heightened. To see how this came about, however, it is necessary to go back to the sudden but short-lived explosion of aspirations which followed the end of the First World War.

'The war', wrote Keynes in 1919, 'has disclosed the possibility of consumption to all and the vanity of abstinence to many.'[1] In

[1] J. M. Keynes, *The Economic Consequences of the Peace* (London, 1919), p. 19.

the aftermath of victory, the same theme was reiterated, if less succinctly, by a succession of writers pronouncing upon the state of Britain. The *Economist,* in its Commercial History and Review of 1919, saw the wage-earners encouraged in their insistence on more pay and shorter hours by the 'orgy of extravagance' in which the well-to-do were indulging.[2] Seebohm Rowntree, in the Preface to the revised edition of his pre-war study of *Poverty,* declared of the workers of 1922 that 'though they often are compelled to fall below the standard which the war made possible, they are determined to regain it at the earliest opportunity. Meanwhile they claim as a right a better maintenance than they would once have begged as a privilege.'[3] 'It would be well', warned C. F. G. Masterman, in the sequel to his book of 1909 on *The Condition of England,* 'if those who are spending would realize that it is necessary to go softly and behind closed doors, and to realize that they are being watched by thousands of eyes, awakened to criticism by the grim education of war.'[4] These examples could readily be multiplied. All observers, however they might differ about what ought to be done, seemed agreed about the changes that had happened. The pre-war pattern of reference groups had been disrupted for good.

The First World War, therefore, needs to be seen as having ended an epoch if only because it was seen like this by those who lived through it. But, of course, a good deal of qualification is necessary. It is a commonplace that history can never be so neatly partitioned, and historians will have to continue to argue what might have happened if war had not broken out in the summer of 1914. Dangerfield, whose *Strange Death of Liberal England* paints perhaps the most lurid picture of Asquith's government groping through its last pre-war years, goes so far as to describe the War as having hastened everything, but started nothing.[5] This categorical statement is a little extreme. But those who, in the aftermath of the bloodiest war in Europe's history, looked back to the order and stability of the Edwardian world were sometimes apt to forget the ferment of industrial and social unrest with which Asquith's government had been confusedly trying to deal. Lloyd George, in a speech delivered on July 17th, 1914, had declared that if the threats of the Irish Rebellion and the Triple Industrial Alliance were to materialize, then in such an event 'the situation will be the gravest with which

---

[2] *Economist,* Feb. 21, 1920.

[3] B. Seebohm Rowntree, *Poverty* (rev. edn.; London, 1922), p. xv.

[4] C. F. G. Masterman, *England After War* (London, 1922), p. 97.

[5] George Dangerfield, *The Strange Death of Liberal England* (London, 1935), p. viii (and cf. e.g. Roger Fulford, *Votes for Women* [London, 1957], p. 298).

any government has had to deal for centuries'.[6] Sir George Ask-with, the astute and patient mediator of the fierce industrial disputes of 1911 to 1914, told the Cavendish Club in Bristol in November 1913, 'That the present unrest will cease I do not believe for a moment; it will increase, and probably increase with greater force. Within a comparatively short time there may be movements in this country coming to a head of which recent events have been a small foreshadowing.'[7] Ernest Bevin, at the Shaw Enquiry of 1920, said of 1914 that 'It was a period which, if the war had not broken out, would have, I believe, seen one of the greatest industrial revolts the world would ever have seen.'[8] The shrewder observers of Edwardian England were well aware that they were living in a period of rapid social change whose outcome it was impossible to foresee. In sketching the background, therefore, to a sample survey of 1962, it is legitimate to begin at 1918 only if the break is not seen as quite so abrupt as the war itself had made it appear.

But the break was nonetheless a real one. Indeed, 1918 can be legitimately taken as a landmark for other reasons than the ending of the War. Not only was it in February of 1918 that the Labour Party Conference adopted the constitution which is generally held to mark the emergence of Labour as an established, powerful and non-revolutionary left-wing party. In addition, it was only after the Representation of the People Act of 1918 that Britain could be properly regarded as a political democracy with (bar only the women in their twenties) a fully enfranchised working class. And thirdly, it was in 1918 that the Fisher Education Act made schooling compulsory until 14. Thus the date is significant enough for inequalities alike of class, status and power. It is necessary, even in a superficial résumé of the period between the wars, to go back occasionally to the situation as it was before 1914. But 1918 may fairly be taken as the starting-point of the changes in the pattern of social inequality which did or, more surprisingly, did not follow from the altered reference groups which were the legacy of the War.

THE INTER-WAR YEARS

The principal change was the change in economic expectations and standards summarized by Keynes. But in addition to purely monetary aspirations, there were relative deprivations of both status and

[6] Quoted E. Halévy, *A History of the English People in the Nineteenth century, VI: The Rule of Democracy 1905–14,* Book II (London, 1952), p. 486.

[7] Lord Askwith, *Industrial Problems and Disputes* (London, 1920), p. 349.

[8] *Report of the Transport Workers' Court of Enquiry* (Cmd. 936, 1920) I, 495, cited hereafter as Shaw Enquiry.

power which the war had done much either to create or to promote. Women, for example, had begun to expect an equality of status beyond the simple equality of franchise so fiercely fought for before the war and so lightly granted during it. The trade unions were demanding not only an increase in economic rewards for their members, but a recognition of their heightened position in the hierarchy of power. The pressure on facilities for secondary education, due partly, in the view of the Board of Education, to high war wages and partly to the cumulative changes which had been 'working silently and unsuspected beneath the surface',[9] increased with a startling suddenness. In 1919, it was the feeling of post-war indulgences deserved which (in contrast to the self-conscious austerity of 1946) pushed the aspirations of all sections of society so high.

There was, however, a major difference between the aspirations of the Labour movement and those of the employers. To Labour, the aspirations whose realization had been earned were aspirations to standards which the war appeared to have made possible. The aspirations of the employers, by contrast, were for a return to what they meant by 'normalcy'—that is, for the world of high profits, plentiful labour and minimal government control which they remembered from the years before 1914. Thus the unanimity of public pronouncements about what should be done after the war concealed a fundamental divergence. There was a marked contrast between the seeming receptivity of governmental and public opinion to the egalitarian demands of Labour and the return in practice to a 'normalcy' which meant a denial of working-class interests. Arthur Henderson and G. D. H. Cole, in a memorandum submitted to the Joint Committee of the National Industrial Conference of 1919, quoted what Lloyd George had said to a Labour Party Deputation about 'a really new world', and argued that 'In view of the attitude now adopted by the Government in regard to industrial reconstruction, these words of the Prime Minister must be regarded as a material cause of Labour unrest.'[10] The failure to meet the demands of Labour, therefore, was not simply a frustration by economic necessity of purposes which an unlucky government had done its best to fulfil. This description would fit more appropriately the situation of Ramsay MacDonald's second government than Lloyd George's. In 1919 there was, rather, the awareness among the representatives of Labour that it was not the hopes of the working class that the government was seriously trying to realize.

[9] *Report of the Board of Education for the Year 1923–24* (Cmd. 2443, 1925), p. 23.

[10] *Report of Provisional Joint Committee Presented to Meeting of Industrial Conference, Central Hall, Westminster, April 4th, 1919* (Cmd. 501, 1920), Appx. I, p. ii.

A detailed account of how the grievances of Labour were placated or withstood without its demands being granted is beyond the scope of a brief summary. The skill of Lloyd George, the erratic economic conditions and the actions of individual unions and employers are all a necessary part of the story. What is interesting from the standpoint of relative deprivation is simply that the placation was successfully achieved. At the end of the war, the sense of relative deprivation among the working class was unmistakably high, not only in terms of class, but of status and power. The story of the period between the two wars, therefore, is of a decline or, at least, a considerable appeasement of relative deprivation among the less fortunately placed; and by egalitarian standards, at any rate, it is a story of a continuing discrepancy between objective situation and the level of relative deprivation which could, from this point of view, have been expected to accompany it. The gap between the promises of the Coalition and its subsequent actions is one of the most notorious in the long history of English social reform. Yet this failure, far from arousing a strong and cumulative resentment among those for whom a 'really new world' was to be built, never led to the degree of militant egalitarianism which such failure might be thought bound to evoke.

The outburst of industrial unrest which followed the War did not last beyond 1921, and the actual number of strikes declined after 1920. If, as a different index of industrial unrest, we take the number of workers involved in strikes and the number of days which strikes lasted, then the decline does not occur until 1922; but this marks the effective onset of the Depression. The General Strike of 1926 was, of course, still to take place. But the General Strike must be looked at principally in the light of the unhappy history of the coal industry, and it would be a mistake to take it as of itself an indicator of too widespread or intensely felt discontents. It did afford a notable demonstration of Labour solidarity; but this is a different matter. It was only in the period after the war that the manifestations of Labour unrest were such as to invite comparison with the disturbances which had characterized the immediate pre-war period. This is not to say that strikes are at all a straightforward or unambiguous indicator of resentment of inequalities of class. But if a broad generalization is possible, the periods of intensive strike activity in Britain during the twentieth century coincide less with the periods of severest misery than with the periods in which economic expectations once raised have been disappointed. This is partly because when times are hardest no one can afford to go on strike; but it is at the same time partly because frustrated expectations are less readily tolerable than consistent hardship. Between 1919 and

1921 the Government succeeded in diverting the threat of severe labour unrest without either embarking on any large-scale reorganization of industry or doing more than a prudent minimum (as in the police and rail strikes) to meet the workers' wage demands. Once the Depression had set in, diversion became less necessary. The Depression served to pare down reference groups as effectively as the war had served to heighten them.

This does not mean that either hardship or suffering were lessened. Hardship was in many ways sharply increased, and workers may have been just as anxious to strike in 1922 as they had been in 1919 if only they could have felt sufficient economic security to do so. But to emphasize that prosperity is a necessary permissive condition of many expressions of discontent is only to emphasize the importance for the sense of relative deprivation of what are seen to be the limits of feasibility. The Depression reduced rather than heightened the magnitude and intensity of relative deprivation because few of its victims felt it to be obviously avoidable. This does not apply in the notable cases of what was felt as extreme injustice in particular industries or areas or among particular categories of people. The miners, for example, who felt cheated of governmental promises of reform and victimized by wage-cuts which differed arbitrarily from district to district, felt progressively more aggrieved as the Depression wore on.[11] So did those of the unemployed and their dependants who were the victims of severe anomalies in the often haphazard welfare provisions introduced or amended by successive governments. But many of the victims of the Depression, or even the majority, seem to have thought of themselves as victims of misfortune rather than injustice. If redress of hardship is seen to be feasible, then the greater the hardship the greater the sense of relative deprivation. But the less feasible redress appears to be, the less relative deprivation is felt and the more the frame of reference is restricted to such few advantages as might still be retained.

To read the Parliamentary Debates of the period is to be forcibly reminded of the helplessness of all sections of opinion in the face of the obstinate continuance of unemployment. The spokesmen of successive governments held out perennial hopes of a forthcoming

[11] Within the mining industry, however, there were notable regional variations in unrest: the miners of Northumberland and Durham throughout the century have been less prone to strike than the miners of South Wales. But this too may be partly explained in terms of relative deprivation, since the contrast between pre-war prosperity and post-war depression was much more severe in South Wales. On the difference in the attitudes of employers and employees to each other in the two areas, see e.g. Asa Briggs, 'The Social Background', in A. Flanders and H. A. Clegg, eds., *Industrial Relations in Great Britain* (Oxford, 1954), pp. 17–18.

revival in trade. The limited recovery at the end of 1923 not only encouraged ministerial optimism but persuaded the unions that they might be able to regain some of the wage-cuts forced on them in the previous two years. The return to the Gold Standard announced in Churchill's budget of 1925 seemed to symbolize a recovery at last of pre-war stability. The General Strike could be disproportionately blamed for any gloomy figures in the trade returns for the period which followed it. There was another twitch of apparent prosperity in 1927–28. But the signs of recovery turned out every time to be illusory. In June 1929, when the second Labour Government took office pledged to deal 'immediately and practically' with the problem of unemployment, the promise did not seem implausible. But the Government was less than half a year old when the short-lived period of calm turned out to be as illusory as the rest. Wall Street crashed at the end of October. In November, the unemployment figure was still a little lower than it had been the year before; but the seasonal rise in unemployment, instead of falling off again in the spring, only mounted still higher. By the end of 1930, when Labour had been in power for a year and a half, the percentage of insured workers registered as unemployed was roughly twice what it had been when Labour took office—nearly 20% as compared with under 10%. In spite of the diversity of remedies proposed—or perhaps precisely because they were so various—neither the Government nor the Opposition nor the employers nor the trade unions could offer a sufficiently convincing diagnosis. Unemployment seemed the consequence not of a detectable blunder but rather of an incurable disease. Its victims did not appear to be the victims of remediable injustice so much as of an Act of God.

Anyone brought up under the benign shadow of the Beveridge Report and its conclusion that the privations of the inter-war period were, in Beveridge's phrase, a 'needless scandal', cannot but be startled to read how oppressive and widespread was the feeling of pessimism and helplessness. This was true as much on the Left as on the Right. Beatrice Webb, in her diary for September 20th, 1927, asked

'And is there any practicable solution, should this unemployment prove to be not only chronic but also progressive? If such a disaster is actually imminent, will any change in administration, policy and procedure avail to alter the result? Might it not be a question of muddling through, curbing and checking the present Poor Law administration until a lowered birthrate, emigration and even a higher death-rate brought about a new equilibrium of population with natural resources?'[12]

[12] *Diaries, 1924–32* (ed. M. I. Cole; London, 1956), pp. 153–4.

These despondent queries are typical of a widespread feeling that a high rate of chronic unemployment was a natural calamity which the political nostrums of any faction or party could do no more than mildly alleviate. Lloyd George's programme for the election of 1929 did, it is true, embody much of what was later to be accepted as orthodox remedy: deficit financing, public works, central manipulation of credit and the extension of government control over industry. But not only was it dismissed by his opponents at the time ('rather vainglorious', said *The Times*);[13] after the events which followed, and particularly after Labour's failure to make good an equally confident pledge, the remedies later considered the right ones were seen merely as a few among many conflicting and equally credible proposals. There was, if anything, too much advice available rather than too little. The schemes proposed ranged all the way from draconian wage-cuts to road-building in the Highlands to colonization in Western Australia. The net result was to reinforce the conviction that there was no good answer except to sit tight.

It may be that the attitude of the country at large would have been different if some of the leading personalities involved had acted differently: if, for instance, Snowden had not been so indissolubly wedded to the 'Treasury view', or if Mosley had been more adroit in persuading the Labour Party to accept his ideas. Despite the real and unavoidable decline in Britain's trading position, it must, at least, remain arguable that events might have made it possible for those whose proposals now seem most enlightened to try to implement them. But this speculation leads to controversies which are still unsettled and which are in any case irrelevant to the present argument. All that matters is that none of those whose remedies might have been efficacious commanded a following sufficient to make the country as a whole feel that unemployment was not only an intolerable hardship but the 'needless scandal' it was later to appear. If the Keynesian answer was available in embryo, it was far from being seen as such by his contemporaries in general.[14] The far Left could likewise be claimed to have been nearer the solution than Snowden or the bankers: their speeches contain numerous such recommendations as Brockway's that 'there must be an increase of the purchasing power of the mass of the people before there can

[13] *Times*, March 13, 1929.

[14] A reading of the Minutes of Evidence of the Macmillan Committee (*Committee on Finance and Industry* [Cmd. 3897, 1931]) makes it clear that the Keynes of 1931 was not yet the Keynes of the *General Theory*. See in addition Alan Bullock, *The Life and Times of Ernest Bevin* (London, 1960), I, pp. 425 ff., and in particular the remarks in Private Session quoted on p. 431.

be any reduction of unemployment',[15] or Maxton's that what was needed was 'to improve the trade of this country by improving the purchasing power of the common people'.[16] But here again, there was no argument sufficient to empower this viewpoint to overcome the prevailing orthodoxies. Ernest Bevin had been saying the same thing since 1921,[17] but nobody's mind had been effectively changed by it. Manual workers and their families had little cause to think in other terms than the hope that things would not get still worse.

The various accounts of the Depression all make one wonder, at first sight, why discontent was not much more vehement. The failure of the General Strike turned the Labour movement away from industrial action and for some years strengthened the hand of the advocates of parliamentary gradualism. But as unemployment, instead of decreasing, grew more severe under a Labour Government there was an increasing incentive to return to less gentle methods. Convinced Socialists, already bitterly hostile to MacDonald, were pushed still further towards militancy by the 'betrayal' of 1931. Among the intellectuals of the Left, few but the most resolute Fabians saw the political tendency as other than Marxism had predicted—a progressive intensification of the class struggle leading towards ultimate revolution. 'It is not now a question of the "inevitability of gradualness",' said Stafford Cripps at the Labour Party Conference of 1931. 'The one thing that is not inevitable now is gradualness.'[18] And yet it is hard to see in retrospect that English gradualism was really threatened by the Depression, even at its worst. Militant discontent was never widespread, and was organized almost entirely by the Communists, not by the Labour movement. Wal Hannington, who led the National Unemployed Workers' Movement and published his own account of it in 1936, had to concede despite the claims he made for the influence of his organization that 'at no time has the standing membership approached even ten per cent. of the vast masses of the unemployed'.[19] Orwell brusquely described the membership

---

[15] 248 H.C. Deb., c. 710.

[16] 231 H.C. Deb., c. 707.

[17] See the Minutes of the Dockers' Union Executive Council, 4–11 February, 1921, quoted by Bullock, *op. cit.*, p. 164.

[18] *Report of the 31st Annual Conference of the Labour Party*, p. 205.

[19] W. Hannington, *Unemployed Struggles 1919–1936* (London, 1936), p. 323; and cf. the letter of Sid Elias, the chairman of the N.U.W.M., written from Moscow in 1932, in which he complained that the hunger marches involved 'at the most one or two thousand out of the millions of unemployed' (quoted by Pelling, *The British Communist Party* [London, 1958], p. 65).

figures of the extremist political parties of the period as 'pathetic'.[20] Wight Bakke, who came from the United States to study the workings of unemployment insurance in England, found in Greenwich that 'the talk of revolution is conspicuous by its absence', and the publicity given to demonstrations of the unemployed 'is out of proportion to their importance as indications of unrest'.[21] A more representative picture would seem to be given by Priestley's description in his *English Journey* of a couple he visited in Blackburn: 'Both of them good independent folk, insisted that they didn't want to ask for anything. Lots worse off than them. They all say that.'[22] There could hardly be a more graphic expression than this of a restricted reference group comparison.

During the Depression, therefore, relative deprivation among manual workers and their families appears to have been low in both frequency and magnitude. The authors of one of the earliest systematic studies of inter-war unemployment, after remarking that 'It is noteworthy that the local reports reveal little of the political unrest resulting from unemployment which accompanied pre-war depressions', went on to observe that 'There would seem to be some recognition of the abnormal character of the depression, a disposition to grin and bear it, and a distrust of panaceas from whatever quarter they are offered.'[23] This stolid reaction to the first heavy onset of unemployment remained the pattern for two decades. This is not to say that at certain times and places there were not strong demonstrations of working-class militancy, most notably among the miners of South Wales. But not all the militancy, even among the miners, was due to feelings of relative deprivation of class. There was, for instance, an extremely bitter and protracted dispute in the Nottingham coalfields in the winter of 1936–37. But the bitterness which made this strike notable was not caused by a sense of injustice with reference to the rich or the better-paid, but by the separate and inflammatory issue of company unionism.[24] Similarly, the London busmen were a particularly militant group during the 1930's—considerably more so than their official leaders; but they were also a relatively well-paid one, and their case seems rather to support the correlation between radicalism

[20] George Orwell, *Inside the Whale* (London, 1940), p. 164.
[21] E. Wight Bakke, *The Unemployed Man* (London, 1933), pp. 60–62.
[22] J. B. Priestley, *English Journey* (London, 1934), p. 281.
[23] *Third Winter of Unemployment* (London, 1923), p. 74.
[24] See Ronald Kidd, *Report to the Executive Committee of the National Council for Civil Liberties* (March, 1937), quoted by K. G. J. C. Knowles, *Strikes* (Oxford, 1952), p. 86.

and prosperity.[25] The Depression imposed severe and sometimes intolerable hardship on large sections of the working class and many non-manual workers also; but it did not heighten their feelings of relative deprivation in the way that both wars did. Particularly severe wage-cuts were, as one would expect, resisted, notably in the textile industry. But the disposition to grin and bear it remained much more widespread than the disposition to storm the barricades.

Even in the most severely depressed industries, it was only in certain regions (and these not necessarily the hardest hit) that militant discontent was high. The unrest in South Wales can be largely traced to the history of its industrial relations, and as already noted, the contrast with pre-war improvement was more marked in Wales than elsewhere. The comment of the Pilgrim Trust investigators towards the end of the Depression serves to illustrate both the disposition to grin and bear it and the non-correlation of hardship and grievance: 'The Durham miner', they observed, 'who has been out of work for five years has not a perpetual sense of grievance, but rather—though he is actually rather poorer than the unemployed man in South Wales—a determination to make the best of things'; and they found in the mining community studied, although its misfortunes were typical of the 'special areas', a spirit which they summarized as 'this sturdy refusal to give up'.[26]

The argument that economic grievances in the working class were a function of limited reference groups is further borne out by the one episode when discontent was most notably vehement, widespread and successful. This episode is the uproar which followed the introduction of new scales of relief under the Unemployment Act of 1934. Under the Act, the newly-created Unemployment Assistance Board was to take over the responsibility both for 'transitional payments'—payments, that is, to those no longer entitled to the standard insurance benefit—and, eventually, for all the able-bodied unemployed, insured or not, who had been the previous responsibility of the local Public Assistance Committees. The P.A.C.'s, so-called, which were the successors to the old Poor Law Guardians abolished by Neville Chamberlain's Local Government

[25] The bus strikes cannot, of course, be explained purely in terms of standards heightened by prosperity. Union politics had something to do with it; so did the resentment at 'speeding-up' (A. Hutt, *The Condition of the Working Class in Britain* [London, 1933], p. 174), although the London General Omnibus Company was a better employer than many; so perhaps did irritation resulting from fatigue. On this, see Lloyd Davies, 'Strikes', *British Journal of Industrial Medicine* III (1946), p. 49, cited Knowles, *op. cit.*, p. 179, n. 2, C. R. Wason, *Busman's View* (London, 1958), p. 101, and cf. the letter to the T.G.W.U. journal *The Record* (Christmas, 1961), p. 6.
[26] Pilgrim Trust, *Men Without Work* (Cambridge, 1938), p. 75.

Act of 1929, had been autonomous in the fixing of scales of benefit in accordance with their own assessments of need. This meant, in effect, the continued possibility of what became known after 1921 as 'Poplarism'—overspending on relief by local Councils. The old problem had been the allegedly excessive disbursement of local funds; it was against this practice that Neville Chamberlain had introduced legislation in 1926 whereby the Guardians in West Ham, Bedwellty and Chester-le-Street were replaced by government appointees. After 1931, the funds administered by the local authorities for transitional payments were not their own, whether borrowed or not, but came directly from the Treasury. But there was still no central regulation of scales of relief, and thus two P.A.C.'s—those of Rotherham and County Durham—were replaced, just as the Guardians of West Ham, Bedwellty and Chester-le-Street had been, by appointees. The Act of 1934 accordingly established, in the words of Sir Ronald Davison, 'a new kind of centralized Poor Law'[27] whereby the relief of poverty arising from unemployment was to be centrally directed, uniformly fixed and removed from the vagaries and dissensions of party politics. The scales of payment were to go into operation on January 7th, 1935, having been fixed, after the framing of the Act, during the autumn of 1934. It was foreseen by the Government that the known regional variations in scales of relief would mean that some recipients might find their benefits reduced; but in the absence of any accurate survey, it was assumed that the majority of recipients would gain small increases while those who had been receiving more than the new standard rates would probably have either deceived or been pampered by their local P.A.C. On the appointed day, January 7, *The Times*' first editorial smugly declared that 'Everything points to the prospect that 1935 will be a distinctly happier year for most of those who, in spite of the industrial recovery, will not be able to find work.'

What happened in fact was that the recipients rapidly realized that a very great many of them would have their benefits reduced. The extent and volume of protest was, by English standards, spectacular. By the time that Parliament reassembled, the National Council of Labour was issuing a statement saying that 'public anxiety and disquiet have been aroused to a degree never known before'.[28] There had been an uproar in the industrial areas most affected, particularly in South Wales. Meetings were held, protests sent, and demonstrations organized. Members of all parties returned from their constituencies with reports of unexpected suffering and

[27] R. C. Davison, *British Unemployment Policy since 1930* (London, 1938), p. 41.
[28] See the front page of the *Daily Herald*, Feb. 2nd, 1935.

vociferous resentment. In the Commons debates, the Minister of Labour was conciliatory and even apologetic. There were scenes in the public galleries which George Lansbury, speaking as Leader of the Opposition, said he could not without hypocrisy deplore. For a short time, the Government was under heavier parliamentary criticism from all sections of opinion than at any time in the inter-war period. In the face of the continuing pressure, it gave way. A standstill order was issued on February 5th whereby applicants for unemployment assistance would be given the best of both worlds. The increases were allowed to stand, but the reductions annulled. The centralized scale was not put into effect until the autumn of 1936. Public opinion had forced the Government into the virtually immediate reversal of a measure long prepared and confidently planned. For the only time, a militant sense of relative deprivation was aroused among the unemployed; and the manifest failure of the Government secured for them prompt and unequivocal redress.

The episode is worth narrating in some detail because it provides a striking illustration of the extent to which the frustration of modest expectations led not only to a more intense and widespread sense of relative deprivation than, for instance, the cuts of 1931, but also earned the victims of the new dispensation more outspoken and influential support than they would have been accorded if their hardships had not been compounded by the Government's fallacious predictions of improvement. A similar but less dramatic example of how expectations, rather than objective hardship, pro-vided the more effective stimulus to discontent is the mounting pres-sure during the later 1930's for an improvement in the economic position of the old age pensioners. Even as late as 1938, when the worst of the Depression was long over, it could be argued that people living on fixed incomes were relatively better off than their predecessors had been during the years after contributory pen-sions had first come into effect. Prices fell steadily after 1924, and although they rose again after 1932 they were still considerably lower in 1938 than 1924. The cost of living as measured by the Ministry of Labour's index only reached in 1939 a level as high as it had been at in 1930.[29] But this, of course, was not the point. What-ever opposition there might originally have been to the principle of either contributory or non-contributory pensions, the right to a pension was now built into the social context from which those of pensionable age were selecting their reference groups. They thought of themselves not simply as 'old people' but as 'pensioners', and as

[29] See the *Statistical Abstract for the U.K., 1924–38* (Cmd. 6232, 1940), Table 137 and *Annual Abstract of Statistics* No. 84 (1938–1946), Table 302.

such they felt entitled to an equivalent share in the increasing prosperity of the country. Even in 1936, pensioners were likely, despite the help of public assistance, to be in poverty as defined by the revised but still not lavish standard adopted by Seebohm Rowntree in his second study of York. Since then, moreover, the cost of living had been rising. Thus it is not to be wondered that in the summer of 1939 the Labour Party introduced a motion of censure on the Government which could, in the words of Chamberlain himself, 'be considered as the climax in this House of an agitation which has for some time past been carried on with ever increasing vehemence in the country'.[30]

The Government did not in fact grant any increase of pensions, and the debate, already overshadowed by international affairs, was soon obscured altogether by the outbreak of war. But the agitation to which it gave expression is a good example of a relative deprivation on the part of a self-conscious membership reference group; it was engendered by the pensioners having, as pensioners, expectations which were not being fulfilled. If pensioners were expressly entitled to the help of the State, if they were on rates which had not risen with the cost of living (irrespective of arguments about the rate being higher in real terms than it had been when first introduced), and if the State was spending increased amounts on rearmament and claiming at the same time that prosperity was being restored, then why should they not receive an increase? 'One is asked on all sides,' said Mr. Graham White in the Commons debate, ' "If you can spend so many hundreds of millions upon armaments, why is it that you can do nothing for us? You can give subsidies to sugar, to herring, to oats, to a dozen other things, and yet you have not either the time or the ability to take care of the old people." '[31] It might be true that at the end of the 1930's the old age pensioners were better off than they had been for much of the period after the Acts of 1919, when non-contributory pensions were raised to 10/-, and 1925, when contributory pensions were introduced. But in the actual context of 1939, they had effective reason to feel relatively deprived: they were in greater hardship now than they had been when times in general had been claimed to be worse, and they could not see why an increase in their scales of benefit should not be feasible. This, once again, was the impulse behind their discontent, not simply the fact (however true) that they were living in serious hardship.

In general, the welfare provisions of the inter-war period helped

[30] 350 H.C. Deb., c. 1706.
[31] *Ibid.*, c. 1721.

to keep the level of relative deprivation lower than the actual hardships imposed by the Depression might appear to warrant. This is in part because the provisions for relief were, if not enough for even a rigorous standard of minimum needs, still enough to show that some attempt to remedy poverty was being attempted. If laissez-faire had been allowed to operate untrammelled, there can be little question that relative deprivation would have been both widely and intensely (or even dangerously) felt. By the 1920's, the poverty resulting from unemployment could not be plausibly argued to have fallen only on the thriftless or lazy, and there was precedent enough, particularly in the out-of-work donations made to ex-servicemen and war-workers, for those hardest hit to feel that they had a just claim on the community for relief. But at the same time the magnitude of working-class relative deprivation was kept low because the provisions for relief were not greater—or, more precisely, because they were granted according to the principles that they were. There was never any suggestion that the purpose of such relief was a reduction of inequality of class; it was an ambiguous mixture of fixed benefits as of right and minimum provision against destitution. There was nothing to make the unemployed worker take as a comparative reference group the sections of society more fortunate than his own. Maxton's arguments that justice required a redistribution found no response in the policies of either Conservative or Labour governments. If the provisions made had been such as to encourage the suggestion that the duty of the state extended to ensuring that the hardships of the Depression should fall as heavily on the rich as on the poor, then the level of relative deprivation might once again have risen alarmingly high. But this never happened. In the matter of welfare, there was little or no inducement for those most affected to take a comparative reference group from outside their own stratum.

Manual workers certainly felt that they had a claim on the state. But their demand was not 'soak the rich' so much as 'work or maintenance'. It was in terms of working-class comparisons that their deprivations were felt. The successive legislation which extended the state's responsibility for their welfare neither aimed at social justice in a redistributive sense, nor was enacted as a concession to such a feeling. It proceeded by a series of almost haphazard precedents, none of which were such as to encourage hopes that concessions of a revolutionary nature might be forced from the government under the pressure of articulate egalitarianism. The two principles on which legislation was based throughout the inter-war period remained insurance against the short-term unemployment to which even those 'genuinely seeking work' might be liable, and provision for the barest needs on a Poor Law basis. The two principles, insofar as they were articulated at all, were not consistently applied, and it is the occasional breaches forced in them which are the most significant chapters in the story of the continuing, if uneven, progress towards the post-war 'Welfare State'. But their immediate result was that relative deprivation, in the context of social welfare, was restricted to comparisons close to people's immediate situations and minimum needs.

One measure which might seem in retrospect to foreshadow the 'Welfare State' was the Act of 1921 whereby unemployed workers were allowed for a statutory period to draw 'uncovenanted' benefit beyond what was covered by their contributions. Both this and the provision for dependants enacted a few months later were, in effect, a concession to the principles of provision according to needs irrespective of insurance. The authors of *The Third Winter of Unemployment* observed that 'it is doubtful whether "uncovenanted benefit" is not more properly to be regarded as relief pure and simple'.[32] But although it might be detected that the insurance principle was something of a pious fiction, it was a fiction stoutly maintained. 'Uncovenanted benefit', said the Ministry of Labour in the same year, 'has certain features resembling those of Poor Law relief . . . Nevertheless, the distinction remains that only persons who are normally insured can draw uncovenanted benefit; this benefit is, in fact, in the nature of an advance made on the faith of future payment of contributions.'[33] The insurance principle, however threadbare, was resolutely patched up by government spokesmen as the need arose, although attacked both from the Left (because the Exchequer paid too little) and from the Right (because the Exchequer paid too much). It was emphatically retained after the recommendation of the Holman Gregory Commission, and was incorporated after 1945 into the principle of the 'Welfare State'. It was greatly preferred by the recipients of welfare to a criterion of needs, since a criterion of needs involved a test of means rather than a benefit as of right. But the insurance principle was at once anti-revolutionary and anti-egalitarian. It was anti-revolutionary because it served to restrict comparative reference groups within the class of eligible beneficiaries, rather than extending them to those whose wealth might appear to be available for welfare through stiffened progressive taxation; it was anti-egalitarian because it ran directly contrary to the maxim of 'from each according to his capacities, to each according to his needs'. It

[32] *Op. cit.*, p. 39.
[33] *Report on National Unemployment Insurance to July, 1923* (1923), p. 14.

meant that the unemployed, far from being relieved by the community at large for a misfortune for which they were not responsible, were dependent in large part upon the members of their own class who were in work. The working class was still required to try to support itself by what could be described as a tax on wages.[34]

In this climate of principles and policies, the reference groups of the recipients of welfare were virtually bound to remain within the broadly delimited area of potential fellow-beneficiaries. It was the anomalies within this area which were the focus of successive grievances, not the relative prosperity of people not obviously comparable. The agitation for legislative changes was largely directed towards the inclusion of categories of workers not yet covered by insurance, notably the agricultural workers who were not brought in until 1936. This case provides by itself an instance of how reference groups are a more important influence on policy than an appeal to principles. The claim made on behalf of the agricultural workers was based almost entirely on the argument that if other wage-earners were covered, they should be also, although their wages were too low for them to be readily able to afford the contributions, and their rate of unemployment was too low for their need to be as great as that of some better-paid non-manual workers. Indeed, they were likely to do better from the existing scales of assistance than from benefit as of right. They were included under a special scheme, together with workers in horticulture and forestry, for a complex of reasons which included both the wish of the government to attract workers into agriculture and a feeling of relative deprivation of status on the part of the agricultural workers themselves, who wanted 'the prestige which, since 1931, had come to be attached to the insured status'.[35] There was no argument on either side that their claim to insurance rested on the principles either of greatest need, or of social equality, except in terms of their claim to be accorded an equivalent status to the rest of the working class.

Thus the welfare provisions of the inter-war years did not aim at a conscious diminution of economic inequality; and despite their provision of a 'safety-net' minimum, they did not greatly diminish

[34] There is no adequate evidence for how many of the contributors took this view, though it was claimed that some did: see the remarks of William Greenwood in the Commons debate of October 24, 1921 (147 H.C. Deb., c. 533). It was found in 1926 that nearly half of contributors had drawn no benefit since 1921, so that for these the term could be claimed to be appropriate. But the contributory method seems agreed to have been generally thought acceptable by the contributors as a whole.

[35] Davison, *op. cit.*, p. 56. Cf. the remarks of G. E. Hewlett of the Agricultural Workers at the Trades Union Congress of 1925 (*Report*, p. 282), and for a general claim for equality with other workers, R. Wagg at the 1936 Congress (*Report*, pp. 353–4).

it in practice. There was certainly some resentment of the rich, and a widespread feeling that benefits should be higher. The claim that the more prosperous classes of society should bear a greater share of the cost of relief had been argued by Clynes in the House of Commons during the early measures of 1921, and was repeated by various Labour spokesmen throughout the period. Indeed, Snowden himself had argued in the debate on pensions in 1908 that they should serve a redistributive purpose. But the principle that the employed working class should, through compulsory insurance, support as far as possible the unemployed working class was never seriously challenged, and seems to have been broadly accepted by the members of the working class themselves. The alternative was relief with a means test, and as we have just seen, insurance was preferred to this even at a potentially lower rate of benefit. The share of contributions borne by industry might be argued to involve some distribution of the cost among the rich. But it was likely to be passed on to the consumer rather than to be borne as a cut in distributed profits. There are several slightly conflicting estimates of just how much was in fact being redistributed from the rich to the poor by public finance. But it seems agreed that although by the late 1930's an appreciable redistribution was taking place, it was not such as could be described as a large-scale transfer. Colin Clark's estimate is that whereas in 1913 the working classes were actually contributing more in the various forms of taxation than they were receiving in benefit from the various social services, by 1935 there was a net redistribution of some £91 millions in their favour.[36] But this is not by any standards a revolutionary redistribution; and on Clark's estimate, the working class was still paying some four-fifths of the cost of the services from which its members benefited.

It is undeniable, however, that the condition of the working class was better in the inter-war period than it had been before the War. Quite apart from the increasing provision, however haphazard, for social welfare, real incomes and wages were rising, despite the fall after 1929.[37] By the last inter-war years, the country was, except

[36] *National Income and Outlay* (London, 1937), pp. 147–8. See also T. Barna, *Redistribution of Incomes Through Public Finance in 1937* (Oxford, 1945), pp. 233–4, and the more pessimistic remarks of G.D.H. and M. I. Cole in *The Condition of Britain* (London, 1937), p. 349, who conclude that the poor were 'being called upon to pay an increasing share in the taxes and rates out of which these services are provided for them'.

[37] Real incomes, having fallen between 1929 and 1932, rose steadily and steeply thereafter: A. R. Prest, 'National Income of the United Kingdom 1870–1946', *Economic Journal* LVIII (1948), pp. 58–9 (Table II). Real wages, however, are calculated to have still fallen slightly after 1932 by E. C. Ramsbottom, 'The Course of Wage Rates in the United Kingdom, 1921–1934', *Journal of the Royal Statistical Society* XCVIII (1935), p. 661.

in a few particular areas, enjoying some fair measure of relative prosperity. But if there had been an improvement relative to what had gone before, by egalitarian standards the differences of class were still very great. The several studies of industrial poverty carried out in the inter-war period are ample testimony of this. Unfortunately, there is no comparable evidence for the prosperous manual workers in the most flourishing areas of the Midlands and South (although Bristol, which was studied in 1937, was enjoying a boom, despite the poverty found there). But as far as the evidence goes, it suggests an improvement sufficient to allay the more excessive relative deprivations of the pattern of 1911-14, but not sufficient to arouse the demands of a revolutionary egalitarianism.

Aspirations had, perhaps, risen; but the level of relative deprivation was still much lower than it would have been if reference groups had begun effectively to extend across the manual/non-manual line. Working-class standards were gradually rising as the country began to recover from the Depression. But by any yardstick, there remained wider inequalities of class than manual workers and their families appeared to realize or resent. There were still several million people who were poor enough to fall below Bowley's 'bare subsistence' standard or Rowntree's standard not as revised in 1936 but as applied in his original investigation in 1899.[38] But the causes of it were now such as to inhibit the sense of relative deprivation more than the causes of the poverty of 1899. The principal cause of poverty during the inter-war period may be summarized in the words of the authors of the Merseyside survey: 'Poverty usually comes to a man not because he is underpaid but because he is underworked.'[39] Unemployment was not the sole major cause, for a working-class family with several dependants was likely also to fall below the line; it has even been said that 'Having three or more children before the war in the working class was practically sufficient to guarantee poverty.'[40] But both causes are significant for the discrepancy between objective inequality and relative deprivation. Where poverty is due either to unemployment, or to dependent children, rather than to inadequate wages, the comparative reference groups most likely to suggest themselves are other people who are in work, or who have fewer children, rather than those who are relatively better paid. The situation described by

[38] See Rowntree, *Poverty and Progress* (London, 1941), pp. 108-9.

[39] D. Caradog Jones, ed., *Social Survey of Merseyside* (Liverpool, 1934), I, p. 167. For the period of recovery, cf. H. Tout, *The Standard of Living in Bristol* (Bristol, 1938), p. 45: 'Unemployment is outstandingly the most important reason for family income falling below "needs".'

[40] PEP, 'Poverty: Ten Years after Beveridge', *Planning* XIX (1952-3), p. 25, and cf. the Beveridge Report itself (Cmd. 6404, 1942), p. 7.

Rowntree in 1899 had been that the wages paid for unskilled labour in York 'are insufficient to provide food, shelter and clothing adequate to maintain a family of moderate size in a state of bare physical efficiency'.[41] In this situation, the obvious comparison for the poor would be with the better paid, and there would be likely to be (as there was) a strong feeling of an explicitly egalitarian kind for the upgrading of the wages of unskilled workers to a level closer to that of the skilled. In the inter-war Depression, however, the demand among the unskilled was more likely to be for work or maintenance than for an equalization of rewards. In fact, the time-rates for the unskilled as a percentage of those for the skilled did noticeably fall.[42] The workers in all trades may have been anxious to improve their wages; but they were more concerned with resisting wage-cuts in their particular industries and securing some diminution of unemployment than with the question of differentials, whether within or between classes.

On another issue also relative deprivation was, as far as can be inferred, less in magnitude and frequency than the objective inequalities might lead one to expect. It might be that by the later 1930's standards had so far risen as to arouse at least some new feelings of relative deprivation: the number of strikes, and particularly of unofficial strikes,[43] rose steadily from 1933 to 1937; electoral support was visibly accruing to the Labour Party; the National Unemployed Workers' Movement held in 1936 a larger hunger march and demonstration against the means test, with official Labour backing, than at any time during the worst of the Depression. But such symptoms of rising expectation still did not lead to reference group comparisons between rich and poor. In particular, they did not lead to comparisons in terms of the greatest economic inequality of all—the distribution of property. This is a topic on

[41] Rowntree, *Poverty* (London, 1901), p. 133. Cf. A. L. Bowley and A. R. Burnett-Hurst, *Livelihood and Poverty* (London, 1915), p. 46.

[42] K. J. G. C. Knowles and D. J. Robertson, 'Differences between the Wages of Skilled and Unskilled Workers, 1880–1950', *Bulletin of the Oxford University Institute of Statistics* XIII (1951), p. 111.

[43] Accurate statistics on unofficial strikes are hard to come by; but see Knowles, p. 33 n. 2 and the statements of the Minister of Labour there quoted. For the view that the number of working days actually lost in 1933–7 was *less* than one would expect in a time of recovery see J. H. Richardson, 'Industrial Relations', in *Britain in Recovery* (London, 1938), p. 115. It may be argued that the number of workers involved in strikes shows the extent of relative deprivation, and their duration its intensity. But the uncertainties of such interpretation should again be stressed; the duration of strikes is at least as likely to be a function of union organization on the one hand and negotiating machinery on the other.

which simple lack of information is likely to inhibit any very extensive or explicit feelings of relative deprivation. The distribution of property has always been a matter of some mystery, and there is good reason to think that the estate duty figures, which constitute the basic source, consistently underestimate the true extent of inequality. In the 1930's, however, there was in addition to this a widespread and almost certainly erroneous belief about the distribution of small savings and property among the less prosperous majority of the population. Without sample survey evidence, no definite calculation is possible; but if only on the basis of systematic post-war information, it is highly probable that small savings among the working class were very much rarer, and smaller, than many people supposed at the time.

The only figures readily available are figures for the total amounts held in savings banks, friendly societies and so on, and for the total numbers of members or depositors. All that can be calculated from these is an average, and averages are notoriously misleading in contexts of this kind. John Hilton, who tried as far as possible to answer the question in 1938, concluded that the great majority of deposits in the Post Office, Trustee Savings Banks, Building Societies and the rest were very small, and that the average should rather be explained by the much larger deposits made by a very few people. He was able to quote some figures of Post Office accounts showing that at the end of 1934, 70% of the holdings concerned were under £25, and the average of these was barely over £4.[44] If any plausible inference can be drawn from all the systematic evidence collected for the 1950's, it is that almost all working-class families of the '30's must have been propertyless. Yet the apparent growth of small saving could lead not merely a Liberal spokesman to talk about 'the great mass of the people'[45] becoming the possessors of savings, or a manager of Harrod's about the strong working-class demand for clothes, furniture and even motor-cars,[46] or the managers and actuaries of Trustee Savings Banks about the prosperity of their working-class clients,[47] but even induce Evan Durbin of the Fabian Society to conclude, despite reservations, that 'a very large distribution of small property has taken place'.[48]

[44] John Hilton, *Rich Man, Poor Man* (London, 1944), p. 60.
[45] Walter Runciman as reported in *The Times*, March 11th, 1929.
[46] Cited R. Lewis and A. Maude, *The English Middle Classes* (London, 1949), p. 79.
[47] Hilton, *op. cit.*, p. 63: 'Excellent and knowledgeable men they are, but invariably they hold the view that the average family is one with a good round sum laid by'.
[48] E. M. F. Durbin, *The Politics of Democratic Socialism* (London, 1940), p. 116.

There seems to have been the same sort of misapprehension about home-ownership. It was, of course, perfectly true that a number of working-class people, particularly in certain districts, were in this way property-owners. But to talk of 'an immense number'[49] was without question an exaggeration. Hilton quotes a survey by the British Institute of Public Opinion which showed that of families with incomes of £200 and under, 90% were rentpayers, while even among those with incomes between £200 and £500 the proportion was still 68%.[50] A sample budget enquiry conducted by the Civil Service Research Bureau in 1938–9 revealed that over three times as many civil servants, local government officials and teachers had bought or were buying their houses as urban insured workers.[51] Moreover, during the Depression homeowning was sometimes not an asset at all, but a liability, since it could prevent people from emigrating from some of the areas hardest hit.[52] It might be true that the working class of the 1930's was relatively better off in both income and savings than the working class of 1913. But the distribution of property was still extremely unequal. If there was a considerable discrepancy between the distribution of incomes and the extent, or degree, of relative deprivation among the working class, there was a still wider one as regards the distribution of wealth. There might be enough small, or very small, savings among manual workers for a few of them to be affected by the 'savings scare' of the 1931 election. But the concern of the great majority was for security, not property—that is, for a steady job without the threat of unemployment, and a guarantee of unemployment relief without a means test. The unequal distribution of property was something of which they were too little aware to resent it.

Expectations, then, were rising by the late 1930's, but they were rising among manual workers and their families only in terms of limited reference groups. The real income of the average working-class family was 37% higher in 1938 than it had been in 1913,[53] and might have been expected to go on rising. But it was still not feasible for a working-class family to aspire to anything approaching the standards of the family of the middle-class salary-earner. The average salary-earner was not only spending more on what could be regarded as luxuries; he was also better clothed, better

[49] Walter Runciman, as above.
[50] *Op. cit.*, pp. 68–9.
[51] Marian Bowley, *Housing and the State* (London, 1945), p. 177.
[52] Hilda Jennings, *Bryn Mawr* (London, 1934), pp. 856; *Readjustment in Lancashire* (Manchester University, 1936), p. 24.
[53] Mark Abrams, *The Condition of the British People, 1911–1945* (London, 1946), p. 86.

housed and better fed. Above all, he was economically more secure. Even the prosperous wage-earner was still insecure for both of the two most familiar reasons: first, he was much more likely, even in a prosperous trade, to risk being unemployed, and second, he had no full and guaranteed insurance against the causes which, apart from unemployment itself, might at various stages of his life force him close to or below the poverty line. The most obvious comparative reference group for the prosperous manual worker was still other workers less fortunate than himself.

THE SECOND WORLD WAR AND AFTER

In both these respects, working-class reference groups were altered by the Second World War. There was a rise in wages, as there had been in the First. But it was in the area of communal provision that a revision of standards chiefly took place. Both work and maintenance became not aspirations but fixed expectations. The revolution in social policy has been often described: the pre-war standards were dispelled because, in the words of the official historian of social policy, 'the area of responsibility had so perceptibly widened'.[54] In addition, the awareness of the actual situation of others was enormously heightened by the simple fact of physical movement and broader social contacts. This was true not only of those who had been called into the armed forces, who are generally believed (although there is no statistical evidence) to have voted strongly Labour in 1945. According to some estimates, the rate of movement of the civilian population during the war may have been double what it was in the '30's, and movement across district boundaries may have involved close to two-thirds of the total population: 'Evacuation', in the words of one author, 'had, in fact, lifted the lid'.[55] The enforced contacts which resulted from it were not always harmonious,[56] but they forced on many people, however unwillingly, comparisons which they would not otherwise have made. It was at one time fashionable to see the advent of the Welfare State as the culmination of a steady and inexorable trend in first liberal and then explicitly socialist doctrines. But in practice unforeseen need and improvised precedent were at least as strong determinants. As it is summarized by Professor Briggs, 'the experience of war seems to have been as relevant as the appeal of socialism in determining

[54] Richard M. Titmuss, *Problems of Social Policy* (HMSO, 1950), p. 506.
[55] H. C. Dent, *Education in Transition* (London, 1944), p. 11.
[56] See e.g., H. Orlans, *Stevenage: a Sociological Study of a New Town* (London, 1952), pp. 160–63.

the practicability and the popularity of comprehensive welfare proposals'.[57] Thus standards of comparison were once again disrupted by the impact of war, and the magnitude and frequency of relative deprivation heightened. The slogan 'work or maintenance' was displaced by the slogan 'fair shares for all'. By contrast with 1918, the demand for social justice was much more clearly defined; the Beveridge Report had furnished the authoritative depiction of how a juster society could be organized in terms both of higher wages and of collective provision. Redistribution of incomes was not, as it happened, an issue in the 1945 election; although Dalton raised the surtax in Labour's first budget he at the same time reduced the standard rate of income tax. But by 1950, when the emphasis on nationalization and controls had been moderated, Labour's election campaign rested heavily on the claim to have secured an equitable distribution of resources. Against the accusation that resources had been squandered and prosperity delayed, Labour spokesmen and canvassers argued that what there was had been fairly parcelled out.[58] 'Fair shares for all' appeared in 64% of Labour election addresses.[59] Yet despite the widespread belief that the Labour Government had pursued, and achieved, a policy of large-scale redistribution of wealth, the actual inequalities of class were still such as to suggest that relative deprivation was out of correlation with the facts.

Throughout the period of the Labour government, relative deprivation was much more widely felt among the non-manual stratum than the manual. When Dalton introduced his surtax proposals, Sir John Anderson, his Conservative predecessor as Chancellor, told the House: 'Social equality has very little to do with the Budget. I would venture to say that the pursuit of economic equality, which certainly has something to do with the Budget, is rather a questionable doctrine . . . Is a man to be reproached because he wishes and strives to do better than his neighbour?'[60] This sort of repudiation of egalitarianism on principle was directly coupled with the conviction that a large-scale redistribution of incomes was taking place. In March of 1946, the *Economist* published an article which was avowedly introduced as 'a plea for mercy on behalf of the middle

[57] Asa Briggs, 'The Welfare State in Historical Perspective', *Archives Européennes de Sociologie* II (1961), p. 223.

[58] A team of American observers found that 'Great emphasis was placed—especially in door-to-door work—on the way the Labour people had equitably divided what there was of food, gasoline, houses and the like': J. K. Pollock *et al.*, *British Election Studies, 1950* (Ann Arbor, 1951), p. 3.

[59] H. G. Nicholas, *The British General Election of 1950* (London, 1951), pp. 219–20.

[60] 414 H.C. Deb., c. 2022.

range of the earned incomes'. The writer conceded that 'the incomes concerned are unquestionably high in comparison with the average of all incomes', but went on to say: 'But they are the incomes, and they have hitherto represented the standard of living that can reasonably be aspired to by the professional man.'[61] By 1949, Messrs. Lewis and Maude were writing in their study of *The English Middle Classes* about a 'huge redistribution of wealth' having taken place.[62] The Board of Inland Revenue reported in 1950 that a comparison of the income distribution between the fiscal years 1938–9 and 1948–9 showed a 'very considerable redistribution'.[63] By the time that the Conservatives were returned to power, it had come to be extensively believed not only that the poor were no longer with us, but also the rich.

To the resentment of many of the non-manual stratum at the redistribution of incomes there was added a resentment at what was felt to be the excessive and unmerited redistribution being effected by the provision of social services in kind. This may seem surprising, since at the General Election both parties had offered the voters a National Health Service and a system of social insurance along the lines of the Beveridge Report. But there was a considerable resurgence of the sort of feelings already expressed during the inter-war period by those who felt that the social services were somehow enabling other people to get something for nothing. There was perhaps no one prepared to pronounce in public, as one witness to the Shaw enquiry of 1920 had done, that the working class had not borne its share during the War. But there was certainly a feeling among many middle-class people that the working class was getting more than its fair share of the benefits of the peace thanks to the indulgence of a government too little aware of the proper ordering of economic priorities.

Yet just as the noticeable feature of the inter-war period was the discrepancy between hardship and resentment in the manual stratum, what is noticeable in the post-war period is a resentment among the middle class which closer examination of the facts does not entirely warrant. After the onset of the Depression, manual workers and their families did not have reference groups sufficiently far from their own situation for them to be turned by their deprivations into revolutionists. After 1945, non-manual workers and their families expected too much not to feel resentful at the diminution of what they saw as their legitimate differential advantages. Very

---

[61] *Economist,* March 16, 1946.
[62] *Op. cit.,* p. 24.
[63] Board of Inland Revenue, *92nd Annual Report* (Cmd. 8052, 1950), p. 86 (and see Tables 85 and 86, p. 83).

often their grievances were quite explicitly expressed in these terms. Because, they maintained, their legitimate expectations were higher and their accustomed way of life more expensive to maintain, a fair equivalence in reward between themselves and manual workers entailed a higher net sum for themselves.[64] The working class, therefore, was seen as doing too well not because it was not legitimate or even desirable that its members should be enabled to improve their standard of life, but because a corresponding gain, or maintenance of position, was being denied to non-manual workers.

There were, however, a number of ways in which this sense of relative deprivation was not proportionate to the facts. During the period of most vociferous middle-class complaint, the unions were voluntarily accepting a policy of wage-restraint, rather than securing for themselves such rewards as a freer operation of the market system would have yielded to them. It was true that many members of the non-manual stratum were in relative hardship. But so, it could be claimed, were many members of the manual stratum who had an unfulfilled claim on a share of the general improvement of living standards entitling them to higher aspirations than would have been feasible a generation before. Moreover, the benefits accruing from the social services were as advantageous to the non-manual as to the manual stratum, if it did not disdain to make use of them. The differentials of reward had certainly narrowed; but had they so far narrowed as to constitute a claim for social justice on behalf not merely of the hardest hit among the retired or lower-paid salary-earners but on behalf of the non-manual stratum as a whole?

During the Depression, it had already been argued that the middle class, or at any rate the larger and less affluent part of it, was suffering as much as the working class from economic hardship and governmental or entrepreneurial exploitation. This claim was advanced on the one hand by non-manual workers who felt that too little attention was paid to their claims by comparison with those of manual workers, and on the other by Marxists who saw in the Depression the inevitable tendency, predicted by Marx, for the capitalist system to drive the salariat and the petty bourgeoisie into the ranks of the proletarians. But despite the many cases of individual hardship, this view, whether held by intellectuals who hoped and expected to see the white-collar workers assimilated to the proletariat, or by white-collar workers themselves who hoped and ex-

[64] See e.g. the article of Mr. Graham Hutton in the *News Chronicle*, Nov. 21, 1949, cited by Barbara Wootton, *The Social Foundations of Wage Policy* (London, 1955), p. 40, or Lewis and Maude, *op. cit.*, Chapter 12.

pected not to be, could not be adequately supported by the evidence. In assessing the position of clerical labour, in particular, between the inter-war years and the 1950's it is instructive to compare the Marxian forebodings of Klingender's *The Condition of Clerical Labour in Britain,* published in 1935, with Lockwood's *The Black-coated Worker,* published in 1958. It was simply not true that clerical workers were, as a class, as hard hit by the Depression as manual workers. Colin Clark, using the data provided by the 1931 census, showed that the incidence of unemployment during what was generally considered the depth of the Depression varied sharply and directly with occupational class. The figures which he gives are: unskilled manual workers, 30·5%; skilled and semi-skilled manual workers, 14·4%; personal service workers, 9·9%; salesmen and shop assistants, 7·9%; clerks and typists, 5·5%; higher office workers, 5·1%; proprietors and managers, 1·3%.[65] Despite the unexpected and sometimes lasting unemployment which affected in particular the older clerks who were unemployable elsewhere,[66] Klingender's predictions were not borne out in the event. Not only was the general level of unemployment much lower among clerks than manual workers, but the higher the clerk the less likely he was to be unemployed. General commercial clerks suffered somewhat, but bank clerks, for example, hardly at all.[67] The security of clerical labour was still its major attraction in the eyes of the working class. 'If', commented the Pilgrim Trust investigators, 'working men and women seem to be unduly anxious to make their sons and daughters into clerks, the anxiety behind it is not for more money but for greater security.'[68] Although the '30's were a very bad time for clerical workers by comparison with their traditional expectations, and although they were right to fear a narrowing of the gap in earnings between themselves and manual workers, their class-situation nonetheless remained much the more advantageous one.

All differentials were further narrowed by the War; but in the same way, the fact that after the War many members of the middle class were being disappointed in their traditional expectations and saw themselves being approached or even overtaken in salary by wage-earners should not be taken to mean that their own class-situation might not still be preferable. When all the factors of superannuation, promotion, hours and conditions are taken into account,

---

[65] *Op. cit.,* p. 46 (Table 19).
[66] F. D. Klingender, *The Condition of Clerical Labour in Britain* (London, 1935), pp. 91–9; Lockwood, *The Blackcoated Worker,* p. 56.
[67] Lockwood, (*ibid.,* p. 55) cites the *Bank Officer,* June 1932, p. 7, to the effect that in 1932 there were only twelve or fourteen cases of bank clerks out of work out of a guild membership of 21,000.
[68] *Op. cit.,* p. 144.

there is room for a possibility of continuing relative deprivation on the part of manual workers. Lockwood, in comparing the situation of clerical and manual workers during the inter-war period, concludes that, up to 1939, while some clerks were earning less than some manual workers, only skilled artisans could approach the earnings of the average male clerk, and some clerks were earning a good deal more than any artisan.[69] During and after the War, this difference in earnings was noticeably narrowed: when earnings, as opposed to wage rates, are compared, it appears that by the 1950's the average male clerk and the average manual worker were at just about the same level. There were, indeed, two other respects in which the clerical worker might now feel relatively deprived in view of the traditional differentials between manual and non-manual labour: in the first place, he could point to the faster rate at which wages seemed to be advancing[70]—the result, perhaps, of more aggressive trade unionism; in the second place, he could not help being aware that whereas before the War only a skilled artisan could rival him in earnings, now it was even the unskilled manual worker who was catching up to him. But despite these manifest changes, there were other comparisons which gave a more accurate and perhaps less uncomfortable picture than the discrepancy suggested by the simple comparison between traditional differentials and present rates of pay.

It is difficult to establish just what comparison would give the least biased picture. It is well-known that the average earnings of all clerical workers is a misleading figure in view of the number of women in lower-paid clerical work who cannot be counted as long-term members of the clerical labour force. Equally, it is well-known that wage rates for manual workers are an inadequate guide because of overtime and piecework. But in every feature of class-situation other than actual earnings, there can be little doubt that the clerical worker of the 1950's was still better placed than the manual worker. Even the claim that wages were advancing faster than salaries could not be effectively maintained.[71] The manual worker who was now enabled by overtime to reach or overtake the white-collar worker's earnings was obliged to work considerably longer hours in order to do so: in April 1960, male manual workers over

[69] *The Blackcoated Worker*, pp. 44–48. The two years for which adequate data are available are 1924 and 1930.

[70] See e.g. the Institute of Office Management, *Clerical Salaries Analysis, 1962*, p. 14, where comparisons are put forward to show the greater relative increase in real earnings of manual workers over the past ten years.

[71] The Ministry of Labour's index started in 1955 at a baseline of 100·0 shows wages to have reached 141·8 by 1962, but salaries 147·7.

21 in all industries were averaging a 48-hour week.[72] He was less favoured in terms of holidays: a study by the Industrial Welfare Society in the early 1960's found marked differentials in favour of non-manual workers. Manual workers were the 'least favoured group' in 67% of the firms studied, and the maximum holiday granted to any manual worker was still two weeks, even after long service, in 46·5% of the firms.[73] The white-collar worker remained much better placed for retirement: Lydall found that in 1952 very nearly twice as many non-manual as manual employees were contributing to pension schemes.[74] Moreover, as noted by the authors of *Social Conditions in England and Wales,* whereas many schemes for white-collar workers are based on a capital payment and a pension tied to peak earnings, arrangements for wage-earners are generally based only on length of service.[75] For 1956–7, Professor Titmuss calculates that of male employees in the private sector 86% of salaried staffs had some private occupational cover as against 20% of wage earners,[76] and finds that there is a good deal of evidence that 'for the middle and upper-middle classes the proportion of those with non-contributory benefits of various kinds rises with income'.[77] In amenities at work, the white-collar worker remains clearly favoured: nobody who has been on a tour of a car factory or walked from a dockside to a shipping office can fail to have noticed the differences not only in conditions of work but in meals, furnishings

[72] Ministry of Labour *Gazette,* August 1960, p. 314. By October, 1962—that is, after the time of the sample survey to be described—the number of hours had dropped to 47.

[73] Industrial Welfare Society, *Holidays—Current Practice and Trends* (December, 1963), pp. 18 and 4. A maximum of two weeks for non-manual (non-supervisory) workers was found in only 13% of the firms (p. 6).

[74] H. F. Lydall, *British Incomes and Savings* (Oxford, 1955), p. 117 (Table 55). The actual percentages are 40% for non-manual and 21% for manual employees. In the sector of public administration and defence, a further 15% of workers are entitled to non-contributory pensions, and most of these are non-manual. In mining and quarrying, a National Coal Board pension scheme is largely responsible for a notably higher figure for manual employees than in other industries. It should also be noted that Lydall's figure is likely to include many female clerks who might have schemes available to them, although not in fact contributing.

[75] A. M. Carr-Saunders *et al., A Survey of Social Conditions in England and Wales as Illustrated by Statistics* (Oxford, 1958), p. 198.

[76] Titmuss, *Income Distribution and Social Change* (London, 1962), p. 155, n. 2. Some picture of what the difference may mean in practice is given by Willmott and Young's findings in Woodford: of retired men in their old age sample, a quarter of manual workers were receiving an employee's pension as against three-quarters of non-manual workers, and the average drop in incomes was noticeably bigger for manual than non-manual workers (*op. cit.,* pp. 62–63).

[77] *Op. cit.,* p. 152.

and sanitation. On the question of promotion, which is perhaps the biggest of the differences in the class-situation of the manual and clerical worker, it could even be argued that it was becoming more, not less difficult for the manual worker to rise into management; the more potential managers are pre-selected by education, the less it is likely that manual workers will be able to follow the proverbial career of the self-made man.[78]

Thus an equivalence of earnings between manual and white-collar workers should certainly not be taken to mean that they are equal in class-situation, let alone that the manual worker has reached a position of 'doing better'. Even in the matter of earnings, the figures are misleading, since averages take too little account of the significance of the higher clerical salaries. In October, 1960, the average weekly earnings of administrative, technical and clerical employees in firms employing 25 or more persons were £14 15s. 0d. for men paid by the week;[79] this figure may be compared with the average earnings in April, 1960 of men over 21 in the principal manufacturing and non-manufacturing industries, which were £14 17s. 0d.[80] This shows the weekly-paid clerical worker actually at a disadvantage; but the October, 1960 figure for administrative, technical and clerical employees paid by the month is a good deal higher—£23 15s. 4d. This is more than the earnings of manual workers in even the best-paying industries such as vehicle-building and printing, where the average in October 1960 was still well under £20, with the single exception of certain printers earning £20 2s. 5d. Of course, for the clerk whose earnings are low and who is aware that he will not in fact be likely to achieve promotion, the manual workers of his own age or younger who are earning noticeably more provide an obvious reference group in terms of which he will feel relatively deprived. Given full employment, he may well envy the earnings of the artisan. He may even prefer an artisan's career for his children, just as the artisan of the 1930's was attracted on behalf

[78] See e.g. R. V. Clements, *Managers: a Study of their Careers in Industry* (London, 1958). The study by Clements does not yield exact figures for the relative chances of a manual and a non-manual worker reaching a managerial position in British industry, but it gives a good picture of the reasons why the chances are loaded against the manual worker. It is tempting to contrast with it the conclusion of S. J. Chapman and F. J. Marquis, 'The Recruiting of the Employing Classes from the Ranks of the Wage Earners in the Cotton Industry', *Journal of the Royal Statistical Society* LXXV (1912), pp. 293–306 that two-thirds or more of Lancashire managers had risen from the bottom. The cotton industry, however, is in several ways atypical, so that it would be unwise to draw any general statistical conclusion for the difference between the 1950's and the 1910's.

[79] Ministry of Labour *Gazette,* June 1961, p. 241.

[80] *Ibid.,* p. 242.

of his children by the security of the clerk. A study carried out in Western England in 1956–7 found that only 3·2% of a sample of 208 clerks wanted their sons to be clerks, and nearly a fifth looked to a skilled trade as offering a better career than their own.[81] But if the classes as a whole are to be compared, the comparison between average manual and clerical earnings is only a part of the total picture.

Once, therefore, a comparison is made which takes into account all the aspects of the relative class-situation of the manual and non-manual strata, it becomes apparent that the egalitarian trend of the post-war period was not so marked as was widely believed. It is true that there was more of an overlap between the two than there had been before the war. But not only were comparisons between ostensible earnings likely to be misleading. In addition, the official statistics of income distribution, which constitute the principal evidence for the claim that a large-scale redistribution has taken place, can be strongly criticized. The problems of classification and analysis which are involved are fairly intricate. But as has been shown by Professor Titmuss,[82] the figures given by the Board of Inland Revenue are demonstrably inaccurate as a picture of the real distribution of net annual increment in economic power among the adult population; and there is a considerable number of sources of net increment which are not covered and which almost certainly yield greater benefits per capita to the middle than the working class.

The two topics on which manual workers might be thought to have most reason for some relative deprivation of class are first, fringe benefits, and second, remissions or bounties from the Exchequer. It is, as Titmuss emphasizes, impossible to make an accurate estimate of the extent of fringe benefits, but it is certain that these are considerable and it is a plausible guess that they are principally enjoyed by non-manual workers. Titmuss's own conclusion is that 'in the United Kingdom as in other modern economies there has been a marked growth in the provision of benefits in kind during the last twenty years or so, and, secondly, that for many groups in the occupied population the receipt of such benefits rises sharply with income'.[83] Such benefits are not, of course, confined to non-manual workers. Many firms spend considerable sums in industrial welfare benefits for their manual employees, and provide, for example, subsidized canteen lunches for them at the same time as providing tax-free expense allowances for their executives.

[81] J. R. Dale, *The Clerk in Industry* (Liverpool, 1962), pp. 21–23.
[82] In *Income Distribution and Social Change, passim.*
[83] *Ibid.*, p. 171.

In addition, manual workers in different industries may be entitled to free perquisites of one sort or another; those mentioned in the report of the Radcliffe Commission include a railwayman's free travel, a domestic servant's board and lodging, a miner's traditional free coal allowance and the issue of free or reduced rate consumer goods to the employees of many factories.[84] But the overall evidence on the scale and nature of such benefits makes clear that the higher grades of earners are the principal beneficiaries. Such benefits as houses, cars and entertainment allowances, which amount to a considerable loss of tax revenue to the Exchequer, are certainly not likely to be accruing to manual workers, and although the total spent on fringe benefits to manual employees may be high, the value of the benefits available to the individual employee is a good deal higher in the non-manual grades. Any estimates on this topic can only be guesswork. But such evidence as there is suggests that much the greater benefits accrue to members of the non-manual stratum.[85]

The question of tax reliefs is still more complicated. It is obvious that the surtax relief granted by the Conservative government in 1957 and 1961 served to widen the gap between manual and non-manual earnings, but other fiscal inequalities are more elusive. Accurate estimation is for several reasons impossible. But such evidence as there is all points in the direction of a similar conclusion. Deferred payments of various kinds, the redistribution of income within families, and the conversion of income into capital gains, are all legal devices which are likely to operate only for the benefit of the higher range of earners, and certainly not for manual workers and their families. The more notorious manipulations, such as the ploughing back of large earnings into private companies or heavy investment in farms organized as private companies with children as major shareholders, are probably common only among the very small number of people in the higher range of surtax income.[86] But the total effect of all forms of tax avoidance serves

---

[84] Royal Commission on the Taxation of Profits and Income, *Final Report* (Cmd. 9474, 1955), §209. A. Rubner, *Fringe Benefits: the Golden Chains* (London, 1962) includes as fringe benefits absenteeism, featherbedding, length of service concessions of various kinds, vocational training and tea breaks, all of which apply to manual workers. But even if the notion of 'fringes' is extended to cover all these, there is no evidence to show that they, or their equivalents, benefit manual workers more than non-manual.

[85] Published evidence about the higher grades of non-manual workers is, unfortunately, particularly scarce. For example, fringe benefits for higher executives below the boardroom level in 1963 have been analyzed for a sample of 117 firms by a firm of London management consultants, but the circulation of the results is restricted to the participating firms.

[86] L. R. Klein *et al.*, 'Savings and Finances of the Upper Income Classes', *Bulletin of the Oxford University Institute of Statistics* XVIII (1956), p. 314.

markedly to reinforce inequality of class. In remissions or allowances from the Exchequer, which include both deductible expenses
and schemes for provision for retirement, the non-manual worker
gains much more than the manual. Despite the widespread belief
that the 'Welfare State' is designed to benefit, if not explicitly the
working class, at least the less prosperous sections of the community,
the net benefits accruing to the individual from the Exchequer in
matters of 'welfare' are likely to be higher in the higher ranges of
income. There is not merely the objection, often voiced in Parliament and elsewhere, that flat rate contributions constitute in effect
a system of regressive taxation, since the burden is relatively greater
the poorer the person contributing.[87] It is also demonstrable that
considerably higher benefits can accrue to persons with higher incomes. Titmuss gives an example based on the rates per annum
for 1955–6 for child awards: a man with two children under 15
earning £2,000 a year receives £97, while a man earning £400
receives £28; over the lives of the two families, the first will receive
a total of £1,455, while the second will receive a total of £422.[88]
There is no need to summarize further calculations of this kind
which could be taken from the writings of Titmuss and others.
There is a variety of ways in which the British fiscal system pre-
serves or enhances the inequalities of class-situation between
manual and non-manual workers particularly at the higher levels
of non-manual work. Any conclusion about the egalitarian trend
of post-war Britain drawn from income statistics must, therefore,
be severely qualified.

If it was true that income, as opposed to ostensible earnings, had
not been so extensively redistributed by the 1950's as many writers
supposed, it was truer still that the distribution of property remained
markedly unequal. The estimate of Lydall and Tipping is that 'in
1954 the top one per cent. of British adults owned 43 per cent. of
total net capital and the top 10 per cent. 79 per cent'.[89] This figure
cannot, perhaps, be taken by itself as evidence for the unequal
class-situation of the manual and non-manual strata; the concentration of large amounts of capital in a few hands can still leave the
bulk of the non-manual class as propertyless as the manual. But it
can safely be said that only among the non-manual class is there

---

[87] See e.g. the remarks of Mrs. Castle in the discussion of the National
Health Service Contribution Bill in 1961, 635 H.C. Deb., c. 1035.
[88] Titmuss, *Essays on The Welfare State* (London, 1958), p. 47, and cf. the
memorandum submitted by the T.U.C. to the Radcliffe Commission (*Minutes
of Evidence*, p. 239).
[89] H. F. Lydall and D. G. Tipping, 'The Distribution of Personal Wealth
in Britain', *Bulletin of the Oxford University Institute of Statistics* XXIII
(1961), p. 90. (The Gini coefficient of concentration is ·87).

any significant accumulation of wealth, and to attribute any sizeable proportion of savings to the working class would be as mistaken for the 1950's as for the inter-war period. The Oxford Savings Surveys of 1953 and 1954 found that a third of income units had no liquid assets at all, and over 12% were actually in debt.[90] Moreover, when net worth and personal assets (defined as total assets minus the value of businesses) are analysed by occupation of head of household, it becomes clear that in this respect the class-situation of all non-manual workers was noticeably better than that of manual workers. Although the mean gross income of the clerical and sales workers in the 1953 sample is lower than that of the skilled manual—£403 as against £466—even the clerical and sales workers are better off by nearly a third in terms of mean net worth —£394 as against £299; and when a comparison is made in terms of mean personal assets, the figure is £479 as against £368.[91] As one would expect, the unskilled working class is much worse off, and the managerial and technical and self-employed classes very much better off. When holdings of stocks and shares are analyzed, the distribution is still more unequal. The mean among the skilled manual class is £4, with less than 1% owning stocks and shares worth more than £100; the mean among the clerical and sales class is £50, with 2·6% owning more than £100; the mean among the technical and managerial class is £842 with 17·8% owning more than £100 worth.[92] It is thus evident not only that the distribution of assets is very unequal, but that the skilled manual worker is in a less favourable position than even the lower grades of non-manual workers.

Not only were the rich not so far levelled down after 1945 as was widely supposed, but in addition poverty was by no means eliminated. If poverty is defined simply as the current level of National Assistance, then the actual number of people in poverty rose steadily during the early 1950's, declined somewhat in the late 1950's, but rose again in 1959–60 to almost exactly what it was in 1954–5—1,874,000.[93] The most striking characteristic of the recipients is the proportion of them over pensionable age. In 1960, this proportion was 69%.[94] If before the First World War the poor were the underpaid, and between the wars the underworked, then after the Second World War they were those past working. The

[90] T. P. Hill, 'Incomes, Savings and Net Worth—the Savings Surveys of 1952–54', *Ibid.* XVII (1955), p. 155.
[91] K. H. Straw, 'Consumers' Net Worth: the 1953 Savings Survey', *Ibid.* XVIII (1956), pp. 12, 14 (Tables VII and VIII).
[92] *Ibid.*, p. 19 (Table X).
[93] *Annual Abstract of Statistics*, 1960, Table 49.
[94] Ministry of Labour *Gazette*, July 1960, p. 281.

evidence of official statistics supplemented by survey data has been summarized as follows: 'By and large, then, three-quarters of the people drawing National Assistance are living for long periods of time at the best a few shillings above the basic Assistance scale rates including rent. This represents about 4 per cent. of the population—perhaps 6 per cent. of all households. The great majority, probably two thirds or more, are old people: the rest are divided among the long-term sick and disabled, the long-term unemployed, and women who have lost their husbands.'[95] It is known, however, that a good many people entitled to National Assistance do not draw it,[96] and it can also be argued that a more useful measure is one based on the total amount of income actually accruing to the recipients of National Assistance. With these further considerations in mind, it has been calculated by Townsend from the Ministry of Labour's budget data for 1960 that 14% of the population were then below a line drawn at 40% above the basic assistance rate plus rent.[97] When Rowntree's income standards were adjusted to 1953 prices and applied to the Ministry's budget data for 1953–4, it was found that 5·4% of households were in poverty by Rowntree's definition.[98]

These various findings all reveal that the redistribution of wealth which took place in post-war Britain was not as extensive as was believed at the time. Given this general belief, and what was certainly an advance on the part of the manual workers, there is nothing surprising in the resentments voiced by members of the middle class. The knowledge that manual workers, however few, could now earn upwards of £20 a week, and be the possessors not merely of television sets but of motor cars, was enough by itself to exacerbate their fears of a decline in terms of traditional middle-class standards. The further effect, however, of the belief that a major redistribution had taken place was to restrict the relative deprivation felt by manual workers who might otherwise have been led to compare themselves with non-manual.

The widespread conviction that the major evils of the 1930's had been remedied after 1945 also exerted its influence on the feelings of working-class families. Prosperity, although it heightened some expectations and therefore some discontents, was not so swift or

[95] Dorothy Cole Wedderburn, 'Poverty in Britain Today—the Evidence', *Sociological Review*, n.s. X (1962), p. 263.

[96] *Ibid.*, citing D. Cole with J. Utting, *The Economic Circumstances of Old People* (London, 1962), pp. 94–5, and giving an estimate of one old person in three.

[97] Peter Townsend, 'The Meaning of Poverty', *British Journal of Sociology* XIII (1962), p. 215, n.,2.

[98] *Ibid.*, p. 212.

violent as to set off an upheaval of standards and norms comparable to the War. The awareness of 'never having had it so good'—a slogan which became associated with Macmillan's government as much as 'fair shares' had been with Attlee's—was sufficient to make new comparisons feasible; but by these comparisons, the better-paid manual workers were likely to feel relatively gratified rather than relatively deprived. This would not prevent their pressing claims for higher wages. But the knowledge that manual workers could earn more than many white-collar workers—whatever other differences might be less apparent—together with the popular impression of working-class prosperity in general, tended to give non-manual workers and their wives the greater sense of grievance. Manual workers and their wives were much more likely to compare their lot with that of themselves and their parents during the Depression, and by this comparison to count themselves fortunate.

At the same time, and perhaps more important still, there was little if any awareness of the kinds of inequalities analyzed by Professor Titmuss. There was, in fact, no occasion for manual workers to make the sort of cross-class comparisons likely to suggest themselves to academic investigators examining the statistical evidence. The Government Social Survey conducted an enquiry for the Radcliffe Commission in 1952 about the attitudes of manual workers to taxation and their possible effects on productivity; its conclusion was that although attitudes to tax might have some slight effect of the kind suggested, they were 'completely uncorrelated with the facts', and 'No adequate structure exists in the informants' minds to enable them to consider and regard the subject as a whole'.[99] A survey carried out prior to the general election of 1959 by Research Services Ltd. found that when somewhat disingenuous hypothetical examples were presented, there was as much sympathy for the rich as the poor; when respondents were asked whether they thought that three hypothetical men, each with two children, were paying too much, too little or the right amount of income tax at their respective levels, 29% of the sample thought that 'Mr. A', earning £600 and paying £3, was paying too little, and 52% thought that 'Mr. C', earning £5,000 and paying £2,199, was paying too much. Only 4% thought Mr. C was paying too little, and only 6% thought that Mr. A was paying too much; and when the answers were analyzed by party, it was found that as many as 47% of

[99] Royal Commission on the Taxation of Profits and Income, *Second Report* (Cmd. 9105, 1954), pp. 120, 107. The sample consisted of 1429 workers in operative and supervisory grades in England and Wales. Cf. also the statement made to the Commission on behalf of the T.U.C. (*Minutes of Evidence*, questions 2634–7).

Labour supporters thought that Mr. C was paying too much, and 27% that Mr. A was paying too little.[100] These two pieces of evidence taken together lend further support to the impression that few people, and, in particular, few manual workers outside of the diligent readers of their union journals,[101] were likely to make Professor Titmuss's kind of comparison. Inequalities of class were becoming increasingly invisible.

Where survey data are unavailable, the best remaining source from which to look for evidence about relative deprivations of class is the terms in which wage or salary claims are put forward by different occupational groups. There is certainly a noticeable change between the inter-war and post-war periods. In the inter-war period the greater number of disputes were about either the level below which wages would not be regarded as providing subsistence or the changes made possible (or necessary) by the economic situation of the particular firm or industry concerned. After 1945, the achievement of full employment and the governmental policy of wage restraint which was in part a result of it altered the language and assumptions within which wage disputes were conducted. Appeals to justice came more often to be based on differentials; and the relation of wages to the cost of living, although it had been a topic of contention from 1920 onwards, became almost the standard rationale for a steady cycle of demands. But despite these changes the relation of grievance to hardship remained anomalous. Principles other than subsistence were more freely and frequently invoked. But they did not at all provide a yardstick by which manual and non-manual work could be directly compared. The wage-claims made seldom rested on any broad principle of egalitarianism.[102] Even where explicitly championed as 'just' or 'reasonable', the majority of claims continued to be based either on relativities of limited scope, or on the need to maintain a previously established position. Cross-class reference groups, or appeals to explicit principles of overall comparison, remained as infrequent as ever.

[100] Communicated by Dr. Mark Abrams in correspondence; a breakdown by class is not available but it may be plausibly assumed that the majority of Labour supporters were working-class.

[101] See e.g. the Record (the journal of the T.G.W.U.), Nov. 1961, p. 23, for awareness of inequalities in welfare. But for evidence of how few members of the T.G.W.U. ever read the *Record*, see *The Dockworker* (University of Liverpool, 1954), p. 134.

[102] An unusual case where a specific comparison is made across the manual/non-manual line is in the claim of the post office workers submitted to the Royal Commission on the Civil Service of 1953–5: see the *Minutes of Evidence*, p. 462 and cf. p. 306.

There have been a number of official pronouncements about principles relating to levels of reward, but none have been such as to suggest that an unrestricted choice of reference groups would be legitimate. In particular, none have laid down principles of comparison between manual and non-manual work. The first of the Fair Wages Resolutions was passed by the House of Commons in 1891, but its central phrase—'such wages as are generally accepted as current in each trade for competent workmen'—cannot be made to yield any criterion of comparison beyond the existing market rate for the job. A new clause, passed under Labour pressure in 1909, substituted for the criterion of current wages the criterion of wages recognized by employers and trade unions, or, failing this, the practice of 'good' employers. But this was only to substitute the rates established by collective bargaining for the rates established by the free market, and although the resolution was embodied in some subsequent legislation, such as the British Sugar (Subsidy) Act of 1925 or the Bacon Industry Act of 1938, it remained as empty a principle as its predecessor. In 1924, the Agricultural Wages (Regulation) Act passed by the Labour government set up county wage committees which were to establish agricultural wages 'adequate to promote efficiency and to enable a man in an ordinary case to maintain himself and his family in accordance with such standards of comfort as may be reasonable in relation to the nature of his occupation'. The vagueness of these phrases, however, hardly needs demonstration; the only clear inference is that no comparisons would be considered appropriate which extended across class or occupational lines. A third Fair Wages Resolution was passed by the House of Commons in 1946, but this did not do more than establish collective bargaining as the criterion of fairness without reference to the 'good employers' of the 1909 clause. In 1948, the Government issued a *Statement on Personal Incomes, Costs and Prices*[103] which explicitly asserted that traditional differentials might be based on irrelevant or even undesirable criteria, but the criterion now substituted was that of an efficient distribution of labour, not a just system of rewards. After 1948 governmental pronouncements on the principles of wages policy continued to make primary reference to the need for restraint, so that all advances became by implication exceptional. No general principles were laid down by which traditional differentials might be effectively assessed. At the Trades Union Congress of 1952, a resolution calling on the General Council to consider a greater co-ordination of wages policy 'with a view to providing greater equity and fairer relativities'[104] was overwhelm-

[103] Cmd. 7321.
[104] *Report*, p. 505.

ingly rejected. The role of reference group comparisons in wage demands is too obvious to need comment; but the scope and relevance of such comparisons continues to be determined by precedent, convention and habit, not by appeal to a principle established by either the legislature or the unions whereby cross-class relative deprivations could be shown to be justified.

As well as the fair wage resolutions, there have been a number of attempts to establish a standard for the fair remuneration of government employees. But the search for a principle has been just as unsatisfactory, and the various Royal Commissions which attempted to establish criteria of 'fair comparison'[105] have reflected the conventional framework of reference groups more than they have sought to establish criteria by which any one type of job could be related to any other. After the Second World War, the extended role of the Government as an employer led to considerable discussion about the appropriate standards by which the pay not only of civil servants in the ordinary sense but of doctors and dentists, policemen, and railwaymen should be assessed.[106] But the conclusions reached were neither based on broad comparisons between manual and non-manual work nor did they result in a widened choice of reference group by those whose claims they considered. The Pilkington Commission compared doctors with architects, and the Willink Commission policemen with skilled manual workers. The choice of comparisons made both by the claimants for higher reward and those adjudicating their claims continued to rest on established differentials within the manual and non-manual strata. By the 1960's, there was a widespread awareness of how far the differences in earnings had narrowed. But perhaps for this reason, manual workers seldom rested their claims for higher wages on a comparison with non-manual occupations. If there was a sense of relative deprivation generated by comparisons across the manual/non-manual line, it was more likely to be on the part of the less well-paid non-manual workers who wished to preserve a diminishing difference and were likewise more conscious of earnings than of those other features of class-situation by which a 'fair' comparison would have to be made.

From this summary of the decades leading up to 1962, it is clear that the magnitude and frequency of relative deprivation has seldom been in close correlation with the facts of inequality of class. Each of the two world wars has set off a disturbance of reference groups

[105] See e.g. the Royal Commission on the Civil Service, 1929–31, *Report* (Cmd. 3909, 1931), pp. 81–3; and cf. the report of the 1953–55 Commission (Cmd. 9613, 1955), pp. 23 ff.

[106] See H. A. Clegg, 'The Scope of Fair Wage Comparisons', *Journal of Industrial Economics* IX (1961), pp. 194–214.

and an upsurge of expectations. But after both of them, other influences have inhibited the mounting egalitarianism which had been aroused. After the First World War, the Depression and its apparent irremediableness prevented manual workers and their families from seeing it as feasible that they should demand comparable rewards to those for non-manual work. After the Second, relative deprivation was damped down by the achievement of some gradual amelioration of the class-situation of manual workers and the conviction that a greater redistribution was taking place than did in fact occur. If the account which I have given is correct, then we should expect the evidence of the 1962 survey to show that in terms of inequalities of class, the respondents least likely to express relative deprivation will be those at the top of the manual stratum; working class reference groups will not often be taken from the other side of the manual/non-manual line; and an awareness, or even disapproval, of the greater prosperity of others will be more frequent among middle-class people looking at working-class people than the other way round. There is not yet, however, any conclusion to be drawn as to whether a similar relationship will hold between inequality and relative deprivation of status.

V

ATTITUDES TO STATUS

THE problem of measurement is not the only reason why inequalities of status are harder to describe than inequalities of class. It is obvious that monetary comparisons can be far more accurately made than even ordinal comparisons of prestige. But in addition, it can always be questioned how far a particular difference in style of life does in fact constitute an inequality of status. English people might speak or dress differently from each other, or spend their leisure in different pastimes, without such differences providing any occasion for a sense of inequality or resentment. Why do differences in style of life have to constitute or even exemplify a hierarchy of social esteem? But there is in practice a close and pervasive connection. There may be no inherent inequality in the preference of one man to watch polo instead of dog-racing, to drink wine instead of beer or to wear a bowler instead of a cloth cap when he goes to work. But such differences do directly affect the pattern of inequalities, since however neutral they may be as simple preferences of taste, their effect is further to compartmentalize different strata into status-groups whose divergent styles of life inhibit their recognition of each other as equals. That this is so in England can, I think, be accepted without argument. Differences of status may not be suspectible of measurement; but they are easy to demonstrate, and the fact of them in English life poses exactly the same question as do inequalities of class about the relation between relative deprivation and inequality.

The answer, however, is different. In Britain since 1918, the relation between inequality and relative deprivation of status has been clear in outline and consistent in direction. As the manual stratum has advanced towards greater equality with the non-manual (without yet reaching it), relative deprivation of status among working-class people has increased in both magnitude and frequency. Indeed, on the topic which lies closest to the roots of inequality of status—education—there is an exact parallel with the promotion example from *The American Soldier*. When few children of manual workers

95

were receiving secondary education, few working-class families took the recipients of secondary education as a reference group, comparative or normative. But as more children of manual workers stayed on at school beyond the minimum age, more working-class families began to feel relatively deprived of education and of the status (apart from the job opportunities for the individual child) associated with it. On other topics relevant to status, the spread of aspirations is less easily demonstrable. But I shall argue that the evidence all points in the same direction. The magnitude and frequency of relative deprivation of status in the manual stratum has, on the whole, risen as inequality of status has declined.

There is a further difference in the analysis of status from that of class: the distinction between fraternalistic and egoistic relative deprivations is more important. Where inequalities of class are concerned, there has been little to modify the tendency of working-class people to 'fraternalism'; middle-class people may have come more often to feel fraternalistic relative deprivations, but the nature of the differences between the class-situation of manual and non-manual workers has meant that fraternalism has remained the normal mode for the manual worker. In the matter of status, it is no less true that the two strata cannot be described as equals; but there is a greater likelihood of a change from fraternalistic to egoistic relative deprivation. Either kind can in principle be felt by a working-class person on topics relevant to status. He may, on the one hand, feel that he and all his fellows should be accorded equal status with non-manual workers, that secondary modern education should have parity of esteem with public or grammar and that all snobberies of dress, accent and style of life should be abolished. On the other hand, he might simply want for himself and his family the status which he sees as enjoyed by the families of non-manual workers, and be more concerned that his children should go to a grammar school than that their secondary modern school should have parity of esteem. Relative deprivation of status can extend just as far or as fast in aspiration for individual status mobility as in subscription to the ideals of egalitarian Socialism. The comparative reference group may be the same in either case. But if it is also a normative reference group, then the relative deprivation felt will be egoistic; and the frequency of the one or the other may have an influence both on the way in which the status-structure changes and on how far the relative deprivations felt within it can be vindicated by reference to social justice.

It may be difficult to press the distinction in practice, even with the help of a sample survey. A man who wants for himself or his family the status which he sees as accorded to others may not know himself whether he wants it on behalf of all the members of his membership reference group or whether he would be prepared to leave them behind. But the distinction must be applied as far as it can. Between 1918 and 1962 the relative deprivations of status felt in the working class were often of both kinds. But it is necessary to ask whether the relative deprivation of status felt by manual workers in 1918 became more or less fraternalistic as well as how far it increased in frequency and magnitude.

In the aftermath of the War, many observers noted signs of a breakdown in the status-hierarchy as it had been prior to 1914. The working class was demanding fuller educational and cultural opportunity; the middle class could no longer keep resident servants in the way that it had been accustomed to do; the great country houses were up for sale. Orwell, in *England Your England*, commented on the emergence after 1918 of an indeterminate class (i.e., status-group) whose position could not be at once inferred from their clothes, their manners and their accent.[1] But the changes were small in comparison with the remaining inequalities. Since style of life is a function of income, the income distribution was already likely to ensure this. Although many middle-class families were undoubtedly worse off than they had previously been, it is important to remember that (in Schumpeter's useful simile) a class or a status-stratum is like a bus or hotel—always full, but of different people.[2] There might, in 1920, be many members of middle-class status-groups and even of the aristocracy who were relatively deprived by reference to their former expectations. But this was not a necessary reason to prevent the emergence of just as many 'new rich' to replace them in the appropriate categories of status as well as of class; nor did it by any means make them the status equals of manual workers.

The advertisements of country houses up for sale and the complaints (however justified, in relative terms) of the self-styled 'new poor' should be set against the jokes in *Punch* about the purchase of peerages by war profiteers and the swollen waiting-lists of the public schools. There is a resemblance here between the aftermaths of the two world wars. After both, there was a widespread and articulate feeling among the middle and upper status-strata that their privileges had been undermined, that they were no longer properly respected by their inferiors and that the style of life to which they were accustomed had come to be denied them. But neither in 1919 nor 1945 should this feeling on the part of those for whom it might well be true be taken, as they themselves were apt to take it, as evidence of a social revolution. From the point of view of the manual worker,

[1] Orwell, *England Your England and Other Essays* (London, 1953), p. 223.
[2] Joseph Schumpeter, 'The Problem of Classes', in *Imperialism and Social Classes* (New York, 1955), p. 126.

such changes were merely changes in the composition of the status élite. If the manual worker had attained some greater measure of economic equality with reference to the lower-middle class, this was largely a separate matter from the recognition by the strata above him of his equal status as a 'gentleman'. It could hardly be expected to matter to him that different people were now taking holidays on the Riviera, or sending their sons to schools where they would learn to speak with an educated accent. The 'new poor' might resent what they saw as the untoward rise of the working class; but they were hardly more likely, after the First War or the Second, to treat a factory worker as a social equal and invite him to a meal in their homes.

But if in 1920 the inequalities of status between the two strata had diminished much less than was sometimes supposed, there was still a demand for a greater measure of equality of status than manual workers had ever aspired to before the War. The War itself was one cause of this; so was the successful emergence of the Labour Party. In particular, the demand for educational equality began to be forcibly expressed. I have already quoted the opinion of the Board of Education that the startling upsurge in demand for secondary education was in part the culmination of tendencies which had been invisibly at work for a period of some twenty years. The demand by the working class for universal secondary education can be traced back before the war and even before the turn of the century. But in the 1920's, it became suddenly more insistent and more widespread. For the more prosperous working class, education was beginning to be a feasible aspiration whose denial would constitute a relative deprivation. 'I do not decry education', said Ernest Bevin in 1920. 'I lament the lack of it and I curse the other class for monopolizing it.'[3] By the time of the Hadow Report of 1926, there was in both strata a growing body of opinion which held that it was not only desirable but feasible for the monopoly to be broken.

Such a view might not be shared by the more resentful members of the non-manual stratum—the people described by Sir Cyril Norwood as 'those who attribute the scarcity of domestic servants to the unreasonable institution of elementary education, by which they are made to pay for the teaching of other people's children'.[4] But more recent and systematic research has made it clear not only that

[3] D.W.R. & G.W.U., *Minutes of the Triennial Delegates' Conference*, Plymouth, 18–22 May, 1920, pp. 129–36, quoted by Bullock, *op. cit.*, pp. 132–3.

[4] C. Norwood, *The English Tradition of Education* (London, 1929), quoted D. V. Glass, 'Education', in M. Ginsberg, ed., *Law and Opinion in 20th Century England* (London, 1959), pp. 325–6.

(contrary to much middle-class opinion) the ability of many work-ing-class children was going to waste, but also that middle-class families were, in effect, the greater beneficiaries from the spread of public education. It is true that in the inter-war period many more sons of manual workers received a secondary education than they had done before the First War. Indeed, their progress can in one sense be described as greater. But this is only because it is an in-crease on what before the war had been so tiny a proportion. The opportunities for secondary education made available to the sons of manual workers between the Education Acts of 1918 and 1944 did not mean that they achieved such an education in anything like a proportion corresponding to the proportion of middle-class children. The figures best illustrative of this are given by Jean Floud in a study completed in 1949. Of working-class boys born before 1910, it was found that 4·0% had received a secondary education; the proportion of middle-class boys was 27%. Of working-class boys born between 1910 and 1929, 9·8% had received secondary educa-tion; the proportion of middle-class boys was 38·9%.[5]

Although by the end of the 1920's the political parties were agreed in principle that some form of full-time secondary education should be made available for all children up to the age of 16, the practical achievement of this aim remained hardly more than visionary. In the matter of the school-leaving age, both Labour and National govern-ments were unexpectedly and abruptly frustrated. The second Labour Government announced in 1929 that the age would be raised to 15 from 1931, but their Bill collapsed over the question of build-ing grants for the voluntary schools. The Education Act of 1936 passed by Baldwin's government provided for the raising of the age to take effect in 1939, but by an almost extravagant irony the appointed day was the day on which the wartime evacuation of children from London was set in motion. It could despite this be claimed that the proportion of children between 14 and 17 receiv-ing secondary education, although lower as the Depression wore off than it had been at its height, was a great deal higher than it had been twenty years before: in 1938, the proportion was 19·6%[6] and the Spens Committee estimated that the number of pupils in recog-nized secondary schools was well over half a million.[7] But this was very far short of the goal of four years of secondary education for

[5] Jean Floud, 'The Educational Experience of the Adult Population of England and Wales as at July 1949', in D. V. Glass, ed., *Social Mobility in Britain* (London, 1954) pp. 120–1.
[6] *Statistical Abstract for the U.K.*, 1924–38, Table 40.
[7] *Report of the Consultative Committee on Secondary Education*, 1938 (Spens Report), p. 91.

all. In particular, it was far short of this goal for the children of manual workers. Although the number of free places increased steadily during the '20's, it did not follow that this, any more than the simple extension of numbers, benefited the children of manual rather than non-manual workers. Although the Board of Education described the free place system as designed to bring the advantages of secondary education 'within the reach of the poorer classes, and to place them on the same footing as pupils whose parents were in a position to pay the school fees',[8] the social survey of Merseyside carried out not long thereafter came to a more disillusioning conclusion: 'our figures indicate, what is not commonly realized, that in fact barely half those who receive free education in secondary schools come from manual working class homes'.[9] Not only did the improvement (which it was) in secondary education fall short of what governments of all parties had hoped for. As far as it went, it did not even achieve what was thought to be its principal aim both by the egalitarian reformers and by the more resentful members of the middle class. Relative deprivation might be spreading among manual workers as education did; but neither was yet spreading very fast.

The principal reason for this was, once again, the permissive condition of money, meaning not merely the lack of public funds but the lack of sufficient resources to enable a working-class family to afford to keep a child on longer at school.

'Having made primary education compulsory,' wrote Kenneth Lindsay in 1926, 'it was found that many children were uneducable owing to neglect, disease and other causes. It may be said of secondary education that, with its rapid growth, particularly since the war, many children either cannot take advantage of it owing to inability to afford the money, or cannot continue it, having entered the schools, for the same reason.'[10]

The *New Survey* of London found that educational handicaps consequent on the poverty of parents 'have only been partially removed by maintenance scholarships'.[11] The claim that the granting of free places was not in itself enough continued to be made in the '30's also. After the General Election of 1935, the subject was raised by Attlee in the Debate on the Address, and it is worth quoting from his speech if only because of the unimaginativeness of his interruptors: the raising of the leaving age, said Attlee, was

'a minor matter, because there is to be no question of seeing that

[8] *Report*, 1926–27, p. 23.
[9] Caradog Jones, *op. cit.*, III, p. 187.
[10] Kenneth Lindsay, *Social Progress and Educational Waste* (London, 1926), p. 45.
[11] *New Survey of London Life and Labour* (London, 1930–35), I, p. 259.

the poor as well as the better off shall be able to stay at school.
[HON. MEMBERS: 'Why not?']. Because, as I understand it, there
is no provision for a subsistence allowance, and without that, as
everybody knows perfectly well, the poorer families cannot afford
to let their children stay on at school.'[12]
Indeed, it was not simply a question of subsistence for the child
remaining at school. As the economy recovered from the Depression, it was increasingly a question of the family also losing a
potential earner—a loss much less easy for working-class families
to sustain, since they were likely to be not only poorer but larger
than middle-class families.

Thus the continuing failure of secondary education to spread
fully among the children of manual workers was largely the result
of continuing inequalities of class. But it was also due partly to
continuing inequalities of status. For a working-class child to go to
a grammar school could mean leaving his status-group for a stratum
not merely foreign to him but often less desirable in the eyes of his
parents. I have already quoted in the conclusion of the Pilgrim Trust
investigators that in the Depression it was security, not money (let
alone, one may infer, status) which was the attraction of clerical jobs
to the parents of working-class children. It is probably rash to de-
duce too much about attitudes to education from parental preferences for their children's jobs. But it is certainly plausible to suggest
that the association of secondary education with a clerical occupation, and the unwillingness of many working-class parents to see
their sons go into a lower clerical rather than a higher artisan's job,
was a significant factor in the refusal by parents of the offer of free
places at secondary schools for their children.[13] Martin still found
in 1950 that the most common occupational preference among
manual workers for their sons was for a skilled trade or craft—that
is, 'for an occupation which stands high in the hierarchy of manual
work, but which does not involve too marked a change of
status'.[14] It may well be, therefore, that a reluctance on the part of
manual workers for their children to receive a grammar school education was partly responsible, even during the period of maximum
expansion of opportunities, for the preservation of the inequalities
of status which derive from unequal education.

But if status inequality was preserved in this way despite the

[12] 307 H.C. Deb., cc. 62–3. Cf. the T.U.C. *Report*, 1936, pp. 276–8, where
not only is the question raised about maintenance, but the sense of grievance
in the matter of education has been intensified by government expenditure
on rearmament.
[13] Lindsay concluded (*op. cit.*, p. 11) that 'where secondary education is
free, the number of refusals of free places exceeds the number of accept-
ances'.
[14] *Op. cit.*, p. 69.

spread of education, relative deprivation of status could still be gradually extended and heightened because of it. Although the traditional reference groups of manual workers and their families inhibited many of them from wishing to take advantage of the opportunities by which these reference groups would be most effectively changed, the progressive extension of education down the status hierarchy carried with it an influence disproportionate to the small numbers involved. Such effects are very difficult to document, let alone to measure; but by the middle 1930's there was a distinct impression of a change of this kind.[15] The Depression itself sometimes provided an awareness of the benefits of education to workers who would not otherwise have been exposed to them. Not only the Workers' Educational Association played a part in this, but also the residential centres providing educational opportunities for the unemployed: 'as some men have put it', said the annual report of Wincham Hall for 1935–36, 'they did not realize there were so many things a man could do with his life'.[16] Only a tiny fraction of manual workers were affected by schemes of this kind; but any change of attitudes towards education as such was likely to be self-perpetuating. Working-class parents who had themselves been beneficiaries of secondary education were likely to bring up their children in the expectation that they likewise would stay on at school over the minimum age. The survey carried out in 1957 for the Central Advisory Council for Education disclosed that only 8% of fathers who had stayed at school beyond the minimum age allowed their own children to leave at the minimum.[17] An investigation in Hertfordshire and Middlesbrough in the early 1950's also found a noticeable correlation in all classes between examination performance and the education of parents: the educated parents of the successful children 'favoured a longer school life, preferred further education of the academic type for their children (i.e. at a university rather than a technical college) and looked forward to seeing their children enter non-manual rather than manual occupations'.[18] The more working-class children came to receive a secondary education, the more they were likely to act as catalysts for the relative deprivation of status of both their fellows and their fellows' parents.

[15] On the 'upthrust of new strata of the population' into the secondary schools see e.g., G. A. N. Lowndes, *The Silent Social Revolution: an Account of the Expansion of Public Education in England and Wales, 1895–1935* (London, 1937), pp. 128 ff.

[16] Quoted Pilgrim Trust, *op. cit.*. p. 351.

[17] Ministry of Education, *15–18: A Report of the Central Advisory Council for Education (England)*, 1962 (Crowther Report) I, p. 9.

[18] Floud *et al.*, *Social Class and Educational Opportunity* (London, 1957), p. 88.

At the same time, the extension of mass communications was sufficiently rapid and widespread to expose many more members of the working class to the possibility, at least, of a middle-class style of life. Such effects are, once again, very difficult to document, and without the evidence of surveys virtually impossible to estimate. Moreover, the influence of the mass media was in some ways an ambivalent one. The BBC is generally argued to have done rather more under Reith's direction to bolster the established system than to undermine it; and much of the portrayal in the popular papers of the more affluent strata of society was not of a kind to induce a genuine reference-group comparison on the part of their readers. It is, in a way, surprising to glance through the *Daily Herald* of the 1930's and find that it seems to be little less full of photographs of yachts at Cowes or society weddings than *The Times*. But these were likely to be enjoyed by the readers of the *Herald* precisely because they did not constitute a genuine reference group; like the film stars, 'society' was too close to a fantasy world to engender feelings of relative deprivation. Relative deprivation was more likely to be induced by either the front-page news about the progress of the Labour movement or by the advertisements for consumer goods. It was in this way that the extension not only of education but of information conveyed by the media of mass communication was likely to lead to an awareness of the possibility of greater equalization of status between the two strata. Such improvement might not be a sufficient condition of equality, but it was at any rate a step towards it; and like educational change, it was likely to be self-perpetuating. 'These children', said a speaker at the T.U.C. in 1929, 'with their new outlook, with their cultural development, with their habits of refinement and good taste, are not going to be satisfied with the standard of 1905, and we ought not to expect them to be.'[19]

Throughout the inter-war period, therefore, there were enough influences at work within the status hierarchy to sustain a steady movement towards some greater measure of equality, even if there were at the same time enough restraints to make it likely that change would be gradual. Circumstantially, educational and cultural development was inhibited by lack of the necessary resources at the appropriate times. Socially, it was inhibited by all the traditional barriers between the strata and the feeling as much among the manual as the non-manual stratum that working-class education was a separate matter and should properly be kept so. During and indeed well after the 1920's, at the same time as the movement for secondary education for all was steadily growing in strength, the

[19] *Report*, p. 449.

T.U.C. was more frequently making representations to the Government about specifically working-class education than about a free secondary education, let alone an equal secondary education, for every child. Traditional standards of reference in terms at once of the existing educational structure and of the overall hierarchy of status meant that relative deprivation of status extended only slowly within the manual stratum. But retrogression, however small the advances made, was unlikely or even impossible; economic inequalities once narrowed could easily widen again, but not inequalities of social esteem. Whatever inequalities remained, the general status of manual workers and their families was rising slowly but continuously throughout the inter-war period within the established hierarchy of English society.

This advance towards equality of status is perhaps best illustrated by the assimilation of the trade unions into the conventional system of honours and prestige. A number of influences underlay this assimilation. The increased responsibility handled by union leaders during the war, their accession to cabinet rank under Lloyd George and subsequently MacDonald, the role played by Bevin and others on such bodies as the Macmillan Committee, all played a part in heightening the status as well as the influence of the Labour movement within the community as a whole. When Asquith had made the decision which brought the first Labour government into office, there was a flurry of popular speculation as to how far the new ministers would conform to the conventions of the status-system. What would they wear? How would they behave? Would they be polite to the Royal Family? In the event, even the strictest sticklers for etiquette need not have been so fearful. Some ministers, such as Henderson, regarded these matters as unimportant.[20] Others, and most notoriously MacDonald himself, revelled in them; his fondness for duchesses and a white tie and tails has been attested by a succession of anecdotes supplied by his acquaintances and colleagues. Jimmy Thomas was depicted by the political cartoonists as permanently attired in evening dress; Frank Hodges played golf with the future George VI.[21] Some of Labour's supporters resented this easy transition to the mores of their traditional enemies: Hamilton Fyfe, the editor of the *Daily Herald,* wrote in the *Socialist Review* that the wearing of court dress by members of the Labour movement was 'a gain for the Old Gang'.[22] But despite the disgust of the

[20] M. A. Hamilton, *Arthur Henderson* (London, 1938), pp. 237–8.
[21] R. W. Lyman, *The First Labour Government 1924* (London, 1958), p. 104.
[22] *Socialist Review,* October 1924, p. 114; cf. e.g., the dockyard heckler described by J. Paton, *Left Turn* (London, 1936), p. 168.

militants there is little evidence that this feeling was very wide-spread. 'As a matter of fact', Snowden wrote in his autobiography, 'the constituents of the Labour members who appeared in the full uniform were rather pleased to see the photographs in the news-papers of their representatives arrayed in all this glory.'[23] A Ger-man socialist who was present in London during the first weeks of the Labour Government wrote that 'among the workers, in a circle stretching far beyond the party organization and the Socialistic electorate, there prevailed a naive and rapturous pride that by men of their class, and in their name, the mightiest empire of the world was ruled'.[24] Only a minority of the Labour movement, either within Parliament or without, seems seriously to have expected that the movement should reject, let alone overthrow, the traditional status system. It was enough, as implied by such autobiographical titles as George Barnes's *From Workshop to War Cabinet* or John Hodge's *From Workman's Cottage to Windsor Castle*, that men who had once been manual workers should rise to high places within it.[25]

The issue of whether or not members of the Labour movement should accept knighthoods and peerages provided in one form a continuation of the arguments of 1924 about ceremonial dress, a continuation which lasted more or less until the Second World War. It was to some extent bound up with the question of the reform or the abolition of the House of Lords, and with the arguments as to whether or not the implicit support of a hereditary second chamber preserved an unjust apportionment of power as well as of status. But it was chiefly a dispute about whether the implicit sup-port of the status hierarchy was not at variance with the fraterna-listic tenets of a Socialist party. The acceptance by Walter Citrine and Arthur Pugh of knighthoods in 1935 was attacked in these terms at the annual meeting of the T.U.C. and the general topic was raised at the Labour Party Conference of the same year. But on neither occasion was there evidence of significant opposition. In-deed, it was the acceptance of honours by trade unionists from a Conservative rather than a Labour government which touched off the formal objections; there had been no opposition when Ben

[23] P. Snowden, *Autobiography* (London, 1934), II, pp. 662–3.

[24] E. Wertheimer, *Portrait of the Labour Party* (2nd edn.; London, 1930), p. xii.

[25] The most celebrated example is David Kirkwood, a militant shop steward from Clydeside who entered Parliament in 1922, and in his memoirs, published in 1935 with a foreword by Churchhill, went so far as to say that 'Class-distinctions [i.e. status-distinctions] are fast losing their importance as the standard of judgement . . . Snobbery has almost gone.' (*My Life of Revolt* [London, 1935], pp. 265–6). In 1951, on his retirement from the House of Commons, he accepted a peerage.

Turner of the Textile Workers accepted a knighthood in 1931 together with James Sexton and Robert Young. The ordinary members of the movement seem to have been less critical than proud: Pugh wrote in his union journal of his 'keen appreciation for the large number of messages of congratulations . . . received from members, branches and branch officers'.[26] After the accession of a Labour Government in 1945, the acceptance of knighthoods by trade unionists became a matter of routine. Indeed, Miss Godwin of the Women Clerks and Secretaries, the mover of the resolution in which Citrine was implicitly criticised in 1935, became a Dame of the British Empire in 1962, under a Conservative Government, as chairman of the General Council of the T.U.C.

Thus the attitude of the majority of the Labour movement towards the aspects of the status system most closely bound up with ritual and snobbery was not that of wishing to abolish them but rather to make them open to all sections of society. Although the abolition of the House of Lords played a prominent part in Labour's earlier programme—even as expounded by Jimmy Thomas[27]—the only measure in fact taken against it was the further curtailment of its powers in 1949 by a Labour Government whose leader subsequently joined it. The wish to abolish the hereditary principle as a criterion of selection was not confined to the Labour party.[28] Nor was the refusal of peerages: Neville Chamberlain, for example, refused one as well as Ernest Bevin. In the same way, the abolition of the public schools did not come to be seriously attempted in practice, despite the resolutions occasionally introduced at Labour Party Conferences; and the Education Act of 1944 was an all-party measure resting on meritocratic rather than egalitarian principles. The attitude of the Labour movement to the traditional status-structure was as much that it should be opened as that it should be levelled. The official ambitions, as it were, of the Labour movement were for advancement within the established system; and this advancement was progressively attained from the First War onwards in such a way as to heighten the standards of feasible aspiration without, or perhaps instead of, promoting a desire for the system's overthrow.

It is, however, much more difficult to find evidence for the feelings of the population at large than for those of Labour ministers and spokesmen. How far there was an acquiescence by the bulk of

---

[26] *Man and Metal,* June 1935, quoted by V. L. Allen, *Trade Union Leadership* (London, 1957), p. 35.

[27] J. H. Thomas, *When Labour Rules* (London, 1920), p. 47.

[28] See R. T. McKenzie, *British Political Parties* (London, 1955), pp. 223 ff. for evidence on the views expressed by the Conservative National Union.

manual workers and their families in the status hierarchy as it directly affected them is very hard to guess. There is, nonetheless, one topic on which some evidence is available and which sheds some light on changes in the status hierarchy: this is the topic of resident domestic service. It is interesting because it is a symptom not only of the expectations of the richer non-manual families that they should be waited on, but of the readiness of members of the working class to engage in an occupation carrying with it an overtone, whether resented or not, of personal servitude beyond the purely economic relation between employer and employee. There is an obvious economic determinant of the numbers of people engaged at any one time in domestic service: there must be employers with enough money to spend on their wages and upkeep, and there must be potential employees sufficiently in need of the money to choose this as a job. But the changing pattern both of recruitment and attitude reflects also a change in the temper of the social relations between the strata from which the employers and employees in this particular occupation were drawn.

In 1921, the Minister of Labour was able to comment on 'the amount of heat to which this domestic servants' question gives rise on both sides of the House'.[29] By 1960, when a court case was brought to decide whether *Lady Chatterley's Lover* was obscene, a question by the prosecuting counsel to the jury as to whether they would wish their servants to see the book in their house was widely treated as a joke. It would not have been so regarded forty years before. To the readers of *Punch* in 1920, what was quaint was not that middle-class families should have resident servants but that they should not. Themes for cartoons were furnished by 'lend-a-hand parties' where guests were expected to help with housework, or by the daughters of the house having to pose as maids.[30] In 1923, a non-parliamentary committee on the *Supply of Female Domestic Servants* was set up by the Ministry of Labour to investigate the complaint frequently voiced in letters to the newspapers that domestic servants were unobtainable because of the payment of unemployment benefit to women suitable for such work. The committee in fact concluded that this had little to do with it. The shortage should be attributed rather to the lack of adequate standards of wages, hours and leisure, and the solution was the professionalization of domestic work. The committee recommended, moreover, that all domestic workers should be brought within the scope of unemployment insurance. But despite this report, the same complaints were being made with, it appeared, as

[29] 147 H.C. Deb., c. 476.
[30] *Punch,* June 2 and June 9, 1920.

107

little foundation twelve years later,[31] and the recommendation about unemployment insurance was not implemented until 1938. Professionalization was never successfully achieved. By the end of the Second War, the low status of domestic service in the eyes of its potential recruits was officially recognized,[32] and the economic pressures on them had for the most part relaxed. By the 1950's, it was plausible to suggest that the visible luxury spending of the rich might be due not necessarily to tax avoidance but to the change in patterns of expenditure resulting from the lack of resident domestic servants.[33] Even when considerable economic incentives were being offered, they appeared now to be inadequate to overcome a very widespread unwillingness to accept this particular relationship between employer and employee.

The change was not entirely continuous. The authors of the Merseyside survey found that despite the sharp decline revealed in the census figures, 'the absence of any big alternative forms of employment for women on Merseyside had made the supply of domestics large in relation to the demand and their wages low, so that many families have been able to keep servants on Merseyside who would not do so in other Northern towns', and observed that although there was a falling-off in the number of girls entering this form of employment, there was a tendency after 1921 for women to re-enter it, perhaps as a consequence of the Pensions Act of 1925.[34] But despite such local or short-term variations, resident domestic service became progressively more of an anachronism. The *New Survey* of London concluded at the beginning of the '30's that it was certain that

> 'the marked tendency to a decline among the number of domestic servants in London has not slackened during the post-war period'.[35]

When the census figures for 1931 and 1951 are compared the percentage of women employed in domestic service is shown to have more than halved, and when a comparison is made of the proportion of consumers' expenditure on goods and services which went on domestic service in 1938 and 1956, the drop is from 2·7% to ·7%.[36] This decline cannot be taken to mean that by the 1950's there

---

[31] Ministry of Labour, *Report for the Year 1935* (Cmd. 5145, 1936), p. 16.

[32] *Report on the Post-War Organization of Private Domestic Service* (Cmd. 6650, 1945).

[33] Barna, *Journal of the Royal Statistical Society* CXXII (1959), I, p. 38, commenting on Lydall, 'The Long-Term Trend in the Size Distribution of Income', *ibid.*

[34] *Op. cit.*, II, pp. 300–302.

[35] *Op. cit.*, II, p. 429.

[36] Carr-Saunders *et al.*, *op. cit.*, p. 158.

had come to be an equality of status between the former employers of resident domestic servants and the sort of people who would a generation before have been their employees. But it is certainly a symptom of the modification of the status hierarchy and the spread of relative deprivation of status: the working class might not feel themselves to be the equals of the rich, but they did not feel themselves to be their servants either.

The more significant change of reference groups, however, is in the relation between manual workers and the stratum of non-manual workers closest to them. There is little reason to look for a mutual relation of equality between white-collar workers and the unskilled working class: there is too much evidence of status barriers between unskilled labourers and artisans, as between clerks and directors, for such a degree of equality to be plausible. But despite the evidence that the manual/non-manual line retained its importance in the hierarchy of status, it is still pertinent to ask if there was not a major change between 1918 and 1962. I have already quoted Orwell's remark to the effect that after the First War there began to emerge a status-stratum which could not be immediately placed in terms of clothes, manners and accent. In the same passage, written in 1941, Orwell went on to talk of an 'intermediate stratum at which the older class distinctions are beginning to break down', and to argue that despite all the unjust distinctions of privilege which remained, 'in tastes, habits, manners and outlook the working class and the middle class are drawing together'.[37] Similarly, Carr-Saunders and Caradog Jones, writing in 1937, asked: 'Is it not a misreading of the social structure of this country to dwell on class divisions when, in respect of dress, speech and use of leisure, all members of the community are obviously coming to resemble one another?'[38]

Such impressionistic arguments could be supported in several ways. First of all, a definite assimilation in styles of life was taking place: the more prosperous worker, earning about £4 a week and with not more than two dependent children, could enjoy many kinds of pastime which would have been out of the question for him in 1913. He might not have a car, or a telephone, or eat out at restaurants, or play golf or tennis; but he was probably spending money on holidays, the cinema, a wireless licence, perhaps a pet, and perhaps even a visit by his wife to the hairdresser. Second, there were the slow but significant educational changes which I have described. Third, there was the explicitly egalitarian propaganda

[37] *England Your England*, pp. 222–3.
[38] Carr-Saunders and Jones, *A Survey of the Social Structure of England and Wales* (2nd edn.; Oxford, 1937), p. 67.

which became increasingly diffused during the later 1930's, the product at once of heightened social conscience and the persuasiveness of Marxist doctrine: for example, the Left Book Club, founded by Victor Gollancz in 1936, acquired 50,000 subscribers within a year—to the surprise, apparently, of its founders.[39] Fourth, there was the increasing support for Labour both among middle-class voters and among middle-class recruits to the Parliamentary Party.[40] Finally, there was the changing pattern of recruitment into the lower-grade white-collar occupations. Whatever the misgivings of many working-class parents about the desirability of a clerical career for their children, an increasing number of working-class families were coming to have a white-collar worker among them. Very often this was a daughter rather than a son; Klingender, using the data of the *New London Survey* for 1929–30, found that the proportion of young clerks living in working-class families was 30%, with the proportion for the two sexes more or less equal.[41] There was also a fairly high rate of intermarriage—one of the best indices of equality of status between different economic classes. Lockwood's conclusion, based on an analysis of data collected for the London School of Economics in 1947, was that 'clerks as a group are definitely not endogamous' and that the spouses of clerks were 'quite likely' to come from working-class families or have working-class jobs.[42] Moreover, despite the attractions of greater security, many of the children of clerks might enter a skilled manual occupation, and throughout the inter-war period as many as a fifth of secondary school boys might do so, or in some districts more.[43] The authors of the Merseyside survey, having remarked that a considerable number of sons of clerks were found to have become skilled or semi-skilled manual workers, concluded this to be 'an indication of the change that has been taking place in recent years in the division between social classes on Merseyside as elsewhere'.[44]

There is thus little question that some modification at once of the status-structure and the pattern of reference groups deriving from it was taking place by the time that Orwell wrote. Moreover, any feelings of nascent egalitarianism which had been aroused by the social changes of the inter-war period were much heightened by the

[39] C. L. Mowat, *Britain Between the Wars* (London, 1955), p. 526.

[40] Except in the electoral setbacks of 1924 and 1931, middle-class strength in the Parliamentary Party increased steadily between the wars: M. Harrison, *Trade Unions and the Labour Party since 1945* (London, 1960), p. 264.

[41] *Op. cit.*, p. 65.

[42] *The Blackcoated Worker*, p. 116.

[43] See the figures reproduced by Olive Banks, *Parity and Prestige in English Secondary Education* (London, 1955), pp. 169 ff.

[44] *Op. cit.*, II, p. 336.

Second World War. No statistical or experimental evidence is needed to support the assertion that status-differences tend to lose some of their importance in an air-raid shelter. The hope that a greater measure of status equality would result from the war found a partial expression in legislation, not only in the Education Act of 1944 but in the New Towns Act passed by the Labour Government in 1946. There was a good deal of feeling among urban planners that a deliberate attempt was called for to remedy the residential segregation of the one-class neighbourhoods which were themselves, in part, the outcome of inter-war housing legislation. Silkin, the Labour Minister of Town and Country Planning, was quite explicit about the intention of ensuring that different strata of society should mix,[45] and the final report of the New Towns Committee under the chairmanship of Lord Reith[46] was frank in recognizing that its terms of reference required a confrontation of the problem of class (i.e., status) distinction. There was a widespread belief, as after the First World War, that the hierarchy of status had been fundamentally altered. Status barriers had been visibly diminished by the combined impact of war and economic change.

But if inequality of status had diminished it had by no means disappeared; and if relative deprivation of status was increasing, it was still not proportionate to inequality. It was not true that the strata had fused, only that there was less 'objective' inequality of status and a consequent spread of relative deprivation of status on both sides of the manual/non-manual line. The hope that war-time egalitarianism had made possible the harmonious establishment of 'blended' communities turned out to be naive. Indeed, the planners (or, for that matter, Orwell) might have seen from the similar ventures of the inter-war period sufficient evidence to convince them that, however much they might be struck by visible changes in the hierarchy of status, these were not enough to bring about a full equality between manual and non-manual workers or even between manual workers themselves. Ruth Durant, who conducted a survey of the Watling housing estate shortly before the war, concluded that 'it seems to have been inevitable that the growth of the Estate and the constant turn-over of its population would make apparent differentiations of income, of social status and of outlook'.[47] 'There is a tendency', wrote the author of a letter to the *Watling Resident* in February, 1931, 'on the part of certain groups of people to regard

---

[45] L. Silkin, 'Housing Layout in Theory and Practice', *Architects' Journal* (July, 1948), p. 45, quoted by Orlans, *op. cit.*, p. 82.
[46] New Town Committee, *Final Report* (Cmd. 6876, 1946).
[47] Ruth Durant, *Watling: a Social Survey* (London, 1939), p. 47.

themselves as the "aristocracy" of the Estate, because they happened to wear clean collars, pressed trousers and speak with a tolerable air of assurance.'[48] F. J. Osborn was forced to conclude of the 'garden cities' of Letchworth and Welwyn that although there was less segregation than in other towns, 'whatever the town planner may desire, people have a marked tendency to segregate themselves by class or income'.[49] The clerical workers, of whom there were never very many on housing estates, were found to be the likeliest to move away from them.[50] The Government Social Survey conducted an investigation in 1946–7 among the housewives of Willesden, from which many future New Town residents were expected to be drawn, and found that 'It was clear that most Willesden people preferred to have as neighbours others of their own social status.'[51] In the mood of 1945, town-planners were optimistic enough to forget that much friction, as well as sympathy, had been engendered by evacuation, and that in 1934 a wall had actually been built at Cutteslowe, in Oxford, to separate a private from a council estate.[52] But they were soon forced by experience to the conclusion that whatever the disadvantages of homogeneous neighbourhoods, the principal result of an attempt at mixing would be to create tensions or resentments directly deriving from the conscious distinctions of the traditional status hierarchy. By 1961 it could be said that 'Most new towns now accept, though sometimes with reluctance, that an attempt to promote social mixing by building "managerial" houses scattered throughout the town and its neighbourhoods, without the alternative of such houses built in groups, has failed,'[53] and in rural communities the change was almost negligible. A study of the village of Gosforth in the 1950's found that although· in England in general the decline of the large country houses might have contributed to a greater belief in equality of status, in Gosforth attitudes were virtually unchanged; even the generalization ventured earlier about domestic service does not apply here.[54]

[48] Quoted *ibid.*, p. 46, n. 1.

[49] F. J. Osborn, *Green-Belt Cities* (London, 1946), p. 93.

[50] R. Jevons and J. Madge, *Housing Estates* (Bristol, 1946), p. 65.

[51] B. Hutchinson, *Willesden and the New Towns* (Social Survey: London, 1947), p. 2, quoted by Orlans, *op. cit.*, p. 91.

[52] The episode is described by Peter Collison, *The Cutteslowe Walls* (London, 1963), who refers also to a similar episode in Cardiff in 1955 (p. 17).

[53] J. H. Nicholson, *New Communities in Britain* (London, 1961), p. 132, quoted Peter Willmott, *The Evolution of a Community* (London, 1963), p. 114.

[54] W. M. Williams, *Gosforth: the Sociology of an English Village* (London, 1956), pp. 118–9.

Inequalities of status, therefore, were still a fact, but relative deprivation of status among manual workers and their families had so far
been extended and heightened as to be less disproportionate to
them; as greater equality was attained, the awareness of such inequalities as remained was heightened. These statements, however,
are still incomplete without some reference to the fraternalist/egoist
distinction. In part, the spreading sense of relative deprivation of
status was fraternalistic. Working-class people increasingly felt that
they did not owe deference to their traditional superiors in status,
and compared the prestige accorded to the working class as such
with the prestige accorded to the middle. Manual work was more
and more widely regarded as entitled to an equal recognition and
prestige with clerical. But relative deprivation of status was spreading in the home as well as at the place of work; and here the tendency was towards aspirations of status which entailed a detachment
from the status-stratum of 'ordinary' manual workers. It is difficult
to say how far a divorce from the traditional working-class subcul-
ture either resulted from or led to the taking by manual workers and
their wives of middle-class reference groups, whether comparative or
normative. As I have already emphasized, there is no warrant for
assuming that because working-class families approach the style of
life of some middle-class families they are therefore trying to be
accepted by them as equals. But to the extent that changes in style
of life were bound up with changing aspirations of status, these
aspirations were likely to be of the egoistic rather than the fraternalistic kind.

The changes in style of life are fairly well documented. There is
a substantial literature on the 'traditional' working-class community,
and its distinctive features are well known—the sense of communal
loyalty, the lack of intimate friendships outside the family, the in-
frequency of entertaining non-relatives at home, the low membership
of voluntary organizations that are not specifically working-class,
and so on. In a socially homogeneous working-class community,
such as a mining village, this pattern is unlikely to be disrupted even
by considerable advances in earnings.[55] Where earnings are at the
same time low, it is virtually certain that, as found by Madeline Kerr
in 'Ship Street', Liverpool, the rate of change will be very slow
indeed.[56] But in a more heterogeneous community, a sufficient degree
of prosperity is likely not only to enable manual workers to acquire
some of the consumer goods which were formerly the prerogative
of the middle class, but also to modify their attitudes and way of life

[55] For example, the Yorkshire community described by Dennis *et al.*, *op.
cit.*
[56] M. Kerr, *The People of Ship Street* (London, 1958), p. 189.

in such a way as to make them resemble more closely the members of non-manual status-groups.

In the first place, it has been noticed that the sense of community, and the frequent public, although not intimate, social contacts which characterize it, have given way to a greater reserve and home-centredness and an increasing awareness of distinctions of status within the working class itself. This had already been noticed by Jevons and Madge in Bristol,[57] and was confirmed by studies of other localities after the war. Mogey, studying two contrasting districts in post-war Oxford, noticed how in Barton, the Council estate on the outskirts of the town, working-class families were both less communally friendly and more open to influences from outside the traditional working-class pattern than families in the long-established central area of St. Ebbe's.[58] In addition, the extended kinship network of the traditional working class, whose importance was noted by Young and Willmott in a study of Bethnal Green, was shown liable to be replaced by a set of social relations approximating more closely to the middle-class pattern. In particular, the segregated conjugal roles of the traditional working-class husband and wife were found to be giving way to a greater measure of joint activity both in leisure pastimes and in tasks connected with the management of the household.[59] By the 1950's, some, at least, of the stepping-stones to status-equality with the non-manual stratum were being crossed by the more prosperous working-class families; and this was by individual status mobility, not by the achievement of a collective equality between the traditional middle-class and traditional working-class subcultures.

Collective equality between the two strata was in any case inhibited by the feelings of non-manual workers and their families. As well as the attitudes of the kind found by Willmott and Young in Woodford, the tendency of non-manual workers to move away from working-class districts provided unmistakable evidence of this, and was found no less true by Willmott in Dagenham in 1958–9 than by Jevons and Madge in Bristol a generation before. The upwardly mobile, including not only those in professional and white-collar jobs but also some manual workers prompted by higher incomes and aspirations of status, were found consistently likely to move away from a traditional working-class district, and those staying behind were found happy enough to see them go.[60] Often, to

[57] *Op. cit.*, pp. 69–70.

[58] J. M. Mogey, *Family and Neighbourhood* (Oxford, 1956), pp. 152–6.

[59] Young and Willmott, *Family and Kinship in East London* (London, 1957), pp. 15, 107–8; Zweig, *The Worker in an Affluent Society* (London, 1961), pp. 30–32.

[60] Willmott, *op. cit.*, Chapter V.

judge by the interviews reported by Willmott, the emigrants might explicitly express their desire to 'better themselves' socially, and in Woodford, Willmott and Young found an equally explicit disdain on the part of middle-class residents for working-class residents who, in their view, lowered the district's 'tone'.[61] Despite all talk of manual workers 'becoming middle-class', there was no evidence that the changes brought about by the prosperity of the 1950's were yet sufficient to overcome the traditional barriers of status.

Further evidence of the attitudes of the non-manual stratum is provided by a different source, which, although not reliable as a substitute for survey evidence, nevertheless gives an insight into the fears of the lower grades of non-manual workers that their relative position in the status hierarchy was being threatened by the advance of the manual workers. The journals of white-collar unions, such as *Bank Officer* or the journal of the Civil Service Clerical Association, *Red Tape*, contain during the post-war period numerous references to the declining status of the white-collar worker vis-à-vis the manual. This is not a topic which makes its appearance only in the post-war period. But in the period between the wars clerical workers, despite the hardships which they regarded as comparable to the hardships of manual workers, had no reason to regard their position in the hierarchy of status as seriously threatened. Although Socialist militants both within and outside their ranks regarded them as forced into awareness of their equivalence in class-situation to the manual workers, any concession of a common identity of interest was still a concession made from a higher rung on the ladder of status. After the war, by contrast, they began to see themselves not as forced down among the manual workers but rather as overtaken by them, with the result that condescensions of status might even come to be the other way round. Equality of status might not yet have been reached; indeed, the fears about status on the part of clerical workers might be one of the factors helping to inhibit it. But a sufficient change of attitude had taken place for Lockwood to conclude in 1958 that 'The official standard of emulation for the blackcoated worker is now the skilled workman in the export industry, not the rentier in his seaside resort.'[62] Whether or not they were now persuaded by Marxist arguments that they were as much proletarians as the machinist or even the navvy, clerical workers began to feel that many of the community no longer regarded them

[61] *Op. cit.*, p. 119.
[62] *The Blackcoated Worker*, p. 105. See e.g. the remarks of the President of the C.S.C.A. on the 'fallacy' that the fashionable emphasis on productivity means only more coal or more cars. 'Those who render a service, such as civil servants, can also make a contribution by their greater efficiency.' (*Red Tape* [July, 1957], p. 636).

as entitled to pretensions of status.[63] This change might serve to heighten rather than lower their resistance to status-assimilation with manual workers; but this was precisely because the superiority of non-manual work could no longer be unquestionably assumed.

It is possible to see further evidence of this change in the pages of *Punch*. Looking through its cartoons during the inter-war period, it is hard sometimes not to be uncomfortably suspicious that to the middle-class readers of *Punch* there was something intrinsically funny about working-class people. It sometimes looks as if the only point of a drawing or caption lies in the inherent quaintness, to the middle-class reader, of manual workers and their families. One example may serve: in a cartoon of 1932, two working-class children are depicted in a fashionable area of London with the girl saying to her small brother 'Come now, Alf—this ain't the Mile End Road. If yer can't walk proper try and look as if yer knowed *how*.'[64] It is difficult to imagine such a caption being published twenty years later. In the post-war period, jokes about manual workers were more likely to be jokes about their affluence. Whether accorded with nervousness or approval, a recognition of the heightened status of the manual worker becomes discernible in the newspapers, films and magazines of the 1940's and '50's. Once again, the change was not such as by itself to 'deproletarianize' the working class; but by comparison with the 1920's it reflected an unmistakable modification of the assumptions which underlay the traditional differences of status, and it helped to heighten among those on both sides of the line a sense of relative deprivation of the social recognition due to them.

The limited advance towards equality and the consequent spread of relative deprivation continued to be visible during the 1940's and '50's in the sphere of education. In higher education, a university degree began to be ᷄ feasible aspiration for an important minority of working-class children very much as a grammar-school place had begun to be in the inter-war period.[65] In secondary education, the Act of 1944 ousted from the grammar schools some of the less able of the lower-middle-class children and spread the available places and the aspiration for them increasingly widely among the manual stratum. Even after 1944, the children of unskilled manual workers continued to be under-represented in the grammar schools, but the

[63] See e.g. *Bank Officer* (June, 1952), p. 1; (February, 1953), p. 9; (April, 1953), p. 8; or *Red Tape* (May, 1957), p. 573.

[64] *Punch*, January 30th, 1932.

[65] See e.g. the T.U.C. *Report*, 1948, p. 165 for the beginnings of this mounting trend.

skilled working class attained a much more adequate representation.[66] At the sixth form level, the Crowther Report found in 1959 that nearly half the sixth form boys and girls in direct grant and maintained grammar schools were the children of manual workers.[67] The changed attitudes of parents can also be documented. Mrs. Floud and her collaborators found that in South West Hertfordshire and Middlesbrough in 1952 and 1953 'surprisingly strong' minorities of working-class parents wanted their children to attend grammar schools—some 50% in Middlesbrough and 46% in Hertfordshire—and that in the matter of the leaving age there had been 'something like a post-war revolution in the views of working-class parents'.[68] Despite the number of working-class families still uninterested in a grammar school education for their children, the evidence points an unmistakable contrast with the inter-war period when the combined effects of inequalities of class and of status led to the frequent refusals of free places for working-class children, and a leaving age of 18 was the aspiration of only a small fraction of them.

But the educational aspirations which were spreading among the manual stratum were inevitably of an egoistic rather than a fraternalistic kind. Working-class parents who wanted their children to have a grammar school and perhaps university education wanted their children to rise out of the manual status-stratum, not with it. This might not have been so if the three types of secondary education established by the 1944 Act had been accorded the 'parity of esteem' officially intended for them, or if the comprehensive schools, which were seen by some members of the Labour Party as the solution to inequality of status, had become universally established. But few local authorities were building comprehensive schools in the 1950's —the Crowther Report estimated that even by 1965 comprehensive or bilateral schools would contain only 11% of secondary school pupils in England;[69] and parity of esteem within the tripartite system had certainly not been achieved. Ellen Wilkinson, the Labour Government's Minister of Education, told the Party Conference in 1946 that 'If the teachers get the same pay, if the holidays are the same and if, as far as possible, the buildings are as good in each case,

[66] See H. T. Himmelweit, 'Social Status and Secondary Education Since the 1944 Act: Some Data for London', in D. V. Glass, ed., *Social Mobility in Britain* (London, 1954), p. 158.

[67] *Op. cit.*, p. 230.

[68] Floud *et al.*, *op. cit.*, p. 79.

[69] *Op. cit.*, p. 27 (Table 8). For the opposition to multipartite education during the inter-war period, see e.g. the T.U.C. memorandum submitted to the Spens Committee (*Report*, 1934, p. 145). At the time of writing, however, there is a strong trend in favour of comprehensive education among local education authorities of both political parties.

then you get in practice the parity for which the teachers are quite rightly asking.'[70] But other speakers were less optimistic. One of them, although arguing against a resolution (which was carried) urging the Minister to 'reshape educational policy in accordance with socialist principles', still found her 'very complacent' in assuming that parents would not now mind to which of the three types of schools their children went.[71] This judgment was amply vindicated by subsequent experience; 'secondary modern education,' said a speaker at the 1953 T.U.C., 'has not yet taken shape or size . . . All of you who have got children round about the age of 11 will know whether there is equal esteem or not'.[72] Educational equality, in other words, was spreading in a very different sense from that implied by the egalitarian phraseology of its pioneers. It was not equality of esteem which was furthered by the 1944 Act, but equality of opportunity. More and more working-class children were aspiring to, and achieving, a middle-class education. But this is very different from a progressive equality of esteem between the education leading to manual and non-manual jobs.

It is true to say, therefore, that between 1918 and 1962 inequality of status was diminishing and relative deprivation of status growing more widespread. But careful qualification is necessary. A narrowing of inequalities could be observed (although not measured); but it did not go so far as to vindicate the assertions sometimes made in the 1950's that manual workers had now 'become middle-class'. Aspirations both spread and heightened among the families of manual workers; but they often did so—particularly in the matter of education—in a way which was more suggestive of an egoistic than a fraternalistic sense of relative deprivation. Parental aspirations are, of course, feelings of relative deprivation only in a vicarious sense; and the children themselves may well be motivated by relative deprivation of class as much as of status. But it is a fair assumption that parental attitudes to education are, like attitudes to intermarriage, a meaningful guide to attitudes towards inequality of status. There is no numerical evidence for the changes in working-class reference groups, and it is impossible to say to what extent non-manual status-groups furnished comparative or normative reference groups for working-class people. But it is plausible, at least, to

[70] *Report*, p. 189.

[71] *Ibid.*, p. 194.

[72] *Report*, p. 315; cf. the memorandum submitted to the King George Jubilee Trust in 1954 (*Report*, p. 185). For the strains imposed by status mobility within the educational system, see Brian Jackson and Dennis Marsden, *Education and the Working Class* (London, 1962), a study of 88 children in a Northern City; and cf. Ministry of Education, *Early Leaving* (1954), Ch. VI.

suggest that this occurred increasingly often in both senses. More working-class people had occasion to compare themselves to middle-class people and at the same time to take their standards from them. If a generalization can be attempted at all—and there is enough evidence for the attempt to be at least worth making—it suggests a very different relationship between inequality and relative deprivation of status from that which was found between inequality and relative deprivation of class.

VI

INEQUALITIES OF POWER AND THE DECLINE OF MILITANCY

I HAVE said that I would deal less fully with the relation between inequality and relative deprivation of power. But although the evidence of the sample survey is, except for its treatment of party preference, restricted to inequalities of class and status, the changes in attitudes about the distribution of power between the two strata are a necessary part of the background to it. At the beginning of this century, the situation of the manual worker was visibly inferior in power as well as class and status. Indeed, a relative deprivation of power was the principal motive behind the formation of the Labour Party, for its founders saw the working class to be not yet securing an adequate parliamentary representation for its interests by comparison with the representation enjoyed by its superiors. Although manhood suffrage was by then effectively established, and the right of combination had been secured by the trade unions, the Labour movement could scarcely feel that it was accorded its fair share of power within either the political or the industrial system. Half a century later, however, it was possible for many people to believe that this and more than this had been conceded to it. The distribution of power and, more important, beliefs about the distribution of power, had so far changed as to account for some considerable part of the decline in proletarian radicalism and the heightening of middle-class feelings of relative deprivation. The relation between relative deprivation and inequality was different in this dimension of inequality from either of the other two; and this helps in turn to explain why working-class militancy was not, by the 1960's, more vehement. We must therefore ask first, whether there has in fact been a broad realignment of power between the manual and the non-manual strata, and second, how far the relative deprivation felt by the two strata has been proportionate to it. The answer, in brief, is that the relative deprivation felt by the manual stratum has declined as its power has appeared to increase; but this increase has been often exaggerated both by its supposed beneficiaries and by its pretended victims.

In the early years of the century, the principal issue in the hierarchy of power had been the legal position of the trade unions. The two Acts of 1906 and 1913 resulted from the two legal judgements which turned out to be most significant for the future of the British Labour movement—the Taff Vale judgement of 1901 and the Osborne judgement of 1909. By the first of these, a union became liable to be sued for damages arising out of the actions of its members or officers during a strike; by the second, the unions were debarred from political action, and in particular from contributing from their funds to a political party. Both decisions were taken to reflect an opposition to, and even a fear of, trade unions on the part of the employing class,[1] but their most significant effect was to help those who wished to foster in the Labour movement an organized campaign for the parliamentary representation of the Labour interest. Some of the more hesitant but influential sections of trade union opinion were only persuaded by the Taff Vale decision to support the Labour Representation Committee in its efforts to send members to Westminster, and only in 1909 did the 'Lib.-Lab.' miners' M.P.s join what had by then been christened the Labour Party. Thus the effect of the opposition to trade unions by employers and the law at the turn of the century had been as much to make the Labour movement aware of its need and capability for political representation as to weaken, for a short time, a part of its strength. At the same time, the industrial unrest was mounting which led to the great strike period of the pre-war years. By the time of the sudden outbreak of the War, the relative deprivation of power felt by the trade union movement was intense, widespread and increasingly threatening.

The War, however, did not only put into abeyance the industrial grievances of the unions. It also brought them into a formal relation of consultation with the Government—a relation resulting from the need for a much more centralized control of both materials and men than had been needed or even thought of before the War. By the end of the War, the unions were not only more respectable but

---

[1] It has been shown, however, that the Taff Vale judgement, which at the same time reflected changes in legal opinion on the matter of corporate liability, should be seen as the end rather than the beginning of a trend going back to 1889. See J. Saville, 'Trade Unions and Free Labour; the Background to the Taff Vale Decision', in A. Briggs and J. Saville, eds., *Essays in Labour History* (London, 1960), pp. 317 ff.

more influential than they had been when the Syndicalist movement had been most alarming and widespread. But unionism was still as different from what it became by 1939 as it was from what it had been in 1914. The Labour Party representation in Parliament was increased, but it was not such as to encourage great optimism among those who hoped soon to see the working class gain control of the Government through constitutional means. The unions had agreed to co-operate as they did with the Government only on the explicit understanding that when the war was over they would resume their demands for whatever they might feel to be their due. 'Direct Action'—that is, a strike for a purely political purpose—was a much more serious threat in the immediate post-war period than the 'Bolshevism' mistakenly attributed to MacDonald by his detractors. The unions were perhaps a little less politically outcast than they had been, but they were not very much less frustrated of the power to which they felt their position entitled them.

The history of the inter-war period has, therefore, come to be seen as the history of how the trade unions started by trying to coerce the Establishment and ended up by joining it. The success not of revolutionism but of respectability assuaged the relative deprivation of power which might have threatened the social order in the autumn of 1914. The story can be symbolized in the career of Ernest Bevin, who in the summer of 1914, as an organiser in the National Transport Workers' Federation, was giving 'three ringing cheers for the Social Revolution' in the Dockers' Hall at Swansea, and in the summer of 1940 became Minister of Labour under Churchill. Between these two dates had occurred the Depression and the General Strike, two minority Labour Governments both regarded by the Labour movement as failures, and a more or less unceasing dispute between the different factions of the Labour movement itself. But in retrospect, the electoral setbacks, the outbreaks of industrial unrest and the threats to constitutional gradualism all came to seem less significant than the movement's steady progress to apparent power within the fabric of established government.

There are a number of might-have-beens which make it permissible to wonder why Labour did not embark in the immediate years after 1918 on a direct, deliberate and explicitly political challenge to the Government's authority. The Government was not in a position to resist all challenge: it gave in to the railwaymen in October of 1919, and under pressure from the railwaymen to the miners in October of 1920. The threat of 'Direct Action' may have helped to restrain the Government from intervention against Soviet Russia in the summer of 1920. 'Black Friday'—the 15th of April, 1921, when the railwaymen and transport workers withdrew from the strike called in support of the miners—could, but for an odd mistake on the part of the Miners' secretary, have turned instead into a General Strike five years ahead of time. If Frank Hodges had not, for no reason ever effectively disentangled, admitted to a House of Commons meeting the possibility that the miners would consider district agreements, there would have been no question of the miners being betrayed (as they felt it to be) by their allies. Even in the General Strike itself, if the Labour movement had been better organized, had prepared itself more fully in advance, and had entrusted the General Council of the T.U.C. with more effective powers, it is sometimes suggested that it need not have failed as it did. But the actual outcome of these events makes it more plausible to doubt whether the Labour movement could ever have coerced the Government into doing what it was determined not to do. Baldwin gave way in 1925 when he agreed to a coal subsidy and the maintenance of wages for nine months. But 'Red Friday', as it was called, was not the defeat it was represented to be; it was, as the shrewder members of the Labour movement were aware, simply Baldwin's decision not to fight until a time of his choosing if he could help it—which he could.[2] In any case, the might-have-beens are irrelevant to the events which in fact determined the relation between inequality and grievance. What happened was that Labour's aspiration to power was channelled away from the attempt to impose its wishes through 'Direct Action'. The trade unions came to the standing they now enjoy by immaculately constitutional means, the 'Councils of Action' and the General Strike notwithstanding; and their aspiration for power was assuaged, not further heightened, by this gradual and cautious success.

1925 is generally taken to mark the high point of militancy in the Labour movement. At the annual congress of the T.U.C., a motion was carried which explicitly called on the Congress to organize for the revolutionary overthrow of capitalism.[3] Michael Tomsky, who had been invited as a fraternal delegate from Soviet Russia to the Congress of 1924, once again addressed the delegates, and subsequently told a *Daily Herald* reporter that the Congress's decision showed the British trade unions to have 'taken their stand on the ground of the class struggle, not of class co-operation'.[4] Alonzo Swales, who was the President of the Congress, and had been

[2] As was admitted quite explicitly by Churchill in a speech of December 1925: see W. H. Crook, *The General Strike* (Chapel Hill, 1931), p. 296; and cf. Baldwin's own remark quoted by G. M. Young, *Stanley Baldwin* (London, 1952), p. 99 that 'we were not ready'.

[3] *Report*, p. 437.

[4] *Daily Herald*, Sept. 15, 1925.

talking in June about a 'rising of the people', asked the Congress to strengthen the powers of the General Council so that it could more effectively pursue a militant policy.[5] The militant trend found expression not only at the Congress. A. J. Cook, who had succeeded Hodges as secretary of the Miners' Federation, had already been making what *The Times* captioned 'another threat': if Baldwin had not given way, said Cook on September 12th, 'Take it from me, there would otherwise have been a revolution'.[6] Extravagant pronouncements were likewise made by the more left-wing members of the Parliamentary Party. 'A. J. Cook on behalf of the T.U. Left', wrote Beatrice Webb in her diary for September 16th, 'and Maxton and Wheatley on account of the Clyde, talk about immediate revolution—whilst George Lansbury thunders threats of the immediate dissolution of "capitalist civilization".'[7] Wheatley even said things which were, perhaps, to be interpreted as meaning that the workers ought to arm.[8] Throughout the late summer and autumn, the speeches of both Labour leaders and Government spokesmen reflected an awareness of the possibility that when the moratorium of 'Red Friday' had expired, a direct and dangerous trial of strength would ensue. 'If', said Baldwin, defending the granting of the subsidy in the House of Commons, 'we were again confronted with a challenge of the nature I have described, let me say that no minority in a free country has ever yet coerced the whole community . . . I am convinced that, if the time should come when the community had to protect itself, with the full strength of the Government behind it, the community will do so.'[9]

The story of the General Strike has often been told. All that needs to be repeated is first, that it failed unconditionally, and second, that it failed in an atmosphere of moderation which has helped to make proverbial the British predilection for restraint and compromise. The strike did not pass off entirely without violence,[10] but there was by any standards remarkably little. Everyone knows about the football match arranged between strikers and police. There is a good deal of evidence, indeed, to show that most of the General Council and the Labour movement as a whole were not merely opposed to any suggestion of violence but would have preferred to avoid the out-

[5] *Report*, p. 68.
[6] *Times*, Sept. 14, 1925.
[7] *Op. cit.*, pp. 70–71.
[8] See Bevin's criticisms in the *Daily Herald* of Aug. 24 and Sept. 17.
[9] 187 H. C. Deb., c. 1592.
[10] For left-wing charges of 'licensed brutality on the part of volunteer special constables', see e.g. R. Milliband, *Parliamentary Socialism* (London, 1961), p. 136.

break of the strike altogether. The workers generally—and even the Communist Party[11]—seem to have been much more caught by surprise than the Government. It was the tougher-minded members of the Government, not the General Council, who wanted a pretext for a trial of strength. The determined quest for negotiation and the lack of organized preparation are enough to show that the militancy of the Scarborough conference was of words more than intentions. Even the Scarborough Congress, when it came to the point, had been unwilling to vote for amalgamation, or to empower the General Council to call for a levy and order a stoppage.

The General Strike might, at first sight, be regarded as the fruition of a syndicalist belief in the power of organized labour. Perhaps the unions half believed that Labour could really force decisions on a recalcitrant government which would, in the end, give way not only to the demands of social justice but to the pressure of countervailing force. As the last and biggest expression of 'Direct Action'—however much the General Council disavowed its political purpose—the strike could be seen as the climax of a trend which dated back before the War: set back by 'Black Friday', delayed for a breathing-space by 'Red Friday', the working class finally put 'Direct Action' into practice in 1926. But it is more realistic to see 'Direct Action' as already rendered harmless by Lloyd George. It is, at best, very questionable if it could even then have coerced the Government into more than such limited industrial concessions as were needed to buy time. The General Strike was only a sort of apologetic postscript to the explosive doctrines of Daniel De Leon or Tom Mann. Far from putting into practice the precepts of revolutionary syndicalism, the unions were being described by their opponents as political revolutionists when they had merely been driven to collective strike action to further what they saw as justified grievances of class. They had not the least intention of trying to overthrow the authority of the government. They were not trying to reverse, and scarcely to disturb, the established hierarchy of power in favour of the manual stratum. On the contrary, they felt only that they might now have sufficient power to compel the Government to mitigate the economic hardships which were being forced on the miners, with the Government's acquiescence, by greedy and incompetent owners. In 1920, perhaps, they could have been described as bidding for power, but not in 1926. 1926 was not an exception to the decline of militancy, but a symptom of it.

In any event, if there had been unionists who hoped by industrial action to set right the unjust distribution of power, the failure of the General Strike helped to channel their ambitions towards

[11] See the remark of J. T. Murphy quoted by Crook, *op. cit.*, p. 368, n. 3.

parliamentary methods. If there had been much less threat to constitutional government in 1925 than there had appeared to be, there was not even the appearance of it after 1926. The combination of the Depression and the 'betrayal' by MacDonald in 1931 did, as we have already seen, lead to talk about the futility of gradualism. But this was more vehement among the intellectuals than the unions, and found little response in the working class at large. The unions remained resolutely respectable. After 1935, and the expected electoral recovery which Labour made, a parliamentary majority seemed sufficiently close for there to be little inducement to take as a normative reference group those revolutionists who in other places had seemed to show that only violence could bring the working class to power.

In the aftermath of the General Strike, the introduction of the Trade Disputes Bill and the acrimony with which it was debated helped to preserve the illusion that a struggle for power was at stake. But the fiercer sanctions embodied in the Act were never invoked at all. It is odd in retrospect to see debated in the House of Commons such an issue as whether the leaders of strikes declared illegal should be entitled to jury trial, or a labour spokesman talking of 'the most contemptible government of modern times . . . using its power for the establishment of slavery'.[12] The more significant feature of the bill was the reversal, long desired by the more militant Conservatives, of the 'contracting-out' provision of the Act of 1913. After 1913, unionists unwilling to contribute to their union's political fund were required to contract out, rather than those willing to contribute having to contract in. This was a real issue if only because of the financial difference to the Labour Party. Although the statistics published by the Registrar of Friendly Societies are not adequate to yield an accurate figure, it has been calculated that the repeal in 1946 of the 1927 Act was worth some two million contributions to the Labour Party per year.[13] Whatever the rights and wrongs of principle, this is some evidence, at least, that the Conservatives were not wholly foolish in opposing the repeal of the 1927 Act as vehemently as they did. But even so, the issue was more important for its symbolic value. It would be hard to show what tangible power the unions lost by contracting-in or regained by contracting-out. Labour could scarcely be said to have needed contracting-out to win in 1945, and its restoration did not prevent

[12] 206 H. C. Deb., c. 1118 (17th May, 1927). There is a particular irony in this choice of quotation, since the speaker is Oswald Mosley.

[13] Harrison, *op. cit.*, p. 36. (In 1959, the political levy varied from 1/- or less in 25 affiliated unions to over 4/6 in 4.).

their losing in 1951.[14] The Conservatives pledged themselves to reverse the situation once again, but in fact did not do anything of the kind. The one severe curtailment of the unions' power which there has been since 1918 was the emergency provisions passed during the Second World War, and in this, given the restrictions necessarily imposed on the community at large, the unions had no occasion to feel relatively deprived. The threat of prosecution against strikers which was embodied in an Order of 1940 was last used in February of 1951, under a Labour Government. Under the pressure of the 'grave misgivings' of the T.U.C.[15] the threat was withdrawn. Except in wartime, there has been in effect no restriction on the freedom to strike; and only this would have provoked the Labour movement to a militant feeling of relative deprivation of power.

Even in the 1920's, the right of industrial action was never seriously threatened. The Emergency Powers Act of 1920 had, it is true, been designed to protect the Government against the coercion implicit in alliances between the separate unions in different industries. But it still contained no suggestion of directed labour; and thereafter, the authority of the unions became more and more explicitly recognized. In a decision generally regarded as symptomatic, the court in *Reynolds v. Shipping Federation* (1924) refused to regard a rigid closed-shop agreement as an actionable conspiracy. Still more clearly symptomatic of the change were the Mond-Turner talks of 1928. These were a series of conversations, instigated principally by Sir Alfred Mond of I.C.I. and Lord Weir, between a group of leading industrialists and representatives of the T.U.C. under Ben Turner, then President of the National Union of Textile Workers. The talks did not come to very much. But unlike Lloyd George's abortive Industrial Conference of 1919, they did exemplify a modification of the relations between organized labour and its employers. They were evidence of a genuine recognition of the entitlement of the unions to consultation about the organization and control of the industries supported by the work of the unions' members.

The talks provoked angry recriminations within the Labour movement. But the anger of the Left neither found much response within the movement itself nor aroused much counter-antagonism outside it. The attitudes of Left and Right within the unions can be summarized by two quotations taken from the debate on the talks

---

[14] On the overstatement by Conservatives of the political levy as a factor in Labour support, see e.g. the comments of D. E. Butler, *The British General Election of 1951* (London, 1952), p. 23.

[15] *Report*, 1951, p. 233.

at the Trades Union Congress of 1928. The official view was succinctly stated in a speech by Citrine: 'We cannot await the advent of the breakdown of capitalism before we start marching towards control.'[16] But this, of course, was just what was most strongly disputed by the Left: this principle, said Cook, 'is going to bind us with shackles to capitalism, which is the thing we want to break'.[17] In the event, it could scarcely be said that the talks did either the one thing or the other. They neither secured for the unions a greater measure of control nor bound them any more tightly to capitalism than they were bound in any case. In the crises that followed 1929, neither side had any interest in discussion of this kind, nor did they any longer share the feelings which had made them possible. But what came to be recognized as significant about the talks was the fact that they could occur at all. They did not give the T.U.C. more power, but they gave its authority more recognition; and this can serve as well, or sometimes better, to mitigate feelings of relative deprivation of power.

If they did have a tangible result, it was that of helping the General Council to restore the authority within the Labour movement itself which it had been in danger of losing after the failure of the General Strike. But in the same way, what is significant about this is that it was a re-establishment of authority effected, first, by successful resistance to the Leftward inclinations that had seemed to be dominant in 1925, and second, by a visible demonstration that through the authority of the General Council it was possible for the union movement to meet and to talk to representatives of the employers as more or less equal partners within the established social fabric. In addition to the recognition accorded to it by the employers the T.U.C. continued under Citrine's leadership steadily to expand its role towards the Government. In 1931–2, there was only one Governmental Committee on which the General Council was represented; by 1938–9, there were twelve, and by 1948–9 sixty.[18] By the time that Bevin was called into the Coalition cabinet, the trade unions had ceased to be a challenge to the authority of the Government. On the contrary, they appeared to have become a part of it.

Thus the situation of the unions at the end of the Second World War differed from their situation at the end of the First both because a Labour Government was in power and because the unions were now immutably respectable: 'when we look up at the platform

[16] *Report*, p. 413.
[17] *Ibid.*, p. 437.
[18] V. L. Allen, *Trade Unions and the Government* (London, 1960), pp. 32–3, 34

from the Press table,' said Miss Margaret Stewart at the end of the 1947 Congress, 'we really feel we are in the presence of the boss class.'[19] If, after 1945, there was a section of the community which felt relatively deprived of power, it was the non-manual stratum more than the manual. It might be true that the success of the unions had appeased their relative deprivation of power without in fact upsetting the traditional hierarchy. But even if the traditional hierarchy had not been fundamentally upset, many members of the middle class were ready to be convinced that it had.

Some middle-class grievances against the Labour Government were specific enough. The doctors, for example, who felt that their freedom would be curtailed by the provisions of the National Health Service Bill, had a clearly defined resentment against the Party that was bringing this about. Similarly, the issue of governmental controls inevitably antagonized the entrepreneurial class, for the situation after the Second World War was almost exactly the opposite of what it had been after the First. As Tawney remarked of the entrepreneurs of 1918, 'Control was odious to them, not merely because it contracted the scope for remunerative business, but as the expression of an antithetic creed, which challenged their power, as well as their profits.'[20] The entrepreneurs of 1945 may likewise have felt that control was odious and that their power was challenged by it; but they now had little effective resistance against it, and their sense of resentment was proportionately more intense.

But apart from the threats to 'liberty' identified with Socialism by its opponents,[21] there was a strong, if less specific, feeling in the middle class that the unions, through the Government, had too much the upper hand. There was, as we have seen, a considerable resentment at the reduction both of economic differentials and of some traditional differences in status. But in addition there was the feeling that the unions had too powerful an influence, that the Government was unwilling to bring pressure to bear on them, and that the Government was explicitly aiming to curtail the power of the business and professional community. The *Economist* during the period of the Labour Government voiced a series of protests against 'the streak of vindictiveness towards the non-Socialist classes which runs through so many of the Labour Government's actions'.[22]

[19] *Report*, p. 561.
[20] R. H. Tawney, 'The Abolition of Economic Controls, 1918–1921', *Economic History Review* XIII (1943), p. 14.
[21] Most notoriously in Churchill's broadcast of June 4th, 1945 which inaugurated the election campaign and in which he went so far as to say that 'no Socialist system can be established without a political police' (*Times*, June 5, 1945).
[22] *Economist*, April 13, 1946.

Reasonably or not, there was among the non-manual stratum a strong feeling of relative deprivation not only of class and status, but of power. The middle class, said the *Economist* in 1948, should have 'more than its numerical weight in British politics—instead of less, as at present'.[23]

This feeling was not new. Masterman, writing in 1909, remarked that 'No one fears the Middle Classes, the Suburbans; and perhaps for that reason, no one respects them'[24] and he went on to give a vivid description of the 'suburbans' ' fear of the proletarians whom they saw as a threatening mob of potential revolutionaries who might at any time rise up and trample their neat suburban gardens underfoot. Masterman paints a similar picture of the England of 1922;[25] and although reliable evidence is hard to come by, the General Strike certainly brought out a number of manifestations of the sort of hostility which he describes.[26] In the coal crisis in 1921, when the Government called for volunteers for a special 'Defence Force', 75,000 people came forward in the ten days before recruiting was stopped.[27] The short-lived 'Middle Classes Union' advertised itself as having been formed 'to protect the great, hitherto unorganized Middle Classes against the insatiable demands of Labour, the Power of Capital, the indifference of Governments'.[28] Nor was there any difficulty in recruiting special constables either before or during the General Strike. If it is true that recruitment to the Fascists during the '30's was chiefly from the middle class and particularly the blackcoated workers,[29] then this provides further

[23] *Economist*, Feb. 14, 1948.

[24] *The Condition of England*, p. 68.

[25] *England after War*, pp. 54–5.

[26] See e.g. the letter to the *Bank Officer*, April 1934, quoted by Lockwood, *The Blackcoated Worker*, p. 180, n. 3: 'Am I forever to witness bank clerk Fascists helping to break the General Strike, or bank clerk Special Constables waiting to wipe up a few hunger marchers?'; and cf. the interviews with special constables published in the *News Chronicle*, November 2nd, 1932, quoted by Klingender, *op. cit.*, p. 82. Railway clerks, however, solidly refused to blackleg in the General Strike (Crook, *op. cit.*, p. 395), although in the strike of 1919 *The Times* claimed that 'but for the loyalty of the clerical staffs it would have been impossible to overcome the difficulties of resuming a train service' (*The Times*, Oct. 3, 1919)—a comment which would seem to contradict the claim of the *Railway Service Journal* (December, 1919), p. 262, accepted by Lockwood, p. 159, that the members of the Railway Clerks' Association refused to blackleg despite offers of 'loyalty pay'.

[27] Mowat, *op. cit.*, p. 121.

[28] A. Gleason, *What the Workers Want* (New York, 1920), p. 17.

[29] This is asserted e.g. by Mowat, *op. cit.*, p. 473; but see Lockwood's remark in *The Blackcoated Worker*, p. 195, n. 1, that Mowat 'gives no evidence on this score, and I have been unable to find a single piece of evidence which would indicate the relative importance of clerks and others, such as

evidence for a conscious and militant desire to curb the power of the working class. But all these were manifestations of a fear of violence more than of a sense of relative deprivation of established predominance. After 1945, not even the most extreme Conservative opponents of the Labour government could seriously suppose that there was a possibility of violent class conflict.[30] What they resented was not the threat of proletarian revolutionism, but the deliberate reversal, by peaceful means, of the preeminent position of the middle class.

The unions, therefore, from being the subjects of relative deprivation of power had become the objects of it. Up to the Second War and through the immediate post-war period public sympathy tended on the whole to be on the side of the unions. Except, perhaps, for the General Strike, all but those with a direct interest in restricting wages to a minimum came increasingly to see the working class as subjected to misfortunes for which it could not be held responsible and victimized by governmental inaction which amounted to a direct denial of social justice. The trend reached its climax in 1944, when the Beveridge Report was selling in thousands and the wartime experience of the population had led to the demand for legislation which would prevent the 'needless scandal' of the inter-war years from occurring again. But over the subsequent decade, opinion shifted. The spectacle of increasing working-class prosperity, the adverse publicity attaching to strikes, and the feeling that individual workers might sometimes be the victims rather than the beneficiaries of their union organization all contributed something to the change. By 1959, George Woodcock, then the Assistant General Secretary of the T.U.C., was forced to observe in a broadcast talk that 'the trade unions have lost the general sympathy that the public usually reserve for the underdog; and the reason for that is that the trade unions do not now give to the public the impression that they are the underdogs any

---

members of the *lumpenproletariat* and retired army personnel'. There are certainly many claims made to the effect that the British Fascists 'swelled in numbers by an increasing flow of middle-class recruits' (Frederic Mullally, *Fascism Inside England* (London, 1946), p. 25), but there does not seem to be any accurate evidence on the social composition of the movement.

[30] Extravagant statements were, of course, made: see for example Viscountess Davidson's assertion in the Commons debate on the National Health Bill that 'no majority should exercise its mandate beyond the endurance of the public or bitterness will result, and may lead to civil war' (422 H.C. Deb., c. 91). But remarks like this one are obviously not to be taken seriously—much less seriously, to make the obvious comparison, than those of A. J. Cook in 1925, however unreal his predictions may have been.

longer'.[31] A Gallup Poll of the same year reinforced this view: by the end of the 1950's, the unions still enjoyed the strong support and approbation of their members, but their support among the public at large had markedly dwindled.[32]

At the same time, there was another noticeable change in the attitude of the courts. The change after the First War was that the courts began to protect the unions against the employers; the change after the Second was that the courts began to protect individual members against their unions. This further change, which Woodcock himself described as 'unmistakeable', is generally taken to be most clearly exemplified in the case of *Bonsor v. Musicians' Union* (1956), where it was established that a member of a union operating a closed shop could successfully claim damages for wrongful dismissal. Already in 1950, it had been established by *Birch v. National Union of Railwaymen* that a union member who had contracted out of the political levy could not thereby be excluded from any union office involving partial discretion over the management of the political fund. By *Spring v. National Amalgamated Stevedores and Dockers* (1956) it was established that unless an expulsion was permitted by rule, it could not be carried out simply on the instruction of the Disputes Committee of the T.U.C. In all these cases, the courts seem to have reflected a change in opinion whereby the unions were seen not so much as the rightful contenders for sectional power as the potentially unjust wielders of it.[33]

It is significant, moreover, that the expansion of unionism during the 1950's was more among non-manual than among manual workers, and higher among women than men. This was the outcome of various industrial changes whose analysis lies outside the scope of the present chapter; the slight fall in the overall percentage of employees organized which took place during the 1950's partly reflects a movement of workers to less unionized occupations and districts.[34] But the tendency to unionization in non-manual occupations is well attested. It has been attributed to a variety of causes, notably the

[31] George Woodcock, 'The Trade Unions and Public Opinion', *Listener* (July, 1959), p. 120. For a partisan, but also symptomatic, view from the other side, see the Inns of Court Conservative and Unionist Society, *A Giant's Strength* (London, 1958).

[32] See W. McCarthy, 'The Future of the Unions', *Fabian Tract No. 339* (1962), p. 1. For a finding that 'more than half' of a sample of urban workers agreed that 'unions have too much power', see R. T. McKenzie and A. Silver in the *Observer*, September 6, 1964.

[33] At the time of writing, further evidence for this has been furnished by the House of Lords decision in *Rookes v. Barnard*.

[34] PEP, 'Trade Union Membership', *Planning* XXVIII (1962), pp. 154–8.

role of the Government as an employer, the narrowing of differentials, the bureaucratization of large-scale industry and the increasing number of non-manual workers of working-class origin. But whatever the varied influences behind this change, a relative deprivation of power became increasingly felt by kinds of workers who had previously felt no need or desire for collective organization on the proletarian pattern. It may be that difficulties of organization and recruitment have inhibited the growth of white-collar unionism as much as either a middle-class disdain for 'unions' as such or a feeling of sufficient superiority to the manual unions for similar collective action to be unnecessary. But although this may continue to be true in particular occupations,[35] the increase in white-collar unionism is sufficiently noticeable to suggest a new sense of fraternalistic relative deprivation of power among non-manual workers. Not only did the public after the Second World War come to be resentful of the power enjoyed by the unions; the lower grades of non-manual workers came to realize some of the advantages of imitating them.

It would, however, be hard to demonstrate that the legislation enacted by the Labour Government between 1945 and 1950 in fact promoted the working class to such a primacy of power as some of Labour's opponents affected to suppose. It was true that this had been one of its motives: Attlee has remarked, for instance, that his retention of controls was directed to such an end,[36] and a similar motive underlay much of the enthusiasm for nationalization. But as it soon turned out, nationalization was not going to reverse the inequality of power inherent in the relationship between employers and employees. Nor was it going to give the workers that control of industry which had been one of the traditional ideals of democratic socialism. 'Joint consultation', of which much was hoped by some of the partisans of industrial democracy, turned out on the whole to be successful only where it was unnecessary—where, that is, relations between unions and management were already good; and even where joint consultation is successful, it remains true that 'the status and power of the ordinary worker is virtually unaffected'.[37]

[35] See e.g. the remark of an American observer that 'the history of USDAW since 1947 is evidence that a high degree or organization of industrial workers does not lead easily or inevitably to the rapid spread of unionism among retailing employees': R. E. L. Knight, 'Unionism among Retail Clerks in Post-War Britain', *Industrial and Labour Relations Review* XIV (1961), p. 527; and the argument that work-situation is not adequate to explain the failure of the Bank Officers' Guild advanced in V.L. Allen and Sheila Williams, 'The Growth of Trade Unionism in Banking, 1914–1927', *Manchester School* XXVIII (1960), pp. 314 ff.

[36] C. R. Attlee, *As It Happened* (London, 1954), p. 163.

[37] H. A. Clegg, *A New Approach to Industrial Democracy* (Oxford, 1960), p. 90.

It certainly did not serve to draw workers into control. The authors of *Coal is Our Life* concluded that 'joint consultation, meant to be a method of drawing workers into the management of the collieries, is a failure, if only because the vast majority of the men are not drawn into it, so that their relation to the direction of work has not changed one iota'.[38] It is much the same with 'co-partnership' as with joint consultation. The Ministry of Labour reported in 1956 that if co-partnership is defined in terms of profit-sharing then 'at the end of 1954, there were in the United Kingdom 421 schemes being operated on a prearranged basis by 408 undertakings. The aggregate number of employees shown as entitled to participate in these 421 schemes was 389,433.'[39] As a proportion of the total labour force, this number is almost nugatory. Predetermined redundancy policies, which constitute one of the workers' principal safeguards against the inequality of power between employers and employees, remained hardly less common: the International Labour Organization calculated in 1959 that 'It is probable that predetermined redundancy policies exist in somewhat less than one-third of the industrial firms in the United Kingdom.'[40] None of these scattered observations need to be taken to mean that the overall position of the organized worker had not improved since 1918; but they serve as a reminder that this improvement, however great, still did not constitute any fundamental reversal in the hierarchy of power. Relative deprivation of power was less intensely and probably less widely felt; but the accession of the unions to an established position did not mark quite the degree of equalization of power between manual workers and their superiors which this decline in relative deprivation would warrant.

It is not the purpose of this chapter to try to measure the discrepancy between inequality and relative deprivation which remains in the dimension of power. But whatever middle-class critics of the unions might suppose, there is a good case for saying that the Labour government of 1945–51 did not leave the power-situation of the manual worker greatly different from what it had been in 1938 or even 1918. 'Workers' control' was no nearer to achievement; the legal position of the unions was in essentials the same; the bargaining position of organized manual workers was better as a result of prosperity more than of changes in the formal hierarchy of power; the fundamental inequality in the relation between employer and employee was unchanged, even if the employer might more

[38] Dennis *et al., op. cit.,* p. 77.
[39] Ministry of Labour *Gazette,* May 1956, p. 166.
[40] ILO, 'Dismissal Procedures—V: United Kingdom', *International Labour Review* LXXX (1959), p. 352, n. 2.

often be the Government itself. But to establish how far manual workers were more unequally placed than they resented or even supposed would be a far more complicated and specialized task in considering industrial relations than incomes or educational opportunities. A summary of the period up to 1962 can do no more than suggest that in the third dimension of social stratification, the relative deprivation felt by the manual stratum tended to decline as the Labour movement appeared to grow steadily more powerful.

If this conclusion is correct, it is not only interesting in showing that the relation between inequality and relative deprivation is different in each of the three dimensions of social inequality. It also helps to explain why the level of 'fraternalistic' feelings of relative deprivation of either status or class was no higher at the beginning of the 1960's than it was. The aspirations of the trade unions have always been for economic gains at least as much as for an increase in power for its own sake. But as they appeared to have established themselves not only within the structure of industrial relations but within society as a whole, it became more difficult for egalitarian resentment to be aroused against the bosses as the untrammelled agents of the exploitation of the working class. The unions might continue to press wage demands with at least as much insistence and determination as they had shown in the inter-war years. But their role was that of delegates in the established and broadly successful process of collective bargaining; not even their most militant members could plausibly regard them, as they might have done in 1925, as the vanguard of the working class in its struggle against the power of the bourgeoisie.

There is a parallel with inequalities of status. It might be true that more manual workers and their wives were now eager for a social position and style of life which had previously been the prerogative of middle-class families. But the seeming achievement of a greater equality of power was itself one of the influences which made working-class aspirations in general less a common resentment of the subordinate position of manual work as such and more an individual pursuit of middle-class prerogatives. This pursuit did not have to be motivated by a deliberate imitation of non-manual workers; but it was accompanied by an increasing detachment from the lateral loyalties of a proletariat still resentful of its powerlessness as well as its poverty or its lack of social esteem.

VII

THE IMPLICATIONS OF PARTY CHOICE

THERE is one final topic which is closely linked to the relation between inequality and relative deprivation but cannot be effectively broken down into its separate implications for relative deprivation of class, status and power. This topic is voting, and particularly the voting of manual workers and their wives. In a country with the political history and social structure of Great Britain, the vote is an obvious source of evidence for attitudes to social inequality. Where the left-wing party is explicitly working-class, Socialist and egalitarian, a Labour vote can be plausibly interpreted as implying the view that wealth ought to be more equally distributed, the status of the manual worker heightened, and the trade unions given a maximum of influence within the industrial system. The persistent rejection, therefore, of the Labour party by a substantial minority of working-class voters is a further aspect of the complex relation between inequality and attitudes towards it. It is true that many voters may be voting for reasons wholly unconnected with social inequalities in any of the three dimensions. They may attach greater importance to some specific issue such as foreign affairs, or they may vote out of personal reasons or habits with which egalitarianism has nothing to do, or they may even feel that the inequalities to which they are subject will be better remedied by the Conservative Party. But for a working-class person not to support the party dedicated to the working-class interest suggests, in the absence of special explanation, a discrepancy between his situation and his attitude to the inequalities in the social structure.

With the help of the survey, I shall suggest that reference groups —or, more specifically, self-rated 'class' seen as a normative reference group—can help to explain working-class Conservatism, and thereby shed some further light on how inequality is related to attitudes towards it. But any analysis of working-class voting requires some reference to the electoral background of the previous decades.

136

The election results from 1922 onwards might seem to tell a story of Labour's steady advance until 1945 and steady decline until 1964. But this view is very much too simple. Not only is the distribution of parliamentary seats a wholly misleading guide to changes of opinion within particular strata, but it is not even an adequate guide to changes of vote. Labour was stronger in 1931, weaker in 1945, and stronger between 1951 and 1959 than the results of the General Elections showed. Throughout the period between 1918 and 1962, there has been a body of Labour support in the manual stratum whose allegiance has been much more consistent than the changing parliamentary majorities would suggest. At the same time, the substantial minority of working-class Conservatives has remained almost as consistent in its loyalties, despite the impact of historical events, the varying policies of the parties and the demographic changes in its own composition. It is this which needs to be explained more than the short-term changes, however important their impact on election results, if the relation between inequality and relative deprivation in twentieth-century England is to be further explored.

In the aftermath of the General Election of 1918, it seemed to the Labour Party's leaders a hopeless task to win the working-class electorate to an awareness of its true political interests. Labour had increased its parliamentary representation from 42 seats to 59, but Parliament was still overwhelmingly dominated by members returned under the 'coupon' in support of Lloyd George's coalition. The Labour party was divided within itself; its three most notable members—MacDonald, Snowden and Henderson—had all lost their seats; and the Socialist wing of the party was discredited in the eyes of the electorate by its opposition to the War. The Representation of the People Act seemed to have enabled the Coalition to exploit the underlying conservatism of the working class more than to have encouraged the working class to vote into power the party formed to champion its cause. 'Conservatism', wrote MacDonald in 1920, 'no longer resists but welcomes a democratic franchise because experience has shown it that it can manipulate that franchise.'[1] In 1920, the prospect of Labour holding office seemed more or less chimerical; MacDonald was himself to describe it to the Labour Party Conference of 1924 as 'that apparently insane miracle'.[2] If the working-class Conservative vote was to be interpreted as an acquiescence in the existing order, then the existing order seemed firmly entrenched.

Yet the 'apparently insane miracle' did happen. Two years after

[1] J. R. MacDonald, *A Policy for the Labour Party* (London, 1920), p. 53.
[2] *Report*, p. 106.

137

MacDonald had lamented the ease with which Conservatism could manipulate the franchise, Lloyd George had fallen for ever from power, and Labour was established as the Opposition party; and within a further two years Labour was itself in power. By April, 1927 Beatrice Webb could write in her diary: 'Deficient in brains and money, it is a miracle that the Labour Party steadily grows in voting power. The impression left on the observer's mind is of a slow underground social upheaval, moving independently of leaders or organization—propelling a lower strata of society into a more dominant position.'[3] Labour's first tenure of office had, in the event, been short-lived, and its second was to be cut almost as short by the disasters of 1931. But looking back to 1918 from Labour's triumph in 1945, it was plausible for Labour's supporters to see their progress very much as Beatrice Webb had described it—a progress, that is, made in spite of the parliamentary weakness of the movement, the preference of many of its members for industrial action, and the folly or even treachery of its leaders. To compare the electoral success of Lloyd George with the failure of Churchill was to see the election of 1945 as the climax of the 'underground social upheaval' which had at last brought the under-privileged to an egalitarian awareness of their interests.

But the victory of 1945 was not nearly so climactic as the large parliamentary majority and the surprise with which it was greeted might suggest.[4] It might in one sense seem plausible to describe it as a working-class victory. But just as a Conservative government cannot come to power without the support of a sizeable minority of manual workers and their families, so a Labour government depends on the support of a sizeable minority of the middle class. In 1945, millions of middle-class voters supported Labour, but millions of working-class voters still did not.[5] The swing to Labour from the Conservatives averaged 12% over the country as a whole, and their average percentage of the poll per opposed constituency rose by 10%; but although these figures are high, there had been a ten-year interval since the previous General Election, and the swing reflected the penetration of Labour into regions traditionally hostile to it rather than a large-scale conversion of working-class voters. Labour

[3] *Diaries 1924–32* (ed. M. I. Cole; London, 1956), p. 138 (April 5th, 1927. 'strata' *sic*).

[4] For evidence of this surprise, see e.g. R. B. McCallum and A. Readman, *The British General Election of 1945* (London, 1947), p. 243; George VI to Gloucester, Sept. 13, 1945, quoted by J. W. Wheeler-Bennett, *George VI* (London, 1958), p. 649; Attlee, *op. cit.*, p. 148; P. J. Grigg, *Prejudice and Judgement* (London, 1948), p. 398.

[5] For an estimate based on Gallup Poll results, see John Bonham, *The Middle Class Vote* (London, 1954), p. 168.

did not win by establishing its hold gradually higher up the occupational scale from the unskilled to the skilled to the white-collar. It won by overcoming local habits of support for either the Conservative or Liberal parties among both manual and white-collar occupations.[6] Its share of the working-class vote was significantly larger in terms of swing; but in overall percentage terms, it was not so very different.

In the same way, the decline in Labour's electoral strength after 1945 was not the result of large-scale defections by working-class voters, whether because of austerity under a Labour government or prosperity under Conservative ones. Between 1945 and 1959, the great bulk of Labour support remained loyal. The heaviest losses sustained by Labour after 1945 were in the dormitory suburbs and particularly in the London area. This is not by itself a conclusive demonstration that the working-class vote remained faithful. But for the post-war period, survey evidence is available as well as the sometimes hazardous conclusions suggested by regional correlations. According to a calculation based on samples taken by the British Institute of Public Opinion, the largest change between 1945 and 1950 was a rise of 9% in middle-class support for the Conservatives —a rise which was partly at the expense of Labour and partly a reduction in the proportion not voting at all.[7] Although the Conservatives increased their parliamentary majority at all three of the elections of 1951, 1955 and 1959, the Labour vote remained more or less solid. After the election of 1955, David Butler rightly concluded, despite the Conservative victory, that 'if prosperity was rapidly driving the working class into middle-class habits of consumption, it was only very slowly driving them into middle-class attitudes to voting'.[8] The further Conservative victory of 1959 seemed to some observers to indicate that the traditional working-class Labour vote was at last being undermined: Butler and Rose, indeed, were now prepared to talk of traditional working-class attitudes as having been 'eroded by the steady growth of prosperity'.[9] But although it might be true that some attitudes had been changed and some resentments mollified by the growth of prosperity, there was still no warrant for concluding that events had brought about a fundamental alteration in the pattern of party support. There were, perhaps, some signs of restlessness among the electorate. As many as one in six of all voters changed their minds between 1955 and

[6] Cf. Bonham's conclusions for London and Birmingham, *ibid.*, p. 162.
[7] Nicholas, *op. cit.*, p. 296.
[8] Butler, *The British General Election of 1955* (London, 1955), p. 164.
[9] D. E. Butler and Richard Rose, *The British General Election of 1959* (London, 1960), p. 2.

1959, and the Gallup Poll found that 12% made up their minds how to vote during the course of the campaign.[10] In addition, there was a strong Liberal revival in the trough between the general elections of 1959 and 1964. But such signs of apparent fickleness should not be interpreted as signs of fundamental change. It would be truer to say that the small percentage of working-class defections from Labour to Conservative at a general election—bye-elections apart—were conditional defections. Despite the appearance of a lasting swing, and the crucial importance for the distribution of seats of even very small fluctuations, the underlying pattern of party support had hardly changed. Election results, however important to the nation's destiny, are no answer at all to the question why people vote as they do.

The newer methods of voting study inaugurated in 1944 by the publication of Lazarsfeld's *The People's Choice*[11] have accustomed us to see the principal reasons for party support not in campaign issues so much as in underlying social determinants which change little from one election to the next. Working-class Conservatism cannot be explained by the 'Zinoviev letter' scandal of 1924, or the rearmament issue in 1935, or the charismatic appeal of Churchill in 1945 or Macmillan's slogan 'never had it so good' in 1959. Such things can alter the outcome of elections, but they neither create nor destroy the strong and complex network of influences by which the votes of four-fifths of the electorate are determined long in advance of any particular campaign. Even in 1931, when Labour's parliamentary representation was shattered from 288 seats to 52, the drop in its average percentage of the vote per opposed candidate was only 5·7%. This is, to be sure, a large change for a two-year period; indeed, it is not to be wondered that a National Government headed by the former Labour Prime Minister and asking, in MacDonald's phrase, for a 'doctor's mandate' should have defeated Labour as heavily as it did. But it is a measure of the stability of the electorate and the loyalty of Labour's supporters that even a sequence of events as damaging to a political party as the events of 1931 should have resulted in less than a 6% drop in its average percentage of votes per constituency. Throughout the whole period from 1922 to the time when the sample survey to be described was conducted—and, indeed, thereafter—there has been a recurring two-thirds of the manual electorate who have supported the Labour party and a recurring one-third who have not.

The elections from 1922 to 1935 cover a period when sample survey evidence is still unavailable, and diagnosis is further compli-

[10] Butler and Rose, *ibid.*, pp. 196, 200.
[11] P. F. Lazarsfeld *et al.*, *The People's Choice* (New York, 1944).

cated by the presence of three national parties each securing a substantial percentage of the total vote. A number of unsubstantiated and conflicting things have been said about the elections of the period, not least by those most intimately involved in them. But more systematic statistical analysis has, so far as it goes, confirmed that even then the movements of opinion were much slower and less violent than the distribution of seats implied. The key to understanding the fluctuating fortunes of the parties is not the conversion of the manual stratum to Labour so much as the consistent decline of the Liberals. If 1931 is left aside, Labour's average percentage of the vote per opposed constituency hardly varied at all between 1922 and 1935. In 1924, it dropped by nearly 3%. But if we are trying to explain the allegiances of the working-class electorate in the decades before 1962, the change is negligible, and it was in any event largely due to the increased number of hopeless seats which the Labour Party chose to contest.[12] The election result of 1924, in which the defeat of the first Labour government was too hastily attributed to the 'Zinoviev letter', was due rather to the decline in support for the Liberals which characterized the entire decade. The solid majorities enjoyed by Baldwin in 1924 and 1935 were certainly based on some substantial measure of working-class support, but this does not mean that working-class Labour supporters were fickle in their allegiance; it means rather that Liberal support was declining among all sections of the electorate except in those few regions where local Liberalism was particularly strong.

It is true that a big change occurred between 1935 and 1945—a bigger change, indeed, than between 1929 and 1931 or between 1931 and 1935, and much bigger than was generally predicted. Yet Labour's victory still cannot be interpreted as a solid mandate for Socialism—however the different shades of opinion within the Labour Party may have understood the term. McCallum and Readman calculate that if, after allowance has been made for double-member constituencies and unopposed candidates, the total anti-Socialist vote (including the Liberals) is subtracted from the total pro-Socialist vote, the margin is only 65,880.[13] This is not, by any standards, an overwhelming victory. Given that the potential changers are always a very much smaller proportion of the electorate than used to be supposed, the change since 1935 may be remarkable. But if we are to explain the attitudes of the working-class

---

[12] Butler, *The Electoral System in Britain, 1918–51* (Oxford, 1953), p. 177; and cf. the conclusion of S. R. Graubard, *British Labour and the Russian Revolution, 1917–1924* (Cambridge, Mass., 1956), p. 284 that Labour had no hope whatever in 107 constituencies of which 71 were nonetheless contested.

[13] *Op. cit.,* p 252.

electorate, it hardly carries the matter any further. Who were the 30% of working-class voters who still did not vote Labour, and why? Of course, the result of the election was in a way the culmination of an 'underground social upheaval' such as Beatrice Webb had foreseen. It was a victory which could not have been achieved without a radical change of opinions among a proportion of the community which, however small in absolute numbers, was of crucial importance at the polls. But in the broader terms of the British social structure and the attitudes of those within it to their own unequal location, the minority of changeable voters are less important than the larger and more consistent minority of working-class voters who have steadily refused, ever since the emergence of a Socialist party avowedly dedicated to their interests, to see these interests as the official leaders of the Labour movement have seen them.

Up to a point, the answer seems obvious. Many voters, within the manual as well as the non-manual stratum, are wholly uninterested in issues of social reform even if ostensibly directed to their own benefit. When the country is prosperous and their own position is improving, will they not be likely to feel that a Conservative government will maintain this state of affairs more successfully than a Labour one? The Conservatives, moreover, have always based their appeal on better representing the national, as opposed to some sectional, interest, and there is evidence to show that their claim to be the best executants of a resolute and competent foreign policy finds a response at all levels of the electorate. But to state these well-worn propositions is still not to answer the question. We have seen that radicalism can be a product of prosperity as much as of hardship; and however many intelligible reasons there may be why working-class voters should not respond to the appeal of the Labour Party, who exactly are those who do not? Stated in this way, the question is impossible to answer accurately without the help of sample surveys. But there are several long-term influences known to have an effect on working-class Conservatism which account in part, at least, for the apparent discrepancy between inequality and grievance, and are required to supplement the correlations with social characteristics which the survey may disclose.

Some of these influences have long been familiar to political observers—for example, the strength of Conservatism in rural districts, or the correlation between religion and party. In addition, the evidence from particular constituencies and regions often reveals the extent to which working-class Conservatism is a response to local tradition. These conclusions cannot be too far generalized from one

district to another, and the evidence may reflect the pattern of support at different times when different short-term influences have
been at work. But as I have already emphasized, the effect of even
violent short-term influences is negligible by comparison with the
long-term social determinants, and the study of individual communities can help to account for the working-class Conservative
vote in a way which has implications outside of a single place and
time.

In many areas, such loyalties can be readily traced to historical
causes. In some parts of North-West England, manual workers
joined Conservative clubs in the late nineteenth century as a reaction against their Liberal employers in the cotton industry, and
the tradition has persisted. In Birmingham, the influence of the
Chamberlain family lasted well into the twentieth century; the
swing to Labour was higher in Birmingham in 1945 than anywhere
else in the country, which attests the extent to which that influence
had retarded a change which would otherwise have taken place
earlier and more gradually. Birch, studying Glossop in the early
1950's, found strong traces of a connection between religion and
politics which had been forged in the years between 1884 and
1918.[14] Margaret Stacey, studying Banbury, on the Southern fringe
of the Midlands, at about the same date, found that working-class
Conservatives tended to be workers in small, long-established local
industries where there was direct personal contact between employers and employees rather than in newer and larger industries
where most of the labour force was not native to the town.[15] These
are the kinds of entrenched loyalties which explain much more of
the working-class Conservative vote than superficial correlations
with either national prosperity or short-term political events. Whatever their specific origins, they can be summarized as local traditions
of Conservative support which cut across or override loyalty to the
working class as such, and outlast the day-to-day ups and downs of
the parties' fortunes.

But even when this is said, there remains much to be explained.
Why does the hold of such loyalties continue to be so strong when
their origins are largely outdated? Who are those voters who most
readily respond to them? And what of the working-class Conservative vote which cannot be explained by reference to local tradition?
Where there is such a tradition in a static and long-established community, the influence of the family will account for many habits
and attitudes. But perhaps these attitudes ought also to be seen as
the reflection of a deeper acquiescence in the traditional social

[14] A. H. Birch, *Small-Town Politics* (London, 1959), p. 111.
[15] Margaret Stacey, *Tradition and Change: a Study of Banbury* (London,
1960), p. 46.

structure which the vestiges of a local political tradition reinforce rather than engender. Is it not possible that the social correlates, however consistent, of working-class Conservatism are less important than the notorious 'deference' of the British electorate upon which Bagehot first remarked[16] and which explains much of the persistent discrepancy between relative deprivation and inequality which working-class conservatism implies?

That 'deference' is in some way peculiarly characteristic of the British nation has been pointed out by many writers since Bagehot and is not difficult to demonstrate from a variety of examples drawn from English social history and mores. The gradualism of the British Labour movement, the survival of hereditary institutions, the failure of extremist parties are all symptoms of a willingness on the part of a British public to accept its traditional institutions and leaders as self-evidently entitled to the positions which they hold in the social structure of the country. This willingness has without doubt served to mitigate the relative deprivation felt among the subordinate strata of British society, and particularly that 'fraternalistic' sense of relative deprivation which finds expression in left-wing working-class politics of a radical and militant kind. But although it is a pertinent observation to say, as Bagehot did, that the British are a deferent nation, this is to state the problem with which we are concerned rather than to resolve it. Working-class Conservatism is the expression, not the result, of acquiescence in the social system. Of course, not all working-class Conservatives need be personally 'deferent' in any sense of the term: as I have emphasized, people's reasons for supporting one party or another may have nothing to do with social equality at all. But in the absence of such an ulterior explanation, working-class conservatism expresses an acquiescence in the existing system of social inequalities and a rejection of fraternalistic relative deprivation on behalf of manual workers as such. To attribute this to 'deference' is not to explain it unless the question is also asked who these people are.

One suggestion is that those working-class Conservatives who think of themselves as 'working-class' are 'deferent' while those who think of themselves as 'middle-class' are 'aspiring',[17] but this is once again to confuse the issue. An attitude of 'deference', however defined, can just as well be found among those manual workers who think of themselves as 'middle-class' as those who think of themselves as 'working-class'. There is certainly a difference between

[16] For the revival of Bagehot's notion as applied to more recent British politics, see R. T. McKenzie, 'Bagehot and "The Rule of Mere Numbers" ', *Listener* (November, 1959).

[17] See S. M. Lipset, 'Must Tories Always Triumph?' *Socialist Commentary* (November, 1960).

those working-class Conservatives who describe themselves as 'middle-class' and those who describe themselves as 'working-class', but it is not a difference between those who are deferent and those who are not so much as between two different kinds of 'deference'. Both acquiesce, by implication, in the existing system of inequalities. The significant difference is that those who describe themselves as 'middle-class'—whatever of a number of different things they may mean by this—are likely to be the 'egoists' of the typology of relative deprivation: they accept the existing system, but either wish to rise, or feel that they have risen, within it. Those who describe themselves as 'working-class', on the other hand, are likely to be those who have no wish to rise out of their present membership reference group. In the typology of relative deprivation, this means that they are likely to belong with Type A—those who feel satisfied not only on behalf of their group but also within it. Both, therefore, are 'deferent' in the sense of accepting the existing system, or the sense given to 'traditional' by Margaret Stacey. 'The essence', says Miss Stacey, 'of the traditional attitude is an acceptance of the traditional class system. This means that a man accepts his position in it, although he may improve his lot by thrift and individual effort, and accepts also the right of those in higher classes to lead. The lead the middle classes give is towards conservatism'.[18] The further distinction which needs to be drawn is not between the more and less traditional or deferent so much as between those who in fact want to improve their own lot within the existing system (or feel that they have done so) and those who are content with a fixed position within what they recognize as a subordinate group.

The determinants of these two attitudes may be many and various; but a distinction in terms of normative reference groups and, by implication, relative deprivation, suggests a division into two broad kinds of working-class electors who do not feel relatively deprived as members of the subordinate stratum. Those workers and their wives who respond to the Conservative Party's appeal—who believe, that is, that it will make the country as a whole more prosperous and conduct the business of government more effectively—will either be those who are ambitious in the terms of the Conservative ideology of individual effort, or those who accept by habit or tradition not only the Conservative ideology but also their own fixed position within the hierarchy justified by it.

It might be argued that only the second kind of working-class Conservative should be labelled 'deferent', since 'deferent' carries overtones of 'submissive' and 'unambitious'. But there may be just

[18] *Op cit.*, p. 47.

145

as many working-class Labour as Conservative supporters who are unambitious. The essence of 'deference' is a positive acquiescence in the existing system of political inequalities, and this is common almost by definition to all working-class Conservatives except those who either do not think about these matters at all or else believe that the Conservative Party will in fact do more to reverse the relative position of the two strata than will the Labour Party. Acquiescence in the system is not, of course, peculiar to manual workers and their wives. If, indeed, it is made synonymous with 'deference' than there is at least as much 'deference' in the non-manual as in the manual stratum. But, as the analysis of the historical evidence has shown, the manual stratum is not yet the equal in class, status or power of the non-manual, and therefore the 'deference' of working-class people in particular remains the cardinal problem in the relation between relative deprivation and inequality.

Too much cannot be made of the distinction in terms of normative reference groups. A manual worker may, for example, both identify with the non-manual stratum and support the Conservative Party because his father was in a non-manual occupation and a Conservative: it may have nothing directly to do with his wish to 'improve his lot by thrift and individual effort'. Similarly, he may be fully aware of proletarian membership and yet be both a Conservative supporter and a man of strong personal ambition. But his choice of reference group can provide a clue to the interpretation of party preference as an attitude to inequality, and it is along these lines, as I shall try to show, that the 'class' to which manual workers and their wives assign themselves may be able to supplement the sort of evidence presented so far.

There is, however, one specialised sense which has been given to the notion of 'deference' and which has a bearing both on the nature of working-class relative deprivation and on the changes in the nature of working-class Conservatism during the present century. In interviewing a sample of manual workers in six English cities in 1958, McKenzie and Silver classified them as 'deferent' or 'secular' according to whether they expressed a preference to be led by someone born into the élite or by a self-made man.[19] They found that the 'deferent' voters, so defined, were more frequent among the older working-class Conservatives and 'secular' voters among the younger. This finding suggests two conclusions. First, just as local

[19] R. T. McKenzie and A. Silver, 'Conservatism, Industrialism and the Working Class Tory in England' (paper read at the Fifth World Congress of the International Sociological Association; Washington D.C., 1962).

or familial traditions of Conservative support may have progressively weakened between the 1920's and the 1950's, so may the attitudes of respect for the traditional élite which can well have been bound up with them. Second, this difference between the older and younger respondents confirms the argument that relative deprivation of status is now more frequent among manual workers. This may, presumably, have the effect of converting some of them from Conservative to Labour support. But McKenzie and Silver demonstrate that a rejection of the traditional status structure is still perfectly compatible with belief in the efficacy of the Conservative Party; indeed, they suggest that this has been a necessary condition for the Conservatives' continued success.

It is obvious that this sense of 'deference' means something over and above a simple acquiescence in the system of inequalities. This is more than a difference of degree, for to assume that 'wealth and rank', in Bagehot's own words, are symbolic of the 'higher qualities' which entitle some men to rule others[20] is 'deferent' in a further sense than that of 'accepting the right of those in higher classes to lead'. Whether many people are Conservative supporters because they are deferent in this more extreme sense would be hard to establish—this would probably be a necessary condition only in some special cases of the relationship between personality and party choice. But if it is true that over the decades before 1962 working-class Conservatism was becoming less and less bound up with subservience to inherited rank and more and more with 'secular' feelings of self-interest, then this is a further reason for expecting to find that many working-class Conservatives do not so much acquiesce in a subordinate position as feel indifferent to the Labour Party's ideology of 'class', as opposed to 'individual', mobility.[21]

Without the evidence of previous surveys, however, there is no way of being certain how far the psychological composition of the working-class Conservative electorate changed in the decades after 1922. It is possible to say with confidence only that despite either psychological or any other changes, about a third of manual workers and their wives have throughout rejected the explicitly egalitarian appeal of the Labour Party. In order further to test whether the social characteristics and normative reference groups of the working-class Conservatives of 1922 may help to elucidate the relation between relative deprivation and inequality, it will be necessary to examine the evidence of the survey.

[20] McKenzie, 'Bagehot and "The Rule of Mere Numbers" ', p. 871.
[21] Cf. Stacey, *op. cit.*, p. 47.

PART THREE
THE 1962 SURVEY

VIII

SELF-ASSIGNED 'CLASS'

WE are now in a position to turn to the 1962 survey with several specific questions in mind. Without the survey, generalizations about the relative deprivation felt by different groups could only be drawn from very indirect inference. With it, generalization is still a matter of inference, but it can be rather more solidly based. The survey made it possible to ask a cross-section of the adult population of England and Wales questions bearing directly on the topics discussed so far, and to relate the answers both to the social characteristics of the respondents and to their answers to other questions about their attitudes. This still will not yield a precisely delineated picture of the magnitude, frequency or intensity of relative deprivation in the manual and non-manual strata; nor can it show exactly how far people's feelings about class and status correspond with their own location. But it does provide some useful and otherwise unobtainable evidence for the relation between inequality and relative deprivation, and if my interpretation of it is correct, it furnishes some confirmation for the tentative generalizations which have been advanced in the preceding chapters.

The sample, which is described in detail in Appendix 1, was a stratified random sample taken from electoral registers. 2,000 names were drawn at random from two wards within each of 50 constituencies in England and Wales, and 1,415 respondents interviewed. The questionnaire had been previously tested on a quota sample of 100 respondents in four different areas. Respondents in the main survey were classified as manual or non-manual on the basis of occupation; wives were classified according to their husband's occupation, and retired or unemployed people on the basis of their last occupation. The criteria of classification were based on the standard procedure used by Research Services Ltd., who carried out the interviewing, coding and preliminary cross-tabulations. The classification is more fully discussed in Appendix 3. Applied to the 1,415 respondents, it yielded a ratio of 919 manual to 496 non-manual.

151

The interview schedule contained three kinds of question: factual questions, such as those about age or income; pre-coded attitude questions, where the interviewer circles one of a range of alternative answers formulated in advance by the designer of the questionnaire; and open-ended questions, where the interviewer notes down a verbatim answer and these answers are subsequently sorted into categories drawn up after the questionnaire has been administered. The open-ended procedure, which is discussed in greater detail in Appendix 4, was used particularly for the questions from which it was hoped to draw some direct evidence about reference groups. This attempt poses considerable difficulties. It is obviously useless simply to ask the question 'what are your comparative, normative and membership reference groups when you consider inequalities of class, status and power respectively?' People do not think naturally in these terms, even if their replies may help to confirm the validity of doing so, and conclusions about reference groups can only be elicited by the interpretation of questions which are much more colloquially worded. In the present study, no attempt was made to see how far respondents' pictures of the social structure could be categorized in terms of class, status and power models. The questions used were rather designed to elicit a broad idea of how respondents saw their position in the social structure, and then to relate this general self-assessment, whatever model or mixture of models might underlie it, to some of the questions asked. People were not asked to describe the social structure in detail in whatever terms might seem to them most appropriate; instead, they were asked about their picture of society in terms of an explicit distinction between 'middle' and 'working' class.

The practice of asking the respondents in sample surveys to what 'class' they would assign themselves is often criticized on the grounds that the vagueness of the term, and its lack of precise meaning to many of the people who use it, make the resulting distribution of answers dangerously misleading.[1] It can certainly be shown that where different forms of question, and particularly different forms of multiple-choice question, are used, very different patterns of response may be obtained. These difficulties, however, can largely be avoided if respondents are first of all asked an open-ended question as to which 'class' they think they belong to, and if, after those who are unwilling to assign themselves to any class have been further prompted, all the respondents are asked some question which will throw light on what they mean by the terms being used.

[1] See e.g. the criticisms of the Centers study made by Milton M. Gordon, *Social Class in American Sociology* (Durham, N.C., 1958), pp. 193–202, and cf. the remarks of Goldthorpe and Lockwood, *op. cit.*, pp. 143–145.

The following four questions were therefore asked: first, 'What social class would you say you belonged to?'; second (for those who did not give an initial answer), 'If you had to say middle or working class, which would you say?'; third, 'What sort of people do you mean when you talk about the middle class?'; and fourth, 'What sort of people do you mean when you talk about the working class?'. In answer to the purely open-ended question, a small proportion of respondents were unwilling to assign themselves to any class; but the number who remained unwilling even when prompted was only 1% of the total—including, ironically enough, the only titled lady in the sample.

The questions about meaning produced, as was to be expected,[2] a wide diversity of replies. Many were in terms of occupation. Some of these were very loosely phrased, while others drew a precise—but variously placed—line between 'middle-class' and 'working-class' occupations. Some rested on a personal criterion of approval or disapproval, which might or might not be linked to occupation. Some were so broadly expressed in terms of 'average' or 'ordinary' people that no clear picture of the social structure could be inferred from them. A few people gave answers which were puzzling or even incomprehensible, and a few said that they did not know what they meant by 'middle' or 'working' class.

This diversity makes it clear that there is no warrant for inferring from a manual worker's description of himself as 'middle-class' that he either is or wishes to be *'embourgeoisé'*. In the same way, a person in a non-manual occupation who describes himself as 'working-class' may mean something very different from the sort of self-conscious proletarianism which the phrase might suggest. But although people may mean different things by their self-assigned 'class', it would be as much of a mistake to suppose that no conclusions about their attitudes to inequality can be drawn from their self-rating as to base on it ambitious and unsubstantiated generalizations about the fusion of the manual and non-manual strata.

A good many of the replies given suggest an uncertainty or ambiguity of attitude. But none suggest a total distortion or reversal of the social hierarchy as normally viewed. Some people defined the middle class to include skilled manual workers, or the working class to include clerks or professional men or even 'everyone who works'. But nobody assigned unskilled labourers to the middle class, or described the middle class as skilled manual workers while describing the working class as business and the professions. It is fair, therefore, to expect that manual workers or their wives who

[2] Cf. the findings reported in Martin, *op. cit.* Comparison with the present study, however, is impossible, since not only the form of questions but also the coding categories are different.

describe themselves as 'middle-class' will be distinguishing themselves in some sense, however minimal or confused, from the 'ordinary' or 'lower' or sometimes 'rough' working class. Similarly, a person in a non-manual job who calls himself 'working-class' is in some sense likening himself to at least a section of the manual stratum. Both these types of respondent may in practice assimilate almost everyone to the class to which they assign themselves.[3] But although any generalization based on self-assigned class must be carefully qualified in the light of the meaning given to 'working' or 'middle' class, it seems legitimate to regard a manual worker who describes himself as 'middle-class' or a non-manual worker who describes himself as 'working-class' as departing to some degree, at least, from the orthodox and widely-held distinction between the non-manual stratum, or 'middle class', and the manual stratum, or 'working class'. Provided that the necessary qualifications about meaning are made, self-assigned 'class' can still help to throw light on the relation between relative deprivation and inequality.

It was found that nearly all the replies to the questions 'What sort of people do you mean when you talk about the ———— class?' could be assigned to one or other of seven categories. Of these seven, five corresponded to an equivalent category in each of the two 'classes'. In the tables which follow, the seven categories are designated by abbreviated and somewhat elliptical phrases, but some more detailed comment, together with quotations from the verbatim replies, may help to show just what range of meanings has been subsumed under them. For the meanings given to 'middle-class', the following coding categories were used: first, non-manual workers; second, 'between top and bottom'; third, actual manual jobs mentioned; fourth, 'rich'; fifth, personal approval; sixth, personal disapproval; seventh, middle-class style of life. For the 'working class' the categories used were: first, manual workers; second 'ordinary' people; third, actual non-manual jobs mentioned; fourth, 'poor'; fifth, personal approval; sixth, personal disapproval; seventh, 'everybody'. Those replies which could not be assigned to any of the seven categories were classified either as 'other' or as 'don't know'.

The first category—manual or non-manual workers—was defined to cover not merely specific occupations such as 'labourers' or 'clerks', or general categories of jobs such as 'professions' or 'a man who works at the bench,' but any form of phrase which seemed clearly suggestive of manual or non-manual work. Thus the category of manual workers includes a number of replies such as 'wage-earners', where it seems plausible to suppose that it is not non-

[3]Cf. Martin, *op. cit.*, p. 64.

manual workers paid by the week who are meant. The most tenuous of the replies coded under this heading were either such loose phrases as 'anyone under the professions' (which might, after all, mean clerical as well as manual workers in the eyes of the informant) or such literal descriptions of the 'working class' as 'people that are forced to work for a living'. Where phrases like this seemed in context to suggest the 'working class' in the orthodox sense, the replies were generally included by the coders with 'manual workers'. Sometimes, however, references to 'working' shaded over into the second category of definitions of the 'working class'—the category which I have labelled 'ordinary'. This was so defined as to include not only the explicit use of words like 'ordinary' or 'average person' or 'the man in the street' but also references to 'working' which did not seem to carry any particular implication of either manual or non-manual work. 'Anyone that works for a living', said a bar steward at Kodaks, 'a doctor is very much a working man.' 'People who work for a living', said the wife of an economic adviser to a bank who assigned herself to the working class. 'Everybody who works', said a compositor in his fifties, 'no particular class—most people have to work these days.' More detailed questioning might have revealed that these replies were symptomatic of very different models of the social structure, but for the purposes of the survey any general definition of the working class as 'people who work' was included in the category of 'ordinary'.

The definition of the 'middle class' as 'between top and bottom' was also more widely drawn than the literal expression might suggest. It includes both specific references to differences of income— 'people who get an average wage, £16 to £20 per week'—and to differences of status—'decent hardworking people just a bit above the labourer'. Any answer, however, which clearly implied a stratum both below and above the 'middle' was assigned to this category. 'People who aren't poor and aren't well off', said the wife of an electrician inspector. 'Just in-between', said a young shorthand typist. 'Just a little better than poor', said the wife of a marsh man in South Norfolk. 'Not living in the slums', said the wife of a driver in the food industry, 'but not having their own house.' Very few of these answers specified clearly where the respondent drew the line between the middle and working class, but all had in common some notion, whether implied or explicit, of 'in-betweenness'.

The categories 'rich' and 'poor' likewise include many replies where no clear dividing line was specified; but all had in common at least an implicit reference to money. The definitions of the middle class coded under 'rich' included such phrases as 'people who have money in the bank' or 'independent people not requiring any assistance' or 'those that have something behind them'. The definitions of the working class coded under 'poor' included 'people who live on their income from hand to mouth', 'not quite so well off as us' (this from a miner who described himself as 'middle-class'), 'them that's used to poverty' and 'used to be the very poorest'. Sometimes, however, the answers coded in these categories were difficult to distinguish from references to style of life. For the definitions of working class, where no 'style of life' category was used, this means merely that 'poor' includes some answers which relate only indirectly to money. Thus, the wife of a storekeeper in the engineering industry who described the working class as 'people who live in slums' was coded in this category; this is stretching the category a little, but the coding is supported by her reference at a different point in the interview to the 'working class and poor class'. For the question about the middle class, however, the overlap between 'rich' and 'style of life' is more blurred than the figures given in the tables suggest. For example, the coders assigned 'people who can afford to have a holiday and have a nest egg' to 'style of life', but 'those who live fairly well' and 'people who can afford all the amenities we've spoken about and money to spare' to 'rich'. There is a discernible difference, perhaps, but it is not a large one. Some of the answers belonged very clearly to 'style of life': for example, a small-holder's wife in a rural district in the South said 'Well, I go by the way they live at home, not by the money they earn'. But very few of the replies emphasized status rather than class as explicitly as this.

The two categories of personal approval and disapproval included for the most part answers of a predictable kind. Approving definitions of the middle class included 'people who try to better themselves', 'chapel people, not those who go to bingo—they have no sense', and 'it depends on ideals and standards'. Disapproving definitions included 'people who think they are better than what they are', 'people who are reaching for something they can't get and keeping up appearances' and 'there are not a lot of middle class, but some people think they are'. Approving definitions of the working class included some phrases also used in favourable definitions of the middle class, such as 'respectable', but also some which carried a distinct flavour of traditional lateral solidarity such as 'people who give a helping hand when needed'. Disapproving definitions of the working class often referred to spending habits or lack of ambition, but some of them were less explicit: 'the rougher people living in the slums', said a salesman's wife: 'rough and ready types', said the wife of an insurance manager, 'who don't bother about things'. These phrases, however vague, are clearly pejorative; but some of the replies which were coded under the heading of a personal criterion only just, if at all, carried a visible overtone of approval or disapproval. This was particularly so where the working class was defined by reference to a lack of education. For example, the description of the working class as 'without GCE O Level' is not necessarily pejorative, but for coding purposes it is in the same category as 'type of person who will watch TV all night'—the answer given by a young storekeeper in the shoe industry who described the middle class as 'people whose minds are alive'. Thus the category of 'personal disapproving', although it does contain many outspoken expressions of disapproval, should not be assumed always to carry a strongly pejorative sense.

The category of 'everybody' for the working class is obvious enough. Some people, however, gave this answer for the middle class, although it is not used as a separate coding. The reason why it was not used for the middle class as well is simply that the initial sub-sample drawn from the answers showed that it was very much rarer for the middle than for the working class; but a few of the definitions of the middle class coded as 'other' would have come under this heading if it had been used. Otherwise, the two 'other' codings cover a diversity of replies which could not be assigned to any of the principal categories. Some were hopelessly vague, such as 'people we mix with'; some were specific, but not codable—'those who have worked up from the working class'; some were merely eccentric, as when the wife of an unemployed hosiery worker who had described herself as working class gave as a definition of the working class 'people earning very high salaries'. Lastly, the 'Don't Knows' include some people who actually said they didn't know, but more often people who were unable to give any definable answer at all.

Each of the categories used, therefore, covers a fairly wide range of meanings. But although the range is sufficiently wide to demolish at once any theory that a manual worker who describes himself as 'middle-class' has therefore become 'bourgeois' the answers still demonstrate that most people do have a definable picture of their place in the social hierarchy, and that almost all of these pictures can be coded into a small number of broadly defined categories. The percentage figures are shown in the three tables which follow. The first shows the pattern of responses to the two questions initially asked— 'What social class would you say you belonged to?' and, for those who did not give an answer, 'If you had to say middle or working class, which would you say?'. The second and third tables show the distributions of the meanings given to the 'working' and 'middle' class by those who assigned themselves to the one and the other respectively. For these two questions, more than one answer was sometimes given, so that the percentages total more than 100%.

TABLE 1

Self-assigned 'class'; by occupational stratum.

	non-manual %		manual %	
Upper or upper-middle	6		*	
Middle	51		22	
Lower-middle	10		7	
Working	19		52	
Don't know, other, none	14 = Middle	7	19 = Middle	4
	Working	6	Working	14
	Don't know	1	Don't know	1
		14%		19%
Total	100% (N=496)		100% (N=919)	

*=one person

TABLE 2

'What sort of people do you mean when you talk about the middle class?'; by self-rated class within occupational stratum.

	non-manual		manual	
	self-rated middle %	self-rated working %	self-rated middle %	self-rated working %
Non-manual workers	49	51	16	43
Those 'between top and bottom'	11	3	14	6
Actual manual jobs mentioned	1	1	6	0
Rich	7	23	8	27
Personal criterion of approval	16	2	27	2
Personal criterion of disapproval	0	2	0	6
Middle-class style of life	10	10	12	10
Other	8	8	16	5
Don't know	3	8	6	10
Total	105% (N=365)	108% (N=124)	105% (N=303)	109% (N=610)

TABLE 3

'What sort of people do you mean when you talk about the working class?'; by self-rated class within occupational stratum.

| | non-manual | | manual | |
| | self-rated middle | self-rated working | self-rated middle | self-rated working |
	%	%	%	%
Manual workers	65	28	34	42
Ordinary people	9	40	13	29
Actual non-manual jobs mentioned	1	3	0	2
Poor	5	7	9	9
Personal criterion of approval	1	10	5	12
Personal criterion of disapproval	11	1	15	1
Everybody	3	1	7	1
Other	4	10	7	5
Don't know	7	7	16	4
Total	106%	107%	106%	105%
	(N=365)	(N=124)	N=303)	(N=610)

Several interesting comparisons emerge from Tables 2 and 3. First of all, the group least likely to define the 'middle class' as non-manual workers is the group of manual workers who say that they are themselves 'middle-class'. Similarly, the group least likely to define the 'working class' as manual workers is the group of non-manual workers and their wives who say that they are themselves 'working-class'. This finding bears out that of Martin, although the codings used are different.[4] Only 28% of non-manual respondents who describe themselves as working-class give manual workers as their definition of the working class, thus seeming by implication to assimilate themselves to the proletarian stratum; this group is liklier to give a criterion of 'ordinariness', implying rather a common membership of a group including everyone but the extremes. In the same way, even fewer of the manual respondents who describe themselves as 'middle-class' define the middle class by a non-manual criterion. Only 16% of this group seem to imply a conscious assimilation to the non-manual stratum; they are likelier to give a purely personal criterion, and several of them—slightly more, indeed, than of the non-manual self-rated middle class—give the sort of more or less literal answer coded as 'between top and bottom'. This group is also likeliest to give some criterion which could not be assigned to one of the pre-defined categories.

There is, however, a difference between these two groups in their definition of the opposite class: manual respondents describing

[21] Cf. Stacey, *op. cit.*, p. 47.

themselves as 'middle-class' are less likely by 17% to see the working class as manual workers than non-manual respondents describing themselves as 'working-class' are likely to see the middle class as non-manual workers. This reinforces the argument that although many manual workers see themselves as different from the traditional working class, this does not mean a conscious assimilation to the white-collar or salaried stratum. On the other hand, non-manual respondents describing themselves as 'working-class' may, to this extent, be likelier to share the perspective of those who are in fact manual workers. A further difference is that non-manual respondents describing themselves as 'working-class' are very unlikely to give a personal criterion of disapproval for the 'middle' class (2%), whereas 15% of the manual respondents rating themselves 'middle' give a personal criterion of disapproval for their idea of the 'working' class. Non-manual respondents describing themselves as 'working-class', therefore, seem to have their class-situation more in mind; manual respondents describing themselves as 'middle-class' seem likelier to feel detached from the working class in terms of status.

Yet another difference is in the definitions given in terms of 'rich' and 'poor'. A definition of the working class as the poor is relatively rare among any of the groups, and the differences here are not striking; the only small difference is that members of the manual stratum, however they rate themselves, are more likely than members of the non-manual stratum to give this definition. The definition of the middle class as the rich, however, is very much commoner among those who describe themselves as working-class, not only among manual but also among non-manual respondents. It need not be true that those who describe the middle class as rich assign themselves to the working class for this reason; but it is not implausible to suppose that the non-manual respondents who assign themselves to the working class and describe the middle class as 'rich' are doing so because they see themselves as closer in income to the skilled artisan than to the businessman or professional.

The percentages suggest, therefore, that although self-assessments in terms of 'class' may vary widely, even when people share a common position in the hierarchy of occupations, this variety is neither meaningless nor random. It is wide enough to show the futility of bracketing all the self-styled 'middle' or 'working' class under a single heading, or attributing to them a uniform social perspective. But it is quite coherent enough to enable conclusions to be drawn from it. Only one further precaution needs to be taken. The one danger which is concealed by the tables shown is that even if the codings are legitimate, some of the pairs of replies may be mutually inconsistent. The pattern of answers separately given for the 'middle' and 'working' class does not reveal how many respondents gave pairs of answers which when taken together suggest a much less coherent view of the distinction between 'working' and 'middle'; indeed, the imposition of this dichotomy may have led some respondents to give answers which were much more apparently coherent than a freer form of questioning would have shown. A further question was, however, included in the interview which makes possible some check on this. After a question in which people had been asked what income they thought necessary for 'a proper standard of living for people like yourself', the open-ended question was asked: 'What sort of people are you thinking of as "people like yourself"?'.

This question not only makes it possible to check the answers given against the answers about 'class'. It also gives an idea of the extent to which other membership reference groups may be uppermost in people's minds. An old age pensioner, for example, although he may be willing to assign himself to one or other of the two 'classes' may nonetheless think of himself chiefly as an old age pensioner, and it may be this much more than his self-assigned 'class' which furnishes his membership and perhaps also his normative reference group. As it turned out, the majority of answers among both the manual and non-manual strata included a reference to occupation, whether or not specifically tied to a class or manual/non-manual distinction. There were, however, a number of other replies given, as shown in Table 4.

The replies to this rather different question were almost without exception coherent and straightforward, and the proportion of 'Don't Knows' is small. But a number of them turned out to be in contradiction with the answers given later in the interview to the questions about 'class'. For example, the wife of a turbine pump driver answered this question by saying 'respectable working class'. But when asked about 'class', she assigned herself to the middle 'class' which furnishes his membership and perhaps also his norma-ing class' she defined simply as 'working people'. Her answers all fall neatly enough into the coding categories; but none of the percentage tables reveal that she in fact means very little by her self-assigned 'class'. It is obviously necessary, therefore, to discover just how many such people there may be.

A detailed examination of the individual schedules revealed several people whose self-assigned 'class' did not have very much meaning. They fell into two main categories: first, those whose answers showed that although they were prepared to assign themselves to one or other class they in fact made little or no distinction between them; second, those whose answers to the questions about

TABLE 4

'What sort of people are you thinking of when we talk about "people like yourself"?'; by occupational stratum.

	non-manual %	manual %
'Working class', manual workers	12	41
'Middle class', non-manual workers, professions, business	42	7
Personal criterion ('good sorts', 'self-respecting', etc.)	11	9
Old, retired, pensioners, widowed	8	12
Young *or* middle-aged	1	1
'Ordinary'	4	7
Self-made	2	1
Same job, class but no specific manual/non-manual reference	12	10
Friends, neighbours, others in similar area or district	2	2
Particular family situations (e.g. number of dependents)	4	7
Other	2	2
Don't know	4	5
Total	104% (N=496)	104% (N=919)

class and the question about 'people like yourself' were directly contradictory. There were also a number of respondents who assigned themselves to the 'middle class' although describing 'people like themselves' in such phrases as 'ordinary working people' or 'skilled workers' or 'skilled working people'; but those who gave this sequence of answers, although they were generally coded under the heading labelled 'working class, manual workers' in Table 4, were not being inconsistent; they were simply drawing the line between middle and working class below the skilled manual worker. Some of those whose answers showed that they drew no meaningful distinction whatever appear in Table 3 among those who defined the working class as 'everybody'. But this coding does not cover by any means all of the respondents whose answers showed that their self-assessment meant very little. The total arrived at by an individual examination of all the interviews was 83 (6% of the sample). This is not an altogether negligible proportion. But at the same time it is not enough to upset the conclusion that self-assigned 'class' has at least some meaning to almost everyone. Since the 'anomalous' replies could not be selected by any strict formal criterion, it is possible that a selection made by someone else would be a little larger; but it would certainly not be so much larger as to

162

exceed 100 (i.e., 7% of the sample). When the 13 respondents who refused to assign themselves to either class and the 62 who said that they did not know what they meant by their self-rating are also added, the proportion rises to 11%. But it is still true to say that virtually nine out of ten adults in England and Wales have some sort of definable and coherent view of their place in the system of 'class'.

A few examples will be enough to give some idea of the respondents who had to be counted as anomalous. First, there were the replies which were consistent as between the answers to self-assigned class and 'people like yourself' but were shown by the definitions given for the 'working' and 'middle' classes to have little meaning in terms of a distinction between the two. Thus the wife of a retired accounts manager who both described 'people like yourself' as 'middle-class' and also assigned herself to the 'middle class' defined the working class as 'more like ourselves'; she also gave as her reason for supporting the Labour Party that 'they have helped the working class since I was a girl—I'm better off than my mother was'. Clearly, therefore, her self-assessment—which she defined in terms of personal approval—is not as clear-cut as the coded answers would imply.

Other respondents were inconsistent in both respects. Thus, the proprietor of a fish and chip shop assigned himself to the middle class but described 'people like yourself' as 'just ordinary working-class people'; in his definitions of the classes he said 'the common working class are what I call middle class', but also 'people who have strived to get ahead are the middle class'. From this sequence of replies, it is obvious that although his self-assignment to the middle class does have some meaning to him, it is matched by a simultaneous attachment to the 'ordinary working class'. Indeed, he should be classified as 'genuinely ambivalent' rather than either indifferent or confused.

Most of the respondents who were inconsistent, however, were consistent in their answers about class but seemed directly to contradict this by their answers to 'people like yourself'. Thus a textile worker in a Northern city described himself as 'working-class' and said that he meant by this 'people who earn their living by their hands'. The middle class he defined as 'those who have it a bit more easy—white collar workers'. Asked about 'people like yourself', however, he replied 'middle class who take it nice and steady'. This might reflect the same sort of genuine ambivalence as the previous example; but it is more likely to reflect a confusion of definition than of feeling.

In an attempt to test further the possible inconsistencies in the self-assessments given, yet another question was included which contained the phrase 'people like yourself'. This second use of the phrase was in the context of questions about voting. As is shown by the example of the retired accounts manager's wife, people may identify with the middle class in their ideas about income and standard of living, yet identify with the working class—perhaps because it is the stratum of their origin—when it comes to habits of voting. Two questions were therefore asked, after the subject of voting had been discussed: first, 'Do you think that most people like yourself vote the same way as you do or differently?' and then, 'What sort of people are you thinking of? How would you describe them?'. Unfortunately, however, this question turned out to be virtually useless. The reason is that examination of the individual schedules showed that the answers were often given not to the intended question 'who do you think of as "people like yourself" in the context of voting?', but as if the question had been 'what sort of people do you think vote the same (or, differently) as you do?'. This danger had not been detected in the pilot survey. But it was clear from so many of the replies in the main survey that the question had been misunderstood that no generalization of any kind can be legitimately based on the replies.

Even without this further check, however, it seems a plausible conclusion that self-assigned 'class' is meaningless for only about 10% of respondents. The meanings differ; but even if this invalidates the rather sweeping conclusions which have sometimes been drawn from self-assigned class,[5] it does not destroy the validity of using it as an independent variable in the analysis of attitude surveys. In particular, it may have interesting implications for the choice of reference groups. If nine-tenths of English adults see themselves as belonging to one or other of two separate social categories, and if these categories carry strong overtones not only of job or income but of style of life, values and outlook, then it is plausible to interpret their self-assigned 'class' as implying a choice of a normative reference group.

There are, however, still two dangers which must be avoided in any attempt to generalize along these lines. No matter what correlations may emerge in the cross-tabulation of the survey, it may be very misleading to speak of attitudes relevant to social inequality as being 'caused' by the choice of normative reference group. This choice may itself be determined by other influences which are themselves the cause of attitudes to inequality, so that self-rating would

[5] E.g. by Mark Abrams, in 'Class and Politics', *Encounter* (October, 1961).

be better described as a symptom of these attitudes than a determinant of them. Furthermore, there may be no reason to expect the choice of normative reference group to affect one way or the other the magnitude of relative deprivation felt by anyone on any particular topic. Two questions, therefore, need to be asked before testing the effects of self-rated 'class' on other attitudes. The first is what social characteristics are likely to influence people's choice of self-rating, particularly manual workers or their wives who regard themselves as 'middle-class'. Only if these prior determinants are located can the effect of self-rating be tested by holding them constant also. The second question is what effect, if any, self-rated 'class' should be expected to have on attitudes to the inequalities in the social structure.

A number of expected correlations were found between a middle-class self-rating by manual workers and their wives and such characteristics as income, place of residence, and father's occupation. The differences in the form of questions used make direct comparison with other studies impossible; but the present results suggest very similar conclusions to those of other surveys on self-assigned 'class'. Most of them, indeed, are what common sense would lead one to expect. But their main interest lies in further confirming that the choice of self-assigned 'class' is seldom meaningless. Indeed, its apparent determinants afford further grounds for interpreting it as in some sense a normative reference group.

One correlation with self-assigned class cannot be demonstrated with the present evidence. It is known that self-assessment varies with the occupational composition of the immediate neighbourhood in which people live; but in a national poll-type sample such comparisons are not feasible. It can only be said that if a comparison is made with either a very proletarian or a very suburban community, then the proportion of manual workers and their wives in the country as a whole who assign themselves to the 'middle class' is closer to the suburban than the proletarian figure. Taking only the people who answered the open-ended question, a comparison can be made with the figures found by Willmott and Young for Woodford and by Willmott for Dagenham. The Dagenham figure is 13% and the Woodford figure 34%.[6] The figure for the present survey, as shown in Table 1, is 29%. It seems safe to suppose that this varies by immediate neighbourhood, but there is no way of showing it for this sample. A regional breakdown, however, does show a distinct variation. Manual respondents were most likely to describe themselves as 'working-class' in the North, and non-manual respondents were

[6] See Willmott, *op. cit.*, p. 102; and cf. Martin, *op. cit.*, p. 56 for the difference between Greenwich and Hertford in 1950.

least likely to do so in the South. The figures are shown in Table 5; here the prompted and unprompted have been combined, but the Welsh respondents have been excluded since there are too few of them for valid comparison.

TABLE 5

Self-assigned 'class'; by region within occupational stratum.

	non-manual			manual		
	North	Midlands	South	North	Midlands	South
	%	%	%	%	%	%
Self-rated 'middle-class'	72	72	77	26	45	35
Self-rated 'working-class'	28	28	23	74	55	65
Total	100%	100%	100%	100%	100%	100%
	(N=127)	(N=76)	(N=273)	(N=311)	(N=188)	(N=380)

These figures seem to accord with the conventional picture of North-South differences, although it is noticeable that the manual respondents who live in the Midlands are likeliest to assign themselves to the 'middle class'; this particular result may be due to the geographical distribution of skilled manual occupations as well as to regional differences in attitudes to status. When a comparison is made in terms of urban or rural residence, there is once again a predictable difference. Among the non-manual stratum, the difference is very slight; but among the manual stratum 35% of the urban residents assign themselves to the middle class as against only 26% of the rural. What is more surprising is that there is not the difference between men and women that one might expect. It is generally held that women are more status-conscious than men. But if status-consciousness implies a middle-class self-rating, then the expectation only holds among the non-manual stratum. 33% of men in the non-manual stratum described themselves as 'working-class' as against only 18% of women. In the manual stratum, by contrast, the proportion of men and women describing themselves as 'middle-class' was exactly the same.

A good deal of the self-assessment of people in the non-manual stratum as 'working-class', and vice versa, can be explained in terms of social origin. The manual respondents whose fathers were in non-manual occupations were much likelier to describe themselves as middle-class than those whose fathers were also in manual occupations: 54% of the former described themselves as middle-class compared with 31% of the latter. A breakdown by sex, however, even when father's occupation had been held constant, still failed to show any difference between men and women. In the non-manual stratum, people whose fathers were manual workers were in the same way much more likely to describe themselves as working-class; but the difference between men and women also remained clearly noticeable. This persistent effect of sex in the non-manual stratum is shown in Table 6. The total number of respondents is a little less than the total of the non-manual stratum, since a few people said that they did not know their father's occupation.

TABLE 6

Self-assigned 'class'; non-manual stratum by father's occupation within sex.

| | men | | women | |
| | father non-manual | father manual | father non-manual | father manual |
	%	%	%	%
Self-rated middle	79	57	92	71
Self-rated working	21	43	8	29
Total	100%	100%	100%	100%
	(N=99)	(N=125)	(N=127)	(N=128)

Within both strata, self-assessment varies to some extent with age, but the pattern of variation is too haphazard to suggest a significant difference between one generation and the next.[7] The one other noticeable difference between the manual and non-manual respondents is the relation between their self-assigned class and their income. For the purposes of the survey, respondents were classified on the basis of either their own stated income or, in the case of married women, their husband's income. The whole sample was then divided into three groups—high, medium and low incomes. The distribution and method of analysis are discussed more fully in a later chapter. For the moment, what is of interest is the effect of income on the likelihood that manual workers or their wives will describe themselves as 'middle-class'. In the non-manual stratum the likelihood of a working-class self-rating does not fall as income rises, which is perhaps unexpected. But in the manual stratum, the frequency of a middle-class self-rating rises with income from 24% to 36% to 41%. This might seem to support the argument that as manual workers become more prosperous they become progressively more 'bourgeois'; but any such conclusion should be

[7] For what it is worth, manual respondents who were in their 20's at the time of the survey, and were, therefore, too young to have any memories of the 1930's were the more likely to describe themselves as 'middle-class'. This may be some support of the argument that the frequency of relative deprivation of status rose between the 1930's and 1960's, but without knowledge of how the older respondents would have replied in the 1930's, such evidence is tenuous at best.

167

treated with caution. The tendency of some working-class people to take the 'middle class'—whatever they mean by it—as a reference group may have a significance for the relation between inequality and relative deprivation. But, as always, the difference between inequalities of class and of status is important. A middle-class self-rating by manual workers and their wives seems to be largely determined by where they live, how much they earn, and what job their fathers had. This may distinguish them in their own minds from other manual workers. But it need not assimilate them to the non-manual stratum, and its effect—or the effect of the influences of which it too is a symptom—is by no means straightforward. If it is true that with few exceptions a middle-class self-rating has some meaning as a choice of reference group, what will be the effect of this choice on the pattern of relative deprivation?

Consider first the implication of a middle-class self-rating by manual workers for relative deprivation of class. The historical evidence suggested that in the England of 1962 the comparative reference groups of manual workers on matters of class are likely still to be taken from the manual stratum; or if comparisons are made to the non-manual stratum, these are unlikely to be based on the true extent of inequality between the two. We have seen that a middle-class self-rating seldom means that a manual worker is directly identifying himself with non-manual workers. His standards of comparison are still likely to be drawn from within the manual stratum, and to help to keep the magnitude and intensity of his relative deprivation low. Indeed he may well feel relatively gratified by comparison with what he means by the 'working class'—the less skilled and less well-paid manual workers. There is no reason to expect that he will feel either more or less relatively deprived than if he thinks of himself as working-class, and if he does, he may feel a no less 'fraternalistic' relative deprivation than the manual worker who explicitly identifies with the 'working class'.

For inequalities of status, however, the expectation is very different. A manual worker who thinks of himself as 'middle-class' will be likelier than one who thinks of himself as 'working-class' to feel relatively deprived of status; and this relative deprivation is likely to be of an 'egoistic' kind. I have argued that relative deprivation of status has both widened in magnitude and increased in frequency among the manual stratum throughout the period discussed, and has done so in such a way as to emphasize the possibilities of individual mobility as much as a collective equality between the two strata. If this is so, then a prosperous manual worker who thinks of himself as 'middle-class' will be likely to have aspirations of status not shared by his fellows who think of themselves as 'working-class'. This still need not mean that he wants to become indistinguishable from members of the non-manual stratum, or that he thinks of himself as resembling them. But he is likely to have aspirations of status which will not be shared by the manual worker who describes himself as 'working-class'.

These two suppositions are phrased in very general and even ideal-typical terms. The attitudes which they deal with are not as simple as this nor as easy to discover, and the generalization which is implied may need to be carefully qualified. But if the relation between inequality and relative deprivation is as I have argued, then some pattern of this kind should emerge from the cross-tabulations of the survey. It is true that there are many topics apart from 'class' itself in which issues of class and status, however different in principle, are in practice inextricably intertwined. This difficulty, however, can be avoided on at least some issues in such a way as to test the validity of my argument. The only topic which must be considered on its own is working-class Conservatism, and, as before, I shall consider it in a separate chapter before going on to specific inequalities of class and status.

IX

THE WORKING-CLASS
CONSERVATIVES

ONCE it has been established that the 'class' to which people assign themselves almost always expresses some coherent view of their position in society, it becomes worthwhile to explore the correlation between working-class Conservatism and self-assessment in order to elucidate further the relation between relative deprivation and inequality. Several studies have shown a correlation between Conservative support and a middle-class self-rating among manual workers and their families, and the present survey fully confirms it. Some commentators have tried to minimize the significance of this correlation.[1] But it is too large to be dismissed as meaningless, and the one way in which it might be plausibly dismissed—a demonstration that it results from a joint correlation with income—can be quickly shown not to hold. An exploration of this relationship, therefore, may throw some light both on the influences behind working-class Conservatism and on the relation between social location and attitudes towards it. It will be convenient to start from the figures for party preference broken down by self-rating within the manual and non-manual strata. I must emphasize that the level of Liberal support is peculiar to the time at which the survey was conducted; it reflects the high-water mark reached by the Liberal revival between the General Elections of 1959 and 1964. But this does not affect the general argument; indeed, it helps to throw further light on the nature of working-class

---

[1] Thus Birch, *op. cit.*, p. 110: 'The fact that needs explaining is that 33 per cent. of the industrial workers voted Conservative in 1951, and it is no help to show that if those who rate themselves as middle class are excluded from the figures, the proportion is reduced to 31 per cent.' The smallness of this difference, however, is a function of the ratio of self-rated middle-class to self-rated working-class manual workers in Birch's sample. Even in this local sample, drawn in 1953, the difference in Conservative vote between the two groups is 13%. In my national sample, drawn nearly ten years later, the difference is half as much again.

political allegiances, as I shall try to show. Table 7 accordingly gives the breakdown of an electorate of which 20% was then expressing support for the Liberals as against 30% for the Conservatives and 37% for Labour.

TABLE 7

Party preference; by self-rated 'class' within occupational stratum.

	non-manual		manual	
	self-rated middle	self-rated working	self-rated middle	self-rated working
	%	%	%	%
Conservative	52	23	36	16
Liberal	25	23	19	16
Labour	11	37	31	55
Other	1	0	0	1
Don't know *or* refuse[2]	11	17	14	12
Total	100%	100%	100%	100%
	(N=365)	(N=124)	(N=303)	(N=610)

These figures clearly confirm that the relationship between self-rated 'class' and party preference is strong. It makes hardly any difference to support for the Liberals. But it makes so much difference to Labour or Conservative support that it reverses the direction of the relationship: non-manual respondents who describe themselves as 'working-class' are 14% likelier to be Labour than Conservative supporters, and manual respondents who describe themselves as 'middle-class' are 5% likelier to be Conservative than Labour supporters. This raises at once the question whether income may not provide the explanation. Since, in particular, we know that a 'middle-class' self-rating becomes more likely among manual respondents the higher their level of income, is it not simply the more prosperous manual workers and their wives who are responsible for the 20% difference? The answer is that it is not. Not only does self-rating make a difference at all three levels of income, but it makes a bigger difference the poorer the respondent: the likelihood of Conservative support among manual respondents who describe themselves as 'middle-class' is in inverse relation to their income. This result must be qualified by saying that Labour support among this group is scarcely affected by income—the figures for Conservative support are rather a function of the differences in support for the Liberals. But as Table 8 shows, the correlation between a middle-class self-rating and Conservative support certainly cannot be explained away by appealing to income.

[2] Refusals amounted to less than 2% of the sample, but they are included in Tables 7, 8 and 13 in order to furnish a complete breakdown.

TABLE 8

Party preference; manual respondents
by self-rated 'class' within income.

	high		medium		low	
	self-rated middle	self-rated working	self-rated middle	self-rated working	self-rated middle	self-rated working
	%	%	%	%	%	%
Conservative	27	18	36	14	41	18
Liberal	29	16	19	15	15	20
Labour	32	55	30	65	33	48
Other	0	0	0	0	0	1
Don't know *or* refuse	12	11	15	6	11	13
Total	100%	100%	100%	100%	100%	100%
	(N=41)	(N=56)	(N=101)	(N=176)	(N=91)	(N=276)

There are other personal attributes than income which show a correlation with working-class Conservatism, and which might explain away the correlation with a middle-class self-rating. But none in fact succeed in doing so, although they show some independent effect. Thus age, which has been shown in other studies[3] to affect the likelihood of Conservative support, does so in the present survey also; and since the old are likely to be the poor as well, a part of the inverse correlation between income and Conservative support will lie here. If manual respondents under 50 are compared with those of 50 and over, there is only a slight difference—6%—in Conservative support. But this simple comparison between young and old conceals a mounting trend among the over-fifties. Of manual respondents, 24% of those in their fifties, 25% of those in their sixties and 31% of those in their seventies expressed support for the Conservatives. Various explanations have been offered for this familiar correlation, apart from the proverbial tendency to radicalism in youth and conservatism in old age. One explanation suggested is the differential death-rate of the manual and non-manual stratum.[4] Another is the comparative immaturity of the Labour Party as the established left-wing party in the two-party system.[5] The probable answer is that the relationship is compounded of several influences of which some, but not all, are dependent on each other. But, whatever the complete explanation of it, it seems to account for at least some small part of the discrepancy between inequality and grievance exemplified by the least affluent of working-class Conservatives. Indeed, it is particularly suggestive for those

[3] See e.g. M. Benney *et al.*, *How People Vote* (London, 1956), p. 105.
[4] R. S. Milne and H. C. Mackenzie, *Straight Fight* (London, 1954), pp. 56–7.
[5] Birch, *op. cit.*, pp. 110–111.

whose party preference cannot be related to their self-assigned 'class'. Out of 79 working-class Conservatives at the bottom income level who described themselves as 'working-class', 78% were found to be 50 or over—a finding which seems to accord, as we shall see, with the greater propensity of this group to give as their reason for supporting the Conservatives a motive of habitual loyalty than a choice of specific policies.

Another of the known influences confirmed by the present survey is sex. Women are more likely than men to support the Conservatives despite the additional finding that working-class women are no more likely than working-class men to describe themselves as 'middle-class'.[6] As Table 9 shows, the difference is small, but it holds good within self-rating. Among Liberal supporters, the pattern breaks down. But the figures for Conservative and Labour support confirm that sex is slightly related to left-wing or right-wing preference, although they show at the same time how strongly the independent effect of self-rating persists.

TABLE 9

Party preference; manual respondents by sex within self-rated 'class'.

	self-rated middle		self-rated working	
	men	women	men	women
	%	%	%	%
Conservative	35	38	14	19
Liberal	17	20	19	15
Labour	36	29	59	54
Other	0	0	1	*
Don't know	12	13	7	12
Total	100%	100%	100%	100%
	(N=135)	(N=164)	(N=270)	(N=327)

*=one person.

Education, likewise, has an independent effect on party preference, although it does not explain away the correlation with self-rating. There are too few manual respondents with more than a minimum of education for them to account for more than a small fraction of the total of working-class Conservatives. But since working-class people who stayed on at school beyond the minimum leaving age are more likely both to support the Conservatives and to describe themselves as 'middle-class', it might be argued that education could explain part of the correlation between self-rating and party support. In fact, when the two are held constant against each

[6] For the influence of sex, cf. Benney, *op. cit.*, p. 107; Milne and Mackenzie, *op. cit.*, p. 38 and *Marginal Seat* (London, 1958), p. 60; Birch, *op. cit.*, p. 102; Stacey, *op. cit.*, p. 47.

other the effect of both is clearly visible; but education makes less difference than self-rating, as shown below in Table 10.

TABLE 10

Party support; manual respondents by self-rated 'class' within education. [7]

	minimum education		education beyond minimum	
	self-rated middle	self-rated working	self-rated middle	self-rated working
	%	%	%	%
Conservative	34	16	49	26
Liberal	20	16	18	15
Labour	34	57	20	51
Other	0	1	0	3
Don't know	12	10	13	5
Total	100%	100%	100%	100%
	(N=253)	(N=558)	(N=45)	(N=39)

On the known correlation between party and religion, the present sample bears out the expectation that low church members will be found least likely to be Conservative supporters; and they are also least likely to describe themselves as 'middle-class'. The proportion of Conservatives among them is 15% as compared with 21% among Roman Catholics and 26% among Anglicans. If church attendance, as opposed to affiliation, is taken as the independent variable, then those who said they had attended within a month are likeliest to support the Conservatives (29%); those who said they had attended within a year are less likely to do so (24%); and those who either never attend or had not attended for over a year are less likely still (17%). The likeliest of all to support the Conservatives were found to be those who said that they would go to church if they could but were prevented by old age or some other reason from doing so; of the 28 people in this category, 36% were Conservatives. Within each denomination, however, the difference made by self-rating continues to hold good. Indeed it turns out that among manual workers and their wives who describe themselves as 'middle-class' the difference between Anglicans and Catholics disappears, and among Nonconformists who describe themselves as 'working-class' the proportion of Conservative supporters falls below 10%. The percentages of Conservatives in the three denominations (excluding the refusals and the people who said they had no religion) are shown in Table 11.

[7] The total number of respondents is one less than in Table 9 due to the exclusion of one respondent whose education was not known.

The Working-Class Conservatives

TABLE 11

Proportion of Conservative supporters; manual respondents by
self-rated 'class' within denomination.

Anglican		Roman Catholic		Low Church or Other	
self-rated middle	self-rated working	self-rated middle	self-rated working	self-rated middle	self-rated working
39%	20%	39%	11%	27%	9%
(N=218)	(N=407)	(N=32)	(N=54)	(N=42)	(N=128)

Finally, it is known that those manual workers and their wives
whose fathers were in non-manual occupations are likelier than
those whose fathers were in manual occupations not only to describe themselves as 'middle-class' but also to support the Conservatives. There is therefore the question, as there was with education,
whether the effect of self-rated 'class' holds good irrespective of
father's occupation. Table 12 shows that there is still a distinct
effect. Of the manual respondents as a whole—leaving out those
who did not know their fathers' occupations—38% whose fathers
were in non-manual jobs were found to be Conservative supporters
as compared with 21% of those whose fathers were in manual jobs.
These figures are almost exactly the same as those found if the
respondents' estimates of their father's 'class', rather than his actual
occupation, are taken as an independent variable. Of those who
said that their father was 'working-class', 19% were Conservatives,
and of those who said that their father was 'middle-class', 38%.
When father's actual occupation is held constant, then the proportions of Conservatives are as shown.

TABLE 12

Party preference; manual respondents by self-rated 'class' within
father's occupation.

	father non-manual		father manual	
	self-rated middle	self-rated working	self-rated middle	self-rated working
	%	%	%	%
Conservative	46	31	34	16
Liberal	19	23	19	16
Labour	21	31	36	57
Other	0	0	0	1
Don't know	14	15	11	10
Total	100%	100%	100%	100%
	(N=57)	(N=48)	(N=237)	(N=525)

If a statistical caricature is constructed from the results of the
survey, then the ideal type of the working-class Conservative is a
woman in her seventies living in a country district in the Midlands

whose father was in a non-manual occupation, who stayed on at school beyond the minimum age, who thinks of herself as 'middle-class', and who would like to attend regularly at an Anglican church but is prevented by age or illness from doing so. This is, of course, only a caricature. Although the manual respondents in the sample included six Anglican women aged 50 or over who had stayed on at school and who described themselves as 'middle-class' and all of them were found to support the Conservatives, more working-class supporters than these are needed to return a Conservative government to power. But the ideal type furnishes a convenient summary of the attributes which are apparent determinants of working-class Conservatism. The implication of a discrepancy between actual inequality and sense of relative deprivation is most striking among those who might be labelled the 'genteel poor'—those who gave their income, or their husband's income, as £10 a week or less but described themselves as 'middle-class'. These people are likely to be old—over half of them are 60 or older. But it seems at the same time plausible to account in part for their political views by interpreting their self-rating as a normative reference group. They may also be influenced by particular questions of policy, or a feeling that things would be no better for them under a Labour government and might even be worse. But the strong independent effect of self-rating is cogent evidence for the view that a choice of normative reference group from higher in the scale of status can inhibit the political radicalism ostensibly appropriate to the poor.

It might be objected that the effect of self-rating is exaggerated by the exceptional strength of Liberal support and its concentration among particular sections of the electorate. The solid Conservatism of the 'genteel poor' is brought into what may be unnatural relief by the greater propensity to Liberalism among the more prosperous manual respondents. But this does not alter the argument. First of all, the most interesting working-class Conservatives are precisely those who are most loyal—who were not, that is, tempted away from the fold even at a time of strong Liberal resurgence. Secondly, the Liberal voters themselves confirm the significance of self-rated 'class' as an independent variable. Among the most prosperous voters, where the proportion of Liberal supporters was highest, self-rated 'class' produced the most marked effect. At the two lower levels of income, its effect is small and contradictory. But its influence at the top level of incomes suggests that Liberalism had its strongest appeal to those manual workers and their wives who no longer felt themselves to be proletarians, but for whom the non-manual stratum was not yet a strong enough normative reference group to lead them to prefer the Conservative party.

But if self-rated 'class' can be shown in this way to have an autonomous and persistent effect, it becomes all the more important to relate this effect to the varied meanings which may attach to one or other 'class'. It may be true that almost all those who described themselves as 'middle-class' were in some sense distinguishing themselves from a stratum which they saw as below them; but the variety of meanings is sufficiently wide for the propensity to Conservative support to be likely to vary to at least some extent according to the meaning given. Those whose self-rating has little or no meaning at all should, if the argument is correct, be visibly different in their political loyalties from those whose self-rating means a definable distinction between themselves and those below them. Similarly, those who meant by the 'middle class' people in actual manual occupations should vote no differently from those who described themselves as 'working-class'. Table 13 accordingly shows the party preference of those manual respondents who described themselves as 'middle-class' according to the definition of the 'middle class' which they gave. Only one respondent has been excluded from the table—the single person in the sample who described himself as 'middle-class' and then gave a criterion of personal disapproval as his definition of the middle class. The numbers shown add up to more than the total of respondents, since there are a few multiple answers.

TABLE 13

Party preference of manual respondents who describe themselves as 'middle-class'; by definitions of the 'middle class'.

	non-manual workers	'between top and bottom'	actual manual occu-pation	'rich'	personal criterion of ap-proval	middle-class style of life	other	don't know
	%	%	%	%	%	%	%	.%
Conservative	47	28	22	37	43	47	33	11
Liberal	14	17	11	17	21	25	16	26
Labour	23	38	56	33	25	22	33	42
Don't know *or* refuse	16	17	11	13	11	6	18	21
Total	100%	100%	100%	100%	100%	100%	100%	100%
	(N=49)	(N=42)	(N=18)	(N=24)	(N=82)	(N=36)	(N=49)	(N=19)

These figures confirm that those who mean workers in manual occupations when they speak of the 'middle class' must be excepted from any generalization about the connection between Conservatism and self-rating. They are, indeed, just as likely to be Labour supporters as those manual respondents who described themselves as 'working-class'. It is equally noticeable that those who did not know what they meant by their self-rating are least likely to be Conservatives. Their support for the Liberals may further imply that they feel poised, as it were, on the upper edge of the 'working class'; but they must in any event be excepted also from the generalization. The third group among whom support for Labour is higher than support for the Conservatives is the group whose definition of the middle class was more or less literally 'middle'. This is the most puzzling finding. Further analysis shows that a big difference is made by age: those under 50 in this group are 6% likelier to be Conservative than Labour supporters, while only those aged 50 or more are nearly three times as likely to be Labour as Conservative. In addition, it is worth remembering that this category includes many definitions of the 'middle class' which imply a low 'middle'— perhaps just above the poor or unskilled working class. It may be that young manual workers and their wives who think of themselves as 'in the middle' mean by this something nearer to the non-manual stratum than their elders do. But the evidence is too slender to support any great weight of speculation. It can only be said that this group, too, must be excepted from the unqualified generalization.

The one other group whose middle-class self-rating does not show a preponderance of Conservative support is the group coded 'other'. This is not surprising, particularly since the coding category includes those who said that the difference is not a real one; but even so, the incidence of Conservative support is almost as high as for the total of manual respondents describing themselves as 'middle-class'. In all the remaining groups, the Conservatives clearly outnumber the Labour supporters. The margin is small among those whose definition of 'middle class' rested on money; perhaps these are people conscious of earning well who nevertheless retain a proletarian or trade-union loyalty. But among those giving a personal criterion, the margin is very substantial, and among those who referred to style of life or those who made an explicit reference to the non-manual stratum, the Conservative supporters outnumber the Labour supporters by more than two to one.

About a quarter, therefore, of the manual respondents describing themselves as 'middle-class' are no more likely to be Conservative than Labour supporters. But among the remaining three-quarters, the propensity to Conservatism is strong, and the pattern brought out by Table 13 does seem to confirm that the 'middle class' to which these people assign themselves is in some sense a normative reference group. This does not, of course, account for more than a section of working-class Conservatism. But the influence of self-assigned 'class' is unmistakable, and bears out the thesis that the way in which people see their location in the social hierarchy is, irrespective of the actual degree of inequality to which they are subject, a major influence on their propensity to radicalism.

Something more, however, still needs to be said about those manual workers and their wives who do not describe themselves as 'middle-class'. For this purpose, it may be rewarding to look at the answers which people gave when asked an open-ended question about their reasons for supporting the party of their choice. This may not only help to show in broad terms why working-class voters vote as they do. It may also show further differences according to self-rated 'class'.

The question was asked in two different forms, depending on whether the respondent had changed his political allegiance at all since 1950. Those who had not changed were asked 'Could you tell me the main reason why you have always supported the ——— party?' Those who had changed were asked 'Could you tell me the main reason why you changed?' Respondents too young to have voted were asked the first form of the question with 'support' substituted for 'have always supported'. The answers were not recorded in full, but were coded by the interviewers into nine categories constructed on the basis of the answers given in the pilot survey. Since the distribution of replies has a certain interest quite apart from the particular question of working-class Conservatism, the figures for the manual and non-manual respondents are shown in full in Table 14.

TABLE 14

Reasons for party preference; by occupational stratum.

	non-manual	manual
	%	%
Job, class or status	14	30
Habit, family or friends	15	20
Party's image as more competent to lead or rule	20	13
Party's other virtues or policies	31	21
Particular personal or family needs	5	7
Candidate	2	2
Would-be Liberal, but no candidate	2	3
Negative attitude to other parties	7	6
Time for a change	2	2
Other reasons	17	10
Don't know	9	10
Total	124%	124%
	(N=479)	(N=901)

It is clear from this table that manual workers and their wives tend to give reasons linked to their membership of a group of some

kind, whereas non-manual respondents tend to give more intellec-
tualized reasons. The pattern does not hold, however, among those
who have changed their political allegiance. There is virtually no
difference between the two strata among the quarter of the sample
who have changed, and the proportion of replies which had to be
coded as 'other' rises sharply. But this also means that among those
whose political allegiance has been stable, the pattern shown in
Table 14 holds even more strongly than appears there. Whatever
reasons may lie behind a change of allegiance, therefore, much of
the consistent Conservatism in the manual stratum must be based
on traditional or inherited loyalties which have outlasted the circumstances which gave rise to them. It may accordingly be useful
to see first of all what sort of reasons working-class Conservatives
give for their preference, and second whether this too is affected by
the introduction of self-rated 'class' into the analysis. Table 15
shows the distribution of the reasons most frequently given by
working-class Conservatives and working-class Labour supporters
according to their self-rating. The Liberals are not included in the
table, first because self-rating makes no difference to the kind of
reasons which they give, and second because their reasons differ
from those of Conservative or Labour supporters in just the way
that could easily be predicted: the party's virtues or policies, and a
negative attitude to the other two parties, are the commonest reasons
given by working-class Liberals, whether or not they describe themselves as 'middle-class'.

TABLE 15

Reasons for Conservative or Labour support;
manual respondents by self-rated 'class'.

	Conservative		Labour	
	self-rated middle	self-rated working	self-rated middle	self-rated working
Job, class or status	12%	5%	58%	54%
Habit, family or friends	20%	35%	25%	24%
Party's image as more competent to lead or rule	36%	27%	8%	4%
Party's other virtues or policies	29%	28%	19%	18%
	(N=109)	(N=100)	(N=96)	(N=336)

Several interesting differences emerge from this table. The largest
difference between Conservative and Labour supporters, irrespective

of self-rating, is on the first and third reasons. Although Conservatives describing themselves as 'working-class' are even less likely to give a 'job, class or status' reason for their choice than those describing themselves as 'middle-class', this kind of reason is, as one would expect, very much more frequent among working-class Labour supporters. Similarly, although Conservatives describing themselves as 'middle-class' are more likely to cite the party's qualities of leadership than are those who describe themselves as 'working-class', this kind of reason is given by hardly any working-class supporters of Labour. This last comparison is some measure of the Conservative Party's success in projecting itself as the party best fitted to exercise the duties of government. It may also furnish evidence for the extent to which working-class Conservatism is based on 'deference', if by 'deference' is meant a conviction that the leaders of a Conservative government will be endowed with superior qualities of leadership. But if this is so, it is significant that those who describe themselves as 'middle-class' are more likely, not less, to give a reason suggestive of 'deference' than are those who describe themselves as 'working-class'. This is further evidence that the connection between self-rating and vote cannot be explained by a simple division of working-class Conservatives into 'aspirers' and 'deferents'. But it does show how the success of the Conservative Party among a section, at least, of the manual stratum may be explained by the party's image as the party best fitted for government.

The one kind of reason, however, where the difference produced by self-rated 'class' is most noticeable and most suggestive is the reason shown as 'habit, family or friends'. Among Labour supporters, self-rated 'class' makes no difference at all to the frequency with which this reason is given. But among the Conservatives not only does self-rated 'class' make a difference of 15%, but this reason is more commonly given than any other by those who describe themselves as 'working-class'. This suggests that although a middle-class self-rating may predispose manual workers and their wives to Conservative support, the substantial proportion of those who think of themselves as 'working-class' and also support the Conservatives tend to do so out of inherited habit and primary group loyalty. There are many others, of course, who give reasons which are just as likely to be found among those who describe themselves as 'middle-class'; self-rating makes no difference to the frequency with which working-class Conservatives mention the party's policies as their reason for supporting it. But of the 16% of manual workers and their wives describing themselves as 'working-class' who support the Conservatives, over a third do so for a reason which the interviewers were able to code as 'habit, family or friends'. 35% of 16% is only a small percentage of the working-class electorate. But it is worth remembering that many more manual workers and their wives describe themselves as 'working-class' than as 'middle-class', so that in absolute numbers those who describe themselves as 'working-class' are as important a constituent of the Conservative vote as those who describe themselves as 'middle-class'. It is likely that a wide variety of influences underlies the ostensible reasons given for party preference. The working-class Conservatives coded under 'habit, family or friends' may be responding to any or all of the influences such as father's occupation, or religious affiliation, or local or regional tradition which have already been shown to have an independent effect on the likelihood of Conservative support. But they have in common that although they think of themselves as 'working-class', they nevertheless have a loyalty to the Conservative Party outside of either 'class' or opinions on particular issues of policy.

One further source of evidence remains in the pattern of changes of political allegiance. I have said that the reasons given for changing were found to be very various—indeed, they account for most of the responses shown under the category of 'other' in Table 14. But however diverse the reasons given, the changes can still throw some light on the extent and nature of working-class radicalism as reflected in party choice. The high level of Liberal support may be symptomatic only of short-term dissatisfaction with one or other of the major parties. But this in itself helps to provide evidence for the way in which voters may be willing to change their allegiance and, in particular, the extent to which working-class loyalty to either the Conservative or Labour Party may be only a conditional one. Table 16 gives a breakdown by self-rated 'class' of all the changes in party preference reported by manual respondents, excluding those before 1950 and covering only the most recent changes by those who may have changed several times within the period. The table is not, given the questions used, a picture of the changes in the working-class vote between any one time and 1962. It is only a picture of the extent to which the pattern of party support at the time of the survey represents a change from some previous allegiance. The six working-class voters who did not assign themselves to either class are excluded from the table: four of them were changers, and one refused to give a party preference. I have also excluded the seventeen who assigned themselves to one or other 'class' but refused to give their party preference. In view of the very small numbers in some of the categories of change, the changers are shown as percentages to one decimal place.

TABLE 16

Changes in party support; manual respondents by self-rated 'class'.

	self-rated middle	self-rated working
	%	%
Lib.–Cons.	·3	1·2
Lab.–Cons.	3·1	1·8
D.K./None–Cons .	·7	·3
Cons.–Lib.	9·0	4·1
Lab.–Lib.	4·1	5·9
D.K./None–Lib.	·7	·8
Cons.–Lab.	3·3	2·2
Lib.–Lab.	·3	·5
D.K./None–Lab.	·3	·7
Cons.–D.K./None	3·7	1·5
Lib.–D.K./None	0	·2
Lab.–D.K./None	2·3	2·5
D.K./None–Other	0	·2
No change	72·2	78·1
	100·0%	100·0%
	(N=299)	(N=597)

The predisposition to Conservatism among those who describe themselves as 'middle-class' is borne out by the higher frequency of changes to the Conservatives shown here, particularly for previous Labour supporters. But although those who describe themselves as 'middle-class' are more likely to be converts to Conservatism, they are also more likely to be defectors from it. The net loss to the Conservatives is larger, and the net loss to Labour smaller, among them than among those who describe themselves as 'working-class'. Among the latter, the net loss to the Conservatives is only 4·5%, as against 10·9% for those describing themselves as 'middle-class'. Among those describing themselves as 'middle-class', therefore, Conservative support is more easily abandoned as well as more easily gained. The self-styled working-class voters, on the other hand, seem to be stauncher Conservatives if they are Conservatives at all—a result which seems entirely consistent with the finding that they are more likely to give 'habit, family or friends' as their reason for being Conservatives.

It might be suggested that the most important influence is still income. Perhaps the more prosperous manual respondents are not only more likely to think of themselves as 'middle-class' but more likely, if they are also Conservatives, to be loyal Conservatives. A further breakdown, however, shows that this is not so. The manual respondents in the top third of incomes—almost all of whom are under 50, so that their changeability or consistency cannot be attributed to old age —bear out the differences found among the manual respondents as a whole. A corollary of these differences is that if those who had ever been Conservatives since 1945 are added to those who were Conservatives at the time of the survey, then the difference between the manual respondents describing themselves as 'middle-class' and those describing themselves as 'working-class' becomes even more pronounced. But while the significance of self-rating is thus confirmed still further, it is an important qualification to it that those who describe themselves as 'middle-class' are more often conditional Conservatives. They are not yet so far assimilated to middle-class norms as to feel a fraternalistic loyalty to the non-manual stratum and the party of its traditional interests. Just as analysis of the meaning of self-rating showed that it need not signify an assimilation to the non-manual stratum, so an analysis of changes in party support shows that working-class Conservatives who think of themselves as 'middle-class' need not have come to share the sort of convictions held by the solid majority of the non-manual Conservative vote. What is clearly true, however, is that the perception which manual workers and their wives have of their position in the social hierarchy is closely bound up with their political preferences. Whatever different things are meant by manual workers or their wives who describe themselves as 'middle-class', the majority of them mean something which can be construed as a sense of being different from the traditional proletarian. These people are not only more than twice as likely to be Conservative supporters as manual workers and their wives who describe themselves as 'working-class'; they are more likely to be Conservative than Labour supporters even at a time when the Liberals, who were drawing more from the Conservatives than from Labour, were at their strongest. The choice of reference group has a consistent and unmistakable effect on the frequency of working-class support for the Conservative party.

Two final questions which were included in the survey shed a little further light on the relation between self-rating and party support. After they had been asked their main reason for their party preference, respondents were asked first, whether they thought that other people like themselves voted the same way, and second, what sort of people they thought voted for each of the three parties. When the answers of the working-class Conservatives are analyzed by self-rating, it turns out that those who describe themselves as 'middle-class' are twice as likely to think that 'others like themselves' vote the same way than those who describe themselves as 'working-class'. Labour supporters, by contrast, are likelier, as one would predict, to think that others like themselves vote as they do if they describe themselves as 'working-class'. It is unfortunate that, as I have earlier described, the follow-up question designed to discover what sort of people were meant was not sufficiently well formulated for reliable conclusions to be drawn from it. But even without this, the figures shown in Table 17 further confirm the suggestion that middle-class self-rating corre-lates with working-class Conservatism because it is a normative reference group. Those who describe themselves as 'middle-class' are clearly aware of assigning themselves to a group in which Con-servative support is the norm.

TABLE 17

'Do you think that most people like yourself vote the same way as you, or do you think they vote differently?'; manual respondents by self-rated 'class' within Labour and Conservative support.

	Conservative		Labour	
	self-rated middle	self-rated working	self-rated middle	self-rated working
	%	%	%	%
Same	40	20	56	62
Differently	42	55	34	24
Don't know	18	25	10	14
Total	100%	100%	100%	100%
	(N=109)	(N=100)	(N=96)	(N=336)

Still further confirmation is furnished by the answers to the ques-tion 'In general, what sort of people do you think vote for the Con-servative (Liberal, Labour) party?' The coding categories used for Conservative supporters included one defined as 'high status, edu-cation' and explicitly distinguished from the category of 'job, class, "rich".' This category of reason was mentioned noticeably more often by those working-class Conservatives who described them-selves as 'middle-class'. Furthermore, the working-class Conserva-tives who described themselves as 'middle-class' were more likely to give as their image of Labour supporters answers which were coded under the heading 'low status, uneducated'. This second difference, however, although it is what one would predict, is not a large one. The two most suggestive differences in Table 18 are first, the difference in the frequency with which Conservatives refer to 'high status, education' and second, the difference in the frequency with which the 'new working class' is cited. These two differences not only suggest more fully the importance of considerations of both status and 'egoistic' achievement in the working-class Conservatism with which a middle-class self-rating is correlated. They also confirm that those working-class voters who do not share the middle-class self-rating which would predispose them to Conservatism are, if they are Conservatives at all, Conservatives who see the party and their support for it in somewhat different terms from those who describe themselves as 'middle-class'. Some of the totals in Table 18 are more than 100% even though the least frequently cited categories of reply have been excluded; the reason for this is that a considerable number of respondents gave a multiple response.

TABLE 18

Image of supporters of (1) Conservative and (2) Labour Parties; manual respondents, by self-rated 'class' within Labour and Conservative support.

		Conservative		Labour	
		self-rated middle	self-rated working	self-rated middle	self-rated working
(1)	Job, class, 'rich'	54%	51%	82%	76%
Conservative	Supporters of policy	7%	7%	2%	2%
Party	High status, education	39%	27%	10%	13%
	'New' working class	27%	15%	5%	6%
		(N=109)	(N=100)	(N=96)	(N=336)
(2)	Job, class, 'workers'	58%	61%	89%	87%
Labour	Supporters of policy	4%	3%	4%	11%
Party	Low status, uneducated	23%	18%	*	2%
		(N=109)	(N=100)	(N=96)	(N=336)

*=2 people

This analysis of working-class Conservatism cannot explain more than in part the working-class vote, nor can it furnish a complete account of how far the working-class vote is symptomatic of a discrepancy between inequality and grievance. But the demonstrable influence of self-rated 'class' has definite implications for both questions. Manual workers and their wives who describe themselves as 'middle-class' and attach some orthodox meaning to this are consistently likelier to support the Conservative Party; the self-rating is to some degree at least a normative reference group, with the result that it leads them to support the political party to which their interests as proletarians are conventionally opposed. Those who think of themselves as 'working-class', by contrast, are much less likely to support the Conservatives; if they do, it is often for reasons which conflict with their position of inequality only in the slightly special sense that they are not much concerned about it. Their acquiescence in the system of inequalities in which they are among the less well placed is most often an acquiescence of tradition and habit.

If, therefore, it is legitimate to see working-class Conservatism as implying some discrepancy between inequality and relative deprivation, and if, in addition, there are good grounds for looking at it in terms of the notion of reference groups, then the answer appears to fall in two distinct parts according to the normative reference group chosen. The particular reasons which lie behind individual Conservative votes may, as I have stressed, be remote from reference group choices. As well as local or familial custom, there are also the particular matters of policy which are given as reasons by respondents themselves and which—whatever social or historical influences may at the same time be at work—there is no warrant to disbelieve. A man who says, as did one manual worker in the sample, that he supports the Conservatives because Labour 'let the blacks in', may be psychologically predisposed to adopt right-wing attitudes; some working-class Labour supporters, after all, feel strongly against coloured immigrants but do not therefore abandon their support for Labour. But where a man changes his vote over a particular issue of policy, it is still fair to regard this as his reason, whatever earlier influences might underlie his response to the particular issue. Party support cannot be simply explained in terms of the social attributes or reference group choices which are shown to correlate with it. But when a whole stratum of the national population is analyzed in the aggregate, it is fair to draw certain conclusions about purely social influences; and this analysis does appear to demonstrate one, at least, of the ways in which the choice of reference groups helps to explain the relation between relative deprivation and inequality in the particular political circumstances of mid-twentieth-century Britain.

X

REFERENCE GROUPS AND INEQUALITIES OF CLASS

THE analysis of survey evidence on relative deprivation of class is in principle straightforward. If, for example, people are asked who (if anyone) they think of as better off than themselves, this information can then be related to the extent of their own wealth and the wealth of the comparative reference group which they have given. There are not the difficulties which bedevil even ordinal comparisons of status, and the actual discrepancy between inequality and relative deprivation can be expressed in quantitative terms. In practice, however, the procedure is less simple. Many people will not say, or even do not know, what their own incomes, or their husbands' incomes, are; other sources of wealth, including not only personal assets but expectations from other members of the family or household, ought properly to be taken into account; and there are arguments for saying that even if incomes can be reliably ascertained, they are not the best of several possible measures of class-situation. I have used people's stated incomes (or, in the case of married women, their husband's income) rather than household income or sub-category of occupation, as my criterion. But some slightly more detailed account of the procedure of analysis is needed.

The manual stratum is sometimes analyzed in sample surveys by being broken down into the skilled and the unskilled, or the skilled, the semi-skilled and the unskilled. These distinctions are certainly a significant aspect of class-situation; but for the present purpose comparative incomes are of more direct interest, and these can be assumed more or less to reflect the differences of class engendered by differences of skill. The total sample, manual and non-manual included, was subdivided into three levels of stated income (or husband's income) after deductions: £10 a week or less; between £10 and £15; and over £15. This subdivision makes possible not only a threefold comparison within each stratum, but also a cross-comparison between members of the two strata at the same level. Three difficulties remain, however: first of all, a considerable minority of the sample could not or would not answer the question about incomes; secondly, neither capital assets nor differences in household per capita incomes are taken into account; and thirdly, what people say to interviewers may be very dubious evidence as to their actual incomes. Even where detailed surveys directed to this sole purpose are carried out it is impossible to be sure of the figures given. There is a known tendency for respondents to understate their incomes, and the different meanings which 'income' can have to different respondents can only be elucidated by intensive and laborious questioning. The form of question used in the present survey was 'Could you give me an idea roughly how much you (your husband) earn(s) each week after deductions?' At the same time as asking this question, the interviewer was instructed to hand the respondent a card on which a range of incomes were printed, rising by intervals of £2 10s. This is obviously unlikely to yield entirely accurate answers; the wide variety of possible sources of income, the ignorance of wives or even husbands themselves (such as small shopkeepers) as to their net weekly revenue, the fluctuations of certain kinds of income and the possible ambiguity of 'deductions' all combine to make the answers only indifferent evidence for the actual distribution of post-tax incomes.

For the purpose of assessing relative deprivation, however, people's estimates of their incomes are if anything more important than their actual incomes; and the ordinal accuracy, at least, of the replies is borne out by the fact that on questions which should be most obviously expected to show a correlation with income, the expectation is vindicated. Provided that the understatement of incomes is a consistent tendency throughout the sample, the accuracy of the figures stated is unimportant. It therefore seems legitimate to use the answers to this question as an independent variable in analyzing the replies to the questions. This must exclude those who, for whatever reason, gave no answers about income. But with these reservations in mind, it may be useful to show the distribution of weekly incomes as stated by the 1087 respondents who gave an answer. In the subsequent discussion I shall refer simply to either 'high', 'medium' and 'low' or 'top', 'middle' and 'bottom' levels of income. But for what it may be worth, the actual distribution is shown in Figure 3.

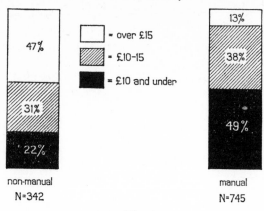

Fig. 3

The distribution shows a considerable overlap between the two strata, but the overlap is still far from being an equivalence. Roughly half of the manual respondents are in the bottom third of the overall distribution, while almost the same proportion of the non-manual are in the top third. Under a quarter of the non-manual are in the bottom third, and only just over an eighth of the manual are in the top third. The discrepancy becomes increasingly marked if we go higher up the scale of incomes. 26% of non-manual respondents said that their, or their husband's, income was over £20 a week; the figure for the manual respondents is 1·6%. Although the figure of £20 might be misleading, given the tendency to understate earnings, the relative proportions are a legitimate reminder that the earnings by some manual workers of up to £30 which are possible in certain industries do not constitute evidence for a large-scale redistribution of wealth. Furthermore, even if the two strata were closer in income than they are, there remains the important difference that many of the lower non-manual earners have expectations of a steady improvement in their incomes; as I have already remarked, this is true only of a handful of manual workers.

There are, however, two qualifications to be made which apply to both strata. The first is the poverty of the old; the responses given in the survey fully bear out the conclusion already cited that in contemporary Britain it is largely the old who are the poor. The second qualification is that in terms of money available to spend the prosperity of a person's household will often be a better measure of his situation than his personal income; even if he is the head of the household, it will make a good deal of difference if other members of it are also contributing earnings. The gain must of course be

190

looked at in proportion to the number of dependents, and working-class households are likely to have more children as well as to have more earners. But provided this also is kept in mind, it is worth setting household income beside personal income in sketching the outline of the relative economic position of the two strata. The distribution of responses to the question 'Could you give me an idea roughly how much money comes into the household per week after deductions?' is shown in Figure 4.

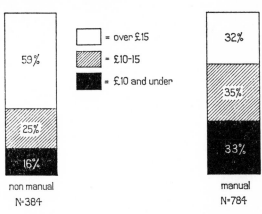

Fig. 4

When income is shown in this way by households rather than individuals, the relative gain of the manual stratum is noticeably greater. If we take incomes over £20 a week, the difference is even more striking. The proportion of non-manual respondents giving a household income over £20 is 36% (as against 26% of individuals); the proportion for manual respondents is 12% (as against 1%). As is known to be true in general, the number both of earners and of dependent children tends to be higher among the manual than the non-manual stratum. Of the 1069 parents in the sample, 35% of the manual respondents have three or more children under 15 compared to 24% of the non-manual, and 20% of the manual have four or more children under 15 compared with 10% of the non-manual. Out of the total of households, 10% of the manual have three or more children under 15 compared with 6% of the non-manual. The number of earners per household is also higher in the manual stratum: only 38% of manual households have only one earner as against 49% of non-manual, while the proportion with any greater number of earners is in each case higher in the manual stratum—there was even one manual household in the sample with six earners.

191

which none of the non-manual households had. Manual housewives are likelier by 11% to work either full or part-time—40% of the 451 working-class housewives in the sample were found to do so as compared with 29% of the 227 middle-class housewives. These figures may not be entirely reliable; but they serve at any rate to give some idea of the relative economic situation of the two strata as represented in the sample, and it is against this background that their relative deprivations should be considered. I shall discuss the replies to those parts of the questionnaire bearing on inequalities of class under three headings: first, relative deprivation of income; second, consumer goods; and third, attitudes to provision by the state.

INCOMES

A sequence of three questions was put to the respondents for the purpose of finding out their comparative reference groups on the topic of income: first, 'Do you think there are any other sorts of people doing noticeably better at the moment than you and your family?'; second (if the person had answered yes), 'What sort of people do you think are doing noticeably better?'; and third, 'What do you feel about this, I mean, do you approve or disapprove of this?' This sequence was chosen in order to tie the answers to people's own immediate situations and to exclude the sort of extravagant or fantastic replies which could not be interpreted as a genuine reference group. It might be thought that even with this wording, so many obvious answers would occur in people's minds that the question would produce long lists of the notoriously rich. Everyone knows, after all, that film stars and industrial tycoons are very much better off than themselves. But in fact, the replies offer ample confirmation that comparative reference groups are limited in scope. On the evidence of this question, relative deprivation is low in both magnitude and frequency even among those who are close to the bottom of the hierarchy of economic class. Over a quarter of the total sample said that there were no other sorts of people that they could think of as doing noticeably better than themselves and their families. The proportion rises, as one would expect, with income. But even in the bottom third of incomes, it is 18% (with an additional 19% of 'Don't Knows'); and in the manual stratum as a whole it is 27% (with an additional 14% of 'Don't Knows') as against 25% of the non-manual (with 14% of 'Don't Knows'). These figures are by themselves a demonstration of a considerable discrepancy between inequality and relative deprivation; and when income is held constant, a comparison of the two strata produces a result very much as the earlier historical discussion suggested. The figures are shown in full in Table 19.

TABLE 19

'Do you think there are any other sorts of people doing noticeably better at the moment than you and your family?'; by income within occupational stratum.

	non-manual			manual		
	high	medium	low	high	medium	low
	%	%	%	%	%	%
Yes	59	66	62	51	56	63
No	31	25	21	39	32	17
Don't know	10	9	17	10	12	20
Total	100%	100%	100%	100%	100%	100%
	(N=160)	(N=107)	(N=75)	(N=99)	(N=278)	(N=368)

At the bottom level of incomes, there is virtually no difference between the two strata. It is still remarkable that so many of the poor should be unable (or unwilling—in either event, their reticence is remarkable) to think of others who are doing better. But the difference between the two strata emerges only at the middle and upper levels of income. At the upper level, the difference is striking if only because the manual respondents who have reached it are nonetheless very much less rich than the non-manual who are shown in the same category. This comparison accordingly supports the argument that for manual workers to reach the top level of incomes will make them satisfied in terms of their traditional comparisons rather than heightening the frequency of relative deprivation among them. In the same way, the greater readiness with which non-manual respondents at the middle level of incomes named others as doing better than themselves suggests that even a modest affluence among manual workers and their wives tends to be seen in terms of traditional working-class comparisons and therefore to lead to a lower frequency of relative deprivation than among non-manual workers at the same level of income. But to interpret these figures more fully, it is necessary to discover who the 'other sorts of people' were who were cited by those who did think of at least some others as doing noticeably better than themselves. Among those who did express a sense of relative deprivation, what was the magnitude of it?

The question used was an open-ended one, and the coding therefore calls for some comment.[1] The replies of particular interest to the argument were those which were explicitly tied to people in either the manual or the non-manual stratum. If my earlier argument is correct, then manual respondents should have in mind

[1] Some further details are given in Appendix 4.

other manual workers more often than non-manual, even though the incomes which are higher than their own occur more often, and are more likely to be very much higher, among the non-manual stratum. This expectation is borne out by the answers given. But the answers most often given by the sample as a whole were references which were not explicitly tied to one stratum or the other. The category shown in Table 20 as 'Higher earnings, etc.' is the general category used for responses of this kind. It covers a diversity of replies, ranging from people with less dependents to people in more prosperous industries to people with unspecified 'better jobs'. They all, however, have in common that the point of the comparison made did not derive from the fact that the reference group was on one side or the other of the manual/non-manual line. Almost all of them imply a comparison close to the actual situation of the respondent. None could be termed in any sense 'class-conscious', and most of them suggest or, sometimes, directly state a comparison based on a particular feature of the respondent's personal situation.

A few direct quotations may bring out both the flavour and the range of the replies coded under this heading. 'People with no children', said a woman with four of them. 'Where there is a man working in the family', said an unmarried woman. 'People who get extra money by letting off part of the house', said an 82-year-old widow. 'Army officers retiring since I did', said a retired army officer. 'People that have good health and are able to be in full time work', said a retired draper. 'People on night work,' said a 63-year-old brazier in the engineering industry, 'I have now had to do day work—I'm getting old.' 'People farming in a bigger way who can get subsidies', said a smallholder, 'I don't have enough acreage to be entitled to any.' 'University research people who went into research instead of teaching', said a schoolteacher's wife.

These replies all relate directly to the immediate position of the respondent, and although they may apply only within one or other stratum this is not the point of the comparison as stated. The answers coded under this heading do, however, shade over into references to occupations where a less personal comparison is implied but where it is unclear whether the respondent has members of the manual or the non-manual stratum in mind. It might have been legitimate to code some of these as either manual or non-manual— for example, a gardener's wife who referred to 'factory people' probably had works, not staff, in mind—but where the reference seemed to be to people in other industries rather than in manual or non-manual jobs as such, they were assigned to 'higher earnings, etc.' This category therefore includes, for example, a grocer's wife who said 'people working in government offices and factories—they get far more money and better hours,' or a joiner who said 'people in the motor-car industry like mechanics, manufacturers etc.', or a bus-driver who said 'people in key jobs in factories down the road'. Some of the replies coded into the other categories could also be interpreted as referring only to the manual or the non-manual stratum: for example, a retired shipping clerk who cited those who had paid in to their firms for a retirement pension presumably had fellow clerical workers, not dockers or seamen in mind. He was, however, coded under the heading of 'welfare beneficiaries' on the grounds that this represented his choice of reference group better than the occupational stratum to which those whom he had in mind in fact belonged. In the same way 'other farmers', when said by a poultry farmer's wife, was coded with 'higher earnings etc.'; but if a factory worker had said simply 'farmers', his reply would have been coded under 'non-manual'.

The distinction is not always easy to draw, and the percentages for the 'higher earnings etc.' category in Table 20 must therefore be regarded as less strict than those shown for questions answered by 'yes' or 'no'. All the answers to this question were, however, individually examined, and the distribution shown in Table 20 is certainly accurate enough to support the argument which follows. Double codings were permitted, but were rarely used. One or two of the more sophisticated respondents gave what amounted to a list of others doing better: a schoolteacher in a secondary modern school cited 'People on expense accounts, professionals with their own practice, shopkeepers, personnel engaged on important industrial work with wives working, newspapermen, publishers, airline pilots'. A solicitor in his early forties listed 'More senior people in professions, professional footballers, judges, television and radio stars, cabinet ministers'. But replies like these were exceptional. Almost all the answers given were short, and most of them suggested limited comparisons which could be directly related to the respondent's personal situation. The full distribution of replies under the codings used is shown below.

The most interesting figures are those for the frequency of references to the non-manual stratum. Not only is such a reference considerably likelier among non-manual than among manual respondents, but the manual respondents are less likely to refer to the non-manual stratum than to their own. If it is true that reference groups tend to be closely circumscribed at all levels of society except under some abnormal stimulus, then this is just what one should expect. But it affords a striking demonstration of the way in which the narrow scope of comparison produces a discrepancy between

TABLE 20

'What sort of people do you think are doing noticeably better?';
by occupational stratum.

	non-manual %	manual %
Higher earnings (including less dependents, more earners in household, opportunities for overtime, more prosperous industries, etc.)	31	39
Non-manual job or class	33	19
Manual job or class	22	25
Friends, neighbours, town or country dwellers	2	2
Specific age group	3	2
Welfare beneficiaries (including paying less tax, retirement pension, family allowances, etc.)	3	2
Educated (including professionally qualified) people	2	4
Everybody else	3	4
Other	4	6
Don't know	4	4
Total	107% (N=304)	107% (N=517)

relative deprivation and inequality. Given the actual distribution of wealth, the answer to the question which would most obviously and naturally accord with the facts of inequality would be a reference by both manual and non-manual workers to those in business or the professions. Although a few manual workers are earning more than some non-manual, the incomes of very many members of the non-manual stratum are far above those of even the most prosperous manual workers. But when asked a question directly tied to inequalities of class, few members of the manual stratum drew a comparison from the other side of the manual/non-manual line. Even if some of those listed under 'higher earnings, etc.' could have been coded as referring by implication to members of the non-manual stratum, less than a quarter of manual respondents, at most, could be described as choosing a specifically non-manual reference group; and this quarter is a quarter of those who were able to name any sort of people as doing noticeably better than themselves—that is, a quarter of only 56% of the manual stratum.

When self-rated 'class' is introduced into the analysis, it makes no difference. A difference is, however, made by income. The likelihood of a reference to the non-manual stratum by manual respondents rises markedly with income; at the bottom level, it is roughly half what it is at the top. This at the same time confirms that reference groups tend to be chosen from close to people's own situation and offers further evidence for the width of the discrepancy between relative deprivation and inequality among the poor. Accordingly, those at the bottom level of incomes are more likely to see some other group as doing better than themselves; but if they do, this comparative reference group is seldom drawn from the non-manual stratum. Those at the top level, by contrast, are more likely to cite members of the non-manual stratum if they cite anybody; but they are the least likely to cite anybody at all.

When those who did see some other sort of people as doing better were asked whether they approved or disapproved of this, there was a slight but interesting difference between manual and non-manual respondents. The proportion coded as 'indifferent' or 'don't know' was almost identical in each stratum. But the non-manual respondents were not only more likely to see some other group as doing better, but more likely, if they did so, to disapprove: 28% of the non-manual respondents expressed disapproval as against 23% of manual. The difference is not a very large one, but it is interesting that there should be a difference in this direction at all. It, too, is unaffected by self-rating. An egalitarian sense of grievance among manual workers and their wives seems to be inhibited not only by circumscribed reference groups but by the lack of intensity with which a relative deprivation of class, if any, is felt. A possible explanation of this might be that middle-class people are more likely to feel that their particular situation is worsening, and this in turn predisposes them to disapproval of others. But although those who thought that they and their families were 'worse off than a year ago' were indeed found to be likelier to disapprove of others, the frequency of disapproval remained higher among non-manual than manual respondents. Irrespective of whether or not they feel that their own position is worsening, middle-class people are more likely to feel the prosperity of others as a grievance.

The frequency of disapproval has, however, little meaning by itself until it is related to the categories of people for whom it is felt. If the comparisons made by the two strata are as I have suggested, references to manual workers will be commoner among manual than non-manual respondents but disapproving references to manual workers will be commoner among non-manual than manual respondents. This expectation is borne out by the figures shown in Table 21. When incomes are introduced into the analysis, manual respondents at the top level of incomes are more likely to express disapproval than those at the middle or bottom. Since this group is at the same time the likeliest to refer to non-manual workers, it might appear that among the most prosperous manual workers and their wives there is, after all, a good deal of disapproval extending

197

across the manual/non-manual line. But in fact, a further break-down shows that those who expressed disapproval and those who made a reference to non-manual workers are not to any significant extent the same people. Even at the top of the manual stratum, disapproval does not extend across the manual/non-manual line to the extent that it does among non-manual respondents who are thinking of manual workers. The kinds of references made to either manual or non-manual workers by members of the two strata are shown below. Perhaps the most remarkable feature of the table is that the disapproving references by manual workers to non-manual are the smallest single category of all.

TABLE 21

Manual or non-manual references; by disapproval or approval/indifference within occupational stratum.

	non-manual		manual	
	approve or indifferent	dis-approve	approve or indifferent	dis-approve
Non-manual reference	36%	24%	21%	15%
Manual reference	16%	37%	24%	32%
	(N=205)	(N=85)	(N=378)	(N=117)

The spontaneous comparisons which people make, however, may not show at all the same pattern as the answers which they give when specific comparisons are put to them. The comparative reference groups spontaneously given have shown first, that there is a wide discrepancy between relative deprivation and inequality; second, that those at the top of the manual stratum are least likely of all to think of any other sorts of people as doing better; and third, that disapproval, and particularly disapproval of manual workers seen as doing better, is more frequent in the non-manual stratum than the manual. But what happens when people are directly asked whether they think that manual workers are doing better than white-collar and whether they think that manual workers ought to be doing as well as they are?

Certain differences between manual and non-manual respondents are readily predictable—the manual respondents will surely be less likely to think that manual workers are doing better, and more likely to think that they ought to be doing at least as well as they are. It can also be safely predicted that age will make a difference to these attitudes—older manual workers and their wives will be less likely than younger ones to think that manual workers ought to be doing as well as they are. Both these expectations are confirmed by the survey; the actual figures are only interesting in that over half the manual respondents agreed that 'manual workers are doing much better nowadays than white-collar workers'. This finding provides abundant confirmation of the way in which this comparison has helped to diminish the relative deprivation felt by manual workers. But what is less predictable is the influence of income and of self-rating.

The two questions used were as follows: first, 'Some people say that manual workers are doing much better nowadays than white-collar workers. Do you think this is so or not?'; and second, 'Do you think that manual workers ought to be doing as well as they are doing compared with white-collar workers?'. When the answers of the manual respondents are more closely analyzed, three interesting differences emerge. First of all, self-rating makes a sizeable difference on the first question, but hardly any at all on the second. Second, the relation with income is uniform only on the first question, and then only among those describing themselves as 'middle-class'. Third, those least likely to agree that manual workers are doing much better nowadays than white-collar workers are those manual workers and their wives who are at the middle level of incomes and who describe themselves as 'working-class'. These results are at first sight puzzling. We saw earlier that self-rated 'class' made no difference to the comparative reference groups spontaneously cited in answer to the open-ended question, and there was, on my argument, no reason to expect it to do so. But when people are asked a question in general terms about the relative prosperity of manual and white-collar workers, it is perhaps more likely that self-rating will have the sort of influence that it did on party choice. A manual worker who is self-consciously 'working-class' is not more likely to see others as doing better, or to disapprove of them if he does. But he is more likely to think that manual workers in general are not doing 'very much better nowadays' than white-collar workers.

Almost two-thirds of manual workers and their wives describing themselves as 'middle-class' agreed that manual workers are doing much better than white-collar, and this proportion is exactly the same among those of the non-manual stratum who described themselves as 'working-class'. Of manual respondents describing themselves as 'working-class', however, under half agreed that manual workers are doing much better. The difference holds good at all three levels of income, and particularly at the top. Of manual workers and their wives at the top level of incomes, 78% of those describing themselves as 'middle-class' agreed that manual workers are doing much better. The figure for those at the same income level who described themselves as 'working-class' is 48%.

It is clear from this that relative deprivation of class of what I have called a fraternalistic kind can be strongly affected by the choice of normative reference group. But there is an important qualification to be made. Self-rating has almost no effect when manual workers and their wives are asked whether manual workers *ought* to be doing as well as they are by comparison with white-collar workers. On the question of party choice, I argued that the correlation with self-rating must not be interpreted to mean that manual workers and their wives who describe themselves as 'middle-class' have become wholly assimilated in political outlook to the non-manual stratum. In the same way, the figures in Table 22 make clear that a middle-class self-rating does not mean that manual workers and their wives will agree with the non-manual stratum about whether manual workers ought or ought not to be doing as well as they are. They may be less likely than those describing themselves as 'working-class' to express a relative deprivation on behalf of manual workers as a whole by comparison with white-collar. But they are hardly more likely to agree that manual workers ought not to be doing as well as they are; indeed, because of the higher proportion of Don't Knows among those who describe themselves as 'working-class', those who describe themselves as 'middle-class' are the more likely of the two to say positively that manual workers ought to be doing as well as they are. Table 22 thus shows both how much and how little the choice of reference group can affect the attitudes of manual workers and their wives to the relative position of manual and white-collar workers in the system of inequalities of class.

TABLE 22

(1) Agreement that manual workers are doing 'much better nowadays' than white-collar workers, and (2) assertion that they ought not to be doing as well as they are; by self-rated 'class' within occupational stratum.

	non-manual		manual	
	self-rated middle	self-rated working	self-rated middle	self-rated working
(1) Yes, doing better	72%	64%	64%	45%
(2) Should not be doing as well as they are	41%	25%	15%	12%
	(N=365)	(N=124)	(N=303)	(N=610)

It is not, perhaps, surprising that income should make no very marked or consistent difference to the answers to the question whether manual workers ought to be doing as well as they are. But it is interesting that on the question about how well manual workers are in fact doing, income makes a difference only among those manual workers and their wives who describe themselves as 'middle-class'. This suggests that those who describe themselves as 'working-class' are expressing a normative reference group which is sufficiently salient to override the effect which income might otherwise have on their propensity to agree that manual workers are doing much better than white-collar. It does not, as we have seen, affect the likelihood that they will be conscious of a comparative reference group such as would cause them to feel relatively deprived. References to either the manual or non-manual stratum are virtually the same whether manual respondents describe themselves as 'middle-class' or 'working-class'. But when a question is asked in general terms about the relative position of manual and non-manual workers, then self-rating makes an important difference. Even those at the top level of incomes who describe themselves as 'working-class' are less likely to say that manual workers are doing much better nowadays by comparison with white-collar workers than are those even at the bottom level of incomes who describe themselves as 'middle-class'.

Those at the middle level of income who describe themselves as 'working-class' are, however, of particular interest. This category of manual respondents shows less agreement that manual workers are doing much better than white-collar than does any other category once income and self-rating are held constant, including those who are poorer than they are but also describe themselves as 'working-class'. The difference is not overwhelming, and is partly explained by the old age pensioners who are at the bottom level of incomes. But it suggests a tentative conclusion which other tabulations seem also to bear out. Manual workers and their wives who have reached the top level of incomes are likely not to feel relatively deprived because in terms of the comparisons natural to them they have done well. Those at a slightly lower level of incomes, however, will be more likely to feel a relative deprivation in terms of what other manual workers have achieved; and if they think of themselves as 'working-class', they will be particularly likely to feel that manual workers in general are not doing all that well. They are, in a sense, the true 'fraternalists' of the manual stratum, for they are not only the likeliest to think that manual workers are not doing much better than white-collar; they are also the likeliest of those who describe themselves as 'working-class' to agree that manual workers ought to be doing as well as they are. Those who think of themselves as 'middle-class' are likelier at any level of income to agree that manual workers are doing much better than white-collar; but among those who think of themselves as 'working-class', those at the middle level of income are least likely to do so. The difference is not large but, as we shall see, there are other questions which suggest that manual workers and their wives at the middle level of incomes show a greater disposition than those at the top to aspirations of a fraternalistic rather than an egoistic kind. The figures for the question whether manual workers are doing 'much better' than white-collar are shown in Table 23.

TABLE 23

Replies to the suggestion that 'manual workers are doing much better nowadays than white-collar workers'; manual respondents by income within self-rated 'class'.

	self-rated middle			self-rated working		
	high	medium	low	high	medium	low
	%	%	%	%	%	%
Yes	78	63	57	48	41	49
No	20	28	31	41	43	33
Other	2	9	12	11	16	18
Total	100%	100%	100%	100%	100%	100%
	(N=41)	(N=101)	(N=91)	(N=56)	(N=176)	(N=276)

There is a further way in which relative deprivations of income may be elucidated, apart from either asking for spontaneous comparisons or testing reactions to a particular comparison which is suggested. Without being conscious of any particular comparison with another group, people may still feel relatively deprived by reference to what their own situation was or, perhaps, ought to be. This is bound to have a relation of some kind to what others are seen as getting; no one has an attitude about personal incomes in a vacuum. But if people are asked what they think is the proper standard of living for 'people like themselves', then this will furnish another and perhaps different conclusion about the relative deprivations of the different strata. It would obviously be foolish to ask 'How much more do you want?', for this does take the question out of any defined social context and into the realm of fantasy. But the gap between what people say they have and what they say they think would be proper for 'people like themselves' may be a better measure of the frequency and magnitude of relative deprivation than a question about others seen as doing better. The question used was worded as follows: 'What income do you think is necessary for you (your husband) in order to maintain a proper standard of living for people like yourself?'

It is often assumed by writers on the distribution of income or wealth that everyone always thinks that they ought to be given a little more than they have at the moment. 'In the American Dream', says Merton, 'there is no final stopping point. The measure of "monetary success" is conveniently indefinite and relative. At each income level, as H. F. Clark found, Americans want just about twenty-five per cent. more (but of course this "just a bit more" continues to operate once it is obtained)."[2] As it is put by Michael Young in his fantasy on *The Rise of the Meritocracy*, 'An early sociologist, a Professor Hobhouse, once stated a profound truth. *Question*: What is the ideal income? *Answer*: 10% more than you've got.'[3] The notion that people's wants can expand indefinitely is not only to be found in both Marx and Freud; it is a good deal older even than Aristotle, who quotes from Solon to just this effect.[4] But in practice, there is a fair proportion of people who will give a desired income little or no higher than their actual income, and, as we shall see, an even higher proportion who will say that they are satisfied with what they are getting. The present question is not, any more than the question about incomes themselves, as reliable a guide as the table by itself might suggest. But when the answers to it are compared with incomes as stated, it is immediately apparent that people do not always think they ought to have a constant percentage more than they do.

The members of the sample for whom the calculation could be made fell fairly neatly into four categories.[5] 303 people said that they thought a proper income would be less than, as much as, or only up to 10% more than their stated earnings (and half of these gave a figure equal to their stated earnings); 329 people gave a figure 15% to 44% more; 281 people a figure 45% to 99% more; and 151 gave a figure twice as high or more. For the rest of the sample, unfortunately, the calculation could not be made, usually because the respondent's income was not known. But there are enough respondents in the first category, and the spread of the answers is sufficiently wide, for it to be clear that it would be a mistake to assume that people think they ought 'properly' to have more in any fixed ratio to what they say they do have. The answers may, of course, be taken as evidence for how far people understate their earnings; it may be naive to suppose that anyone will say that he ought to be getting less than he has. But the discrepancy is hardly less interesting if it arises partly because people are ashamed to say things in an interview which they fear will make them seem greedy; and it is certainly no less relevant to a comparison of the feelings of relative deprivation which the members of the two strata are willing to voice.

[2] Merton, *op. cit.*, p. 136.
[3] Michael Young, *The Rise of the Meritocracy 1870–2033* (London, 1958), p. 127.
[4] *Politics*, 1256b, 33–34.
[5] The frequency distribution is shown in Appendix 5.

If the argument so far advanced is correct, then the most satisfied group in either stratum—in the sense of this comparison—should be the manual workers and their wives who are in the top third of the overall income distribution. These people are likely to have retained working-class standards of income, and since they have done as well as anyone by these standards (but not so spectacularly well as to demolish them altogether) they will more often be content with their incomes than non-manual workers who may be earning a great deal more. We should therefore expect that a comparison between the manual and non-manual respondents at the top level of income will show that the manual workers are more likely to consider their earnings adequate for 'people like themselves', even though the actual earnings of the non-manual workers are considerably higher.

This expectation is confirmed by the responses. Out of the six categories which result from a breakdown by occupation and income, the manual respondents in the top third of incomes are those most likely to give as a 'proper' income a sum more or less equal to what they later say that they (or their husbands) are actually getting. In both strata, the high earners are very much likelier to do so than either the medium or the low earners; but the manual respondents at the top level are still more likely to do so than are the non-manual. The percentages are shown in Table 24.

TABLE 24

Proportion of respondents giving as a 'proper' income (or husband's income) a sum less than, equal to, or under 10% more than stated income; by income within occupational stratum.

	non-manual			manual	
high	medium	low	high	medium	low
43%	15%	12%	56%	26%	22%
(N=160)	(N=107)	(N=75)	(N=99)	(N=278)	(N=368)

A corresponding relationship holds for the percentage in each category giving as a 'proper' income double or more than double their (or their husband's) stated income. Only 2% of the high manual earners did so as against 4% of the non-manual, and more of the medium and low non-manuals also did so than of the medium and low manuals. But even if these figures are representative, they are likely to be misleading, since a much smaller absolute increase will be a percentage increase of 100% for those whose actual incomes are low. In any case, the numbers involved are very small. It is better to observe simply that within each third of the overall income distribution, manual respondents are considerably more likely than non-manual to give a 'proper' income more or less equivalent to what they say that they earn. This is, perhaps, a very obvious illustration of what the difference of standards and expectations between the two strata would lead one to expect. But it is noticeable that the manual respondents in the bottom third of the income distribution are likelier not only than their non-manual equivalents but even than non-manual respondents in the middle third of the distribution to say that they ought to be receiving little or no more than they are. The replies to this question, therefore, confirm the impression given by the answers about 'other sorts of people' doing better: measured either by cross-class comparisons or by reference to the 'proper' situation of the chosen membership reference group, the frequency of relative deprivation of income is lower at all three income levels among manual workers and their wives.

There is one final test, however, which needs to be applied before generalizing too freely. The three questions discussed all support the argument that the comparisons most natural to the different income groups within each stratum are such as to make prosperous manual workers least likely of all to feel relatively deprived. But a person may not think of others as doing better, or have any feelings about manual/white-collar differentials, or think a higher income necessary for a 'proper' standard of living for someone like himself, but still feel dissatisfied with his present earnings. Indeed, a further cross-tabulation shows that roughly a third of the manual respondents who see others as doing better and disapprove of this are still quite willing to express themselves satisfied with their own (or their husband's) income. A question worded in terms of satisfaction with income may not reveal at all the same differences between the two strata as a question where the propriety of particular standards has been deliberately introduced. With this in mind, respondents were also asked the question: 'Would you say you were satisfied with your (your husband's) present position as far as income is concerned?'

A comparison of the two strata on this different question does indeed reveal a different pattern from the answers to the question about other people. More non-manual than manual respondents said they were aware of others as doing better. But when asked a question in terms of satisfaction, fewer manual than non-manual respondents were prepared to express themselves satisfied with their (or their husbands') incomes. In both strata, the proportion is almost suspiciously high—57% of non-manual respondents and 55% of manual expressed themselves satisfied. Married women were particularly likely to express satisfaction, and this may well reflect a marital loyalty which inhibited them from expressing any dissatisfaction with their husband's income to an interviewer. But as before, it is the differences that are interesting, and the comparison with the result of the question about other people suggests that a further analysis is necessary. A slight difference is made by self-assigned 'class', in that manual workers and their wives who describe themselves as 'working-class' are less likely by 5% to express themselves satisfied. But the important difference is made by income. When income is introduced as an independent variable, it turns out that the greater frequency of satisfaction in the non-manual stratum is due entirely to the greater frequency of dissatisfaction among the large number of manual workers and their wives who are at the bottom level of incomes.

We have seen that on the question about other people doing better there was no difference between the two strata at the bottom level of incomes but a distinct difference at the middle and top levels. On the question about satisfaction with income, the direction of the relationship is actually reversed as income rises. At the middle level, and even more at the top level, manual respondents are more likely to express satisfaction, so that the prosperous manual workers and their wives do turn out once again to be the least aggrieved of all. But at the bottom level of incomes, the manual more often express dissatisfaction than the non-manual. The proportion satisfied is still remarkably high—of those who gave their or their husband's income as £10 a week or less, 47% of the manual and 56% of the non-manual nonetheless pronounced themselves satisfied. But the difference at the top level confirms the argument that here the traditional framework of working-class comparisons will produce a high frequency of satisfaction among manual workers and their wives. At the bottom level of incomes, by contrast, manual workers and their wives are just as ready to see others as doing better than themselves (even if these others are not drawn from the non-manual stratum), and they are readier still to express themselves dissatisfied with their incomes. The difference between them and the non-manuals is that the non-manuals are considerably likelier, as shown in Table 24, to say that the 'proper' standard of income for people like themselves is higher than what they are getting. When satisfaction, rather than propriety, is at issue, the distribution of replies at each level of incomes within the two strata is as shown in Table 25.

Those who expressed themselves dissatisfied with their present incomes were then asked the further question: 'Is that because the job you are doing (he is doing) is worth more pay, because you need more money, or for some other reason?'. Of the total in either stratum who had expressed themselves dissatisfied, 17%, of whom the great majority were at the bottom level of incomes, specifically

TABLE 25

Satisfaction with own or husband's present income;
by stated income within occupational stratum.

| | non-manual | | | manual | | |
| | high | medium | low | high | medium | low |
	%	%	%	%	%	%
Yes	63	50	56	72	57	47
No	37	50	41	27	41	51
Don't know	0	0	3	1	2	2
Total	100%	100%	100%	100%	100%	100%
	(N=160)	(N=107)	(N=75)	(N=99)	(N=278)	(N=368)

mentioned retirement and dependence on pensions as their reason.
Among the remainder, the non-manual were likelier by 6% than
the manual to give worth as their reason and less likely by 5% to
give need. This is not a large difference. But it is symptomatic of the
difference in norms and outlook between the two strata, and it suggests what might be a part of the reason why the answers of the
non-manual respondents more often implied not only an awareness
but a disapproval of others.

The questions asked about income, therefore, confirm the expectations suggested by the earlier discussion. Not merely are comparative reference groups among manual workers and their wives so far
restricted as to result in a marked discrepancy between relative
deprivation and actual inequality; their retention of working-class
standards of comparison means that manual workers and their
wives are consistently less likely to feel relatively deprived than are
non-manual workers and their wives who are earning the same (or
at the top level probably a great deal more). Only among the
poorest does this conclusion need to be qualified at all; and even
here, it can only be said that manual workers and their wives are
less often avowedly satisfied, not that they more often feel relatively
deprived.

It is not surprising that at the top level of incomes the standards
of non-manual workers should be very much higher. A wage that
would satisfy a skilled artisan is unlikely to satisfy a managing
director or a high court judge. But the relation between relative
deprivation and inequality is more complex than can be inferred
from this predictable contrast by itself. The survey not only confirms
that the comparative reference groups of the two strata are different.
It also confirms how many qualifications must be made to the
suggestion that prosperity has made manual workers and their wives
'middle-class'. Those few who are in the top third of the overall income distribution are, as we have seen, likelier than the less prosperous manual respondents to have members of the non-manual

stratum in mind. But even when they describe themselves as 'middle-class' and have, therefore, in some sense a different reference group from almost all of those who describe themselves as 'working-class', they are no more likely to see others as doing better. The influence of the reference group is strong only when they are asked whether they agree that manual workers are doing much better than white-collar; only then are those who think of themselves as 'working-class' very much less likely to agree. Without some external stimulus powerful enough to dislodge the hold of traditional standards of comparison, the relative deprivations of manual workers, including even the most prosperous, will derive from very different reference group comparisons from those of non-manual workers and their families. Only when we turn from inequalities of class to inequalities of status shall we see that the pattern of working-class attitudes is different and the influence of normative reference groups very much more strong.

CONSUMER GOODS

In order to find out about attitudes not merely to incomes but to the possession of particular goods, two lists of items were drawn up. The first covered seven obvious and tangible consumer goods: television, telephone, car, refrigerator, washing machine, record player and central heating. The second covered a range of items which it was thought might be more naturally regarded as a prerogative of non-manual households: a house owned (or being bought on mortgage), a fur coat ('for your wife'), foreign holiday travel, a spare bedroom for visitors, first class travel on trains and a private education for children. Respondents were asked first, if they had these items, second, whether they wanted them, third (on the first list only), whether they expected to get those they wanted 'in the next two or three years', and fourth, 'Do you think other people are managing to afford (any items not possessed but wanted)?' Those who answered yes to the last question were then asked the open-ended question, 'What sort of people are you thinking of?'

Actual possession of these goods is shown by the survey to be distributed much as other evidence, where available, suggests, and in a way which confirms the persistent difference in style of life between the manual and non-manual stratum even at the same level of stated income. Thus 80% of households in both strata were found to have a television set. A car, on the other hand, was owned by less than half as many of the manual as of the non-manual stratum, and the difference in the ownership of a telephone was greater still:

208

almost half of the non-manual households were found to have a telephone as against less than one in ten of the manual, and even manual workers at the top level of incomes were found to be less likely to have one than non-manuals at the bottom level. Similarly, three times more non-manual than manual respondents said that they had foreign holiday travel, and six times as many said that they had a private education for their children. These differences are enough by themselves to show that the assimilation of the two strata in style of life is far from complete. But what is more interesting for the present argument is the choice of comparative reference groups among two strata. Who do those who want these things see as having them?

The pattern of the wants themselves presents few surprises. Those who are least likely to want what they do not have are in general those at the bottom level of income in both strata. These people are likely to be the old, or else those in the poorest-paid manual jobs, and in either event few aspirations will seem feasible for them. This produces a marked discrepancy between relative deprivation and inequality, but its explanation is not difficult—there is nothing remarkable in discovering that old age pensioners do not want cars or spare rooms or foreign holiday travel. When a comparison is made between the manual and non-manual respondents, there are again some predictable differences: non-manual respondents who do not have a television set or a washing machine in their household are less likely to want one than manual respondents, whereas they are more likely to want central heating or a telephone. On most items, however, there is relatively little difference between the two. The same proportion of manual as of non-manual respondents without a car said that they would like one, and the difference for both a refrigerator and a record player was only 1%. The big difference between the strata appears when those who want one or more of the items on one or other of the two lists are asked who they think of as being able to afford them.

The way in which comparative reference groups are limited is already suggested by the answers given when those who said they wanted one or more of the items listed were asked whether they thought that 'other people' were managing to afford them. For example, 9% of the non-manual and 16% of the manual respondents who said they wanted foreign holiday travel, replied 'no'; 18% of the non-manuals and 30% of the manuals who said that they wanted a telephone, replied 'no'; and 53% of the non-manuals and 61% of the manuals who said that they wanted central heating, replied 'no'. On the face of it, it is at least as remarkable that there should be anyone answering 'no' to these questions as that there should be anyone saying that nobody else is doing better than themselves. It is one thing not to be able to say, when challenged, just who the thousands of people are who succeed in going abroad every year for their holidays; but to say that no other people are managing to afford to do so suggests an almost wilful ignorance. The numbers involved are small if taken as a percentage of the whole sample. But that there should be any such replies at all is a testimony to the way in which a sense of relative deprivation can somehow fail to be generated even where it would appear to be most appropriate. It is significant also that the percentages are higher among manual than non-manual respondents. The pattern of the differences is the same as on the general question about 'others doing better'. Not only are comparative reference groups not chosen in accordance with the facts of inequality, but such a correspondence with the facts is least likely of all among those who are in fact most unequally placed.

A possible explanation of the limitation of working-class reference groups might lie in the jealousy and resentment with which those trying to 'keep up with the Joneses' are sometimes alleged to view the acquisition by people like themselves of consumer goods. Just as very small differences within a family or a work-group are often more intensely felt than much larger differences outside, so it might be argued that manual workers and their wives who want the items listed are likely to have as a reference group the 'snobs' or 'big spenders' among their fellows whom they see as flaunting possessions which they do not really need and perhaps cannot really afford. This attitude certainly found expression in some of the interviews. Some respondents, particularly the older and poorer, gave answers of this kind, and made pejorative references to those whom they saw as trying to show off, or those who, they claimed, undertook heavy hire-purchase commitments at the expense of more important things. 'Those who are here today and gone tomorrow, who do not save', said a retired engineering worker. 'A lot of these council house people', said a police constable, 'they get the goods on H.P. . . . then when they're on strike, the goods go back.' 'People who think they have money but haven't', said a miner's wife. Other answers of a similar kind included, 'people who owe the lot—no pride', 'they have things that the neighbours have', 'put things in front of food and even children', and 'think that they're a bit above everyone else'. But the number of such answers was not large in the aggregate. The coding presented some difficulties, since not all references to hire purchase, for example, were pejorative, and references to people who had saved up to buy particular items of their choice had to be distinguished from answers in which people were seen as denying themselves or their families basic necessities in order to show off their possession of luxuries. But answers which implied status-seeking, or showing off, or buying what people could not properly afford, were given by only 8% of the manual, and 6% of the non-manual respondents who wanted one or more items on the first list which they saw other people as managing to afford.[6] On the second list, the proportion was smaller still: among manual respondents it was only 3%, and among non-manual as little as 1%. If, therefore, reference group comparisons among manual workers and their wives are limited in scope, it is not because of the frequency of jealousies of this kind.

The answers to these two questions were coded into approximately the same categories as the answers to the question about 'other people doing better'. There are, however, one or two differences. First of all, a number of respondents gave entirely unspecific references to people seen as having more money or higher incomes. Some of the answers to the general question about 'others doing better' were also rather vague; but to answer the question 'what sort of people are doing better than you?' by saying 'people with more money' is vacuous in a way that to say that people with more money are managing to go abroad for their holidays is not. On the two lists of goods, more than 10% of those who wanted one or more of the items gave an answer of this kind. Some of these answers implied a fairly restricted reference group—the phrase 'higher wages', for example, is suggestive of manual rather than non-manual employment; but any answer which was no more specific than this was assigned to the separate category headed 'more money, higher incomes etc.'.

The category of 'more earners, less dependents etc.' contains many answers identical with those given on the general question about 'others'. References to both husbands and wives going out to work were particularly common, but other references were to particular circumstances of work, or to health or age as a limitation on working capacity, or to the age or number of children. There was some overlap between references to children and references to people of a particular age: for example, middle-aged people were sometimes mentioned in a way which implied that their children were now grown up and therefore no longer a financial burden to them. In both the tables which follow, however, I have lumped together the references to age despite the fact that their implications may be very different. Sometimes the reference might be to people younger

---

[6] Cf. the finding of Willmott in Dagenham (*op. cit.*, pp. 98–100).

than the respondent who were seen as having fewer expenses or being less willing to save, while at other times it might be to older people who were seen as having no dependents or as having been able to save in the past. But the percentages were so small that it seemed sensible to add them together within a single joint category.

The list of codings for the table based on the second list contains one category—'very rich'—which does not correspond to any given for the first list. As might be expected, there were a few, although not many, respondents who regarded the items which they wanted from the second list as the prerogative of those at or near to the topmost levels of the social hierarchy. Answers assigned to this category included 'big business people', 'upper class', 'the wealthy people' and 'people like company directors and the big money men'. It was, however, extended to any answer which implied people richer than those coded in the ordinary way under 'non-manual job or class'. References to named sums of £2,000 a year or more were included, together with such unspecific but suggestive answers as 'people who've managed to reach a high income or inherited one' or 'high-ups' or 'people with money and position'. Even with this rather generous definition of 'very rich', only 4% of those in either stratum gave an answer which could be assigned to it. But, like the 'big spenders' or 'status-seekers', it is a category sufficiently distinguishable, and of sufficient interest, to be worth showing on its own.

One other of the smaller categories was slightly different for the two lists. The category entitled 'beneficiaries of welfare, etc.' on the first list includes people with subsidized rents or family allowances as well as people with expense allowances or remissions of tax. The two kinds of beneficiaries of the Exchequer are likely to be drawn from very different levels of the distribution of income or wealth. But there were so few of either that, as with the references to different age groups, it seemed sensible to lump them together. On the second list, however, the small percentage of non-manual respondents coded under 'less tax, expense accounts' all had in mind the sort of bounty from the Exchequer which is chiefly limited to non-manual workers and, as I earlier argued, is seldom considered at all by the great majority of manual workers and their wives.

The codings shown as 'other' include a wide variety of replies, some of which were odd or anomalous, but most of which referred to some category of people which was quite specifically defined but could not be assigned to one or another of the listed codings. Thus references to hire purchase which carried no pejorative or envious overtone are included among these, together with any replies to the effect that those managing to afford the items wanted are simply those who choose to spend their money in this way rather than another. Similarly, replies such as 'those who need these things', or replies linked to a particular item wanted, such as 'people with large houses' (in answer to the question about a spare room), were coded as 'other'. The remaining answers included such diverse replies as 'people who win money—football pools etc.', 'the ones who don't smoke or drink', 'the dark people', and 'catering people attached to the airways'—the answer given by a men's hairdresser who said he would like a fur coat for his wife.

The final category, which covers 'unspecified' as well as 'Don't know', includes those who either said directly that they did not know who else was affording what they wanted, or had no particular sort of person in mind. Thus a reply as vague as 'more people are these days' was included here, as well as 'all sorts' where no further indication was given of what 'sorts' might be meant. Where, on the other hand, there was a clear implication of people in all different grades of occupation the answer was assigned to the category of 'everybody, most people, anyone'. Obviously, those who say 'everybody', even if they do not add any qualifying phrase, are unlikely to have in mind literally everybody, including the old age pensioners and the unemployed. It therefore seemed legitimate to include under this heading those whose answers clearly excepted some people but nevertheless implied that most people in all classes were managing, in their view, to afford the items concerned. This category accordingly includes 'everybody who works', 'a general cross-section of the community', 'anybody except old age pensioners', '80% of the people in all grades', and 'all types of people, even lower working classes'. Only where 'all sorts' or 'all kinds' seemed to carry no implication of 'all classes' or 'all occupations' was it relegated to the 'unspecified' category.

The distribution of answers among the manual and non-manual respondents who both wanted one or more items on the first list and said that they thought that 'other people' were managing to afford them is shown in Table 26.

The remarkable feature of this table is the distribution of references explicitly made to the manual or non-manual stratum. The figures shown should be qualified to the extent that a wide variety of specific comparisons are included in them: the distinction within the manual stratum between skilled and unskilled is, as we have already seen, salient in the minds of many people on either side of it, and it is this comparison which underlies many of the references made by manual respondents to other workers in manual jobs. This is obviously a very different comparison from either that made by a farm labourer between himself and workers in factories or by a

TABLE 26

'What sort of people are you thinking of?' (as managing to afford items not possessed but wanted from first list of goods); by occupational stratum.

	non-manual %	manual %
'Status-seekers', 'big spenders', etc.	6	8
'More money', 'higher incomes', etc.	10	16
More earners, less dependents, etc.	13	16
Non-manual job or class	20	16
Manual job or class	20	27
Friends, neighbours, etc.	8	7
Everybody, most people, etc.	8	6
'Ordinary' people	2	1
'People like self'	4	2
Beneficiaries of welfare	2	2
Age groups	4	3
Other	10	8
Unspecified, Don't know	5	3
Total	112% (N=263)	115% (N=522)

clerical worker between himself and manual workers in general. In addition to this, some of the answers coded under these two headings were very general ones, including the phrases 'middle class' or 'working class' which, as has already been shown, may have a variety of meanings to different people. But these qualifications do not invalidate the conclusion to which the figures point. Manual workers and their wives who want one or more of the items listed are not only less likely than non-manual respondents to take a comparative reference group from the non-manual stratum; they are themselves much less likely to take a comparative reference group from the non-manual than from the manual stratum.

It is, perhaps, arguable that some of the answers given in terms of 'higher income' would turn out under further questioning to lead to a comparison with those very much richer. But against this must be set the likelihood that some of the answers coded under this heading, and many, or even the majority, of the answers coded under the heading 'more earnings, less dependents etc.', embody a comparison with people very close in class-situation to the respondent. A manual worker who replies 'where the wife goes out to work', is more likely to be thinking of workers in similar jobs to his own than clerical or professional workers, let alone big businessmen and company directors. The fact remains, moreover, that whatever might emerge out of the less specific answers under more detailed questioning, the answers spontaneously given were not direct references to those who are in fact most likely to be the possessors of the items on the list. The tendency for the comparative reference groups of manual workers and their wives to be restricted within their own stratum is once again borne out.

It is also noticeable that non-manual respondents are just as likely to mention manual as non-manual workers. It might be possible to argue that the frequency of references by manual workers and their wives to the households of other manual workers is explained by the fact that where several possible reference groups are possessors of the item desired, the group nearest to the respondent is the one most likely to be mentioned. But this clearly does not apply to non-manual workers and their wives. They must be well aware, after all, that even if some manual workers can now afford cars, or fridges, or record players there is at least as high a proportion of non-manual workers who do so. But although they are a little more likely to refer to the non-manual stratum than are manual workers and their wives, they are themselves just as likely to refer to the manual as to the non-manual stratum. This is an obvious discrepancy with the facts of inequality, but given the reasons which I have discussed for the likelihood of relative deprivation of class among the non-manual stratum, it is not to be wondered at. It may be true that only half as many manual as non-manual respondents were the possessors of cars at the time that the survey was conducted. But the awareness that there are some, and perhaps many, manual workers who are car-owners may make them the salient comparison in the mind of a non-manual worker who does not have a car, would like to have one, and is aware that it used to be the prerogative of non-manual rather than manual workers.

The items on the second list, however, are hardly likely to be thought by the members of either stratum to be as readily afforded by manual as by non-manual workers. Some respondents, indeed, specifically up-graded their answer within the same context: for example, an unskilled chocolate maker who cited 'people in engineering' as having the items on the first list cited 'managers in engineering' as having the items on the second. But even on the second list, the distribution of answers is unexpected. The proportion of manual respondents citing members of the non-manual stratum was only 4% more than the proportion citing members of the manual stratum, and 10% of the non-manual stratum gave an answer coded under the heading of 'manual job or class'. Often, foreign holiday travel was the item which respondents had particularly in mind. But although it is true that foreign travel is a luxury which has extended into the manual stratum since the Second World War, nonetheless, it, like all the items in the second list, is very

215

much more common among the non-manual than the manual stratum. If the answers given by the respondents in the survey are accurate, then in 1962 it was exactly three times more common in the non-manual than in the manual stratum, and even among those manual workers and their wives who had reached the top third of the income distribution, it was only 16%. Thus although the proportion of references to the non-manual stratum is higher than the proportion of references to the manual stratum among both manual and non-manual respondents, it is still remarkable that there should be as many references to the manual stratum as there are.

There is, it is true, the additional category of the 'very rich'; but, as I have already remarked, the number of answers which could be coded under this heading, even when generously defined, was very small. The answers given for the items on the second list do not show quite the same pattern of comparative reference groups as the answers given for the items on the first. But given a list particularly selected for items which could be naturally regarded as the prerogative of the non-manual stratum, the answers once again confirm the inhibition on such choices of reference groups as would correspond with the facts of inequality. The distribution of answers for the second list is shown in full in Table 27.

TABLE 27

'What sort of people are you thinking of?' (as managing to afford items not possessed but wanted from second list of goods); by occupational stratum.

	non-manual %	manual %
'Status-seekers', 'big spenders', etc.	1	3
'More money', 'higher incomes', etc.	8	15
More earners, less dependents, etc.	15	14
Non-manual job or class	32	25
Manual job or class	10	21
Friends, neighbours, etc.	6	6
Everybody, most people, etc.	7	2
'Ordinary' people	1	2
'People like self'	2	1
Less tax, expense accounts	3	0
Age groups	9	7
Very rich	4	4
Others	10	8
Unspecified, Don't know	5	5
Total	113%	113%
	(N=258)	(N=527)

216

There is no way of ascertaining in detail from the survey just what influences underlie this restriction of comparisons. If the normal response to economic inequality is to make comparisons only to those closest to oneself rather than to those by contrast with whom one is most unequally placed, then these results need, perhaps, no explanation whatever. But since it is clear that this is not universally true, the question remains to what extent and for what reasons reference groups are so restricted. A glance over the social history of Britain since 1918 reveals some, at least, of the reasons why on matters of economic class—but not status—there has not been a cumulative spiral of aspiration and prosperity since the collapse of the militant radicalism which followed the First World War. But the principal interest of the 1962 survey lies not in demonstrating what influences are at work—this must rest on the historical evidence for the period before the survey was taken—but in revealing to what extent the reference groups of the less well placed are limited in scope, unspecifically defined, and mildly expressed. Several different forms of question were used to elucidate the reference group comparisons made, and each served only to reinforce the same impression. Both the magnitude and frequency of relative deprivation among manual workers and their wives are very much lower than would accord with the facts of economic inequality. The lack of 'class-consciousness' which is sometimes attributed to the British working class is in this sense, at least, amply confirmed.

Indeed, the figures shown in the two tables relating to the posession of goods should be supplemented, like those relating to 'others doing better', by the figure shown earlier for the number of manual workers or their wives who do not feel relatively deprived at all. For the first list of items, only 16% of manual respondents made a specific reference to members of the non-manual stratum, and on the second list, the proportion was still only 25%. But to measure the frequency of relative deprivation felt by reference to the non-manual stratum among the manual respondents, it is necessary to take all of the manual respondents, including those who did not express a wish for any of the items listed. When this is done, the figures are as low as 9% on the first question, and (if the references to the 'very rich' are also included) 17% on the second.

Within the manual stratum, income does not affect the choice of reference groups in any consistent pattern. But when the further question was asked, 'Is there anything I haven't mentioned which you or your household particularly need?', the group least likely to answer 'no' in either stratum was found to be the group of manual workers and their wives at the middle level of incomes. The difference is not large—65%, as against 71% for those at the top level and 70% for those at the bottom—but it suggests a similar conclusion to the finding that those at the middle level were least likely to agree that manual workers were doing 'much better nowadays' than white-collar workers. None of the differences which are not uniform with income—where, that is, a higher percentage of those at the middle level give a particular reply than those at either the top or the bottom—are at all large. But if all the differences of 3% or over are looked at together, they seem to confirm the picture of this group as the 'fraternalists' of the manual stratum, who do not aspire in any sense to rise out of the working class but who do not yet have what they now see as attainable for manual workers as such. Within the manual stratum, those at the middle level of incomes are likelier than those at either the top or the bottom to have the following characteristics or attitudes: to say that they want or need something not mentioned on either of the two lists of goods; to think that manual workers are not doing 'much better' than white-collar workers; to be dissatisfied with their (or their husband's) present income on the grounds of being worth more pay; to think that manual workers ought to be doing as well as they are doing by comparison with white-collar workers; to want, if they do not have, a car, a refrigerator, ownership of a house, a spare room and foreign holiday travel; if assigning themselves to the 'working class' to define this by reference to manual work; to belong to a trade union; to think that the state should provide unemployment pay at full rate without a means test for as long as a man is unemployed; and to support the Labour Party. Given the inadequacy of the figures for the distribution of incomes, these differences cannot be pressed too hard. But they furnish a marked contrast to those results which suggest that where inequalities of status are at issue relative deprivation is more frequent among manual workers and their wives at the top level of incomes, and that this relative deprivation is of an 'egoistic' rather than a 'fraternalistic' kind. This, however, is to anticipate the argument. For the moment, the main conclusion to have emerged is the restricted and even illogical choice of comparative reference groups, particularly in the manual stratum, on matters of economic class.

PROVISION BY THE STATE

A third type of question was also asked to try to elucidate attitudes to economic inequality which are much less directly dependent on comparisons with other people, but can in a different way be suggestive of a resentment at the distribution of wealth or income.

People may feel strongly that their present position is inadequate not so much by direct reference to the situation of other groups as by reference to what they feel should be being done by the government for people like themselves. Such an attitude is likely to derive indirectly from a view of the relative position of others, for as I have already implied, no such attitudes exist in a social vacuum. A feeling that the government is doing too little for one sort of person almost always implies that it is doing too much for another. The form in which a belief of this sort is held, however, may well be such that it will emerge only in answer to a question about the actions of the government, and not in answer to questions about specific comparisons or inequalities. The respondents were accordingly asked, 'Do you think that the present government [in 1962, the Conservative government of Harold Macmillan] is doing enough for people like yourself?' Those who replied 'no' were then asked the further question, 'What more do you think they ought to be doing for people like yourself?'

The use of the phrase 'people like yourself' was designed to tie the replies to some form of collective or social grievance and to exclude purely personal wants which could not be claimed to be felt by the person concerned as a member of any definable group or stratum. In answer to the first question, 43% of the non-manual respondents and 33% of the manual said that the Government was doing enough for people like themselves. Of those who did not, the majority referred to specific personal needs of some kind, such as better housing or security of employment; 63% of manual and 47% of non-manual respondents who thought that the government should be doing more for 'people like themselves' gave an answer coded under this heading. In addition, 11% of the manual respondents and 24% of the non-manual referred to taxation; the frequency here rose sharply with income, particularly among the non-manuals. 14% of respondents mentioned higher wages or pensions, 11% mentioned specific items of government policy, and an altruistic 8% mentioned the needs of some other group than their own. Within the manual stratum, the proportion expressing themselves dissatisfied fell with rising income from 63% to 60% to 54%; but these differences are not particularly large for a question such as this, and in the non-manual stratum there is, surprisingly, no correlation with income. The more interesting differences are in the correlation with party preference.

It is perfectly possible for a Conservative supporter to feel that a Conservative Government should be doing more for people such as himself without feeling impelled to transfer his allegiance to Labour if the Conservatives do not in fact do for him what he thinks they ought. Even a working-class Conservative supporter may feel that although the Conservative government is not doing enough for him a Labour government would do less. Similarly, a Labour supporter can feel that enough is being done for people like himself by the Conservative government even if he would prefer—perhaps for reasons of policy quite unconnected with his personal situation— that the country should be ruled by Labour. But given that the two parties are widely viewed as serving the interests of the middle and working class respectively, there is an ostensible anomaly in replies of this kind which may help to shed some further light on the discrepancy between relative deprivation and inequality. In particular, it will be interesting to see if the self-rated 'class' of manual workers and their wives makes any difference to the likelihood that they will say—even if they are Labour supporters—that a Conservative government is doing enough for people like themselves. The figures for both strata are shown in Table 28 according to party support.

TABLE 28

'Do you think the present Government is doing enough for people like yourself?'; by party preference within occupational stratum.

	non-manual			manual		
	Cons.	Lib.	Lab.	Cons.	Lib.	Lab.
	%	%	%	%	%	%
Yes	63	25	24	57	23	27
No	32	72	69	38	72	66
Don't know	5	3	7	5	5	7
Total	100%	100%	100%	100%	100%	100%
	(N=220)	(N=122)	(N=86)	(N=209)	(N=155)	(N=435)

It is noticeable that the frequency of dissatisfaction with the Government is higher among Liberal than Labour supporters in both strata—a clear reflection of the extent to which the Liberal revival of 1962 represented a 'protest vote'. Over a quarter of all Labour supporters, on the other hand, expressed themselves satisfied with what the government was doing for 'people like themselves'. This is readily explicable among the non-manual stratum if these people are assumed to be 'prosperous altruists'—those, that is, who do not feel relatively deprived either within or on behalf of 'people like themselves' but whose support for Labour represents a conviction that other groups or, perhaps, the country as a whole will benefit by Labour rule. The 27% of satisfied working-class Labour supporters, however, cannot be quite so obviously explained. The relationship with income persists, as one would expect, even after party has been held constant. Among the working-class Labour supporters, the proportion satisfied with what the government was doing for them rises to 35% at the top level of incomes. But it is still as high as 29% at the middle level and 23% at the bottom. Even of those who said that they (or their husbands) had a weekly income of £10 or less, almost a quarter expressed themselves satisfied with what the Conservative government was doing for them in 1962.

There is, perhaps, nothing illogical in such an attitude. Given the diversity of reasons which may lie behind any individual choice of party, it is possible even for the poorest manual workers and their wives to support the Labour party for reasons unconnected with a desire to redress economic or any other inequalities in their own favour. Voters who, at one extreme, vote Labour purely from inherited custom or, at the other extreme, do so on some broad issue of policy which is irrelevant to their own personal situation, can hold the view that a Conservative government is doing enough for people like themselves without any contradiction or inconsistency. But for a working-class person, particularly at the bottom level of incomes, to support the Labour party without feeling that the interests of those like himself would be better served by a Labour than a Conservative government does suggest some discrepancy between ostensibly conflicting attitudes. This may simply be evidence that many working-class Labour votes are the expression more of habit than conviction—a substantial minority of working-class Labour voters did, after all, give this reason themselves, and there may have been others for whom it applied to a greater extent than their answers showed; but even if their answer is not contradictory, it still suggests a further sort of discrepancy between relative deprivation and inequality. A substantial minority of manual workers and their wives did not merely feel that the Conservative government of 1962 was doing enough for people like themselves, but felt this even when holding political opinions which imply an acceptance of the Labour Party's claim to stand for the working-class interest. The survey cannot confirm one way or the other quite why these 27% of working-class Labour supporters feel as they do. But there is one hypothesis suggested by the reference group argument which can be usefully tested even if it does not answer the question in full. We have seen that self-rated 'class', which for the great majority of respondents can be plausibly interpreted as some expression of a normative reference group, is a persistent correlate of working-class Conservatism. If this correlation is relevant to the discrepancy between inequality and relative deprivation in the way that I have suggested, might we not find that it correlates also with the answers to the present question, even when party is held constant? The figures are as shown in Table 29.

TABLE 29

'Do you think the present Government is doing enough for people like yourself?'; manual respondents by self-rated 'class' within party support.

	Conservative self-rated middle	Conservative self-rated working	Liberal self-rated middle	Liberal self-rated working	Labour self-rated middle	Labour self-rated working
	%	%	%	%	%	%
Yes	59	52	25	22	32	25
No	38	39	68	74	60	68
Don't know	3	9	7	4	8	7
Total	100%	100%	100%	100%	100%	100%
	(N=109)	(N=100)	(N=59)	(N=97)	(N=96)	(N=336)

The relationship with self-rating is distinct; indeed, it holds even when income also is held constant. It is not large among either Conservative or, even more, Liberal supporters. Nor can it furnish more than a part of the explanation of the attitudes of those working-class voters who support the Labour Party and yet believe that a Conservative government is doing enough for people like themselves. But it does again confirm the influence of reference group choices on attitudes relevant to inequality. Whatever they may mean by their self-rating, and whatever may be the reasons for their support for the Labour Party, working-class Labour voters are noticeably more likely to think that a Conservative government is doing enough for people like themselves if they think of themselves as belonging to the 'middle class'.

The question asked, however, does have one obvious limitation. There is no way of knowing what, if any, governmental promises bearing on inequalities of class the respondents might have in mind in expressing themselves satisfied. The topic which was accordingly suggested in a separate question was whether certain extensions of 'Welfare State' provision would be approved of by the respondents, and if so, whether they thought that a Means Test should be applied or not. The five particular items selected were: a family allowance for a first child as well as the others, subsidized rent on houses or flats, unemployment benefit paid at the full rate for as long as a man might be unemployed, free legal aid, and a free university education for all who could pass the appropriate exams. A prior question was asked as to whether the respondent approved in principle of the 'Welfare State', but, as might be expected, hardly anyone gave a negative reply: only 6% of the total sample did so, and even among non-manual Conservatives the proportion was only 13%. The more interesting differences of attitude only became visible when the specific extensions of state provision were suggested. Apart from the items suggested, people were asked if there was any other item which they thought the state should provide for them; but the only item mentioned by more than a handful of people was better pensions, and this was only mentioned by those directly affected, who were almost all at the bottom level of incomes in both strata.

The interpretation of the replies is necessarily complicated by attitudes to a Means Test as such. There is a strong tradition of opposition to the Means Test among the families of manual workers, but this does not derive from a feeling about redistribution of income. Indeed, a Means Test is, in principle, a more egalitarian measure than the provision of goods or services without one. But the Means Test incurred widespread odium during the 1930's for three strong reasons: first, the often humiliating severity with which it was administered; second, its penalization of those who had had the diligence or good fortune to accumulate some small savings or property; and third, its damaging effects on the personal relationships within the families affected by it. After the Second World War, there was no cause for these feelings to run as high as they had done during the years of the Depression, and it was no longer to be expected that manual workers and their families should feel that all provision by the state must be made irrespective of means.[7] But although many more of them might favour a Means Test for any extension of state provision than would have done so in 1938, no particular inference can be drawn from this about attitudes to inequality as such. The Means Test may be a more egalitarian measure in principle than universal provision; but it was nonetheless plausible to predict that provision without a Means Test would be generally viewed as the more radical suggestion. In particular, it was still probable that middle-class people would be more often in favour of a Means Test than working-class people.

The expectation that provision without a Means Test would find less favour among middle-class people was borne out by the survey. On all but one of the items on the list, non-manual respondents were clearly less likely to favour provision irrespective of means, and the one exception—university education—is, as we shall see, altogether different. Similarly, on all the items but one—this time, family allowance for a first child—non-manual respondents were more likely to say that the state should make no provision at all. But what is more remarkable (although it is statistically predictable from these other differences) is the correspondence between the proportions of the two strata favouring provision with a Means Test. On each item, this answer was given by roughly between one

[7] Cf. A. J. Willcocks, 'The Means Test', *Sociological Review* n.s. V (1957), pp. 265–286.

third and two thirds of both strata, and the difference between the two did not exceed 5% on any single item. The large differences are only in the proportion of each stratum who think either that provision should be made without a Means Test or that no provision should be made at all.

Where there is a noticeable difference within either of the two strata, it is generally explicable enough. Thus, those who are particularly likely to oppose the provision without a Means Test of unemployment relief at the full rate for as long as a man is unemployed are those at the bottom level of incomes in the non-manual stratum; those in the non-manual stratum who are either intra-generationally mobile—that is, their first job was manual—or inter-generationally mobile—that is, their fathers had manual jobs—are slightly less likely to favour provision without a Means Test; those with at least one child under 15 are more likely to favour family allowances for first children; and Conservative supporters are in general less likely to favour provision without a Means Test. All these differences are predictable ones. But what is more interesting than the direction of the differences either within or between the two strata is the smallness of the differences between them. Even apart from the unanimity on provision with a Means Test, the other differences are not so large as to suggest a widespread feeling of relative deprivation confined to the manual stratum.

Where there is a difference, it is almost always in the direction that one would expect. But the proportion of manual respondents who are opposed to any state provision whatever is high enough to suggest that their sense of relative deprivation on these topics is neither very widespread nor very intense. Thus 40% are opposed to any form of family allowance for a first child; 27% are opposed to any form of subsidized rent; 19% are opposed to full unemployment benefit for as long as a man is unemployed. Only 7% are against free legal aid; but this is within 2% of the figure for the non-manual respondents. If there is a general conclusion which is suggested by the overall pattern of responses, it is the same as the conclusion suggested by the other evidence so far presented: on inequalities of class, the frequency of relative deprivation among the manual stratum is considerably lower than would be consistent with the actual position of inequality of its members. This inconsistency is brought into heightened relief by the evidence for the way in which the non-manual stratum has often benefited from the Welfare State more than the manual. Where there is evidence of resentment, it is more on the part of non-manual respondents for what they see, by implication, as working-class malingering. The full figures are shown in Table 30.

TABLE 30

Attitudes on state provision of items listed; by occupational stratum.

		non-manual %	manual %
	With Means Test	31	29
Family allowance	Without Means Test	18	28
for first child:	Not at all	48	40
	Don't know	3	3
	Total	100%	100%
	With Means Test	47	46
Subsidized rent on	Without Means Test	7	17
house or flat:	Not at all	40	27
	Don't know	6	10
	Total	100%	100%
	With Means Test	67	62
	Without Means Test	19	24
Free legal aid:	Not at all	9	7
	Don't know	5	7
	Total	100%	100%
	With Means Test	46	47
Unemployment pay at	Without Means Test	15	26
full rate for as long	Not at all	30	19
as unemployed:	Don't know	9	8
	Total	100%	100%
	With Means Test	45	48
Free university edu-	Without Means Test	45	45
cation for all who can	Not at all	7	3
who can pass exams:	Don't know	3	4
	Total	100%	100%
		(N=496)	(N=919)

The only item which stands out as an exception to the general pattern is university education. As on family allowances, a difference is made by whether or not the respondent has children under 15: in the manual stratum the difference is 5%, and in the non-manual 10%. But this difference is less striking than the parallel. Non-manual parents are closer in their views to manual parents than they are to non-manual respondents without children under 15. The figures in Table 30 show not merely that there is an almost exact unanimity between the two strata on this item, but that many more manual respondents favour provision without a Means Test on this item than on any other.

This result is a twofold symptom of the social changes of the preceding decades. On the one hand, middle-class parents have come to feel the need for state provision in a matter which was traditionally confined to middle-class families and for which they themselves expected to have to pay. What they feel as the decline in their relative economic position, therefore, has not only led them to feel a greater need for state assistance for something which they can less well afford; it has also led them to feel that if state provision is being made for families which in the past seldom sent a child to university at all, then they are entitled to benefit from this provision also. On the other hand, it is equally unlikely that working-class respondents would have felt about this question in 1919 or 1938 as they felt in 1962. The convergence of attitudes between the two strata is the result of a double change. Middle-class parents no longer feel able to afford to pay for their children to go to university, while working-class parents have come to want it for their children and see it as feasible that they should have it.

The change in working-class attitudes to university education, however, cannot be deduced from this question alone. Obviously, working-class people are likely to feel that if it should be provided it should be provided with a maximum of state aid, for they would be even less likely to be able to afford it than any other of the items suggested in the questionnaire. A working-class family may well feel that it does not need a family allowance for a first child; the feeling that the parents should be able to look after their own children at least to this extent, and the modesty of working-class standards of expenditure relative to what they enjoy, make this a plausible reply even for those who have a child of the age that would benefit. But no working-class family could expect to pay university fees for even one of their children. It is thus readily explicable that more respondents in both strata should have favoured provision without a Means Test on this item than any other. But these figures reflect at the same time the spreading demand among manual workers and their families for education. We have seen how this demand has been steadily rising throughout the century as equal educational opportunity has come nearer to attainment. The present replies furnish further evidence for the conclusion which I have advanced in discussing the relation between inequality and relative deprivation of status as opposed to class. But to pursue this claim requires a fuller analysis of the other questions in the survey which bear on education. These are discussed in the following chapter under the heading of inequalities of status.

XI

REFERENCE GROUPS AND INEQUALITIES OF STATUS

I F MY ARGUMENT about inequalities of status is correct, then the
questions in the survey which bear on it should disclose a very
different pattern from those concerned with differences in income or resources. There is, as always, the difficulty of comparison;
although it is plausible to suppose that the same questionnaire administered in 1938 would not have produced the same pattern of
responses, this can only be a supposition. In addition, there are
still the difficulties inherent in the notion of status itself: people can
be asked how much more money they feel they should have, or what
consumer goods they would like to be able to buy, but they cannot
be usefully asked how much they would like of social esteem. The
topics raised in the survey on inequalities of status are more
ambiguous and less precise than those raised on inequalities of
wealth or income. But if questions can be asked which it is legitimate to interpret as reflecting attitudes towards the hierarchy of
status, as opposed to class or power, these can furnish at least some
further evidence for or against the view that relative deprivation of
status among the less well placed has been progressively increasing
with the advance towards some greater measure of equality.

There are, however, two important differences from the discussion of class. The first is that we are now considering 'egoistic' as
well as 'fraternalistic' relative deprivations. I have argued that
higher aspirations of status have been steadily spreading among
manual workers and their families throughout the period since
1918; but these have in some ways been 'egoistic' aspirations as
much as a sense of relative deprivation on behalf of the working
class as such, and they have been accompanied by a decline in the
sort of intensely fraternalistic feelings characteristic of the traditional working-class militant. Such feelings are still common among
some sections of the manual stratum, and particularly those
workers who are socially isolated by the nature of their work and
for whom an increase in prosperity may well exacerbate feelings of

227

relative deprivation of social esteem. Miners and dockers should both be excepted from any generalization about the spread of a wish on the part of manual workers to rise out of their status-group rather than with it. But the relative deprivation of status felt by manual workers and their families was probably less often and also less intensely fraternalistic in 1962 than in 1919. Even if this could be statistically demonstrated, it still would not mean that the manual workers of 1962 could properly be described as having 'become middle-class'. But as more and more manual workers and their families came to feel heightened aspirations of status, this tended to detach them from those whose more 'traditional' working-class attitudes involved a relative deprivation of status—if any—only on behalf of all manual workers as such.

The second difference is that the questions asked with a view to elucidating feelings about status were mostly asked in terms of how respondents felt about the education and careers of their children (or hypothetical children). This is one of the most obvious ways in which changing aspirations of status are expressed, but it is a very different form of question from those used in asking about attitudes relevant to relative deprivation of class. Many people, when they are asked about their children, will express higher aspirations on their behalf than they would for themselves, and if the respondents in the survey had been asked what they hoped that their children would earn, they might have given a much more extravagant answer than they did when asked about the 'proper' standard of living for 'people like themselves'. The questions about education, therefore, cannot be interpreted as strictly comparable to the questions about income. We shall see, for example, that an overwhelming majority of manual respondents said that they would like 'any son of theirs' to have a university education. It is plausible to suppose that this figure represents a change of attitude since the time when university education was seen as almost entirely a middle-class preserve and some sections of the Labour movement wished not to broaden admissions to Oxford or Cambridge so much as to close them down altogether.[1] But it cannot be used to make any quantified comparison between working-class attitudes to inequalities of status and attitudes to inequalities of class.

It should, however, be possible to show whether normative reference groups, as suggested by self-rated 'class', have an influence on the attitudes of manual workers and their wives towards education and careers for their children. A manual worker may, of course,

[1] See for example Maxton's remarks to the ILP summer school of 1924, quoted G. McAllister, *James Maxton* (London, 1935), p. 157, in which Oxford and Cambridge are referred to as 'those centres of snobbery and exclusiveness'.

think of himself as 'middle-class' and still feel that manual workers as such should be given better educational facilities by comparison with those enjoyed by the entrants into white-collar occupations. But for him to want higher education for his son implies a willingness that the son should rise out of the status group of his birth into another—a willingness which, as we have seen, was probably much less common a generation before.

In the same way, a manual worker's preference that his son should have a non-manual job, particularly if it is no better or even less well paid, can be plausibly interpreted as an attitude to status as much as to class. During the Depression, the attraction of a clerical job to working-class families was, as the Pilgrim Trust investigators commented, its security more than anything else. After the Second World War, this was no longer so. There might be in the minds of some working-class parents a residual fear of unemployment which would lead them to prefer a white-collar occupation for their sons. Some also might be aware of just those reasons cited earlier why the ostensible equality between upper manual and lower non-manual earnings should not be taken to demonstrate a genuine equality in the class-situation of the two. But in an enquiry conducted in 1962 it is plausible to interpret a manual worker's preference for a non-manual job for his son as indicating a wish that the son should rise out of, rather than with, the status-group of manual workers. A preference that the son should take a manual job need not, of course, always mean an attitude of militant fraternalism; it may mean an acceptance of the subordinate status of the manual worker, or a complete indifference to considerations of status, or even a conviction that the manual worker is not accorded any less prestige by society than the non-manual. In any such case, the person belongs to the category which was labelled Type A—the person who feels relatively deprived neither as a member of his group nor on behalf of it. But given the social structure of Britain in 1962, it seems safe to assume that the manual worker who would prefer his son to have a manual job does not do so because he regards it as enjoying higher status. He either does not resent the subordinate status attached to manual work, or, while feeling that manual work is accorded too little status, still does not want a son of his to achieve higher status by 'abdicating' from the working class. If, on the other hand, he would prefer a non-manual job for his son, then this can be plausibly interpreted as some sense of relative deprivation of status of an 'egoistic' kind.

The evidence which can be drawn from the survey about attitudes to inequalities of status is not entirely confined to the questions about education or career for a son. There have already been some

229

implications to be drawn from the analysis of self-assigned 'class', and in addition two further questions were introduced as having some possible implications for attitudes to status. The questions which must, however, bear the brunt of interpretation on this elusive topic are those about attitudes to a hypothetical son.

The actual extent of educational inequality, as opposed to the frequency of relative deprivation aroused by it, can be measured in terms of the proportion of each stratum leaving school at the minimum age, the proportion remaining in secondary school and the proportion going on to higher education. Of the manual respondents in the sample, only 9% had stayed on at school beyond whatever was the minimum statutory age at the time; of non-manual respondents, the proportion was 49%, of whom 22% had had some university or college education. The advance towards actual equality is reflected in the answers given by those respondents with children under 15 when they were asked at what age they expected their children to leave school. Of non-manual parents, only 7% said that they expected their children to leave at the minimum age, while the proportion among manual parents was 36%. The difference is still a large one; but the figure of 36%, even if it reflects some over-optimism among working-class parents, is still evidence of a radical change from the actual experience of the working-class parents in the sample. Furthermore, the proportion rises with income: over two-thirds of working-class parents at the top level of incomes expected at least one of their children to stay on beyond the minimum age. These figures not only provide ample confirmation that in this respect, at least, inequality of status between the manual and non-manual strata is very much less than it was, but suggest at the same time that the frequency of relative deprivation has been rising.

The survey also provides ample evidence for the extent to which the aspiration for higher education is shared by both strata. When asked the question, 'Would you like any son of yours to have a university education?', 82% of manual respondents said 'yes'. The proportion rises with income from 79% at the bottom level to 86% at the middle to 89% at top, and the figure for non-manual respondents is only 6% higher than the figure for manual. This question, however, is perhaps too loosely phrased to afford evidence of genuine aspirations; it may be a little too much like asking 'would you like any son of yours to have a lucrative job?' in order to elucidate attitudes to inequalities of class. But the expectations of the working-class parents in the sample who have children under 15 furnish more tangible evidence of the extent to which educational aspirations have spread. Only at the top level of incomes do as many as half of the manual parents in the sample expect at least one of their children to have some form of education beyond school, and only a further half of these expect this further education to be at a university. But this reflects a large increase in the pre-war pattern not merely of hopes but of expectations of what is seen to be feasible. Furthermore, the replies show an effect made not only by income, but by self-rated 'class'. The working-class parents with children under 15 who described themselves as 'middle-class' were likelier by 10% (39% as against 29%) to expect their children to have some form of higher education than those who described themselves as 'working-class', and likelier by 6% (14% as against 8%) to expect them to go to a university. Educational aspiration, therefore, seems to be affected not merely by the class-situation of the parents, but also by the 'class' to which they assign themselves with its implication of a normative reference group and a concomitant attitude to the hierarchy of status.[2]

A better indicator, however, might be not what parents expect their children to achieve so much as whether they are prepared to contribute fees in order to help their children up the educational ladder. As on all these questions, it cannot be unerringly assumed that such a willingness implies an ambition of status for the children. Since a high-status education normally leads to a non-manual job, it may always be the attraction of a better-paid job for a son, rather than the higher status associated with it, which impels parents to make sacrifices on his behalf. But the link between education and status is sufficiently close for it to be plausible to make some inferences about attitudes to status from attitudes about private education. The matter may be complicated by such individual circumstances as religious denomination or the talents or disabilities of particular children; but there are unlikely to be so many of these as to invalidate the question asked of all the sample, parents or not, about private education.

The proportion of working-class parents with children who attended, or are expected to attend, a fee-paying school at any stage of their educational careers is, predictably, extremely small—6% (and only 8% even at the top level of incomes) as compared to 34% of non-manual parents. But a difference is made by self-rated 'class' even among the handful of manual parents: 9% of those describing themselves as 'middle-class' have children who either have attended, attend, or are expected to attend fee-paying schools, as against 5%

[2] Among non-manual parents, the influence of their own education is strong: 74% of those with children under 15 who had been to a university expected their children to do so also—an effect similar to that found by the Crowther Report (see above, p. 102, n. 17) for secondary education.

of those describing themselves as 'working-class'. A similar difference is visible in the answers to the question 'Do you have (or,
would you like to have) private education for your children?' A
number of people said that they did not know, which is obviously a
reasonable response for those to whom the question was an entirely
unreal one. These 'Don't Knows' to some extent confuse the analysis
of the answers by income and self-rating; but when both are held
constant it is clear that both have an independent influence among
manual respondents. The majority do not (or would not) want any
form of private education for their children. But the proportion
drops between the middle and top levels of income, whatever the
'class' to which the respondents assign themselves, and at all three
levels of income a clear difference is made by self-rating. The figures
are shown in Table 31.

TABLE 31

Proportion of manual respondents who do not (would not) want a
private education for their children; by self-rated 'class' within income.

high		medium		low	
self-rated middle	self-rated working	self-rated middle	self-rated working	self-rated middle	self-rated working
46%	57%	55%	66%	54%	65%
(N=41)	(N=56)	(N=101)	(N=176)	(N=91)	(N=276)

Self-rated 'class' thus shows a clear influence on the answers to a
question which can be plausibly linked to attitudes to inequality of
status. Indeed, those manual workers and their wives who describe
themselves as 'middle-class' are if anything less likely to reject the
idea of a private education for their children than non-manual
workers and their wives at the bottom or middle levels of income.
Only at the top level of incomes, where nearly half the non-manual
respondents would either like or, if they are parents, already have
a private education for their children is there a marked difference
from the manual respondents. Once again, these figures cannot
demonstrate by themselves that there has been a steady spread of
status-aspirations among the manual stratum during the post-war
period; perhaps just as many manual workers and their wives
would have said in 1938 that they would in principle like a private
education for their children. But this is on the face of it implausible,
and the difference between the attitudes of older and younger
manual respondents suggests, as we shall see, a considerable change
in attitudes. Furthermore, the influence of self-rated 'class' on
attitudes to status (unlike attitudes to income) is so far confirmed.

Since, however, questions about education may be misleading as
a guide to attitudes to inequality of status, two questions were asked

about the job which people would prefer for a hypothetical son. The respondents were first of all asked if they would prefer a manual or non-manual job, assuming that they had a son who was at the moment choosing a job; they were then presented with the hypothetical alternative of a job with higher pay but lower status— a factory foreman—or a job with lower pay but higher status—a schoolteacher. As on the question about education for hypothetical children, a good many people were unwilling to express any preference, and in addition some of those who had children replied that it was up to their sons to choose whatever job they would prefer. But the replies nevertheless furnish some convincing evidence for differences of attitude within the manual stratum. Where the question is put in terms of an unqualified manual/non-manual choice of job, then there may be no warrant for inferring that a preference for a non-manual job is based on status rather than class. But where the choice is weighted against the non-manual job in terms of income, then it does seem legitimate to draw some inference about attitudes to the hierarchy of status.

When manual workers and their wives were asked 'If a son of yours was actually choosing a job at the moment, would you rather he chose a manual or a non-manual job?', almost a quarter said that they didn't know, or that it would be up to him, or that they would have no personal preference in the matter; of the remainder, 32% said 'manual' and 49% said 'non-manual'. When, however, they were asked 'If he had the choice of a foreman's job at £20 a week or a schoolteacher's job at £15, which would *you* prefer him to choose?' the proportion of Don't Knows fell from 24% to 19%, and of the remainder slightly more said they would prefer the schoolteacher to the foreman than vice versa—41% as against 40%. Of the non-manual respondents, more than four times as many expressed a preference for a non-manual job as for a manual, and at the top level of incomes more than eight times as many. When the choice of foreman or schoolteacher was put to them, the proportion choosing the foreman rose to 25%, but this is still less than half as many as chose the schoolteacher.

These results are of sufficient interest to call for a slight digression. If I am right about the changes which occurred in Britain in the decades preceding the survey, then this was a period in which relative deprivation of status was rising in both magnitude and frequency as equality of status came closer to being achieved. This period, in other words, corresponds to the rising slope of the hypothetical curve depicted in Chapter Two—the point at which equality has not yet been so far attained that the frequency of relative deprivation starts once again to fall. What, therefore, would happen if equality of status were in fact to be achieved? We can safely assume that the status of the teacher was higher than that of the foreman by the standards of English society in 1962. This difference of status is clearly reflected in the preferences expressed by respondents when confronted with the choice for their sons. A generation or more earlier, however, fewer manual workers and their wives would have chosen the schoolmaster's job for their son, since there was then still less equality of status between the manual and non-manual strata, and the reference groups of the manual stratum were still more limited. Conversely, if equality of status were to progress still further, then the frequency of preference for the schoolteacher ought to fall once again. Since the status of the two is not yet equal, there is no way of testing this for Britain. But it is possible to make the comparison by going to the United States, where there is a very much greater equality of status and this advantage in the schoolteacher's job no longer applies (or, at least, applies very much less than it does in Britain).

A plausible comparison is provided by two questions asked in a Gallup Poll survey of August, 1951.[3] These were worded as follows: first, 'Which of these two jobs would you personally prefer a son of yours to take, assuming he is equally qualified: a skilled laborer's job at $100 a week or a white-collar desk job at $75 a week?'; and second, after the same preamble, 'a college professor's job at $4,000 a year or a factory foreman's job at $6,000 a year?' In answer to both these proposed alternatives, a majority of both manual and non-manual respondents expressed a preference for the manual job. Among both manual and non-manual respondents, the difference was more narrowly in favour of the factory foreman over the college professor than in favour of the skilled labourer over the clerk. But even where the choice was between professor and foreman, the frequency of preference for the foreman was 52% as against 44% among non-manual respondents, and 61% as against 34% among manual. If, therefore, the United States of 1951 foreshadows what the status-structure of Britain may become during the decades after 1962, it may be predicted that the frequency of working-class parental preferences for a non-manual job, even if less well paid, will reach a peak beyond which it will begin to fall back towards its previous level.

It requires to be demonstrated, however, that there is a difference between older and younger manual workers and their wives. If it is true that there has been a marked change in the forty years preceding the survey, then we should expect to find that older manual

[3] I am indebted for these tabulations to the Roper Public Opinion Research Center at Williams College, Massachusetts.

234

workers are less likely to express a preference in favour of a non-manual job for their sons. But since there should also be an effect shown by self-rated 'class', it is necessary to test the effect of both together in order to insure against an overlap. On the initial question about an unspecified choice between a manual and non-manual job for a son, it turns out that self-rating makes the difference rather than age. Age does, however, show an effect independent of self-rating, particularly among those who describe themselves as 'working-class'. Manual workers or their wives who are aged between 21 and 45 are more likely to choose a non-manual than a manual job for a son, even if they describe themselves as 'working-class', and so are those over 45 who describe themselves as 'middle-class'. But those who are over 45 and also describe themselves as 'working-class' are no more likely to express a preference for the non-manual than for the manual job. The figures are given in Table 32.

TABLE 32

Choice for son of manual or non-manual job; manual respondents by age within self-rated 'class'.

	self-rated middle		self-rated working	
	21–45	46+	21–45	46+
	%	%	%	%
Manual	26	28	33	36
Non-manual	51	57	45	36
Don't know	23	15	22	28
Total	100%	100%	100%	100%
	(N=125)	(N=178)	(N=254)	(N=356)

When the specific alternatives of schoolmaster and foreman are suggested, the pattern is slightly different. The effect of both self-rating and age is more marked: those of 45 or under, whatever their self-rated 'class', are likelier to prefer the schoolteacher than the foreman, and so are those over 45 who describe themselves as 'middle-class'. But those who describe themselves as 'working-class' and are over 45 are a good deal more likely to prefer the foreman than the schoolmaster. The figures are shown in Table 33.

TABLE 33

Choice for son of foreman's job at £20 a week or schoolteacher's at £15; manual respondents by age within self-rated 'class'.

	self-rated middle		self-rated working	
	21–45	46+	21–45	46+
	%	%	%	%
Foreman	24	40	33	49
Schoolteacher	61	47	47	28
Don't know	15	13	20	23
Total	100%	100%	100%	100%
	(N=125)	(N=178)	(N=254)	(N=356)

This table provides clear evidence that first, there has been a significant change in attitudes to the hierarchy of status among manual workers and their wives, and second, these attitudes are influenced by normative reference groups as implied by self-rated 'class'. Indeed, the effect of self-rated 'class' persists when either age or sex or education or income or father's occupation is held constant. It does not account for all the variation; each of these other attributes shows an independent effect, and sometimes quite a marked one. But the effect of self-rating is persistent and unmistakable, quite unlike its negligible effect on the questions related to inequalities of class. On questions of income it showed a distinct effect only where those describing themselves as 'working-class' were found to be a good deal less likely to agree to the general suggestion that 'manual workers are doing much better nowadays than white-collar workers'—a question on which the bearing of self-rated 'class' seemed more closely analogous to its bearing on party choice than on direct perceptions of comparative reference groups who are seen to be better off. But on the question which of all those in the survey it is safest to interpret as indicating attitudes to status, self-rated 'class', despite the diversity of meanings which underlies it, shows a strong independent effect.

A corollary of this is that some categories of manual workers and their wives who described themselves as 'working-class' were a good deal more likely to prefer the foreman than the schoolteacher. When a working-class self-rating is combined with either an age over 45, or a father who was in a manual job, or a stated income at the bottom of the three levels, then the person concerned is more likely to prefer the foreman than the schoolteacher. These categories, moreover, comprise a substantial proportion of the manual stratum, and it is they who explain why the preference for the schoolteacher among the manual respondents taken as a whole is so narrow as to be almost negligible. The spread of a preference for the lower-paid, higher-status job for a son, therefore, may have some way to go before it begins to fall again towards the comparable figure found in the United States. Even in the United States the greater equality of status does not mean that every respondent in a national sample will prefer for his son the higher paid of the choice of two jobs. There will always be some whose feelings about a clerical or teaching job will be such that they would prefer their son to choose it for reasons unconnected with the higher status attaching to non-manual work as such. But if the replies of the English sample could be interpreted in this way, rather than as reflecting in the main an attitude which does relate to status, then we should expect to find the preferences for the foreman evenly distributed among manual workers and their wives of all ages and kinds. They would not be concentrated among the declining 'fraternalists', who a generation earlier would have outnumbered those manual workers and their wives whose rising aspirations of status led them in 1962 to choose a schoolteacher's job for a hypothetical son rather than a foreman's.

There are two categories of manual respondents among whom a middle-class self-rating shows a particularly strong effect. The first is women, and the second those at the top level of incomes. I have already remarked that on some questions the popular belief that women are more status-conscious than men does not seem to be borne out by the survey; although women in the non-manual stratum are much less likely than men to describe themselves as 'working-class', even irrespective of their father's occupation, this is not so in the manual stratum. But on the choice of jobs for a son, women who are manual workers or are married to manual workers and describe themselves as 'middle-class' are particularly likely to express a preference for the schoolteacher rather than the foreman. Sex also makes a difference among those who describe themselves as 'working-class', and self-rating, conversely, makes a difference even among men. But both these differences are very small ones. A preference for the schoolteacher is slightly commoner among working-class men who describe themselves as 'middle-class', and both men and women in the manual stratum who describe themselves as 'working-class' are likelier by about the same margin to prefer the foreman than to prefer the schoolteacher. But women in the manual stratum who describe themselves as 'middle-class' are more than twice as likely to prefer the schoolteacher than to prefer the foreman. The figures are given in full in Table 34.

TABLE 34

Choice for son of foreman's job at £20 a week or schoolteacher's at £15; manual respondents by sex within self-rated 'class'.

	self-rated middle		self-rated working	
	men	women	men	women
	%	%	%	%
Foreman	42	26	45	41
Schoolteacher	48	57	37	35
Don't know	10	17	18	24
Total	100%	100%	100%	100%
	(N=137)	(N=166)	(N=280)	(N=330)

Self-rating also makes a particularly marked difference at the top level of income. Here, those manual workers and their wives who describe themselves as 'working-class' are likelier by 12% to express a preference for the schoolteacher than a preference for the foreman—a difference which is the same, within a few per cent., as among those at the middle level of income, whether they describe themselves as 'middle' or 'working-class'. Among those at the top level who describe themselves as 'middle-class', however, the difference is 49%. From the size of this difference, it would appear that manual workers who reach the top level of income will be likely to feel a fraternalistic relative deprivation of status only if they retain as their normative reference group the 'working class' (whatever this may mean to them). If, on the other hand, they think of themselves as 'middle-class' this will make them anxious to distinguish themselves in status from other manual workers. The two are for obvious reasons likely to be bound up together—a middle-class self-rating and a preference for a higher-status job for a son are presumably both manifestations of an attitude to the status hierarchy which, whatever its determinants, is different from that of the majority of those manual workers and their wives who prefer to call themselves 'working-class'. But it would seem that those who have reached the top level of income are not only more likely to describe themselves as 'middle-class' but more likely, if they do, to have attitudes to the hierarchy of status which imply a divergence from the fraternalistic relative deprivations of status of the traditional proletarian.

This strong effect of self-rating among the most prosperous manual workers and their wives emerges also on the one other question which was asked in the survey with a view to elucidating the wish of some members of the manual stratum to rise out of it in status, or at any rate to rise out of the more proletarian sections of it. I have already referred to evidence that one of the principal manifestations of the urge for individual status mobility is the wish to move to a 'superior' residential area. This very often follows from occupational mobility—the sons and daughters of manual workers who move into non-manual jobs are likely to feel not merely the wish to 'better themselves' in terms of class-situation but to 'better themselves' in the sense of moving up in status. But the feeling occurs also among manual workers, particularly skilled manual workers and their wives, who prefer to move out of what they regard as a 'rough' working-class area. Since this attitude has been well documented in the relevant community studies, it is plausible to expect that it will be particularly common among those manual workers and their wives who are at the top level of income and mean by assigning themselves to the 'middle class' either (in a few cases) a direct assimilation to the non-manual stratum, or, more

238

often, some sense of being distinguished from the unskilled or 'rough' manual workers.

Two questions about moving were accordingly included in the survey in order to try to elucidate aspirations of status. People were first of all asked, 'Would you like to move out of your present district?'. Those who said 'yes' were then asked the further question, 'Is this anything to do with the sort of district you think it is?' This suggestion was explicitly made in order to distinguish those whose wish to move could be plausibly interpreted as being socially motivated from those who wished to move for reasons of health, or to be nearer their place of work, or because of particular deficiencies or inconveniences in their present house. It is still possible that those who gave the 'sort of district' as their reason might not have its social composition in mind. But the responses in the pilot survey suggested that with few exceptions some such overtone could be legitimately attributed to those who cited the 'sort of district', and some of the remarks recorded by the interviewers in the main survey provided further confirmation of this. The separate headings of district, house and work were accordingly pre-coded in the main survey, and this method yielded the distribution of answers shown in Table 35. The total percentages come to more than 100% since some of those who said they wanted to move gave more than one kind of reason.

TABLE 35

'Would you like to move out of your present district?', and if yes, 'Is this anything to do with the sort of district you think it is?' (manual respondents only).

No wish to move	65%
Don't know whether wish to move	1%
Wish to move for reason connected with district	17%
,, ,, ,, ,, ,, ,, ,, house	10%
,, ,, ,, ,, ,, ,, ,, work	2%
,, ,, ,, ,, personal reasons	5%
,, ,, ,, ,, other reasons	1%
,, ,, ,, but don't know reasons	1%
Total	102%
	(N=919)

Self-assigned 'class' shows an effect on the reasons given for wishing to move at all three levels of income, but it is only among the manual workers and their wives at the top level that the difference is particularly noticeable. At the middle level of income, it is only 2%; indeed, the proportion of those describing themselves as 'working-class' who give the 'sort of district' as their reason is high enough

239

to upset the correlation with income which holds by a narrow margin among those who describe themselves as 'middle-class'. There is one good reason which might explain a lack of correlation with income, namely the greater likelihood that the more prosperous manual workers who want to move will have done so already; in fact, the manual respondents at the top level of income are likelier by 8% than those at the middle level to have moved at least once between 1945 and 1962. But this will not account for the variations in the frequency with which the 'sort of district' is given as a reason. Those least likely to give this as a reason were found to be those at the top level of income who described themselves as 'working-class', as is shown in Table 36.

TABLE 36

Proportion of manual respondents wishing to move from their present district and giving as a reason 'the kind of district you think this is'; by self-rated 'class' within income.

high		medium		low	
self-rated middle	self-rated working	self-rated middle	self-rated working	self-rated middle	self-rated working
27%	9%	21%	19%	20%	14%
(N=41)	(N=56)	(N=101)	(N=176)	(N=91)	(N=276)

This table offers further confirmation of the way in which the most prosperous manual workers and their wives are sharply differentiated in their attitudes by their choice of normative reference group. Even if it cannot be assumed that every respondent who expressed a wish to move on the grounds of 'sort of district' was expressing a wish to rise in status, it would require several exceptions all in the same direction to invalidate the significance of self-rated 'class'. Some further caution may be called for since the numbers are not very large and there is therefore some risk of statistical misrepresentation; but the difference is nonetheless too large to be accidental. Self-rated 'class' is a persistent correlate of attitudes to status, and the correlation—whether or not it can be properly described as a cause—is particularly marked among the richest manual workers and their wives. The correlation is not, perhaps, remarkable, once it has been shown that what manual workers and their wives mean by assigning themselves to the 'middle class' can, despite the diversity of meanings, be generally interpreted as some sort of self-differentiation in terms of status. But there is a further conclusion to be drawn. Whereas the feelings of relative deprivation of class experienced by manual workers and their wives are a function of the comparisons which most readily present themselves to them, their relative deprivations of status are a function of normative as well as of comparative reference groups. It may be that if a question could be devised to show what comparative reference groups people choose when they have inequalities of status in mind, these would be found to correlate both with aspirations of status and with the choice of normative reference groups. But even if so, this would not alter the finding that the choice of self-assigned 'class' has an effect on attitudes bearing on inequalities of status in a way that it does not on attitudes bearing on inequalities of class.

These questions, however, touch only on a limited aspect of the hierarchy of status. It may be that questions about the education and career of children are valid indices of how people feel about the occupational and educational status of themselves and their families. But just as in asking about relative deprivations of class it was necessary to ask some more general question about inequalities, so it needs to be shown whether some more general question about inequalities of status might not suggest a different picture of the pattern of relative deprivation among manual respondents. In asking about class, the obvious question was whether people felt that the relative position of the two strata, as they saw it, was as they felt it should be. But a general question about inequality of status was rather more difficult to construct. It might be possible to ask whether people felt that either manual or non-manual workers have too much or too little status or prestige, but the familiar difficulties inherent in the notion of status make such a wording of doubtful value. It accordingly seemed more useful to think of an issue directly connected with the hierarchy of status rather than that of class and compare the attitudes of the different respondents to it. As before, this makes any direct comparison with the answers about monetary inequalities meaningless. But it does have two other uses: first, it makes it possible to test whether the influence of self-rated 'class' persists on a general question related to inequalities of status; second, it makes it possible to see whether the egalitarians of class, in the sense of those who think that manual workers ought to be doing as well as they are, are the same people as the egalitarians of status as defined by attitudes on an issue related only to status as opposed to class. The topic chosen was the House of Lords, since it is an obvious and familiar manifestation of a status hierarchy whose élite has no necessary connection with the élite of class. A still more obvious and familiar exemplification of the status hierarchy would be the Monarchy itself, but attitudes to this are so closely bound up with feelings of patriotism that it would provide a very uncertain guide to attitudes to inequality of status. The House of Lords, by contrast, has no such overtones. The question used was accordingly framed as follows: 'Some people think the House of

Lords ought to be abolished on the grounds that it is undemocratic. What do you think?'

Given the political overtones of the question, and the likelihood that it will correlate with party preference, it is necessary to hold party constant before making further comparisons. The correlation with party may itself be connected with overtones of status: some people may be prompted by the same feelings about status rather than class both to support the Conservative Party and to oppose the abolition of the House of Lords. But since the question can be interpreted as touching on political attitudes perhaps as much as attitudes to status by itself, the effect of other characteristics or attitudes needs to be analyzed within the correlation with party preference. When a breakdown is made independent of party, the proportion of respondents who agreed with the suggestion that the House of Lords should be abolished is 18% in the non-manual and 22% in the manual stratum. When party is introduced, however, the group most likely to favour abolition is the group of non-manual Labour supporters. Manual Labour supporters, on the other hand, are less likely to favour abolition than manual Liberals.

The analysis is complicated by the high proportion of respondents who said they didn't know, or expressed themselves frankly indifferent, or gave an answer so qualified that it could not be coded as either a yes or a no. One in five even of non-manual Conservatives came into this category, and the proportion of manual Labour supporters was more than 40%. In the same way, the only consistent correlation with income is that as it rises the proportion of 'Don't Knows' is gradually diminished from 32% to 27% to 19% among non-manual respondents and from 40% to 34% to 30% among manual. In order to bring out the differences in each category, therefore, it is best to exclude the 'Don't Knows' from the table and show the distribution simply of yesses and noes among those who did give one or other of these answers. When this has been done and party has been held constant, self-assigned 'class' can then be introduced in order to see whether it shows the same effect as it does both on party preference and on the questions directly related to status. The result is as shown in Table 37.

It turns out that self-rating makes no difference except among Liberal supporters; and here it is those who describe themselves as 'middle-class' who are more, not less, likely to express a radical view. Clearly, therefore, self-rating and its implication of the choice of a normative reference group does not have the same effect here as it does either on party preference as such or on the questions about education and careers for a son. The only effect is that among

TABLE 37

Replies to the suggestion that 'the House of Lords should be abolished on the grounds that it is undemocratic'; manual respondents with 'Don't Knows' excluded by self-rated 'class' within party.

	Conservative		Liberal		Labour	
	self-rated middle	self-rated working	self-rated middle	self-rated working	self-rated middle	self-rated working
	%	%	%	%	%	%
Yes	24	23	40	32	38	38
No	76	77	60	68	62	62
Total	100%	100%	100%	100%	100%	100%
	(N=83)	(N=72)	(N=45)	(N=65)	(N=61)	(N=188)

the Liberals—those, that is, who appear to represent the non-Socialist protest vote in the working-class electorate—those who think of themselves as 'middle-class' are more likely to reject the traditional status hierarchy as symbolized in the House of Lords. Self-rating, therefore, seems to have little to do with the sort of 'fraternalistic' radicalism which the question was intended to imply.

It remains to be asked, however, how far an egalitarian opinion on this topic correlates with egalitarian opinions on inequalities of class. I have been arguing throughout not only that the three dimensions of social inequality must be separately considered but also that the relation between inequality and relative deprivation in each of them is likely to be different. A further test of their independence, therefore, is afforded by using the results of the survey to measure the extent of the correlation between an agreement with the suggestion that manual workers ought to be doing as well as they are doing compared to white-collar workers and an agreement with the suggestion that the House of Lords ought to be abolished on the grounds that it is 'undemocratic'. For this purpose, those who gave a 'Don't Know' answer on either question were excluded, and the remainder arranged in the form of a four-fold table. The simplest way to describe the correlation is then to use one of the measures of statistical association which have been devised for such tables, and which range from 0 (complete non-correlation) to $\pm$ 1·0 (complete correlation). Since the question about manual versus white-collar workers showed a marked correlation with self-rated class, the self-rated 'middle' and self-rated 'working class' were kept separate. Using Yule's Q as a measure,[4] the correlation of affirmative or negative answers on the two questions was found to be less than ·1 among manual workers and their wives, whether they described themselves as 'middle-class' or 'working-class'. In other

[4] Q is the ratio between the difference between the products of the diagonals and the sum of the products of the diagonals in a fourfold table.

words, attitudes on the two questions are almost completely independent of each other. This does not, of course, amount to a demonstration that attitudes to inequalities of class and status are in general as little correlated as this. But it is worth remarking just how small the correlation is in this one case.

It hardly needs saying that these questions do no more than touch on a few small facets of people's feelings about the inequalities in the social structure. It is possible not only that these are quite different on other topics which were not included in the questionnaire but also that within any one of the three dimensions of social inequality the same people may hold inconsistent or conflicting views. But it can, I think, be claimed on the evidence of the survey both that there is a clearly visible difference between attitudes to class and to status of the kind that the historical discussion suggested, and also that the influence of comparative and normative reference groups is demonstrably different in each case. It is in the light of these differences, therefore, that we must turn to the question how far the relative deprivations which English people were feeling in 1962 could be vindicated by appeal to social justice.

PART FOUR
CONCLUSIONS

XII

THE ASSESSMENT OF
RELATIVE DEPRIVATION

THE ATTEMPT to analyze the relation between social inequalities and the feelings of relative deprivation to which they give
rise has shown, if nothing else, that this relation is both complicated and variable. It is not the same in any two of the three dimensions of social inequality; it can as well take the form of an inverse correlation as a direct one; and of all its various determinants,
one of the least powerful is the abstract ideal of social justice. Yet
the notion of social justice is somewhere implicit in every account of
how people feel about social equality. Any explanation, however
impartially phrased, cannot but involve the question of 'false consciousness', if only to reject it, and at this point the social psychologist or social historian must become, whether he likes it or not, a
political theorist in the philosophical sense. Wherever inequalities
of class, status or power give rise to either a greater or a lesser sense
of relative deprivation than the inequalities themselves would
appear to warrant, there is at once a discrepancy which raises the
question what perception of inequalities is 'natural' or 'reasonable'
or even 'correct'. How is a discrepancy between relative deprivation
and inequality to be assessed? What sort of account are we to give
of the sense of grievance felt by those who, for whatever reason, have
taken more restricted comparisons than in some sense they might
or even ought to have done?

To say that this question is necessarily relevant is not to say that
it is impossible to describe in any way the attitudes of the two strata
to social inequality without some implication as to how far they are
legitimate; indeed, it is a virtue of the language of 'relative deprivation' that it carries no built-in overtones of this kind. But having
once described the extent to which feelings of relative deprivation
are disproportionate to the inequalities which occasion them, it is
then not only possible but necessary to ask how these discrepancies

are to be evaluated. If the reasons for the discrepancies are as I have described them, are they good reasons? Or if not, what sort of language is appropriate to describe them? Is it legitimate to speak of people's perceptions of inequality as 'distorted' or to describe a disproportionate awareness of inequality as 'envy'? Or is there no criterion which could be brought to bear by which the use of any such term could be better justified than any other?

Some social theorists would reply that questions of this kind are not only unnecessary but unanswerable. In the first place, they would say, there are no 'scientific' grounds on which another person's wants or aspirations can be assessed, and it is no business of the academic observer to express his personal approval or disparagement of them. In the second place, some would argue that a notion like justice has no meaning beyond what is felt to be just at a particular time and place,[1] so that it is meaningless to bring it to bear on what people feel about the inequalities to which they are subject. I do not believe, however, that either of these objections is convincing. It is true that the academic observer should be free from bias; but this is a separate matter from the fact that any explanation of people's feelings rests ultimately on criteria which cannot be deduced from within the empirical evidence itself. Similarly, it is true that the meaning given to 'justice' has to be defended against the charge that it is arbitrary; but, as I shall try to show, a modified version of the contractual theory of justice can demonstrate in principle what kinds of grievances could be vindicated as legitimate and what reference group choices could therefore be described by this standard as 'correct'.

The objection against any attempt to evaluate people's wants or feelings is sometimes argued on the grounds that a want is analogous to a pain, so that there is as little point in telling a man that he ought not to want a higher salary or a bigger car as in telling him that he ought not to be feeling a headache. But this is a confusion of the issue. A want is not analogous to a pain for the simple reason that a want must have an object. It is possible for a person to say 'I want something, but I don't know what' in such a way that the analogy with a pain is valid; a statement of this kind is the expression of a feeling of dissatisfaction which the person is unable to pinpoint. But in the ordinary way a want entails an object: to say 'I have a want but I don't know what it is' is as absurd as to say

[1] For example, Pareto: 'When a person says "That thing is unjust", what he means is that the thing is offensive to his sentiments as his sentiments stand in the state of social equilibrum to which he is accustomed.' (*The Mind and Society*, § 1210).

248

'I have an intention to do something, but I don't know what'.[2] To criticize the relative deprivation which a person says he feels is not (except in special cases where his sanity is called in question) to dispute that he wants what he sees his reference group as having. It is to say that he is in some sense misguided in his choice of want; and it is for this reason that some notion of 'false consciousness' becomes relevant.

There is, however, one class of cases where the demonstration that a person is mistaken in what he wants does not involve the difficulties inherent in the attribution of false consciousness to other people. If a person can be shown that what he says he wants will not achieve the purpose for which he says that he wants it, then he may be described as mistaken without any overtones of this kind. Whenever it can be shown on, as it were, technical grounds that a person's interests will be better served by his abandonment of his chosen strategy, then it can be legitimately said to him that he is mistaken in his wants. Trivial examples of a 'mistaken' feeling of relative deprivation arise whenever a man is simply misinformed about his reference group—say, a man who feels relatively deprived of his neighbour's salary but does not realize that his neighbour has to pay out of it far heavier travelling expenses than he does himself. But more sophisticated examples are furnished by those cases where an enforceable contract—say, to obey traffic lights—will be to everyone's greater advantage than the right to drive through intersections as and when they please. Many questions of economic and social policy can be subsumed under this heading,[3] and there may be a number of topics on which a person could be persuaded out of his feeling of relative deprivation by being shown that a social inequality which appears to be to his short-term disadvantage is nevertheless to his long-term interest.

There will, however, be a great number of cases where the feelings of relative deprivation to which social inequalities give rise cannot be shown to be mistaken in this sense, but where the discrepancy between relative deprivation and actual inequality still seems to imply that the magnitude (or frequency or intensity) of relative deprivation felt is in some way disproportionate. It might be possible to argue that all such cases should be subsumed under an

---

[2] See Wittgenstein's remark in the *Philosophical Investigations* (2nd edn.; Oxford, 1958), § 441. 'Suppose I am asked "Do I know what I long for before I get it?" If I have learned to talk then I do know.' Here the deliberate use of a stronger term than 'want' brings the point out clearly.

[3] See e.g., W. J. Baumol, *Welfare Economics and the Theory of the State* (London, 1952).

interest model. Indeed, the 'false consciousness' argument is some-times advanced in a sense whereby the victims of false conscious-ness are said to be blind to their interests rather than failing to see the justice of their unformulated claims. But this is to carry the notion of interest further than what I have called the 'technical' sense to which it should be restricted.[4] An interest model can only be properly applied where the person's own conception of his in-terest will be better realized by his diversion of his present wants to a more expedient object. To tell him that something which he believes to be to his interest is not can be justified only by accept-ing his statement of what he wants and showing him either that the want will be better fulfilled by a different means, or that he is mis-taken about the facts of the situation of the reference group which has aroused his feeling of relative deprivation. It cannot be justified by telling him that his interest is not what he thinks. This is tanta-mount to telling him where his 'true' happiness lies, and although this task may perhaps be legitimately undertaken by moral philo-sophers, it is a task different from either the 'technical' demon-stration of a person's mistaken interest or the task which I propose to attempt here. What requires to be done is at the same time more than to show where people's stated interests can be better served than they are aware and less than to legislate over their spiritual welfare. In order to settle what magnitude or frequency of relative deprivation is 'legitimate' in any given system of social inequalities, it is necessary rather to establish the criterion of social justice whereby these inequalities can be assessed. The legitimacy of the relative deprivation felt (or not felt) can then be established not by showing merely how far it correlates with the positions in the system of those who do, or don't, feel it, but by showing how far it accords with the structure of a system whose inequalities could be vindicated by an appeal to justice.

But what does justice enjoin? What aspirations or wants or envies can it show to be legitimate? In particular, are there certain wants to which people have an absolute entitlement, whether they feel them or not? This suggestion of an 'absolute' entitlement has an added point, because the notion of relativity implied by 'relative deprivation' has led some writers to feel that there must be some wants or needs which could be termed 'absolute' deprivation—

[4] I mean by this the same as the distinction between 'instrumental' and 'ultimate' values drawn by Kenneth J. Arrow, *Social Choice and Individual Values* (2nd edn., New York, 1963), pp. 86-7, but without accepting Arrow's interpretation of the idealist distinction between the 'overtly expressed will' and 'truer desires'. Even claims which can be shown to be just are not the expression of 'truer' desires than any others.

wants, that is, which are independent of the situation of any other person or group, and which can be assessed by appeal to some ideal yardstick such as 'minimum need' or 'subsistence level'.[5] But this idea breaks down under closer scrutiny. There are, perhaps, 'absolute' needs in the sense of what is required by the human organism in order to survive. But they do not furnish a useful definition of 'absolute' either in the sense of not relative or in the sense of universally valid. The level of so-called absolute need can be just as well fixed at one level as another. It may be that progressively more extravagant wants often come to be felt as needs because progressively higher comparisons become plausible; but there is no necessary reason why a sense of need deriving from an external reference group should be less 'absolute' or less valid. Why is education, say, a less 'absolute' need than an adequate diet? It is true that there are certain standards of minimum need which are generally current for all three dimensions of social inequality: few people in contemporary Britain would deny the claim of legitimate need to either a pauper (in the hierarchy of class), an untouchable (in the hierarchy of status) or a slave (in the hierarchy of power). But if challenged, it would be a feeble argument to defend their claims on the grounds that these are 'absolute' deprivations. There have been many societies in which these deprivations have not been seen as any violation of rights, and an argument that they ought to be seen as such is not made any more convincing by labelling the needs of the pauper or the untouchable or the slave 'absolute'. It is also true that some feelings of deprivation are not feelings of relative deprivation: a feeling of hunger is not, as a rule, a relative deprivation. But this is another matter. The way to vindicate a feeling of relative deprivation is not by showing that it would be a legitimate deprivation even if the reference group were not there, but by showing that the inequality which is perceived is one which offends the canons of social justice. And although many people might wish to define justice so as to include the allegedly 'absolute' needs, the vindication rests on what is meant by justice, not on what is meant by absolute.

Only a theory of justice, therefore, can provide an adequate assessment of relative deprivation, and in so doing restate the 'false consciousness' argument in an appropriate form. Once given a theory of justice, there is a valid sense in which the perception or resentment of inequalities can be described as misguided over and above the sense of ignorance of observable facts, or expedient means. This is not because people's interests can be shown to be

[5] A distinction is drawn in these terms between 'absolute' and 'relative' deprivation, e.g. by Dahrendorf, *op. cit.*, pp. 217–218.

other than they think—because, for example, their location in society inhibits them from accepting the Marxist theory of history and thereby modifying their idea of what is to their advantage. The perception of inequalities can be shown to be misguided only in the different sense that if people resent inequalities which are not unjust, they are illegitimately resenting them; and if they accept or are unaware of inequalities which are unjust, then they are waiving, as it were, a right to resent them.

This is not to say that justice is a sole or overriding good. Indeed, few modern writers on justice would argue that it is. A system of social inequalities might be just and at the same time be harmful or degrading or inefficient or a whole number of other undesirable things. But justice is nonetheless a good which in the absence of stronger obligations ought prima facie to be put into effect, and it is this that is implied in saying that the discrepancy between relative deprivation and inequality can so be assessed as to show what feelings of relative deprivation are 'legitimate'. Whatever meaning is given to 'justice', the appeal to justice will distinguish those feelings of relative deprivation which can and which cannot be properly described as a sense of envy rather than the perception of an unfulfilled right. The way in which I shall try to show how this can be done is to apply to the notion of relative deprivation the contractual model of justice as it has been modified and developed in a series of related papers by John Rawls.[6] I am not suggesting that this model makes possible a complete resolution of all the problems traditionally associated with the idea of justice; but it does yield the one most powerful and illuminating question in the light of which relative deprivation can be assessed.

Rawls's conception of justice may be summarized as follows: the essence of justice is fairness, and for an understanding of the concept of fairness a contractual model is the most appropriate. This does not mean in any sense a reversion to the supposition of a social contract historically enacted from the state of nature; it means only that we should ask, in assessing the merits of rival claims, what criteria of assessment would have been established by rational persons if we could suppose them to have been required to agree, from a state of primordial equality, on principles by which they would be prepared both to make claims and to concede them. This agreement is to be supposed to have been on principles, not on

[6] 'Justice as Fairness', *Philosophical Review* LXVII (1958) pp. 164–194; 'The Sense of Justice', *ibid.* LXXII (1963), pp. 281–305; 'Constitutional Liberty and the Concept of Justice', *Nomos* VI (1963), pp. 98–125. I am also indebted to Professor Rawls for permission to consult an unpublished paper on 'Distributive Justice'.

specific practices;[7] and it is to be supposed to have been entered into before the parties to the agreement knew what their relative position would be in the social system within which they would be going to make and to concede their respective claims.[8] To make a claim on the basis of justice, therefore, is not merely to claim what is seen as a right, but to claim what is a right only if it derives from a principle to which the claimant would have subscribed before knowing whether he might not be the loser, rather than the gainer, by the acceptance of it. Thus the principles appealed to in the name of justice must be principles by which everyone would be prepared for his enemy to assign him his place.

The divergences of this line of argument from orthodox contract theory are in some ways more significant than its similarities. Contract theory proper finds its current expression in the theory of games, and the theory of games is, as Rawls himself emphasizes, inadequate to yield the notion of justice as fairness.[9] In this respect, Rawls's notion of justice has a closer affinity to some sort of Kantian 'kingdom of ends' than to the fiction of the historical contract.[10] But his model has the unique merit of disentangling from the criticisms to which it has been rightly subjected the valid insight at the heart of contract theory—the insight that to give meaning to a plea for justice it is necessary to get behind the formation of vested interests. If a person claims that an inequality to which he is subject is unjust, he must be able to give an affirmative answer to the question: 'Is this claim based on a principle to which you would have subscribed even if, as far as you knew, you were as likely to be a loser as a gainer by its implementation?'

[7] The notion of a 'practice' is used by Rawls in a semi-technical sense to mean any activity defined and structured by a system of rules; the term is more fully treated in his 'Two Concepts of Rules', *Philosophical Review* LXIV (1955), pp. 3–32.

[8] A somewhat similar line of argument in the context of welfare economics is given by J. M. Buchanan and G. Tullock, *The Calculus of Consent* (Ann Arbor, 1962), ch. 13, who suggest that the problem that without interpersonal comparisons of utility one Pareto-optimal position cannot be judged better than another can only be resolved by putting decisions back to the 'time of constitutional choice'. Cf. also Arrow, *op. cit,* pp. 107–108.

[9] See 'Justice as Fairness', p. 176, n. 12, where Rawls argues this by specific reference to R. B. Braithwaite's *Theory of Games as a Tool for the Moral Philosopher* (Cambridge, 1955); and cf. the reference to Braithwaite by Richard Wollheim, 'Equality and Equal Rights', *Proceedings of the Aristotelian Society*, LVI (1955–56), p. 299, n. 14.

[10] For the affinity with Kant, see the references given by Rawls, 'Justice as Fairness', p. 193, n. 23, and 'The Sense of Justice', p. 304, n. 16. For the view that Rawls's notion of justice rests, on the contrary, on a 'Hobbesian scheme of self-interest', see D. D. Raphael, 'Conservative and Prosthetic Justice', *Political Studies*, XII (1964), p. 160.

As a theory of justice—that is, as an answer to the question 'What is justice?' with which the whole of Western political theory begins —Rawls's model raises several difficulties which I cannot do more than touch on here. In the first place it is obviously a limited conception of justice: it reduces justice to fairness where others might want to say that justice is a concept wider than or even logically prior to that of fairness. I do not believe that this is an adequate criticism of the model, because it is precisely in this restriction that the virtue of the model lies. But if it could be convincingly shown that justice cannot be made coterminous with fairness,[11] then this would constitute a damaging objection.

A second difficulty is that there may, on Rawls's model, be many situations in which we are faced by a choice of just solutions. Where two competitors for a share of their society's wealth would both be prepared to be losers by the principles behind their own claims but not by the principles behind each other's, whose claim can an appeal to justice vindicate? Where two people hold conflicting priorities in their ordering of principles of social equality—say, needs over deserts or deserts over needs—they could well have disagreed even in a hypothetical state of nature. The resolution of their difference of principle cannot be built into the model without making the argument circular and so destroying its value. Rawls argues that rational men in the state of nature would, before they could know what their positions in society were going to be, agree on two principles of justice: first, 'an equal right to the most extensive liberty compatible with a like liberty for all'; second, inequalities to be treated as arbitrary 'unless it is reasonable to expect that they will work out to everyone's advantage, and provided the positions and offices to which they attach, or from which they may be gained, are open to all'.[12] This second principle, however, looks very like equality of opportunity plus Pareto optimality under another name —that is, the principle that everyone should be made better off provided that nobody is made worse off. But those claims, or feelings of relative deprivation, which most require adjudication are precisely those where some group or stratum stands to lose; and once someone is prepared to lose by his own principles for the regulation of social inequalities, what further appeal to justice is possible? Once again, I do not think this is a damaging objection to the validity of the model, for if it can disclose the point beyond which disputes as to the principles of justice cannot be settled except by some reference extrinsic to justice itself then it will have served its purpose. But I

[11] An attempt is made, for example, by John W. Chapman, 'Justice and Fairness', *Nomos*, VI (1963), pp. 147–169.
[12] 'Justice as Fairness', p. 165.

think that valid objections can be made to Rawls's second principle, as he chooses to formulate it; and although this formulation is not necessary to the theory, if it is required of any theory of justice that it should yield either unique solutions to all social games or even unique orderings of principles for the regulation of social inequalities, then the model may to this extent turn out to be deficient.

A third and related difficulty is that the model might seem to lend itself to interpretation as merely a sort of predefined advantage model in which people are required to see their interests only in a particular way. What does it enable us to say to the man who would be prepared to lose by his principles but for whom a choice of principles is merely a choice of risks among what he envisages as his possible pleasures? Why should he not accept principles for the regulation of inequalities by the light of whether he might sufficiently enjoy, and stand a sufficient chance of attaining, a superior position to make it worth the risk of an inferior one? In the hierarchy of class, he might be willing to take the chance of being a millionaire even at the risk of being a pauper. In the hierarchy of status, he might be willing to take the chance of being a king even at the risk of being an untouchable. In the hierarchy of power, he might be willing to take the chance of being a slave-owner even at the risk of being a slave. Why, therefore, should he not be entitled to his own principles of justice whereby only an entirely random allocation of social positions would be just?

This sort of objection is, I think, the most formidable.[13] It cannot be surmounted by dismissing such a view as irrational in the way that, say, a man who wished inequalities to be determined by the colour of eyes could be dismissed as irrational, without begging the questions which the model is designed to solve. Nevertheless, I think that the objection can be met by visualizing the outcome of such a suggestion if it were made under the conditions stipulated in the model. These conditions need not embody a spurious definition of rationality, but only a requirement that the parties to the hypothetical contract should be capable of argument and endowed with

[13] Not only Rawls's view of social inequalities is threatened by this line of argument. Tawney, for example, seems to have been prepared to admit that there is no answer at all to it: See 'Social Democracy in Britain', in *The Radical Tradition* (ed. Rita Hinden; London, 1964), p. 166: 'If a man affirms that his heart leaps up at the spectacle either of a society in which the common good is defined by the decisions of a totalitarian bureaucracy, or of one like—to mention only one example—the England of a century ago, where, in the unceasing struggle of individuals for personal gain, a conception of the common good cannot easily find a foothold, it may readily be admitted that no logic exists which can prove these exhilarating palpitations to be either right or wrong. One cannot argue with the choice of a soul; and, if he likes that kind of dog, then that is the kind of dog he likes.'

some minimal capacity for a sense of fairness (irrespective of the principles of equality on which it may lead them to decide).[14] This means that the question to be answered is not 'what risks would you be prepared to take before knowing how the game would work out?' but 'what rights would you wish to establish?'. And the person who argued that the second could be reduced to the first would have to justify this by some argument other than that of individual preference.[15] He would have to show that the system of social inequalities which he claims to prefer could accord with principles mutually acknowledged on grounds other than (as in pure games theory) the calculation of risk. I do not propose to try to show the lines which a refutation of this position might be expected to follow. It will be more useful to illustrate the value of the model by showing how principles might be established under its conditions which would make some assessment of relative deprivation possible. Indeed, the model is particularly suited to questions of social as opposed to individual justice for it enables the question 'what is social justice?' to be put in the following form: 'What principles for the regulation of inequalities of first, class, second, status, and third, power would be agreed to by rational men who were ignorant both of what their aptitudes would be[16] and of the chances which they would have of occupying any one position in their eventual social system?'

This model incorporates all of what I have called the 'technical' cases, where a person's ignorance of his interest as defined by himself is formally demonstrable. If a contract (either on principles or on specific practices) will lead the persons concerned to a situation where everyone will be better off by their own definition than if they followed their atomistic strategy, then everyone will accept the contract even before they know what their own position might

[14] See 'The Sense of Justice', *passim*.

[15] A somewhat similar case, but one which also raises the difficulty touched on in the previous objection, is that of the man who honestly believes that Jews should be exterminated even if he is himself a Jew (see R. M. Hare, *Freedom and Reason* [London, 1963], pp. 111, 169–172, 197). This view is likely to be more than a calculation of risk; indeed, we may be obliged, as Hare suggests, to allow it the status of a 'fanatical' moral belief. But however sincerely held, it would surely be as unlikely to be built into the principles of justice by the hypothetical signatories to the contract as the purely random criterion; in the state of nature, there could be no reason for it.

[16] They may, however, be supposed to have some knowledge of the elemental facts of human nature—say, those truisms which furnish the basis for what Professor Hart is prepared to call the minimum content of natural law; see H. L. A. Hart, *The Concept of Law* (London, 1961), p. 195.

be.[17] But the value of the model is that it goes beyond this in making possible the adjudication of those further cases where feelings of relative deprivation require to be vindicated even though the implementation of the claims implied by them would deprive some other group of advantages or privileges which it now enjoys. The test is whether these claims could be vindicated by appeal to principles which would have been mutually acknowledged by men having to settle on the kinds of inequality which they would permit before knowing their own positions. In the following chapter, I shall try to show how the principles which Rawls's model suggests[18] can have a bearing on specifically social inequalities and the feelings of relative deprivation to which they do or do not give rise.

[17] See W. G. Runciman and A. K. Sen, 'Games, Justice and the General Will', *Mind* n.s. LXXIV (1965), pp. 561–2.

[18] I must emphasize that in what follows I use the model in a way that is different from and perhaps incompatible with Rawls's own use of it. He does not apply it under the headings of class, status and power, as I do; and as I have already hinted, I do not regard his second principle of justice, as stated, as entirely satisfactory. Two other qualifications should be made also. First, the model is applied only to the inequalities within, not between, societies. If the parties to the contract were required to envisage themselves as being no more likely to turn out to be citizens of Britain than of China or Sierra Leone, this might not modify their agreement on principles but it would obviously modify the application of them. Second, no mention will be made of the special case of inequalities between adults and children.

XIII

A THEORY OF
SOCIAL JUSTICE

SINCE the agreement envisaged by the contractual model is to be supposed to be on principles, not on practices, it cannot be used to yield any specific formula by which the inequalities in a society should be fixed.[1] It will not yield the provisions of the one and only just Finance Act or Education Act or Trade Disputes Act; nor will it produce a formula for the one just distribution of the gross national product or the only rules to be followed if institutional practices like markets or elections are to be justly conducted. But it does yield a number of agreements on principle which can be applied to particular inequalities of class, status and power, and can thereby vindicate some feelings of relative deprivation as claims to justice while dismissing others as justifiable, if at all, only by some other criterion. I shall, as before, say very much less about inequalities of power, which raise a multitude of difficult questions outside the scope of this study. Rawls argues that the parties to the contract would agree on what could be summarized as the principles of constitutional democracy,[2] and it is not difficult to visualize in outline, at least, how their agrement could extend to limitations on the inequalities of power which might arise between employers and employees, police and citizens, cartels and consumers, and so on. But some brief comment on how the model might apply to inequalities of power is called for if only to show how the requirements of social justice, as well as the empirical relation between relative deprivation and inequality, are different in the dimension of power from that of either class or status.

It is possible to imagine some of the parties to the contract arguing for absolute equality of power—that is, for anarchy. But on

[1] The rejection of a formulaic principle of justice is, of course, long familiar in the theory of justice: it can be found as early as Aristotle's criticism of the formula put forward by Plato in the *Laws* (*Politics* 1266b).
[2] In 'Constitutional Liberty and the Concept of Justice'.

reflection, the model implies rather than at least some inequalities of power can be just. It is understandable how anarchist doctrines can spread under strongly repressive and tyrannical regimes, for no government at all may in such conditions seem preferable to government as it is operating in practice. But if the parties to a primordial contract are debating the principles by which inequalities of power are to be regulated, they will be likely to stipulate not that all authority is illegitimate, but that authority is only legitimate if it does not violate certain principles which would rule out the possibility of repression or tyranny. They will concede that some men must be able to give orders to others, even if they may themselves be among those who receive rather than give them, provided that the contract also limits the scope of the orders that may be given by whoever turns out to be doing so. Conversely, they will forgo the right to give certain kinds of orders even if they should themselves turn out to be those who are in positions of command.

An agreement as vague as this may seem remote from the actual decision in *Rookes v. Barnard,* or the Contracts of Employment Act of 1964 or even the right of combination for which the trade union movement had to fight for so long. But the gap does not in fact yawn so wide if we try to envisage how the discussion of principles in a situation of primordial equality might come to bear on such specific issues. First of all, there are several obvious derivations from the principle of the maximum liberty compatible with a like liberty for all. This not only yields such provisions as a restriction on theft or assault; it also has direct implications for the terms on which employers and employees enter into contracts with one another, the provisions for freedom of association and speech, and the right of appeal before courts of law. Indeed, agreement would extend further than this. If I have no way of knowing what my position or my aptitudes will be, I shall willingly agree to a number of specific grounds on which my liberty should be restricted over and above the restriction on theft, etc. Suppose that I am envisaging an advanced industrial society such as twentieth-century England without knowing what job I shall want or be fitted for or whether I shall turn out to be an employer or an employee. I think it is obvious that I shall want to ensure that if I turn out to be an employee I shall have at least some say in how the organization of which I am part is run, even though I must, to secure this from the state of nature, forgo the possibility of industrial autocracy should I turn out to be a boss. Indeed, a case could be made for arguing that I should agree both to claim and to concede—depending on my eventual situation—a greater measure of employees' control of industrial organizations than has existed in twentieth-century England or, for that matter, has been demanded by more than a minority of militant trade unionists. Such control might well turn out to be outweighed by other disadvantages; but an appeal to the hypothetical contract does suggest how it could be argued that reforms of this kind would at any rate be socially just.

These remarks are no more than a hint of how the hypothetical argument might run, and are introduced only to show how inequalities of power raise issues of their own which cannot be solved by derivation from the principles which might be agreed for the regulation of inequalities of class or status. I shall, however, try to show in rather more detail how the inequalities of class and status for which some empirical evidence has been presented could be assessed in the light of principles agreed under the conditions of Rawls's model. Are the inequalities which have been discussed such that the reference groups chosen represent a correct assessment of entitlement, or are these choices symptomatic of an inhibited or distorted recognition of how far the social structure is unjust? Ought more, or less, manual workers and their wives to feel that they are justly rewarded by comparison with others, or does the disapproval found among some members of the non-manual stratum express a legitimate grievance against narrowing differentials of class? Should manual and non-manual work be accorded equal prestige, or does justice permit certain kinds of talent or position to be more highly regarded than others?

INEQUALITIES OF CLASS

Imagine, accordingly, men capable of argument and of a moral sense who are required to agree from the state of nature what principles are to govern inequalities of class in the society of which they will in due course become members; and suppose further that they are required to envisage an advanced industrial society such as Britain in the twentieth century. Just as it can be shown that the argument for anarchy would be unlikely to be accepted, so it can, I think, be safely said that the agreement reached would not be on a principle of absolute equality of class. If every member of society were annually to receive an equal share of the gross national product, this would mean that a man who turned out to have many more dependents, or whose work was particularly difficult and dangerous, would have no claim to a greater share. A widower with seven children working long hours in a productive industry at personal risk would receive the same as a single man without a job kept by his parents. Faced with this possibility, it is surely plausible to envisage an agreement whereby the parties to the contract will concede that there may be some criteria, at least, by which they would be prepared to concede to others more than they turned out to have themselves in order to secure the right to an equivalent claim should they themselves fulfil these criteria.

But what would these criteria be? It is as clear, I think, that some restriction on inequality would be agreed as that this restriction would not be an absolute one. But further, it is plausible to suppose that three specific principles would be agreed in advance to be capable of justifying such subsequent inequalities of wealth as might occur. These three criteria are need, merit and contribution to the common good. All three appear in various forms throughout the literature on justice. What is distinctive about Rawls's approach is that it makes possible a derivation of these principles of distributive justice and an ordering—although, in my belief, only a weak ordering—of them.

Under the conditions of the model, it is hard not to visualize substantial provision being made for redistribution according to need. If I know that I might, as far as I can tell, find myself unable to support myself and my dependents through no fault of my own, I shall want to reserve the right (which I must also be prepared to concede) to claim some communal provision set aside from the wealth of those more fortunate. I may well, however, be prepared to concede or even to insist on some provision against malingering. This could be built into the definition of 'need': if I could in fact go out and earn a living, I shall be prepared to concede that I do not 'need' money contributed by my fellow-citizens for my support, and I shall expect those whom I might, as it turns out, find myself asked to support to do the same. This does not mean that I might not feel that some provisions in kind should be made by the state for all citizens irrespective of means, such as police protection or even, in a society as advanced as twentieth-century Britain, medical care or education; nor does it mean that there is not room for argument about the level beyond which needs, in the sense of 'supporting myself and my dependents' should no longer operate as a criterion. But it would be agreed that claims of need would be legitimate grounds for at least some redistribution of resources.

There would also be agreement that at least some inequalities of wealth could be justified by the criterion of contribution to the common good. This is not an incentive criterion as such; the fact that a talented man whose talents are valued by his society refuses to exercise them except at some extravagant reward fixed by himself does not mean that that reward is just. But if in the state of nature I were to envisage a society in which some skills were to be highly valued—whether because of their use in augmenting the production of resources or simply because of the pleasure they could afford to others—but I did not yet know which, or whether I should have them, would I not be prepared to claim and concede the principle that valued skills should be differentially rewarded? If I turn out to possess such a skill, I shall surely want to be rewarded for the exercise of it; I shall have been prepared to concede this right, even knowing that I may turn out not to have any skills at all, because of the stipulation that the skill must be such as to contribute to the common advantage of the society in which I turn out to be a member. There is, of course, the added risk that I may turn out not to be personally interested in the product of some skills which my fellow-citizens value; my tastes may be such that I am not interested in augmenting the national wealth even if I shall myself share in the increase. But I am, as far as I know, at least as likely to be in agreement with others in my tastes and therefore prepared, with them, to concede inequalities of reward to those who can gratify those tastes. I can have no reason for refusing to agree that contribution to the common good—however this turns out to be defined in my eventual society—will be a legitimate ground for claiming a differential in income.

This criterion of inequality might seem to include also the criterion of merit, for merit, after all, is socially defined, and society has no reason to reward those skills which are not considered to be of value. It is obvious that the mere possession of a skill will not be agreed to entitle a man to a higher reward. No matter how good someone is at solving crossword puzzles or whistling through his teeth, he will not be entitled to claim a higher income unless other people set a value on the product of his labours or derive an unusual pleasure from watching him engage in them. In the same way, merit in the sense of moral virtue would not be agreed to constitute by itself any justification of a claim to a higher reward. It is perfectly possible that hard work, say, might be regarded as virtuous by society and also be allowed to secure for the industrious man a greater reward than his workmates. But he is being rewarded not for his virtuousness, but his contribution to the common welfare. If his virtuousness were to consist in his perseverance at his crosswords, or his generosity to his friends, or his abstention from gluttony, or his personal modesty, there would be no suggestion that he was therefore entitled to a higher income. The parties to the contract do not, of course, know what their moral attributes will be or what will be the moral standards of their society. But although this will lead them to favour principles of tolerance (deducible, again, from the principle of the maximum of liberty compatible with a like

liberty for all), it will not lead them to a principle justifying inequalities of reward on the sole ground of whatever characteristics
happen to be regarded as virtuous by the other members of the
society in which they find themselves.

But despite this close connection of merit with the common
advantage in the justification of inequalities of wealth, there is still
a case for merit in a sense which cannot be entirely subsumed under
this heading. This is neither the sense of 'pure' skill or 'pure' virtue,
but the sense best expressed by the term 'difficulty'. The most
obvious example is furnished by the kind of difficulty which falls
under the heading of danger. It will surely be agreed as fair by persons having no vested interest that a person doing a useful job which
carries obvious physical risks should be differentially rewarded on
this account. Assuming that such jobs are open to all—and this
stipulation, which Rawls builds into his second principle, would
certainly be agreed under the conditions of the model—I shall not
only prefer, if I find myself wishing to take one of the dangerous
jobs, that it should be more highly paid, but shall be prepared, if I
decide that that risk is not worth it, to concede a differential to
those willing to accept the risk. The same will hold for those occupations which require so much specialized training that the rewards
which they bring are, for a greater or lesser period, deferred. Before
I know if I shall find myself taking a job as a labourer or an
advocate, I shall want to stipulate that I shall be compensated, if I
decide to become an advocate, for the period in which I have not
yet been able to earn what I should be getting if I chose to be a
labourer. Conversely, I shall want to stipulate that if being a
labourer entails demonstrable hardships or sacrifices not entailed
by other occupations, then if I turn out to be a labourer I shall be
entitled to a claim on these grounds. This agreement will not make
it possible to settle in advance whether all advocates should have
more or less than all labourers. But it shows how the principles for
distributive justice will be defined to include 'merit' or 'desert' in
some sense not covered by either need or common advantage.

Starting, therefore, from the assumption that all social inequalities
require to be justified it can, as a minimum, be shown that rational
persons in a state of nature would agree on three broad criteria, or
principles, in the light of which subsequent inequalities of reward
could be claimed to be just. This may not seem very much, but it is
already something. In the first place, it means that the principle of
'absolute' or 'strict' equality may be ignored, since what it contains
of value is embodied in the agreed injunction that all inequalities
need to be justified. Second, such criteria as 'to each according to his
status' or 'to each what the law enjoins' can be dismissed as

irrelevant except to the extent that they coincide with need, or merit, or contribution to the common welfare. Third, it may be taken as established—and this is the kernel of Rawls's own argument—that utility is by itself an inadequate criterion. Fourth, the doctrine that a 'just' reward may be defined by the outcomes of the market mechanism—the underlying notion of the original Fair Wages resolution of the House of Commons—can be categorically dismissed.

It is possible to go further than this. Persons without vested interest would not only agree on the three principles; they would in addition assign a certain priority to needs over the other two. This priority may be initially summarized in the dictum that in a society where anyone is starving it is a crime to have more than enough. If, in the state of nature, I know that I may in due course find myself starving, even though willing to work, while others have the wherewithal to keep me alive, I shall want to ensure not only that I have a claim recognized as just on the basis of need, but that I have a claim which overrides claims made on the basis of either merit or contribution to the common advantage. I shall want to be able to claim a redistribution in my favour no matter how difficult, skilled or dangerous the occupations in which those richer than myself are earning their money, and no matter how much they may by their exertions have contributed to the advantage of everyone including myself. Accordingly, I shall be prepared to say (this being the condition of my right to claim) that if rich I may legitimately be taxed for this purpose. This concession is one which I shall be entirely willing to make as a condition for the right never to starve as long as some wealth is available for redistribution.

But the argument for the priority of needs can be carried beyond the level of starvation. Indeed, it can be carried to the point where it has unmistakable implications for the arguments about minimum provision in the 'Welfare State'. There will be few people who would quarrel with a priority assigned to needs at the level of starvation. Even the administrators of the Poor Law at its most inhumane were prepared to violate Pareto optimality at this level by spending other people's money to keep the most destitute of their fellow-citizens alive. But there is no reason why the parties to the primordial contract would limit the priority of needs to starvation level, least of all when envisaging a society in which the minimum might be very much higher. If we consider how rational persons in a state of nature would try to allow for their ignorance of what a 'minimum' would be going to be, I think it becomes apparent that a limited measure of further agreement on priorities would be reached. It would not be on a predetermined line above which the claim that need outweighs

264

other criteria should be regarded as 'unreasonable'. It would instead be on a principle of appraisal whereby any claim based on need would have priority, in the absence of special considerations, over claims based on desert.

Suppose these rational persons in a state of nature to be considering the suggestion that in the society to be set up everyone shall be free to earn and keep as much as the criteria of merit and of contribution to the common advantage will allow, once some very low minimum of common provision for needs has been made. This minimum may, at this stage of the argument, be only what is necessary to bring up to subsistence level anyone found living below it, and to provide such institutional arrangement as will be agreed to be strictly necessary to guarantee the principle of maximum liberty compatible with like liberty for all. Those arguing against a too strong priority for needs want to be able to claim, if they turn out to be well endowed with talent, the retention of as much of their income as possible, pledging in return that they will forgo the right to claim more than subsistence if they should turn out to be so ill-endowed as to be unable to earn subsistence on their own. Why, they will ask, should they not be free to take such advantage of their talents as they can, once nobody else is actually starving? And if it should turn out that they are not themselves equipped with such talent as to benefit from the principles agreed in advance, then they will be content to have any demand which they make for the wealth of those more fortunate dismissed as a relative deprivation based on envy rather than justice.

The argument is not without force. But a counter-argument can be advanced against it which will be best presented in more concrete terms. The parties to the contract are, after all, required to envisage a society whose general level of well-being is such that not only is nobody starving but a good many people are earning sums very much more than adequate for the current average level of wants. Many of those at or near the bottom of the income distribution may be in possession of consumer goods which would seem to the members of other or earlier societies to be beyond the dreams of avarice. But they may be conscious of being, for example, much less well housed than the majority of their society; and at the same time, they may be aware that a good many of their fellow-citizens have a great deal more than the average income. They accordingly put forward a claim that those earning much above the average should be sufficiently taxed to bring them some way closer to the general level, the money so raised to be set aside in a fund to be used for raising the standard of housing among those whose incomes are least adequate to enable them to approach the average standard.

There is no question of doing away with the rights of the greater contributors to earn more than others in accordance with the criteria agreed in advance. The claim is only that where marked inequalities exist in terms of whatever standard is current then justice requires that some priority should be given to needs (in this sense) over and above the other two criteria.

The argument is necessarily vague. No attempt is made either to establish in advance how marked an inequality constitutes a claim of need, or to legislate over what 'useless' purposes would have to be disallowed as needs. But the search is always for a principle, not a formula. Where some people have genuine needs which are not in any sense 'subsistence' needs but which could be met by some re-distribution of marked inequalities of class, their claim should overbalance the weight which still requires to be given to the other criteria of distributive justice. Rational persons in a state of nature would, I believe, assent to this rather than to the argument that only 'minimum' needs defined in terms of subsistence should constitute a just claim on the fairly earned wealth of the more talented. They would, of course, want to be allowed to make and keep such differential earnings as would be recognized as legitimate. But they would be likely to agree that given an equal chance, as far as they can tell, of being at the bottom as at the top of the hierarchy of class, then the right to claim more than subsistence if they should turn out to be at the bottom will outweigh the right to keep more of what they earn if they should turn out to be at the top.

This line of argument is, of course, far from original. The view that standards of need must change in some approximate ratio to rising prosperity is at least as old as Adam Smith, and the primacy of need as a criterion of distribution can be traced back well before Marx through Louis Blanc and Babeuf to the *philosophes*. But the contractual model makes it possible to integrate these into a theory of social justice which is not restricted to the criterion of need, and can even suggest what weight should be given to it. From this it is possible to derive such specific implications as stiff progressive taxation at the upper levels of earning even where differential earnings are in principle defensible by the other criteria of social justice. Once suppose a state of nature before vested interests have been formed, and it becomes plausible not only to suggest what principles of distribution would have been agreed, but how this agreement would extend to at least a partial ordering of those principles, and how some specific practices could be defended by appeal to them.

There is still room, however, for a conflict over this ordering. Agreement may be reached to the extent that need will be assigned a certain priority. But there may be people who believe, even in the state of nature, that this priority should extend as little as possible into the area of deserts. When picturing a distribution among different jobs or positions at a given level of national productivity, some will want to reward those agreed to be deserving more than those agreed to be needy, and will be willing to abide by this preference even if they turn out to be in one of the needier positions. This is not simply because agreement on principles cannot yield a specific formula or because the definition of 'need' or 'merit' or 'common good' is in dispute. It is possible as a matter of principle—on any meaningful definition of principle—for rational men without vested interest to assign different priorities to the criteria which they agree to be relevant to the allocation of resources in a system in which they will be assigned a place which they cannot foretell. There will, therefore, be a point at which a system of inequalities of wealth cannot be assessed by the standard of social justice; two incompatible views of principle could be legitimately held by rival claimants even if both had had to face the possibility of being so placed that their own principles would make them worse off than before.

This might seem to be a large concession. Having already allowed that the feelings of relative deprivation which people have cannot be assessed by a single formula for the just distribution of income, it now appears that there will be situations where it cannot even be said which of two incompatible principles should be invoked as the relevant criterion of distributive justice. This is not, however, as large a concession as it seems. There will indeed be situations where such a conflict arises which cannot be settled by appeal to justice as fairness. But, as reference to specific examples will show, the scope for dispute between rival interpretations of social justice is enormously narrowed from the welter of conflicting theories which some writers have believed to be insoluble except by invoking a principle extraneous to justice.[3] There will not only be a number of people or groups of whom it can be said that they ought to feel a relative deprivation which they do not; there will also be a number of attempted justifications of existing inequalities which can be shown to be untenable unless some other defence than justice is made for them.

[3] The most famous example is Mill's attempt, in the essay on *Utilitarianism*, to show that the conflict can only be resolved by appeal to utility. The attempt is unworkable; but as Rawls points out in his paper on 'Distributive Justice', Mill was right in holding that to appraise a system of income distribution it is necessary to take a position outside it. For more recent doubts similar to Mill's, see e.g. Perelman, *op. cit.*, Ch. I ('Concerning Justice') or W. B. Gallie, 'Liberal Morality and Socialist Morality' in P. Laslett, ed., *Philosophy, Politics and Society* (Oxford, 1956), pp. 116–133.

Perhaps the most important implication of the contractual model for distributive justice is that in one specific sense it is fundamentally egalitarian. This is not an egalitarianism in the sense either that everyone has a right to an equal amount of wealth or that everyone has an equal right to whatever wealth he can amass once opportunities are open to all. It means rather that no inequalities are to be tolerated except those which can be defended by reference to principles which would have been agreed beforehand under the conditions of the hypothetical contract. It follows from this that in a socially just society there will be a continuous transfer of wealth from richest to poorest except where those above the poorest can vindicate their right to their greater wealth by reference to these principles. In the absence of special claims, there will be a constant regression towards the mean; the richer of any two persons must be able to say that his greater wealth accrued to him through the implementation of principles by which, if he were in the place of the poorer person, he would not feel victimized.

This disposes in one move of several arguments which are sometimes offered to justify inequalities between rich and poor. For example, it is sometimes said in defence of the greater wealth of the rich that if their fortunes were to be redistributed among the rest of the population—if, say, all incomes over £1,000 a year were to be redistributed on a per capita basis—the rest of the population would secure an increase in income so small as to be negligible. Now this is a proposal which no sensible egalitarian has ever made, and has in any case been effectively refuted by Tawney.[4] But a still more forceful refutation is made possible by reference to the hypothetical contract. The point is not whether the richest man's income is more than a drop in the bucket of the gross national product. It is whether there is any reason why the richest man's income should not be transferred direct to the poorest old age pensioner. Given the agreement on needs which I have postulated, the neediest citizens of mid-twentieth-century Britain have a direct claim—provided that they are not malingerers—on the wealthiest, unless the wealthiest can argue that the system of inequalities from which they are the beneficiaries is defensible on the grounds of their need, or merit or contribution to the common good to an extent which they would have agreed even if, as far as they knew, they would find themselves among the poorest. To this the wealthiest might be able legitimately to reply that it would depend on the reasons why the poorest are

[4] *Equality*, p. 132: 'Equality is to be sought not by breaking into fragments the large incomes . . . but by securing that an increasing proportion of the wealth which they at present absorb will be devoted to purposes of common advantage.'

the poorest; they might well, in the state of nature, have argued that it would be just for a man to remain at a very low minimum if his poverty was due to inveterate gambling. But in the absence of such special explanation for the situation of the poorest, the contract provides for consistent redistribution. To argue that the preservation of existing inequalities is just, the richer of any two persons must have been prepared, in Rawls's words, for his enemy to assign him his place in the system.

In the same way, the contractual model disposes of two other related justifications of unequal wealth which I have already touched on—justification by incentive and justification by what the market will bear. It may be that a doctor, or an artisan, or a professional footballer, or an entrepreneur will not be willing to exercise his skills except at some level of reward far in excess of his fellow-citizens. It may also be that the demand for his skills enables him to secure this reward, and that no one questions that it is a contribution to the common advantage. Indeed, it may even be that all the members of his society would prefer to contribute to his excessive differential than that he should cease to practise his trade. But if the price which he sets on his skills and which society is willing to pay is at the same time just, it is so only by coincidence. It is only just if it represents a differential which he would allow to be defensible on the grounds of desert even if he were himself at the bottom level of reward in his society and not a doctor, artisan, footballer or entrepreneur.

Can the supposed agreement on principles then be applied in any detail? From what has been said, it is clear that it cannot. It cannot show whether coalminers should be paid more than architects, doctors than footballers, or musicians than wholesalers, except where it is demonstrable that the differential could not reasonably be justified by appeal to the contractual model. But it does have one more consequence which is of some importance for the evidence on relative deprivation which has been presented in this study; by the standards of justice, the choice of comparative reference groups should be governed only by reference to the principles agreed under the conditions of the contract.

It follows from the model that those debating under its conditions about the inequalities to which they may find themselves subject will have in mind every possible comparison which might turn out to be relevant to their as yet unknown location in their social structure. They will not only ensure that like cases will be treated alike in the sense that one man doing the same job under the same conditions should not get more than another. They will also wish to ensure that if there is a case for a redistribution in any one's favour it should not go by default. It is possible that they might envisage the extent to which reference groups will be restricted by the day-to-day workings of the system, and narrow comparisons be not only more obtrusive but more intensely felt than broad ones. But it will be obvious to them from their situation of primordial equality that if this is relevant to justice at all it is only as an inhibition on the broad view of possible inequalities which is taken in the state of nature where the principles of justice are being settled. All inequalities, they will say, should be fully known and all comparisons regarded as legitimate.

First of all, therefore, the manual/non-manual line should have a very different significance from what it has in practice. It should in no way serve as a barrier to the reference group choices of manual workers and their families. A miner comparing himself with a fitter or a farm labourer with a boilermaker have an equal reason to compare themselves with clerks or businessmen or members of parliament. The facts of habit or precedent or even psychological comfort which prevent them from doing so are nothing to do with the justice of the inequality, and in this sense (and this sense only) 'false consciousness' is an appropriate description of the relation between their feelings of relative deprivation and the structure of inequalities within which their situation is fixed. It may be, of course, that many of the inequalities of which they might be aware, but are not, are inequalities which would pass the test of the contractual model; a miner comparing himself with a surgeon might feel that the surgeon's higher level of reward was one which he would himself, if he had turned out to be a surgeon, have regarded it as legitimate to claim. But he might also be aware of inequalities which would have been redressed in the favour of manual workers by anyone who had, from the state of nature, faced the possibility of being a manual worker under the existing system. There is the further possibility that he might regard all earnings as higher than they should be until some greater redistribution had been effected in favour of those no longer able to work, or of increased medical or educational services. But whatever the detailed outcome at any one level of national wealth, all comparisons would be treated as of equal relevance to any consideration of distributive justice.

In the same way, it might be true that the preoccupation of clerical workers with manual earnings could be vindicated by reference to social justice. But the contractual model makes it more plausible to see this preoccupation as the outcome of vested interest reinforced by precedent. Suppose the parties to the contract to be visualizing twentieth-century England without knowing whether they will find themselves holding a manual or non-manual job in it. It is, I think, doubtful if they would attach particular significance to this distinction. They might soon reach an impasse in attempting to settle particular differentials: is a bus driver's job more difficult than that of a company director? Does an electrician contribute more to the common good than a solicitor? Is the need of an intellectual for books comparable to that of a plumber for tools? The likelihood of such intractable questions as these, however, only breaks down further the importance of the manual/non-manual distinction as such. It might be that in confronting them the parties to the contract would agree that they must in practice be settled at least to some extent by the market value which society turns out to attach to particular skills. But again, if this were to turn out to emphasize the manual/non-manual distinction it would be only by coincidence; and since it is a prior condition of the just society that all positions should be open to all, the scarcity of particular skills would not be a result of unequal opportunity in the way that entry to the professions has, as we have seen, been effectively restricted by the social and educational structure of twentieth-century Britain. There might be no manual job which was more highly rewarded than some non-manual jobs, even when access to all jobs had been made equal. But this would not be because a non-manual job as such was regarded as a prima facie entitlement to a bigger reward.

A third and no less important consequence of uninhibited reference group choice is that much wider contrasts would be drawn in terms of need. We have seen some evidence for the way in which the old have become a self-conscious membership reference group with claims to a redistribution in their favour, and the evidence of the survey confirms the existence of a feeling among the old and poor that their needs after retirement are inadequately met. But their demands, when set against the gap between their incomes and those of others, are modest ones. Some of them, indeed, were prepared to say both that they were satisfied with their present income and that there were no 'other sorts of people' doing better than themselves. But this degree of inequality between pensioners and others would hardly be thought just by the parties to the contract, who have not only agreed on the priority to be given to needs as a criterion of redistribution but are faced with the possibility of being, as far as they know, as likely to be pensioners as anything else. It is evident that the answer in practice would depend on a number of particular circumstances: could a redistribution be effected without an increase in taxation, how many pensioners had declined to participate in an occupational pension scheme, and so on. But this is irrelevant to the validity of a claim to social justice. Assume the typical life history of someone born in England at about the turn of

the century, given a minimum of education, employed in an unskilled manual occupation, and drawn in a national sample carried
out in 1962. Could not such a person, if subsisting on less than £5
a week (including rent) and comparing himself with any or all of
his fellow-citizens, claim that his feeling of relative deprivation was
legitimate by reference to social justice?

The contractual model surely suggests that he could. If I am
faced with an equal chance of being any one such retired labourer
and any one surtax payer, will I not prefer an arrangement whereby
if I am the retired labourer on less than £5 a week I shall have £10
a week more although if I am the surtax payer I shall have £10 a
week less? It can properly be objected that things are not so simple,
for no government could implement such a readjustment between
pensioners and surtax payers simply by waving a wand. But Tawney's point is valid here no less than on the general question of the
redistribution of incomes. If the state of inequalities is such that the
difference between the richest surtax payer and the poorest pensioner
would not be upheld by people faced with either possibility and
having to weight, as far as they could, the agreed claims of need,
merit and contribution to the common welfare, then the poorest
pensioner is entitled to a sense of relative deprivation based on the
inequality between himself and the richest man. There will, of
course, come a point where the implication of the comparison is less
obvious. If the higher earnings of the rich are readily justifiable in
terms of outstanding and arduous contribution to the common good,
then it may be just that they should retain even in old age a larger
sum than is available to the man who had made no such contribution—given always that the poorer man is not at a level of such
relative hardship that any claim based on desert is outweighed by a
stronger claim based on need. But suppose the parties to the contract to be making hypothetical comparisons based on the England
of 1962. I do not think it is stretching the model too far to draw
from it the direct implication that some redistribution from richest
to poorest would be just, and that many more direct comparisons
should be made between manual and non-manual workers in terms
of hours, pensions, holidays and prospects of increasing income
than seem in fact to be generally made.

It will be clear from all this that the contractual model of social
justice is fairly radical in its implications. Even if it cannot demonstrate how far any given distribution is just, the supposition of
primordial equality implies that the holders of greater wealth
would be less well able to defend the differentials from which they
benefit if they had to do so under the conditions which the model
imposes. If asked to envisage the social structure of mid-twentieth-

century England in the knowledge of having to occupy some position within it, but having an equal chance of any single position, who would not want to stipulate some reduction of its inequalities? This applies not only to some redistribution of incomes and to comparisons of conditions of work but even more to those inequalities of wealth which are still less easily visible and still less likely, if only for this reason, to furnish the comparative reference groups on which feelings of relative deprivation might be based. If it is true that only need, merit and contribution to the common good would be agreed in the state of nature to justify inequality of wealth, it is evident that inherited fortunes will not be socially just. They cannot be vindicated by reference to any one of the three; and although it is perfectly possible that such wealth might be put to such uses that the common advantage would thereby be served, the parties to the contract would be unlikely to agree to the right of inheritance. They would be much likelier to stipulate that inherited wealth should pass into a common fund from which it would be either redistributed directly to the neediest or devoted to some purpose of common benefit to all the members of the society. Once again, therefore, the poorest appear to be entitled to a greater magnitude of relative deprivation than the evidence shows them to feel.

The implications of the model can be put in another way by saying that the test of inequalities is whether they can be justified to the losers; and for the winners to be able to do this, they must be prepared, in principle, to change places. However far this leaves us from the one and only just incomes policy, or taxation system, I think it is enough to put the question in this form in order to show that few of the reference groups which people actually take for comparison are those which would be dictated by social justice. It is wholly understandable that such influences as war or depression should have been the effective determinants of the reference group comparisons of the citizens of twentieth-century Britain, quite apart from the hold of habit and precedent. But the model makes it clear that if the reference groups chosen are those which could be vindicated by appeal to social justice, this is, as it were, mainly by accident. Suppose that the social and historical inhibitions on comparison are all removed, and it is required that any and all inequalities be justified to those least well off; it becomes immediately apparent that many more inequalities than are in fact taken for comparison would be difficult to justify in the name of social justice.

There is one final caveat. It follows from the concern of the model with only social, not individual, justice that the feelings of relative deprivation relevant to it are those which I have called fraternalistic rather than those I have called egoistic. Claims to social justice are claims on behalf of a group, and the person relatively deprived within an individual category will, if he is the victim of an unjust inequality, be a victim only of individual injustice. But it does not follow from this that only fraternalistic relative deprivations are legitimate. Many people may have claims to individual equality which could be defended by reference to principles agreed under the conditions of the contract, and even in a just society there may be individual inequalities within a single class or stratum. It is true that if the relative deprivations felt by the less well-placed in twentieth-century Britain were to be those easiest to vindicate by reference to social justice, they would be of a fraternalistic kind—pensioners on behalf of all pensioners, manual workers on behalf of all manual workers, and so on. But this does not make 'egoistic' feelings of relative deprivation illegitimate where inequalities of class are at issue. It is only where inequalities of status are at issue that, as we shall now see, the difference can be important for the implications of social justice.

INEQUALITIES OF STATUS

As soon as we envisage the parties to the contract deliberating about inequality of status, very different problems are raised from those raised by inequality of class. In particular, the case for absolute equality appears at first sight to be very much stronger. Rational men without vested interest might agree on grounds for allowing some people more money, or more power, than others. But would they not hold that every member of a just society would accord equal status to every other, irrespective of variations in role or talent or position? There is a long tradition in political theory which holds that in some sense, however hard to define, all men are equal as human beings and require to be treated as such. Is not this precisely what the parties to the contract would wish to ensure in providing against any inequalities of prestige?

But the counter-argument is also powerful. How can it be unjust for one person to admire another? If, in the social system of which I turn out to be a member, my tastes are such that I want to accord higher status to judges than to dustmen or to dustmen than to judges, what right has society to say that I should not do so? Such an injunction would amount to a restriction on freedom of speech. And even if it should turn out that so many people share the same standards in these matters that one group or another feels relatively deprived of status, what has this to do with social justice?

274

The answer lies, I believe, in a distinction which is not fully drawn either by Rawls or, as far as I know, any other political theorist. This is the distinction between (as I shall use these terms) praise and respect.[5] The first is, in the language of games theory, a zero-sum concept; the second is not. That is to say that to praise two people equally is to praise neither unless there are others by comparison with whom the two are being ranked equal first. To respect two people equally, however, is to respect both. This may seem a trivial statement, but it is not. The notion of equal praise is different both in logic and in practice from that of equal respect. In considering inequalities of class, I have argued that the parties to the contract would agree on three principles justifying inequalities—need, merit and contribution to the common good. In considering inequalities of status, I believe that they would agree not on criteria by which inequalities of status could be justified but rather on a single maxim: free inequality of praise, no inequality of respect.

With the word 'respect', we are of course confronted with a complex of problems long familiar to political and moral philosophers. It is easy to see what language of this kind is trying to express—equality before God, equality as human beings, the dignity of the person and so on. But no formulation of the idea, including Kant's famous precept about treating men as ends but not means, has been found to be satisfactory. The solution, however, is not to attempt another redefinition of 'respect', but simply to show how praise can be distinguished from it. The maxim can be rephrased by saying that in a just society inequalities of status would only be defensible where they could be plausibly shown to be inequalities of praise. Any other inequalities of status would, in the absence of special justification, be accounted inequalities of respect, and as such illegitimate. Any group feeling relatively deprived of respect, therefore, would have a legitimate claim to justice.

A single example is adequate to illustrate the difference. If we suppose the parties to the contract to be envisaging the possibility that different status may be accorded to them in their eventual society depending on the colour of their skin, it is obvious that they will rule out such a system on principle. If I do not know whether I shall have a black skin or a white one, I shall surely be unwilling to agree to any principle whereby either the one or the other will

[5] An apparently similar distinction is in fact made by Bryce in the passage to which I have earlier referred (above, p. 37 n. 2), for the distinguishes between 'equality of social status, or rank' and 'equality of estimation'. But he merely regards the two as slightly different grounds for according prestige, and although his 'equality of estimation' is close to what I mean by equality of praise, his 'equality of status' is not what I mean by equality of respect.

secure for me unequal treatment in the hierarchies of class, status or power. But suppose someone wishes to defend discrimination of this kind as no violation of social justice. It would be absurd for him to try to describe colour prejudice in terms of differential praise. Afrikaaners in South Africa, or white Southerners in the United States, can hardly be described as *praising* each other for the colour of their skins. What they accord to each other, and what the parties to the contract would stipulate against, is differential respect. This would still be true even if the discrimination practised in these places against those with different skins did not include a concomitant denial of equalities of class and power. Even if the only limitation to which they were subject were, say, the denial of admission to the relation of friendship on the sole ground of colour of skin, this would be prima facie evidence of an inequality of status which could not plausibly be justified as an inequality of praise.

There is, on the other hand, a wide variety of obvious inequalities of status which can be readily justified in terms of praise.[6] To applaud the individual excellence of great artists or statesmen or inventors or craftsmen is no denial of social justice. Nor is it illegitimate to extend this admiration even to groups as distinct from individuals. The injunction of respect suggests that it is wrong to assign status to the occupants of particular roles simply because they occupy those roles; if equality between human beings as human beings means anything, it presumably means that they are to be judged independently of the positions which they occupy. But it is perfectly legitimate for any or all of the members of a society to accord higher status to its judges or professors or ministers of state if they are thought to hold their positions because they are the possessors of certain admirable skills or talents. This is not incompatible with praising miners and garage hands for their different skills or even admiring the skills of the miner more than those of the professor; but at the same time, it is not necessary to admire miners as well as professors in order to be absolved of the charge of according differential respect. It is only when such attributions of praise become institutionalized that they violate the maxim —when, that is, one activity or role is assigned higher status than

---

[6] This is not the same argument as that used by Professor Vlastos to show that at least one good may be unequally allocated without injustice. Vlastos claims that the unequal distribution of praise according to merit is just because of the value of praise as 'a practice generating incentives to creative effort'. But this is a poor argument. If the practice of praising turned out not to further creativity, it would still be just to bestow unequal praise. See G. Vlastos, 'Justice and Equality', in R. B. Brandt, ed., *Social Justice* (Englewood Cliffs, N.J., 1962), pp. 63ff.

another irrespective of the praise accorded to the attributes of the person practising it.

Imagine a society in which physical strength is admired above all other attributes. An anthropologist studying this society observes a number of ways in which higher status is bestowed on the strong; how might we suppose him to be able to distinguish those which could from those which could not be properly described as the bestowal of praise? He might notice that the acquaintance of the strong was curried by the weak, that the strong were often cheered or applauded by the weak on their public appearances, that the strong were awarded medals and decorations for their strength, or that a random sample of parents in this society all said that they would prefer their children to be strong than weak. On the other hand, he might notice that when the strong appeared in public all passers-by either bowed or knelt, that the children of the strong were accorded the same deference as the strong themselves, that only the strong initiated conversations or greetings with the weak, not vice versa, or that separate public facilities for washing and eating were provided for the strong and for the weak. In the first case, the anthropologist would surely interpret his observations as evidence for inequalities of praise, but in the second for inequalities of respect. It is possible to visualize behaviour that he might observe which, in the absence of further evidence, could not be assigned to either one or the other—for example, statistics on the frequency of social contact between strong and weak might or might not offer him the evidence which he needed. But the example is, I think, adequate to show the essence of the difference between the two, however difficult it may be to offer a satisfactory definition of 'respect'.

In turning from this hypothetical example to the social structure of twentieth-century Britain, there are two sorts of inequality which we have seen to be particularly relevant and which can, up to a point, be assessed against the maxim derived from the contractual model: inequalities in education and inequalities in the status assigned to different kinds of job. In practice, inequalities in the educational system are tied also to inequalities of class, first because some forms of education are paid for and second because class-situation is increasingly a function of educational qualifications. But it is not difficult to isolate those aspects of the educational system where inequalities of status are those principally at issue and where, therefore, the maxim should be invoked. If we suppose the parties to the contract to be envisaging the educational system of England between 1918 and 1962, there can be no question that they would pronounce it unjust. If I do not know what my own location in society will be or what the aptitudes of my children will be, will I consent to a system whereby the children of the richest parents will be able to get the sort of education which is accorded the highest status? I think there is no doubt that I will not. But the parties to the contract would be able to reach a further agreement than this. They would agree that some educational inequalities would constitute no violation of social justice; but this would be on the condition that 'parity of esteem', interpreted as equality of respect, were strictly preserved.

A complete uniformity of education might be proposed by those parties to the contract who were hostile to too great a differentiation, even by merit; they might attach, as a matter of principle, more importance to equality of status than to the recognition of talent, and be unwilling to allow more talented children to secure higher status even when, as far as they knew, their own children might be the beneficiaries of such unequal treatment. But the answer lies once again in the preservation of strict equality except where justifiable in terms of praise. It will be agreed that everyone will be free to admire such talents or attributes as he pleases; but in accordance with the maxim there will be an injunction against the accordance of institutionalized privilege to any one kind of talent or attribute as such. Some children will be good at music, some at science and some at football. It may well be that equal resources will not be allotted to the cultivation of these various skills, for those talents which will be the proper objects of expensive training will, like inequalities of income itself, have to be justified by contribution to the common advantage. But there is no reason why excellence should not be given rein provided that one kind of excellence is not accorded higher status because one kind of activity is as such accorded more respect.

It could, therefore, be agreed to be just that a common education should be provided for all children up to the age at which some specialization by aptitudes was appropriate; thereafter, further education could be provided for those fitted for it, but those whose talents were not such as to require further formal education would not for this reason be accorded any lower esteem. Those fellow-members of their society who admired only those skills for which further education was necessary would be free, in terms of praise, to look down on them. But they, in return, would be free not to admire those skills associated with further education; there would be no overtone of social inferiority attaching to either. Such a system could be agreed to be fair by persons without vested interest and ignorant of the talents of their prospective children; and for precisely those reasons for which it would be fair, it is clear that the system in twentieth-century England is not.

It is equally unlikely that persons without vested interest would agree to the justice of any educational system in which children were segregated by parental origin. They would naturally wish their children to be free to form their own associations based on whatever lawful grounds they might please. Within a system which provides for parity of esteem there may still be cliques and factions and a graded hierarchy of admiration and friendship. But no parent would agree from the state of nature that the location of parents in the social system should debar any child from this freedom of association. Now this is, it need hardly be said, a persistent criticism voiced against the English educational system during the period under discussion. Indeed, it is a criticism voiced not only by left-wing partisans of radical social justice. Stanley Baldwin wrote in 1929 that 'The classification of our schools has been on the lines of social rather than educational distinction; a youth's school badge has been his social label. The interests of social unity demand the removal of this source of class prejudice'[7] and Harold Macmillan wrote in 1938 that 'It would do nothing but good to the children of every class if the early years of life were spent in the same school.'[8] But however familiar such criticisms might be, and from whatever sources they might have come, they could be as plausibly made in 1962 as in 1938 or 1929; and if inequalities of status deriving from the educational system cannot be shown to be differences in what I have called 'praise', those in an inferior situation are entitled to a feeling of relative deprivation of status. The reasons which would be agreed in the state of nature to justify educational inequality might be such as would correlate in practice with some attribute of the parents; but no parental attribute could be made the reason for the inequality without violating the prohibition on inequality of respect.

Exactly the same applies to the inequalities of status attached to different types of job; and indeed, the two are closely connected. In any society, just or otherwise, the allocation of jobs will be tied to the system of education. But in a just society, although the possessors of some talents and therefore jobs will be more admired than will others, neither the job nor the education which precedes it will be accorded any differential status apart from this. The most obvious implications of this are for the manual/non-manual distinction. If I do not know whether my talents will lead me towards manual or non-manual work, I shall not agree to a

[7] Quoted Lowndes, *op. cit.*, p. 119.
[8] H. Macmillan, *The Middle Way* (London, 1938), pp. 64–5.

system whereby one is assigned more prestige than the other any more than I would agree that the education of my child should be dependent on my income. It is true that the distinction in status between manual and non-manual work is so widespread as to be almost a universal rule; nowhere in the world has it been customary for a 'gentleman' to work with his hands. But however strong the custom, and however understandable the economic and social influences which have produced it, it is hard to see it being agreed to be just by persons with, as far as they know, an equal chance of the one or the other.

It might be objected that there are many manual workers who do not feel any relative deprivation on this account and who have no less self-respect or pride in their work than workers in occupations which are more highly regarded by society at large. Are they to be convicted of 'false consciousness' because they are not disposed to resentment or envy? But it will be clear from the sense which the contractual model gives to the notion of false consciousness that it does not require any individual to be roused to feelings of envy. It means only that if a manual worker, however contented, were to feel that manual workers are accorded too little status by comparison with non-manual, this feeling of relative deprivation would be legitimate. The empirical evidence has shown that there is not an equality of status between the manual and non-manual strata; and since these inequalities are not all such as could be assigned to the category of inequalities of praise, they can for this reason be classified as unjust.

But what of the distinction between egoistic and fraternalistic relative deprivation? The evidence also showed that where relative deprivation of status is felt by manual workers or their wives, it is often of an egoistic rather than a fraternalistic kind; and this is in many instances linked to a choice of normative reference group which implies a conscious differentiation from those seen as in some sense inferior. It follows from the model that on inequalities of status just as much as of class, the choice of comparative reference groups should be free. Not only may the members of any group or stratum legitimately ask whether they are being accorded equal respect with any other person or group, but they are equally entitled to compare themselves with whom they please in matters of praise. The one kind of relative deprivation which an appeal to social justice will not vindicate is a feeling of being entitled to more respect than anyone else. Praise may, of course, be wrongly sought in the sense that an artist who thinks he is as good as Picasso may feel relatively deprived of praise even though all his fellows and critics regard his pretensions as absurd. But this is not a matter of social justice. Social justice arises only when either a relative deprivation of status can be shown to be a desire for unequal respect, or where there is in fact an inequality of respect which calls by definition for remedy.

It follows, therefore, that any wish by members of the non-manual stratum to preserve a difference of respect between themselves and manual workers, and any wish by manual workers to share in such a difference of respect, could not be vindicated by appeal to justice. For this reason, egoistic feelings of relative deprivations of status must be suspect in a way that is not true of class. This does not mean that any manual worker or his wife who describes himself as 'middle-class' is an aspirant for a kind of status which, if attained, would be illegitimate. As we have seen, this implied choice of a normative reference group may mean any one of a number of things, from an awareness of being better-paid or in a more skilled job than other workers to the attribution of purely personal differences of taste and character. Not even the fullest verbatim replies recorded by the interviewers make it possible to classify the replies in terms of the distinction between praise and respect; without more intensive questioning, there is no way of telling whether the phrases typically used expressed an approval analogous to the praise accorded to talent or the respect accorded to each other by people who wish to exclude from contact as equals all but those who share a common attribute. Many of the working-class respondents in the sample who seemed to wish to distinguish themselves from other manual workers might be found to be doing so for reasons entirely defensible as attitudes to praise. But in a society where status is unequally apportioned between occupations in a way which is not readily defensible in terms of praise, an aspiration to the status of the higher positions must carry at least a hint of the sort of aspiration for unequal respect which would not be consonant with the ideals of social justice.

But given that this situation arises because the distribution of status is not yet just, it can be argued that this kind of aspiration, although inconsistent with the ideal of social justice, is nonetheless legitimate in a different sense. A person may be entirely aware that the system is unjust and yet see no reason why, until it has been changed as it should, he should not have as much right as anyone else to one of the superior positions within it. In the same way, where a system of education is unjust, it may or may not follow that every parent must be condemned who would like his child to be a beneficiary of the injustice rather than the child of some other parent who does not even see the system as unjust. The answer to this question lies outside the scope of the contractual model, and could only be settled by appeal to standards of personal morality which are not the concern of this study. But the fact that the question can be asked at all does shed a further light on the sense in which feelings of relative deprivation can be assessed in terms of social justice. The question whether there are good reasons for a feeling of relative deprivation which could not be vindicated by appeal to social justice has nothing to do with what can or cannot be shown to be socially just. The claim to equal rights with the beneficiaries of an unjust system is not a claim to social justice; but this does not make it an unjust claim.

Thus aspirations for individual mobility are not necessarily illegitimate, either in class or status. A coalminer taking as his comparative reference group the holders of high executive positions may be wholly entitled to his aspiration to replace them; and by replacing them, he will move up the hierarchy of status and power as well as of class. But his aspiration for social mobility will be legitimate not because it is a claim to social justice but because social justice has little to do with it. The aspiration for individual mobility entails a claim to social justice only in the sense that the starting position of the coalminer may be the product of inequalities which could be shown to be socially unjust. Beyond this point, it is a matter of individual justice whether he succeeds in his ambition. In a just society, indeed, the wish of a coalminer to become a managing director would be no different in its social overtone from his wish to become a professional footballer. It would be illegitimate in terms of class only if he wanted the superior position because of its unjustly large rewards; and it would be illegitimate in terms of status only if he wanted not differential praise but differential respect.

In a just society, therefore, there would be some inequalities of status just as there would be some inequalities of class. But these would all be inequalities of status in the sense that Picasso has higher status as a painter than does an ungifted amateur, not the sense in which a duke has higher status than a labourer. Many people would look down on others; but this would be in the way that people are looked down on for being unmusical or clumsy or bad at football or even morally wicked, not the way in which they are looked down on for having black skins, or poor parents, or working-class accents. There would be many status-*groups* in the sense of people sharing a common style of life and perhaps common criteria of praise over wide areas of human activity. But there would not be status-*strata*, or castes, whose members could point to some socially institutionalized criterion for disrespecting, or being disrespected by, other people not sharing a common characteristic. Deference would be expressed by some people towards others; but this would be in the sense in which people defer to the opinions of those whom they believe to be wiser than themselves—the sense, in other words, which is synonymous with admiration. It would not be the sense in which the labourer defers to the duke.

In the same way, there would be some educational inequalities in a just society. But no higher status would attach to any one branch of education except to the extent that those qualifying for it were all considered more deserving of praise. It might be that the children receiving a longer or more specialized education than others would all share certain social characteristics; but these would be coincidental—they would not be the reasons for which an unequal education was being given to them. It is even possible that those receiving the most education would go into the better-rewarded occupations (assuming that these differentials were not overriden by claims of need); but those in the less well-paid jobs for which less education was necessary would have had an equal opportunity to choose this education, and would be less well rewarded only if their work was agreed to be less arduous, or to make less contribution towards the common welfare.

It is once again apparent that any decisions of public policy, even if taken by legislators who wished to give the fullest weight to the demands of justice, would have to be settled on other grounds than an appeal to the contractual model alone; and on inequalities of status, there is an additional reason for this which does not apply to inequalities of either class or power. To pass a law whereby it was illegal to accord unequal status except where it could be justified as praise would not only raise formidable difficulties of definition; it would involve extending the scope of legislation into a field which is ultimately immune to it. A government can tax a man, but it cannot force him to regard everyone as his equal in respect. It can secure the overt rights of *isonomia* for all citizens irrespective of status; but where inequalities of status are themselves at issue, justice must, even more than elsewhere, work outside of the statute books and in the hearts of men of good will.

But in any event, the contractual model cannot directly guide the legislator for the reason which applies no less in both the other two dimensions of social inequality. To ask whether inequalities are such that rational men without vested interest would have agreed to principles which would justify them can never yield an answer to specific questions of policy. It can only yield the test which any system must pass if it is not to be categorically dismissed as unjust. This is less, perhaps, than might be hoped by those for whom the answer to 'what is justice?' is Plato's (or any other) ideal republic.

But in doing this and no more than this, the contractual model makes it possible, as far as it can ever be possible, to classify feelings of relative deprivation as 'legitimate' or 'illegitimate' by the standards of social justice.

XIV

REFORM AND ITS LIMITS

SOCIAL justice, then, can be both defined in abstract and brought to bear on observable attitudes to social inequality. But it is not to be wondered that it should play little part in the opinions and feelings even of those whose unformulated claims it would vindicate. Most people's lives are governed more by the resentment of narrow inequalities, the cultivation of modest ambitions and the preservation of small differentials than by attitudes to public policy or the social structure as such. Inequalities which are scarcely visible and difficult to remedy will have little influence on the day-to-day emotions of any but those whose political consciousness is unusually militant or sensitive; and envy is a difficult emotion to sustain across a broad social distance if gratification is nowhere within view. Yet there are times and places at which the resentment of inequality rises to a level where it not merely corresponds with the facts of inequality but even overreaches them. There is no single reaction to a condition of subordination which cannot be documented for some society at some period, from the degraded passivity of a subject race to the incendiary fury of a rioting jacquerie. There is some generalization appropriate to every one of these relationships between relative deprivation and inequality, but there is none which makes any particular relationship the obvious one. For every society, and every group in that society, the question needs to be asked afresh, and it needs every time to be separately asked for each of the three dimensions in which all societies are stratified.

The history of England in these matters is generally explained in terms of its peculiar propensity to gradualism. But to talk of gradualism is, like talking of 'deference', largely to redescribe what requires to be explained. The true explanation leads far further back into English history than the few decades of the present study. Why was there never a revolution in nineteenth-century England? The gradual advance of the British working class to some greater equality with the strata above it has been punctuated by sporadic might-have-beens when an upsurge of feelings of relative deprivation —often the result of rising prosperity rather than hardship—has hinted at the imminence of revolutionary radicalism only to lapse again into acquiescence or even approbation of the established order. Indeed, the relation between inequality and grievance which I have suggested for the period from 1918 to 1962 could perhaps be shown to hold over a much longer period: in the dimension of class, a cycle of mounting resentment followed by passive conservatism; in the dimension of status, relative deprivation spreading steadily but slowly as inequality is reduced; in the dimension of power, a decline in militancy as the legal, electoral and industrial position of the underprivileged has been seen as progressively improving. From these interlacing strands there has been woven a social fabric in which traditional privilege blends with egalitarian socialism, and class-consciousness with a veneration of existing institutions, in a manner which is immediately visible to even the most casual student of Britain but which is very much easier to document than to explain.

The only generalization which can be confidently advanced is that the relationship between inequality and grievance only intermittently corresponds with either the extent and degree of actual inequality, or the magnitude and frequency of relative deprivation which an appeal to social justice would vindicate. But even this modest conclusion raises questions of its own. It may be true that social justice enjoins other attitudes to social inequalities than those which empirical investigation has disclosed. But what follows from this? I remarked at the outset that two opposite conclusions can be drawn from the relation between inequality and relative deprivation, even where the empirical evidence is not in dispute; and in the same way, even a demonstration that this relation does not accord with social justice is not by any means the end of the argument. To the Left, of course, it should be: social injustice calls by definition for remedy, and where people do not perceive it as such it is morally imperative that their false consciousness should be dispelled. But the Right can counter this argument with an argument of its own for which its advocates will offer empirical evidence. Inequality, they will say, is inevitable; to attempt to do away with it will make more people unhappier than they are at present; and if this means that 'social justice' is not done, then all that follows is that there are more important things than 'social justice'.

It has certainly to be agreed even by the most radical partisans of justice that to show a system to be unjust is not to show how it should be changed. This question has always to be decided on other grounds, and it is not the purpose of this chapter to try to answer it for contemporary England or anywhere else. Some political theorists, like Burke, have argued that any attempt to alter the social structure is likely to be for the worse; others, like Lenin, have argued that whatever the costs, they ought to be paid. But this has nothing to do with the prior question whether social justice—irrespective of the ease or difficulty with which it might be realized—is the only or even the most important standard by which social inequalities should be assessed.

It is difficult to deny any appeal whatever to those visions of society in which an ordered hierarchy and close-knit fabric of social relations is linked to a form of economic organization whereby men are not alienated from their work and its products under the de-humanizing condition of 'mass society'. The appeal of such a system was strongly felt even by Marx, for whom its transition was a neces-sary prelude to the Communist society in which some of its virtues would again be exemplified;[1] and it has been felt by anyone, whether on the Left or the Right, for whom modern industrial organization implies a loss or distortion of the values of earlier systems which might have been less mobile and less egalitarian but in which people were (so it is argued) in some way more content. Some writers have claimed to find this contentment still visible among the inhabitants of country districts whose social structure is more hierarchical and paternalistic than that of city-dwellers but for whom this results in, if anything, a greater measure of satisfaction and self-respect. Others have argued that where equality is too obtrusive an ideal, envy and discontent are found to be heightened, for where all are entrants in an open contest, there is a greater disgrace attached to an inferior position. Still others have argued that equality cannot be imposed except by a denial of freedom, since all men who are not incurable dogs-in-the-manger would rather be free to emulate one another than be forced to conform to a tyranny of universal mediocrity. Is there not a strong case, therefore, to be made for ignoring the injunctions of social justice, particularly in a society whose general level of prosperity is as high as that of twentieth-century Britain?

Unfortunately, there is no way of settling arguments about happiness. There are always good grounds for suspecting those in

---

[1] For example, Marx and Engels in the *Communist Manifesto*: 'The bour-geoisie, wherever it has got the upper hand, has put an end to all feudal, patriarchal, idyllic relations. It has pitilessly torn asunder the motley feudal-ties that bound man to his "natural superiors", and has left remaining no other bond between man and man than naked self-interest, than callous cash-payment'. Or Marx in the *Economic and Philosophic Manuscripts of 1844* on the 'human, intimate side' of the relation between feudal workers and their lord, who 'does not try to extract the utmost advantage from his land'.

the more comfortable strata of society who pronounce too glibly about the happiness of their inferiors. But psychology has not yet advanced to the point at which it could furnish a test of the proposition that men are happier in more or less egalitarian societies.[2] This question is answerable only where the choice is so manifestly clear that no argument between the partisans of Left and Right is likely to arise. Yet it would be a mistake to conclude that no further discussion is possible. For the issue rests neither on the happiness of feudal peasants nor on the miseries of alienated, industrial man, but on whether the extent and kind of inequality consonant with the ideal of social justice is necessarily incompatible with those kinds of happiness which are supposed to be found in less egalitarian systems.

Those disposed to answer yes will agree that no adequate comparisons of happiness are feasible; but they will be likely to argue that a socially just and therefore more egalitarian society would be less colourful, more bureaucratic, more inimical to the free play of talent, and less productive of both wealth and culture than a less egalitarian one. Since there is not yet the sociological evidence which would establish this any more than there are the psychological techniques which would make interpersonal comparisons of happiness possible, such an argument will often be reduced in practice to an exchange of immovable preferences—loyalty versus efficiency, variety versus standardization, even benevolence versus justice. But such disagreements are less unarguable than they often seem, not because the evidence is available but because the arguments advanced against egalitarianism are remarkably often irrelevant to the claim that a just society would be a no less happy one. They are apt to be irrelevant for one or even both of the two reasons which I have already touched on: first, social justice does not require a total egalitarianism; and second, the alleged costs of social justice are for the most part costs of achieving justice, not costs which would need to be paid by a society which was already just.

To take twentieth-century Britain and make it socially just might, perhaps, reduce its efficiency, diminish the satisfactions of some people more than it augmented the happiness of others, and entail a form of economic and political organization which would

---

[2] There is some evidence of a kind in the results of small-group experiments carried out in the United States in which a democratic form of organization is shown to be more satisfactory for the performance of group tasks than an authoritarian one. But even if these results are conclusive in their own terms, there are no grounds whatever for inferring conclusions from them about the workings of whole societies. See e.g. François Bourricaud, *Esquisse d'une Théorie de l'Autorité* (Paris, 1961), Pt. I, for effective criticism on this point.

exemplify every attribute which the champions of inequality would deplore. But imagine a society at approximately the economic level of twentieth-century Britain which was already just. What are the grounds for supposing that it would embody such disadvantages or vices as to outweigh the benefits or virtues of justice?

In some ways, such a society might resemble the United States more than any other country. The structure of social relations depicted by Tocqueville and Bryce—excepting always the treatment of the American Negro—was already nearer to what might be envisaged as just by the parties to Rawls's contract than any of the European régimes with which they could compare it. Inequalities of wealth were, as they saw, very great. But inequalities of status were for the most part such as could be classified as inequalities of praise; the individual citizen had a greater say in the decisions by which his life was affected; and despite the possibilities for the exploitation of labour, Tocqueville predicted that equality of social condition would promote, and be in turn reinforced by, a steady rise in the general level of wages. Since Tocqueville wrote, European society has changed in many ways which have confirmed the prediction made by him and his successors that what America is today Europe will become tomorrow. But it would be a mistake to conclude from this that a Britain made socially just would come more than in part to resemble the United States. In the first place, there are several ways in which the American social structure would still be difficult to justify by reference to the hypothetical contract; and in the second, the one ingredient missing in the United States which would follow from the agreement reached under the conditions of the contract is what can best be summarized, despite the dangers of the term, as Socialism.

It is often said that Socialism is about equality; but this catch-phrase has little value unless it is shown what sort of equality is meant and under what sort of conditions it is supposed to follow. I do not mean by Socialism—although it is a more useful definition than many—that a predominant influence is to be assigned to the state in economic affairs. It is possible that a distribution of wealth which would pass the test of the contractual model would be better, or only, achieved by such a form of economic organization, but it is equally possible to visualize a society in which the distribution of wealth was socially just although no industries were nationalized. The sense in which Socialism follows from the primordial contract is the sense in which it is opposed to individualism. In the individualistic tradition, which is better exemplified in the United States than any country in the world, equality is equality of opportunity; in the Socialist tradition, it is equality of communal rights.

The contractual model enjoins Socialism in this second sense through the emphasis which it lays on need. The contract does, it is true, allow inequalities to be justified on other grounds. But whereas the individualistic conception allows inequality to go unchecked once opportunity is open to all, the parties to the contract would have stipulated that any inequalities must be redistributed according to need except those which could be specifically defended. This might in practice lead to forms of centralized bureaucratic organization which would be Socialist in the *dirigiste* sense. But the important difference between the two conceptions of justified inequality is not the form of organization implied by them. It is that the system envisaged by the parties to the contract provides for literal equality except where other principles agreed in advance of vested positions can be shown to apply; whereas on the individualistic view, no inequality needs to be justified except where it has been attained by the illegitimate aid of special privilege.

The claims of social justice, therefore, may be dismissed not only by those who prefer a feudal order in which every person knows his place in a stable network of obligations and rights. They may also be dismissed by those for whom individual effort has a primary value. Such people will argue not for the merits of aristocracy but of unrestricted competition; they will be opposed to what I have called a Socialist conception of equality not because it allows too much mobility but too little; and they will regard a socially just society as mean and drab not because it blights the efflorescence of a civilization based on caste but because it restrains the uninhibited exercise of individual ability. They might agree with Rawls's first principle of the maximum liberty compatible with a like liberty for all. But they would interpret it in such a way as to overrule those principles which would have been agreed by the parties to the contract when setting out the principles by which their eventual society should regulate inequalities of class.

But once again, it would require more convincing evidence than has yet been furnished to argue that a society once made just would destroy the exercise of individual ability and thereby limit both freedom and happiness. In a just society there are three things which the individual is indeed prevented from doing, however talented: first, he cannot amass very much more personal wealth than other people without its being claimed for some communal purpose of need; second, he cannot secure for himself privileges of status other than those symbolic expressions of admiration which can be classified as praise; third, he cannot acquire more power over others than he would have agreed to allow if he had had to envisage that his enemy might be set in the equivalent position of power over himself. But he would otherwise be free to exercise his abilities to whatever extent he chose; if they were such as to contribute to the common welfare, or such that their exercise was at the same time particularly arduous, he would in principle be entitled to some greater measure of personal reward; and the incentive to acknowledged excellence in the eyes of his fellow-professionals or fellow-citizens would be no less than in a system where he was in addition free to secure great wealth, or special privilege, or inordinate power. In a society where inequalities are permitted to the extent that they would have been agreed in advance as legitimate, the virtues on which the individualistic tradition lays so much stress will be restricted only within the limits acceptable to anyone who does not already have a vested interest in more liberty than he would concede to others.

It is therefore possible to envisage a just society with the social and economic lineaments of twentieth-century Britain which would be neither an inchoate and undisciplined rat-race nor an army of sullen and mediocre conformists. In such a society, there would be less inequality of wealth; there would be no inherited privilege; there would be some specialized educational institutions, but none to which admission was based on any social or economic advantage or attribute; there would be no unearned income except that allotted on the basis of need to those unable to earn a sufficient sum; the allocation of rewards would be conducted on a basis whereby any differential from the lowest not only in money but in all conditions of work would have to be justified by the three principles agreed upon; all occupations, offices or positions would be open to anyone willing to undergo the appropriate training and thereafter sufficiently qualified; no deference would be accorded to the occupant of any of these positions except where the individual occupant was being freely accorded praise, and no obedience would be required to the occupant of any position except where the authority vested in him was such as could have been agreed before the relative positions were occupied; all administrative decisions would be taken after the maximum of consultation with those affected by them; and all possible relevant comparisons would be taken into account in judging any claim which the occupants of one social position might bring against another.

Since there is no evidence for how such a society would work in practice, it is always possible that it might turn out to be less productive or less efficient; but it might just as well turn out to be more so. It might show some of the effects of egalitarianism on the manners and customs of the people of Britain such as Tocqueville detected among the Americans; but since other differences would be at least as great as these similarities, there is no ground for predic-tion beyond the obvious points at which the comparison is unneces-sary. Its citizens might, if happiness could be measured, turn out to be less happy; but there is no proof that in such a society happiness might not be increased. There is only one question to which the answer is certainly negative—the separate question whether the change to a socially just society could be either quick or painless.

It is in the transition to a just society, not in a just society itself, that the proverbial conflict of justice with benevolence becomes acute. From all that has been said about the importance of com-parative reference groups it follows that deprivation will be most strongly felt when expectations are disappointed and aspirations will be least disquieting when expectations are low. This much, indeed, is scarcely more than a truism. But it has the important consequence that except where comparisons have been upset by some external stimulus, to attempt to make society just may well cause more un-happiness than it will cure. This can never be an argument for say-ing that an existing system is just; even if slaves preferred to be slaves this would be nothing to do with the injustice of the practice of slavery.[3] But the radical advocate of justice must always face the likelihood that any specific and immediate reform which he pro-poses will be shown to be incompatible with utilitarian criteria of welfare. It need not follow from the fact that society is not just that social justice ought to be done. The sense which I have given to the notion of 'false consciousness' does entail that in a certain sense attitudes to social inequality can be restricted or mistaken. But it does not entail that revolutionism is the duty of the proletariat whose true interest would thereby be served. The long tradition of gradua-lism and deference in the English political consciousness may by its mere continuance be sufficient to inhibit the reference group com-parisons which would be vindicated by appeal to social justice. But it may at the same time be one of the reasons for saying that social justice ought not at once and at whatever cost to be put into effect.

This is one reason why I have been at pains to avoid saying that the working-class Conservatives in twentieth-century England are necessarily mistaken in their choice of party. Many of them may in-deed be unaware of inequalities to which they are subject and which could not be justified by appeal to the hypothetical contract. But although such attitudes may be symptomatic of a relationship between relative deprivation and inequality which is not 'correct' in terms of social justice, it does not follow that those who hold them

[3] Cf. Rawls, 'Justice as Fairness', pp. 188 ff.; and Isaiah Berlin, 'Equality as an Ideal', *Proceedings of the Aristotelian Society* LVI (1955–56), p. 309.

ought to take up any one political attitude or support any one programme of reform. Just as the question of the method by which a
society ought to be changed in order to make it just is separate from
the question whether it is just or not, so the question whether inequalities ought in fact to be redressed at all is separate from the
question whether they are legitimate by the standard of social justice.
There may well be many strong grounds for saying that they ought
to be redressed. But this does not follow from the appeal to justice
itself.

If the respondents to the survey had given answers dictated by the
claims of justice, they would have been very different from those
which I have reported. No old age pensioners would have said that
they were satisfied with what they had; no manual workers would
have cited only other manual workers as being better off than themselves; the pattern of differences between desired and actual income
would have been more extreme; the reasons given for party support
would have been much more politically conscious; many people in
both the manual and non-manual strata would have voiced other
grievances than they did. But this does not mean that they would
have been wrong or foolish had they not at the same time all supported the party more committed to reform. It might be objected at
this point that quite apart from what may follow from it, the evidence of a survey is not adequate to answer what people's real grievances are. Many manual workers and their families may nurture a
latent resentment of the social structure which is more deeply felt
but at the same time more strongly repressed than any doorstep interviewer will be able to discover. Even in Britain, there is a multitude of everyday incidents in the street or on the shopfloor which
can be interpreted as symptoms of the sporadic anger and half-
formulated grievances of the underprivileged. But if there are
suppressed resentments among the British working class, their relevance to the question of 'false consciousness' is as much that they are
suppressed as that they are resentments. An unformulated grievance
or a half-conscious resentment is not a feeling of relative deprivation
as I have been careful to define it. The attitudes to inequality which
an appeal to the contract would vindicate must be at least articulate;
what they do not need to be is programmatic. Whatever latent resentment has failed to emerge in the interviews, this makes no difference to the discrepancy between relative deprivation and inequality
on the one hand and inequality and justice on the other. The 'false
consciousness' argument requires that people should assess inequalities as though they did not yet have any vested position; it only
does not require that they should know, or that it is even possible

for them to know, just what ought to be done about the system in which they find themselves claimants to justice.

If, therefore, the evidence has shown that the British are a people little given either to envy or to radicalism, this is not something which calls at once and without question for remedy. It does not need the evidence of a survey to show that institutions and people are slow and reluctant to change, that habits of class and status die hard, that attitudes are stereotyped and conventions rigid. Modes of behaviour and thought are set both too firm and too early for the members of any social stratum to be readily adaptable to change or even readily open to its appeal. This is no truer a platitude than that once change is under way the clock can never be put back; but perhaps it is in the end a more important one. From the moment almost of birth, attitudes to the social structure are conditioned by pressures in which the ideal of social justice plays little if any part. Not only false consciousness of social inequality but social inequality itself goes back to circumstances far earlier than those which shape the present lives of the respondents to a sample survey drawn only from people of voting age. The denial of equal opportunity begins in infancy, and with it the long process of habituation to inequality without which society would be forever in a state of civil war. But while this is a further argument for saying that the social structure is unjust, and the attitudes to it not those dictated by the injunctions of social justice, it is at the same time an example of the reasons why an appeal to justice cannot show by itself what action ought to be taken. This paradox confronts the reformer in any situation where injustice is not so clear and the movement for redress so strong that the problem of policy is not a problem of what is to be done but only of whether it is going to succeed. Wherever inequalities are unjust, even in the most affluent society, and yet are not seen as such, then attitudes to inequality can be labelled in this sense incorrect; but the correctness of action is and always must be a different matter.

This may seem a wan conclusion to an attempt to show not merely what the attitudes of the English people to inequality have been but how far they are legitimate. But if it is possible to make useful judgements about social justice—and this whole study was conceived in the conviction that it is—then it is all the more important not to expect from them categorical imperatives to political action. There is no single platonic ideal of the good society to which an appeal can be made in order to discover what should be done about social inequality. But it would be equally mistaken to conclude that no argument about political preferences is meaningful or that no assessment can be made of any system of institutions and practices. Any discussion of social justice must rest on some basis of empirical evidence about the inequalities which exist between one stratum and another and the attitudes which the members of these strata have to them. But it is impossible to offer any explanatory account of this evidence without a reference, whether explicit or disguised, to criteria which cannot be derived from within it. In this difficult area where sociology and political philosophy necessarily overlap, it is often as hard to establish just what questions are properly answerable as to discover the means of answering them. But I hope at least to have shown that the answerable questions include not only what is the empirical relation between the inequalities of a social system and the feelings to which they give rise but also how the notion of social justice can be brought to bear on this relation.

Such arguments will not and should not be expected to yield either a comprehensive political theory or a set of mandatory political prescriptions. Social justice is not the sole political good; it does not, even by itself, prescribe one system of stratification only; there is always room for two rival theories of social justice, both of which will pass the test of reciprocity which gives the notion of justice its meaning; and there may always be good reasons why social justice should not be done, even where it can be shown that inequalities are unjust. But only when these limitations are defined and understood can the appeal to justice be usefully made. It is just as important to assess relative deprivation in the light of social justice even if there is not and never will be one canonical theory of the New Jerusalem.

APPENDIX 1

THE SAMPLE

The respondents were selected by means of a three-stage probability sample with stratification at the first and second stages. At the first stage, fifty parliamentary constituencies were selected from a stratified list. This list was prepared by grouping all constituencies according to the Registrar General's standard regions (with London separate), dividing them within each area into those in conurbations and those not, and ranking them within each group constructed in this way according to the percentage of Labour to non-Labour voters at the General Election of 1959. The conurbations in each region were ranked before the other constituencies, and the regions ranked in the following order: Northern, North-Western, East and West Riding, North Midlands, Wales, Midlands, Eastern, Greater London, South-East, South, South-West. Within the first group of constituencies (i.e., constituencies in conurbations in the Northern Region), the individual constituencies were ranked from high to low percentage of Labour voters; in the second group (i.e., constituencies in the Northern Region not in conurbations), the individual constituencies were ranked from low to high percentage of Labour voters; and so on alternately down the list.

At the second stage, the sampling frame was designed in accordance with the techniques developed and published by the Government Social Survey. The sampling units were constructed in terms of wards (or combinations of wards) in urban administrative districts and in terms of parishes in rural districts, the grouping being so arranged as to yield units of roughly 1,000 to 5,000 electors. All the units within each of the 50 constituencies chosen from the first stage were then ranked according to their J-index value, and each constituency divided into two strata in such a way that each stratum contained about the same number of electors. One sampling unit was then selected from each stratum.

At the third stage, 20 names were drawn at random from the electoral rolls for each of the 100 sampling units selected at the second stage. Forty names were thus drawn from each of the 50 constituencies chosen at the first stage. Only those voters shown as resident in a hospital or institution were rejected.

The distribution of the sample by area corresponds reasonably well with the Registrar General's figures for 1961 both for region and for urban rural or district. The figures are as shown below:

	Sample %	Registrar General %
Northern	31	30
Midland	19	18
Southern	47	46
Wales	3	6
Total	100%	100%

Appendix 1

	Sample %	Registrar General %
Urban	82	80
Rural	18	20
Total	100%	100%

Comparison with the Registrar General's figures for age, however, shows a less good fit. This is principally because the Electoral Registers used were at a late stage of their life at the time when the sample was drawn, with the result that voters in their 20's are necessarily under-represented. The figures are:

	Sample %	Registrar General %
21–29	10	17
30–39	18	20
40–49	21	19
50–59	23	19
60+	28	25
Total	100%	100%

Out of the 2,000 voters whose names had been drawn, a total of 247 (12·3%) were either dead, permanently moved, not known or traceable at the given address, or the property was found to be empty or demolished. The effective sample was thus reduced to 1,753. Of these, 169 refused to be interviewed, 71 were not found at home despite successive recalls, 44 could not be interviewed on account of illness, 40 were away temporarily, and 14 could not be interviewed for miscellaneous other reasons. Out of the effective sample, therefore, a total of 338 voters (19·4%) could not be interviewed. In other words, the success of the sample, measured in terms of the productive calls as a percentage of the effective sample, is 80·6%. This figure may be compared with the result obtained by the Institute of Practitioners in Advertising, who carry out a three-monthly readership survey based on a national random sample. Their figure for a total of four samples drawn between July 1960 and July 1961 is 77·2% of an effective sample of 16,464 voters.

298

APPENDIX 2

THE QUESTIONNAIRE

NOTE: Question 4 was included at the request of Dr. Michael Young for a purpose not connected with the present study.

		Codes
ALL INFORMANTS		
Q. 1(a) First of all, could you tell me how long you have lived in this district?	Up to 1 year	1
	Up to 5 years	2
	Up to 17 years (1945)	3
	No move since war	4
INFORMANTS WHO HAVE MOVED SINCE WAR (Codes 1, 2 or 3)		
Q. 1(b) Could you tell me where you moved here from? (Add if necessary—Was that urban or rural?)	Urban–rural	6
	Rural–urban	7
	No change	8
	From abroad	9
ALL INFORMANTS Now could I ask you one or two details about your family?		
Q. 2(a) Are you married?	Married	1
	Single	2
	Widowed	3
	Divorced or separated	4
IF CODES 1, 3 or 4		

Q. 2(b) How many children do you have? Did you have any children who died? (Code total number including those who died)

No. of children	None	1	2	3	4	5	6	7	8	9	10+
Code	Y	1	2	3	4	5	6	7	8	9	X

ASK ABOUT ALL LIVING CHILDREN		
Q. 3(a) How many children do you have under the age of 15 years?	....	
IF CHILDREN UNDER AGE 15		
Q. 3(b) At what age do you expect them to leave school?	Did not attend	5
	At minimum age	1
	Above minimum age	2
	Some of each	3
	D.K.	4
Q. 3(c) How many children do you have over the age of 15?		

299

Appendix 2

		Codes
IF CHILDREN 15 AND OVER		
Q. 3(d) Did they leave as soon as they could or did they stay on at school longer than they needed?	Left as soon as could	7
	Stayed on	8
	Some of each	9
	D.K.	0
	Did not attend	X
ASK ABOUT ALL LIVING CHILDREN		
Q. 3(e) Do or did any of them attend (or do you expect any of them to attend) a fee-paying school?	Yes	1
	No	2
	Depends	3
	D.K.	4
Q. 3(f) Do or did any of them have (or do you expect any of them to have) any education beyond school?	Yes	5
	No	6
	Depends	7
	D.K.	8
IF YES (Code 5 at Q. 3(f))		
Q. 3(g) What kind of further education?	University	1
	Technical College	2
	Evening classes	3
	Other	X
	D.K.	Y
Q. 4 ALL INFORMANTS WITH CHILDREN (INC. ADULT CHILDREN)		
Where was your mother (or if man, your wife's mother) living when your first child was born? HAND CARD A Which one of these would you say? N.B. This question refers to the mother's permanent home at the time.	Less than 1 mile away	1
	1 mile but less than 5 miles	2
	5 miles but less than 20 miles	3
	Further away	X
	Mother/wife's mother dead at time of birth	0
	D.K.	Y
ALL INFORMANTS		
Q. 5(a) What is the job of the head of your household?	AB	1
	C1	2
Occupation..	C2	3
	DE	4
Industry		
....		
N.B. See manual: follow usual social grade rules.		

	Codes

ASK ALL INFORMANTS

Q. 6(a) How many members of your household are there? (Record in space provided)

No. Adults 16+	....
No. Children 5–15	....
No. infants 0–4	....
Total	....

Q. 6(b) How many people, including yourself, are in paid employment, either full or part time?
If informant works ring code X as well as total number working [X]

One	
Two	1
Three	2
Four	3
Five	4
Six	5
Seven plus	6
	7

IF INFORMANT IS HOUSEWIFE ASK

Q. 6(c) Do you work? Is that full-time or part-time employment?

H/W full-time	8
H/W part-time	9
H/W does not work	0

ASK ANY OTHER INFORMANT

Q. 6(d) Does the housewife in your family work? Is that full-time or part-time employment?

ALL INFORMANTS

Q. 7 What was your first job?
N.B. For married women ask about first job before marriage.

Occup...

Indus. ....

AB	1
C1	2
C2	3
DE	4
Never worked before marriage	5

ASK ALL INFORMANTS

Q. 8 Would you say that, generally speaking, you and your family were financially better off, worse off, or about the same as a year ago?

Better	1
Worse	2
Same	3
D.K.	4

301

Appendix 2

	Codes

Q. 9(a) Do you think there are any other sorts of people doing   Yes   1
noticeably better at the moment than you and your   No   2
family?   D.K.   3

IF YES TO 9(a)(Code 1) ASK Qs. 9(b)(c):

Q. 9(b) What sort of people do you think are doing noticeably better?

RECORD ANSWER IN FULL

....

....

....

IF YES TO 9(a)

Q. 9(c) What do you feel about this, I mean, do you   Approve   9
approve or disapprove of this?   Disapprove   0
   Indifferent   X
   D.K.   Y

ALL INFORMANTS

Q. 10(a) Some people say that manual workers are doing   Yes   1
much better nowadays than white-collar   Qualified Yes   2
workers. Do you think this is so or not?   No   3
Other specify: Qualified No   4
   Other   X
....   D.K.   Y

....

Q. 10(b) Do you think that manual workers ought to do   Yes   8
as well as they are doing compared with white-   No   9
collar workers?   D.K.   0

ASK ONLY OF NON-IRISH AND NON-WEST INDIAN
INFORMANTS

Q. 11(a) What about foreign immigrants to this country   Yes   1
such as the Irish or West Indians—some people   No   2
think they are doing too well at the expense of   D.K.   3
British people. Do you think this is so or not?

IF YES AT Q. 11(a) (CODE 1 at Q. 11(a))

Q. 11(b) Has this affected you personally in any way?   Not asked   4
   Yes   5
   No   6

IF YES (Code 4 at Q. 11(b))

302

	Codes

Q. 11(c) In what way would you say it has affected you? Housing | 7
Other specify: Other way | X

....

....

ALL INFORMANTS

Q. 12(a) Does your household have a T.V., telephone, car, fridge, washing machine, record player, central heating?

FOR THOSE ITEMS NOT ALREADY OWNED

Q. 12(b) Would you like one?

ASK (c) and (d) FOR THOSE ITEMS WANTED AT (b) (i.e. code 1)

Q. 12(c) Do you expect to get one in the next 2 or 3 years?

Q. 12(d) Do you think other people are managing to afford......................?

Items	(a) Have			(b) Like			(c) Expect			(d) Other people		
	Yes	No	D.K.	Yes	No	D.K.	Yes	No	D.K.	Yes	No	D.K.
T.V.	1	2	3	1	2	3	4	5	6	7	8	9
Telephone	4	5	6	1	2	3	4	5	6	7	8	9
Car	7	8	9	1	2	3	4	5	6	7	8	9
Fridge	0	X	Y	1	2	3	4	5	6	7	8	9
Washing machine	1	2	3	1	2	3	4	5	6	7	8	9
Record player	4	5	6	1	2	3	4	5	6	7	8	9
Central heating	7	8	9	1	2	3	4	5	6	7	8	9

IF ANY YES's AT (d) (i.e. Code 7's)

Q. 12(e) What sort of people are you thinking of? *Record in full*

ONE ANSWER ONLY

....

....

....

....

ALL INFORMANTS

Q. 12(f) Is there anything I haven't mentioned which you or Yes | 1
your household particularly need? No | 2
 D.K. | Y

Specify: ....

....

....

Appendix 2

Q. 13(a) Could you tell me which of the things on this card you already have?
(Ring one Code in grid below)

FOR ITEMS NOT OWNED

Q. 13(b) Would you like to have a ....?
For items not owned but wanted, 'No' at 2(a) and 'Yes' at 2(b)

Q. 13(c) Do you think other people are managing to afford a ....?

Items	(a) Already have			(b) Would like			(c) Other people		
	Yes	No	D.K.	Yes	No	D.K.	Yes	No	D.K.
(i) A house you own	1	2	3	1	2	3	4	5	6
(ii) A fur coat for your wife	4	5	6	7	8	9	0	X	Y
(iii) Foreign holiday travel	7	8	9	1	2	3	4	5	6
(iv) Spare bedroom for visitors	0	X	Y	7	8	9	0	X	Y
(v) 1st class travel on trains	1	2	3	1	2	3	4	5	6
(vi) Private education for children	4	5	6	7	8	9	0	X	Y

N.B. "A house of your own" includes house being bought on mortgage.
IF ANY 'YES's at (c)

Q. 13(d) What sort of people are you thinking of?

ONE ANSWER ONLY

Specify: ....

....

....

Appendix 2

	Codes

Q. 14(a) Would you like to move out of your present district?   Yes | 1
No | 2
D.K. | 3

IF 'YES' (Code 1 at 14(a))

Q. 14(b) Is this anything to do with the sort of   Yes, district | 4
district (you think) it is?   Yes, anything to do with work | 5
Other reason (specify)   Yes, want another house | 6
                                                         Other | X
....   D.K. | Y

....

IF INFORMANT IS MARRIED WOMAN ASK:

Q. 15(a) Would you say you were satisfied with your husband's   Yes | 1
present position as far as income is concerned?   No | 2
D.K. | 3

IF 'NO' (Code 2 at 15(a))

Q. 15(b) Is that more because the job he is doing is   Worth more pay | 4
worth more pay, because you need more   Need more money | 5
money or for some other   Husband retired, pensions only | 6
reason?   Worth more pay *and* need more money | 7
Code other reasons in full: Other | X
....   D.K. | Y

....

OTHER INFORMANTS

Q. 15(c) Would you say you were satisfied with your present   Yes | 1
position as far as income is concerned?   No | 2
D.K. | 3

IF 'NO' (Code 2 at 15(c))

Q. 15(d) Is that more because the job you are doing   Worth more pay | 4
is worth more pay, because you need   Need more money | 5
more money, or for some other   Retired, pensions only | 6
reason?   Worth more pay *and* need more money | 7
Code other reason: Other | X
....   D.K. | Y

....

305

Appendix 2

	Codes

FOR ALL MARRIED HOUSEWIVES ASK

Q. 16(a) Would you say you were satisfied with your husband's present position as far as prospects for getting ahead are concerned?	Yes No D.K.	1 2 3

ALL OTHER WORKING INFORMANTS
(i.e. Code X at Q. 6(b))

Q. 16(b) Would you say you were satisfied with your present position as far as prospects of getting ahead are concerned?	Yes No D.K.	4 5 6

ASK ALL OTHER UNEMPLOYED OR RETIRED INFORMANTS

Q. 16(c) Would you say you were satisfied with your previous position as far as prospects for getting ahead were concerned?	Yes No D.K.	1 2 3
Q. 16(d) Would you prefer (have preferred) to be in a job where you did have a chance of getting ahead?	Yes No No better chance D.K.	4 5 6 Y

ALL INFORMANTS

Q. 17(a) What income do you think is necessary for you (your husband) in order to maintain a proper standard of living for people like yourself?

	Yearly		*Weekly*		Codes
	Under £350		Under £7.10s.		1
	£351 to £500	Over	£7.10s. to £10		2
	£501 „ £650	„	£10. „ £12.10s.		3
DO NOT	£651 „ £800	„	£12.10s. „ £15.		4
READ	£801 „ £1,000	„	£15. „ £20.		5
OUT	£1,001 „ £1,500	„	£20. „ £25.		6
LIST	£1,501 „ £2,000	„	£25. „ £30.		7
	£2,001 „ £3,000	„	£30. „ £50.		8
	£3,001 „ £4,000	„	£50.		9
	£4,001 „ £6,000				0
	Over £6,000				X
				D.K.	Y

Q. 17(b) What sort of people are you thinking of when we talk about 'people like yourself?'

....

....

....

306

	Codes

Q. 18(a) If a son of yours was actually choosing a job   Manual   1
       at the moment, would you rather he chose a   Non-manual   2
       manual or a non-manual job?   D.K., up to him, etc.   3
       (Probe: Assuming there was nothing
        special he wanted to do.)

Q. 18(b) If he had the choice of a foreman's job at £20   Foreman   4
       a week or a schoolteacher's job at £15,   Schoolmaster   5
       which would *you* prefer him to choose?   D.K., up to him, etc.   6

Q. 19(a) Would you like any son of yours to have a   Yes   7
       university education?   No   8
       (Probe: Assuming you had a son about   D.K., depends, etc.   9
       to leave school now).

Q. 19(b) Suppose you had a son who was able to pass the   Yes   0
       exams, would you expect him to be able to   No   X
       go to Oxford University?   D.K.   Y

Q. 20(a) What social class would you say you   Upper/Upper Middle   1
       belonged to?   Middle   2
            Lower Middle   3
     DO NOT READ OUT LIST   Working   4
        Other, D.K., none, etc.   5

     IF CODE 5 AT Q. 20(a)

Q. 20(b) If you *had* to say middle or working class,   Middle-Class   6
       which would you say?   Working-Class   7
             D.K.   Y

     ALL INFORMANTS

Q. 20(c) What sort of people do you mean when you talk about
       <u>middle/working class</u> (informant's class at (a) or (b))

     RECORD IN FULL...

     ....

     ....

Q. 20(d) What sort of people do you mean when you talk about <u>middle/</u>
       <u>working class</u> (class not coded at (a) or (b)).

     RECORD IN FULL ....

     ....

     ....

Appendix 2

	Codes

Q. 21(a) Could you tell me what your father's occupation was? AB **1**

Occupation... C1 **2**

C2 **3**

DE **4**

Industry .... Not known **5**

Q. 21(b) What social class would you say he Middle, upper or lower **6**
belonged to? Working class **7**

Other, specify **X**

D.K. **Y**

Now could I ask you a few questions about politics?

	22(a)	22(c)

Q. 22(a) If there was a General Election Conservative 1 6
tomorrow, which party would you support? Liberal 2 7

Q. 22(b) Have you always supported....................... Labour 3 8
(party coded at (a)) since 1950? Other 4 9

Refuse Y

D.K., none 5 0

IF CHANGED (Code Y at (b))

Q. 22(c) Which party did you support previously? Always X
(Code in column (c) above) Changed Y

IF NO CHANGE (Code X at (b))

Q. 22(d) Could you tell me the main reason why you have always
supported/support .... party? RECORD BELOW

IF CHANGED (Code Y at (b))

Q. 22(e) Could you tell me the main reason why you changed?
RECORD BELOW

SEE MANUAL Job, class, status 1

Habit, family, friends, neighbours vote that way 2

Party's image—as competent to govern 3

Party's other virtues, policies (any) 4

Informants' needs, welfare benefits, tax remissions 5

DO NOT The candidate 6

READ OUT Would be Liberal but none standing 7

LIST Negative attitudes to other parties 8

D.K., non-voter, no answer Y

Other reasons, specify below X

Double codes
are possible

....

....

....

	Codes

Q. 23(a) Do you think most people like yourself vote the same way as you, or do you think they vote differently?

		Codes
	Same	1
	Differently	2
	D.K.	3

Q. 23(b) What sort of people are you thinking of?
Probe: How would you describe them?

....

....

IF SUPPORTER OF LABOUR PARTY ASK 24(a) FIRST, OF CONSERVATIVE PARTY 24(b) FIRST AND OF LIBERAL PARTY 24(c) FIRST. THEN ASK OTHER TWO PARTS.

Q. 24(a) In general, what sort of people do you think vote for the Labour party?

	Codes
Class, job, income, workers, etc.	1
Supporters of ideology or policy	2
Low status, uneducated, ignorant people	3
Age group, incl. pensioners	4
Region, district	5
Other answers (specify)	X
....	
D.K.	Y

Q. 24(b) In general, what sort of people do you think vote for the Conservative party?

	Codes
Class, job, income, the rich, etc.	1
Supporters of ideologies or policies	2
High status, education, style of life, right minded, sensible, etc.	3
Age group, incl. pensioners	4
Region, district	5
"Getting ahead" new, prosperous wkg. class	6
Other answers (specify).............................	X
....	
D.K.	Y

Q. 24(c) In general, what sort of people do you think vote for the Liberal party?

	Codes
Class, job, income	1
Supporters of ideologies or policies	2
Age group, incl. pensioners	4
Region or district	5
New white collar, prosperous wkg. class	6
People fed up with both other parties	7
People between two other parties	8
Other answers (specify)	X
....	
....	
D.K.	Y

Appendix 2

	Codes

ALL INFORMANTS

Q. 25(a) Do you think the present government is doing enough for people like yourself?

Yes	1
No	2
D.K.	3

IF 'NO' (Code 2 at 25(a))

Q. 25(b) What more do you think they ought to be doing for people like yourself?

Class or job category	4
Personal needs, security, housing, etc.	5
Other (specify)	X
....	
D.K.	Y

Q. 26 Some people think the House of Lords ought to be abolished on the grounds that it is undemocratic. What do you think?

Yes	1
No	2
D.K., indifferent, qualified Yes or No	3

Q. 27 Would you say that you were for or against the Welfare State? N.B. If necessary mention "National Health and so on"

For	5
Against	6
D.K., indifferent qualified Yes or No	7

Q. 28(a) Will you look at the items on this card. They are things which some people think the State should provide. Could you tell me if you think the State should provide them for everybody—with a Means Test, without a Means Test, or not at all?

	With Means Test	Without Means Test	Not at all	D.K. indiff. etc.
(i) Family allowances for the first child as well	1	2	3	4
(ii) Subsidised rent on house or flat	5	6	7	8
(iii) Free legal aid	1	2	3	4
(iv) Unemployment pay at full rate as long as unemployed	5	6	7	8
(v) Free university education for all who can pass exams.	9	0	X	Y

310

Appendix 2

	Codes

Q. 28(b) Is there anything you think the State ought to be providing you or your family with but isn't at present? No/D.K. — **0**

      Yes (1) ....

         (2)..

         (3)..

         (4)..

Q. 28(c) Is there anything you think the State is providing you or your family with that you don't really need? No/D.K. — **0**
         Yes—Family allowance — **1**

      Yes (2)..

         (3)..

         (4)..

      Finally, could you give me one or two more details about yourself?

Q. 29(a) What is your religion?

	Code
Church of England	1
Roman Catholic	2
Low Church	3
None	4
Other (specify)	5

Q. 29(b) When did you last go to church?

	Code
Within a month	7
Within last year	8
Not for over a year	9
Never attend	0
Would attend but can't	X
D.K.	Y

		Yes belong	Yes attend
Q. 30(a) Do you belong to any T.U. club, or other association?	(1)........................		
Q. 30(b) Have you attended its meetings in the last six months?	(2)........................		
	(3)........................		
	(4)........................		
(Check √ in columns provided)	(5)........................		
	(6)........................		

311

Appendix 2

(Club or Association includes any Organization of a formalized nature where people meet each other)

O.U.O. [| | | | | | | | | | | | | |]

		Codes
Interviewer's estimate of informant's style of life	D.K. Not admitted to house	1
	Upper, upper-middle class	2
	Middle, lower-middle class	3
	Working class	4
	N.A.	X
Interviewer's estimate of informant's accent	B.B.C.	5
	Regional	6
	Other	7
	N.A.	Y

CLASSIFICATION DATA

Q. 31(a) What is your age?			Sex		
	21–29	1	*Men*	H/H	1
	30–39	2		Not head	2
	40–45	3	*Women* Housewife		3
	46–49	4	Not housewife		4
Actual age	50–59	5			
. .	60–69	6		Manual	5
	70+	7		Non-manual	6

Q. 31(b) At what age did you finish your full-time education?		
	Minimum school age	8
	Above minimum	9
	University or College	0
	D.K.	Y

		Q. 32	Q. 33
Q. 32 Could you give me an idea	£5 and under	1	1
roughly how much money	Over £5 up to £7.10s.	2	2
comes into the household	Over £7.10s. up to £10.	3	3
per week after deductions	,, £10. ,, £12.10s.	4	4
HAND CARD C	,, £12.10s. ,, £15.	5	5
Q. 33 Could you give me an	,, £15. ,, £17.10s.	6	6
idea roughly how much	,, £17.10s. ,, £20.	7	7
you (your husband)	,, £20. ,, £22.10s.	8	8
earn(s) each week after	,, £22.10s. ,, £25.	9	9
deductions.	,, £25. ,, £27.10s.	0	0
N.B. For married women	,, Over £27.10s.	X	X
ask Q. 33 about *husband*	D.K.	Y	Y
even if wife also works.			

Appendix 2

DAY (Ring)   M1   T2   W3   TH4   F5   S6

INVESTIGATOR'S No.

DATE........:........:........../..........:........./62..........   JOB No.   3289

SERIAL No.

CONSTITUENCY ....

WARD ....

IN BLOCK CAPITALS

NAME Mr./Mrs./Miss.. Initials................................

HOME ADDRESS..

WHERE INTERVIEWED   HOME 1   WORK 2   ELSEWHERE 3

IF AT WORK—ADDRESS..

APPENDIX 3

THE MANUAL/NON-MANUAL DISTINCTION

There are two reasons why no definition of the manual/non-manual distinction can ever be entirely satisfactory. First, whatever definition is used there are bound to be some borderline cases; and second, even a moderately clear-cut line can only be drawn by emphasizing either class or status at the expense of the other. There are several 'objective' criteria which readily suggest themselves, but none is satisfactory by itself. The most obvious is a literal distinction in terms of whether the person works with his hands or his head. But it is difficult to define this in such a way that a stenotypist, for example, is not doing as manual a job as a toolsetter, although a stenotypist is obviously a clerical and therefore 'non-manual' worker. Another significant distinction is between wage-earners and fee, salary or stipend earners. But many clerks are paid by the week just as manual workers are, and if they are not both to be described as wage-earners then some criterion other than the method of payment must be introduced. A third distinction is whether a person is self-employed, an employer or an employee and, if an employee, whether employed in some executive or supervisory capacity. But once again, the distinctions which follow do not by themselves yield a satisfactory dividing-line. There is an evident difference in the class-situation of a plumber who is in business for himself and one who is employed by an enterprise in which he has no share. But many non-manual workers are employees in a capacity which is neither executive nor supervisory; there are many kinds of supervisory positions within the grades of manual work; and the category of the self-employed includes so many jobs which fit the literal criterion of 'manual' that it becomes somewhat implausible to assign every self-employed person to the same stratum. No single characteristic of different occupations can furnish the necessary or sufficient condition for membership of the 'manual' or 'non-manual' stratum.

It follows that the dividing-line will have to be based on a mixture of criteria and will have to be applied to some extent on an ad hoc basis. Even if distinctions in status-situation, which tend to be the hardest to define, are given a minimum of weight as against distinctions of class-situation, it is still possible to make a case for putting a factory foreman or a self-employed cabinet-maker or a ship's bosun or a master-tailor or a market gardener or a prison warder on either side of the line. All that can be done is to adopt a classification which is bound at some points to be arbitrary and to retain it as consistently as possible. The procedure adopted for the present survey was to follow the standard classification by 'social grade' used by Research Services Ltd., in which the dividing-line between grades A, B and C1 on the one hand and C2, D and E on the other corresponds to a distinction between non-manual and manual or 'middle-class' and 'working-class' occupations. The Research Services criteria are at some

314

points different from what could be argued to be most appropriate for the particular purposes of this one study. But such differences are, as I have already emphasized, always arguable, and it seemed in any case better that the interviewers should apply the criteria in which they had been trained and with which they were thoroughly familiar.

In the instructions issued to Research Services interviewers, the grade C1 is described as 'made up of the families of small tradespeople and non-manual workers who carry out less important administrative, supervisory and clerical jobs in general', while C2 'consists in the main of skilled manual workers and their families'. This broad classification would, I think, be agreed by all users of the manual/non-manual distinction, however they might differ over the more difficult individual cases. The Research Services grading is, however, based on several further criteria. In particular, interviewers are explicitly advised to use type of dwelling, amenities and family habits as 'additional guides', with the result that some weight is deliberately given to considerations of status as opposed to class. This turned out in practice to be of most importance in the classification of small farmers. Some were classified by the interviewers as non-manual and some as manual, and these differences were based on the interviewers' own assessment of style of life, rather than the size of holding or number of employees, if any. A classification which assigned all smallholders, irrespective of style of life, to the same stratum would therefore have put ten respondents (·7 % of the sample) into a different stratum from that to which they were assigned by the interviewers.

In the classification of the self-employed other than farmers, the interviewers were similarly free to give weight to considerations of status, so that, for example, the one self-employed plumber in the sample was classified as non-manual but the one self-employed plasterer as manual. In addition, the Research Services general instructions provide for the assignment of proprietors or managers of small shops who do most of the work (i.e., manual work as opposed to sales or accounts) to grade C2. This produces a result similar to that which would have been produced by the criterion of number of employees, but the overlap is not exact. Thus, two men's hairdressers with a staff of two and four respectively were classified as non-manual, and one without any employees as manual; similarly, three grocers with employees were classified as non-manual and three without as manual. But at the same time, one greengrocer with a part-time assistant was classified as manual, a master baker with no staff except his wife as non-manual, and a brushmaker with one employee as manual. Once again, therefore, it would be possible to argue for a slightly different set of criteria by which a number of the respondents would have been put on the other side of the line. Some of the self-employed are likely to be borderline cases on any definition. But if employment status were to be made the sole criterion, so that any self-employed man, even if engaged in purely manual work, were to be classified as non-manual, then 19 respondents (1·3 % of the sample) would be classified differently. If, at the other extreme, any self-employed man doing work which, if he were not self-employed, would classify him as manual, were therefore classified as manual here, then ten respondents (·7% of the sample) would be classified differently.

A similar calculation can be made for the employed. Here, the most difficult cases under any system of grading will be foremen or overseers in the engineering and similar industries. But as well as these, the stipulation in the Research Services instructions that shop managers or assistants 'doing mainly manual work' should be graded C2 meant that a number of respondents who could be graded non-manual by the definition sometimes used of 'clerical and sales' were here coded as manual. If, however, all possible borderline cases in the employed category are added together, the number is still not very large. If all borderline cases which were in fact classified as manual were to be classified as non-manual, nine respondents (·6% of the sample) would cross the line, and if all the non-manuals were to be classified as manuals, nine other respondents would cross the line the other way.

As well as the borderline cases, however, detailed examination of the schedules revealed a small number of codings which could only be categorized as errors—codings, that is, where either the interviewer had given a classification which was flagrantly inconsistent with the criteria given in the instructions and used by the other interviewers, or where a correct classification had been made by the interviewer, but this had been wrongly transferred by the coder to the classification data from which it was punched. There were found to be six of this second type of error, and seven of the first—a total of ·9% of the sample. It is almost inevitable in a survey of this kind that a few errors will have been made, and some were so slight as virtually to be borderline cases. Thus, a night telephonist was classified as manual by one interviewer despite the fact that in the Research Services instructions telephonists are specifically listed as an example of a C1 occupation; but it would not be entirely implausible to argue for a criterion whereby telephonists should, in fact, be assigned to the manual stratum. I do not believe that either the errors or the borderline cases are numerous enough to impugn in any way the results presented in the book. But it is important to emphasize that no definition of the manual/non-manual line is immune from objections, and accuracy requires that the breakdown of the sample into 919 manual and 496 non-manual respondents should be qualified by the figures for the number of erroneous as well as debatable codings.

APPENDIX 4

THE CODING OF THE OPEN-ENDED QUESTIONS

Of the seven open-ended questions used in the interviews (excluding 12f and 28b and c), 23b must be dismissed as a failure for the reasons given in the text. The other five were all more successful. But the technique is open to certain dangers, and if the value of the results presented in the text is to be properly assessed a slightly more detailed account of the procedure used is called for.

In principle, the interviewer who has asked an open-ended question should record a verbatim answer on the schedule. It is obvious that a particularly lengthy answer cannot be recorded in full, but on the questions asked here the interviewers were generally able to record the gist even of long-winded replies. Some interviewers, as is to be expected, tended to write down more of the respondent's own words, whereas one interviewer was found to record phrases sufficiently similar to each other to suggest that a deliberate paraphrase was being used. But whatever differences there may have been of this kind between interviewers, there is no reason to suppose that they were such as to affect the coding of the responses given. The only loss is that some interviewers may have failed to record in full what could otherwise have been quoted in the text as an example of a particular coding.

In one respect, the questions were not entirely open-ended. In the instructions issued to the interviewers, they were specifically told 'There are several questions asking: "What sort of people are you thinking of?" In each case, try to get answers in terms of sorts of people rather than "Mrs. Jones down the road".' This meant that there was bound to be some variation between interviewers in the extent to which they prompted the respondent to give an answer which would seem to be sufficiently in terms of 'sorts' of people. Those interviewers who prompted most persistently were therefore more apt to elicit a response which had to be double-coded than those who were content with less. This carries the risk of introducing a bias since there may well have been other respondents who would, if prompted to the same extent, have enlarged upon their original answer. It seemed better, however, to allow the interviewers discretion to prompt than to be left with a large number of inadequate or unspecific answers which could, with prompting, be legitimately assigned to a specific coding category.

The list of codes for each question was drawn up by myself on the basis of the first 150 completed schedules to be received back from interviewers. The subsequent schedules were then coded by the staff of Research Services Ltd. On questions 17b and 20c and d, the tables in the text show the distribution of answers according to the codings initially drawn up. On questions 9b, 12e and 13d, however, the codings were subsequently revised. On

317

question 9b, it was found that the category of 'higher earnings' had not been defined rigorously enough, so that a number of replies had been assigned to it by the coders although they in fact contained some specific reference to either manual or non-manual occupations. A total of 94 schedules were subsequently altered. This total includes 20 in which an actual error of some kind had been made, and represents 11% of the 821 respondents who had said 'yes' to question 9a. The figures shown in Tables 19 and 20 are accordingly based on the revised coding. It may be worth remarking, however, that even with the earlier coding, exactly the same conclusions were suggested by the figures, although in the original table the 'higher earnings' category was larger by several per cent for both manual and non-manual respondents.

A similar revision was found to be necessary for questions 12e and 13d, but here some additional categories were also introduced. The answers coded under 'higher earnings' were found to include two different and easily distinguishable kinds: those which were, as described in the text, entirely unspecific, and those in which some reason was given for the greater spending capacity of the reference group. At the same time, any answer which contained a specific reference to manual or non-manual occupations but had been coded under 'higher earnings' was transferred to the specific manual and non-manual categories, and some of the smaller categories were more strictly redefined. As on question 9b, the changes between the original and the revised codings were not found such as to alter the conclusions drawn, but the figures presented in Tables 26 and 27 are based on a more accurate and informative classification than was given by the original codings.

On question 17b no revision of the coding categories seemed called for, but the question was such that there were bound to be a number of answers which could be argued to fall into either one of two categories. A total of 50 schedules were found to contain codings which either were errors or, although arguable as borderline cases, were inconsistent with the policy which had been followed by other coders. Roughly half of these 50 schedules contained errors, and half codings which might be argued to be individually defensible but were not strictly consistent with other codings given for similarly-phrased replies. The category of 'ordinary' was, inevitably, particularly difficult, since a number of respondents used phrases such as 'the average working man' which could be argued either to be a reference to the manual class or to belong more properly to the general category of 'ordinary' or 'average' without the implication of a particular stratum. (Cf. the discussion in the text of the meanings given to 'working class'). As is clear from the percentages shown in Table 4, the number of references to 'ordinary' people was not very large. But this category, and the other small category of 'particular family situations', caused some difficulty to the coders, and they did not always adopt the same policy as each other. In summary, it would seem fair to say that a maximum of 2% of the replies to this question were erroneously coded, and approximately a further 2% coded inconsistently.

Questions 20c and d were similarly bound to cause some difficulty for

318

the coders; but as well as problems of coding, a further difficulty arose in 18 of the schedules due to the fact that the schedules were all sent out to interviewers containing a misprint: what should have read 'IF CODE 5 AT 20a' was printed as 'IF CODES AT 20a'. A correction was at once circulated to all interviewers, but it would appear that some of them either did not receive, or else ignored, the correction, since a few respondents were asked both 20a and 20b. Where the same answer was recorded for both, there is, of course, no difficulty; but in some schedules one answer was ringed at 20a and another at 20b. Faced with this, the coders did not always react in the same way, so that as well as the interviewer's error in asking both questions, some schedules were also coded, and therefore punched, in a way that is not only inconsistent but may be entirely misleading. Five different kinds of error were subsequently found to have occurred. In three schedules, 20a and b had been differently answered and 20a had been punched as it should have been, but the codings of 20c and d were inconsistent with this since the interviewer had recorded replies based on the self-assessment given at 20b. In five schedules, 20a and b had been differently answered, but 20b had been punched; in these schedules, the codings of 20c and d were all consistent with the answers to 20b, so that there was no distortion of the kind which resulted from the first sort of mistake, but the interviewers should have asked questions 20c and d on the basis of the self-assessment given at 20a. In three schedules, 20a and b had been differently answered, 20a punched, and 20c and d answered on the basis of the self-assessment given at 20b, but the coder had attempted to correct this by transposing the answers to 20c and d; this was a sensible attempt to undo the interviewer's mistake, but it leaves a result which is still not quite correct since the answers given to 20c and d might have been different if they had been asked on the basis of the self-assessment given at 20a. In five schedules, there was no discrepancy between 20a and b but the coder transposed 20c and d although there was no apparent reason for this. Finally, in two schedules in which there was no discrepancy between 20a and b, 20c and d had not been transposed although it was clear from the answers recorded that they should have been. Thus a total of 1·3% of the 1,402 respondents who were prepared to assign themselves to one or other class were punched onto the cards in a way that to some degree misrepresents the answers which they gave, or would have given if the questions had been correctly asked.

A total of 98 out of the 2,804 responses given to questions 20c and d were found to be either erroneously or inconsistently coded. This represents an overall average of 3½%, which was exceeded in the definitions which people gave of their own class, and counterbalanced by the smaller proportion of errors and inconsistencies in the definitions which people gave of the 'other' class. One word which appeared occasionally in the replies to these questions (and a few times in the replies to 9b and 17b) gave the coders particular difficulty, but this could only have been avoided if it had been so well foreseen in advance as to have been inserted into the interviewers' instructions. The word was 'tradesmen' or 'tradespeople'. This is a term which is sometimes used to mean manual workers in skilled trades and sometimes to mean people engaged 'in trade' such as shop-keepers. This difference is itself likely to be determined by the stratum to which the respondent belongs: an upper middle-class person who talks about 'tradesmen' may be assumed to mean a grocer rather than an apprenticed craftsman, and a manual worker may be assumed to mean an apprenticed craftsman rather than a grocer. But it is not always easy to decide, and the coders had no choice but to try to settle each case on its merits. The category of 'ordinary' people also caused some difficulty, as already described in the text; the coders were not entirely consistent in how they interpreted such phrases as 'people who work' or 'people who work for a living'. But the percentage which I have given is, I think, a fair estimate of the maximum of responses which could be argued to have been wrongly coded. Some errors, some inconsistencies and a good many borderline cases are bound to result from the use of open-ended questions, but a detailed examination of the individual schedules suggests that although the standard of accuracy is not as high as might be hoped for, a very much better representation of people's attitudes on these topics can be obtained than by the use of multiple-choice questions.

APPENDIX 5

THE GAP BETWEEN STATED AND 'PROPER' INCOME

% *Gap*	*Frequency*
Negative	86
0	150
1— 5	6
6—10	61
11—15	—
16—20	27
21—25	84
26—30	147
31—35	—
36—40	71
41—45	—
46—50	10
51—55	4
56—60	149
61—65	37
66—70	5
71—75	49
76—80	24
81—85	—
86—90	3
91—95	—
96—99	—
100+	151
Not calculable	351
Total	1,415

LIST OF REFERENCES

ABRAMS, MARK, *The Condition of the British People, 1911-1945* (London, 1946).

——, *The Changing Pattern of Consumer Spending* (London, 1959).

——, 'Class and Politics', *Encounter* (October, 1961).

ALLEN, V. L., *Trade Union Leadership* (London, 1957).

——, *Trade Unions and the Government* (London, 1960).

——, and WILLIAMS, SHEILA, 'The Growth of Trade Unionism in Banking, 1914-1921', *Manchester School* XXVIII (1960).

Annual Abstracts of Statistics.

ARISTOTLE, *Politics.*

ARROW, KENNETH J., *Social Choice and Individual Values* (2nd edn.; New York, 1963).

ASKWITH, LORD, *Industrial Problems and Disputes* (London, 1920).

ATTLEE, C. R., *As It Happened* (London, 1954).

BAKKE, E. WIGHT, *The Unemployed Man* (London, 1933).

Bank Officer.

BANKS, OLIVE, *Parity and Prestige in English Secondary Education* (London, 1955).

BARNA, T., *Redistribution of Incomes Through Public Finance in 1937* (Oxford, 1945).

——, Comment on H. F. Lydall, 'The Long-Term Trend in the Size Distribution of Income', *Journal of the Royal Statistical Society* CXXII (1959) I.

BARTON, ALLEN H., *Social Organization Under Stress: a Sociological Review of Disaster Studies* (National Academy of Sciences—National Research Council; Washington, D.C., 1963).

BAUMOL, W. J., *Welfare Economics and the Theory of the State* (London, 1952).

BENNEY, M., *et al.*, *How People Vote* (London, 1956).

BERGER, BENNETT M., *Working-Class Suburb* (Berkeley, Calif., 1960).

BERLIN, ISAIAH, 'Equality as an Ideal', *Proceedings of the Aristotelian Society* LVI (1955-56).

BIRCH, A. H., *Small-Town Politics* (London, 1959).

Board of Education, *Annual Reports.*

Board of Inland Revenue, *92nd Annual Report* (1950).

BONHAM, JOHN, *The Middle Class Vote* (London, 1954).

BOTT, ELIZABETH, *Family and Social Network* (London, 1957).

BOURRICAUD, FRANÇOIS, *Esquisse d'une Théorie de l'Autorité* (Paris, 1961).

BOWLEY, A. L., and BURNETT-HURST, A. R., *Livelihood and Poverty* (London, 1915).

BOWLEY, MARIAN, *Housing and the State* (London, 1945).

BRAITHWAITE, R. B., *The Theory of Games as a Tool for the Moral Philosopher* (Cambridge, 1955).

References

BRIGGS, ASA, 'The Social Background', in A. Flanders and H. A. Clegg eds., *Industrial Relations in Great Britain* (Oxford, 1954).
——, 'The Welfare State in Historical Perspective', *Archives Européennes de Sociologie* II (1961).
BRYCE, LORD, *The American Commonwealth* (2nd edn.; New York, 1910).
BUCHANAN, J. M. and TULLOCK, G., *The Calculus of Consent* (Ann Arbor, 1962).
BULLOCK, ALAN, *The Life and Times of Ernest Bevin* (London, 1960) I.
BUTLER, D. E., *The British General Election of 1951* (London, 1952).
——, *The Electoral System in Britain, 1918-51* (Oxford, 1953).
——, *The British General Election of 1955* (London, 1955).
——, and ROSE, RICHARD, *The British General Election of 1959* (London, 1960).
CARR-SAUNDERS, A. M., and JONES, D. CARADOG, *A Survey of the Social Structure of England and Wales* (2nd edn.; Oxford, 1937).
——, et al., *A Survey of Social Conditions in England and Wales as Illustrated by Statistics* (Oxford, 1958).
CENTERS, R., *The Psychology of Social Class* (Princeton, 1949).
CHAPMAN, DWIGHT W., and VOLKMANN, JOHN, 'A Social Determinant of the Level of Aspiration', in Eleanor E. Maccoby *et al.*, eds., *Readings in Social Psychology* (3rd edn.; London, 1959).
CHAPMAN, JOHN W., 'Justice and Fairness', *Nomos* VI (1963).
CHAPMAN, S. J., and MARQUIS, F. J., 'The Recruiting of the Employing Classes from the Ranks of the Wage Earners in the Cotton Industry', *Journal of the Royal Statistical Society* LXXV (1912).
CHARTERS, W. W., JNR., and NEWCOMB, THEODORE M., 'Some Attitudinal Effects of Experimentally Increased Salience of a Membership Group', in Eleanor E. Maccoby *et al.*, eds., *Readings in Social Psychology* (3rd edn.; London, 1959).
CHINOY, ELY, *Automobile Workers and the American Dream* (Garden City, N.Y., 1955).
CLARK, COLIN, *National Income and Outlay* (London, 1937).
CLEGG, H. A., *A New Approach to Industrial Democracy* (Oxford, 1960).
——, 'The Scope of Fair Wage Comparisons', *Journal of Industrial Economics* IX (1961).
CLEMENTS, R. V., *Managers: a Study of their Careers in Industry* (London, 1958).
COLE, DOROTHY, with UTTING, J., *The Economic Circumstances of Old People* (London, 1962).
COLE, G. D. H., *British Trade Unionism Today* (London, 1939).
——, and COLE, M. I., *The Condition of Britain* (London, 1937).
COLLISON, PETER. *The Cutteslowe Walls* (London, 1963).
Committee on Finance and Industry, 1931 (Macmillan Committee), *Minutes of Evidence.*
CROOK, W. H., *The General Strike* (Chapel Hill, 1931).
DAHL, R. A., *Who Governs?* (New Haven, 1961).
DAHRENDORF, RALF, *Class and Class Conflict in an Industrial Society* (Stanford, 1959).

References

Daily Herald.

DALE, J. R., *The Clerk in Industry* (Liverpool, 1962).

DANGERFIELD, GEORGE, *The Strange Death of Liberal England* (London, 1935).

DAVIS, JAMES A., 'A Formal Interpretation of the Theory of Relative Deprivation', *Sociometry* XXII (1959).

DAVISON, R. C., *British Unemployment Policy since 1930* (London, 1938).

DENNIS, N., et al., *Coal is Our Life* (London, 1956).

DENT, H. C., *Education in Transition* (London, 1944).

DURANT, RUTH, *Watling: a Social Survey* (London, 1939).

DURBIN, E. M. F., *The Politics of Democratic Socialism* (London, 1940).

DURKHEIM, EMILE, *Socialism and Saint-Simon* (ed. Gouldner; London, 1959).

The Economist.

EISENSTADT, S. M., 'Studies in Reference Group Behavior, I: Norms and the Social Structure', *Human Relations* VII (1954).

EMPEY, L. T., 'Social Class and Occupational Aspiration: A Comparison of Absolute and Relative Measurement', *American Sociological Review* XXI (1956).

FLANDERS, ALLAN, *The Fawley Productivity Agreements* (London, 1964).

FLOUD, JEAN, 'The Educational Experience of the Adult Population of England and Wales as at July 1949', in D. V. Glass, ed., *Social Mobility in Britain* (London, 1954).

——, et al., *Social Class and Educational Opportunity* (London, 1957).

FULFORD, ROGER, *Votes for Women* (London, 1957).

GALLIE, W. B., 'Liberal Morality and Socialist Morality', in P. Laslett, ed., *Philosophy, Politics and Society* (Oxford, 1956).

General Register Office, *Classification of Occupations, 1960.*

GLASS, D. V., 'Education', in M. Ginsberg, ed., *Law and Opinion in 20th Century England* (London, 1959).

GLEASON, A., *What the Workers Want* (New York, 1920).

GOLDTHORPE, J. H., and LOCKWOOD, DAVID, 'Affluence and the British Class Structure', *Sociological Review* n.s. XI (1963).

GORDON, MILTON M., *Social Class in American Sociology* (Durham, N.C., 1958).

GRAUBARD, S. R., *British Labour and the Russian Revolution, 1917-1924* (Cambridge, Mass., 1956).

GRIGG, P. J., *Prejudice and Judgement* (London, 1948).

HALÉVY, ELIE, *A History of the English People in the Nineteenth Century, VI: The Rule of Democracy 1905-14* (London, 1952).

HAMILTON, M. A., *Arthur Henderson* (London, 1938).

HANNINGTON, W., *Unemployed Struggles 1919-1936* (London, 1936).

HARE, R. M., *Freedom and Reason* (London, 1963).

HARRISON, M., *Trade Unions and the Labour Party since 1945* (London, 1960).

HART, H. L. A., *The Concept of Law* (London, 1961).

HILL, T. P., 'Incomes, Savings and Net Worth—the Savings Surveys of 1952-54', *Bulletin of the Oxford University Institute of Statistics* XVII (1955).

References

HILTON, JOHN, *Rich Man, Poor Man* (London, 1944).

HIMMELWEIT, H. T., 'Social Status and Secondary Education Since the 1944 Act: Some Data for London', in D. V. Glass, ed., *Social Mobility in Britain* (London, 1954).

HOGGART, RICHARD, *The Uses of Literacy* (London, 1957).

HUTCHINSON, B., *Willesden and the New Towns* (Social Survey; London, 1947).

HUTT, A., *The Condition of the Working Class in Britain* (London, 1933).

HYMAN, H. H., 'The Psychology of Status', *Archives of Psychology* No. 269 (New York, 1942).

——, 'The Value Systems of Different Classes', in R. Bendix and S. M. Lipset, eds., *Class, Status and Power* (Glencoe, Ill., 1953).

——, 'Reflections on Reference Groups', *Public Opinion Quarterly* XXIV (1960).

Industrial Welfare Society, *Holidays—Current Practices and Trends* (1963).

INKELES, A., and ROSSI, PETER H., 'National Comparisons of Occupational Prestige', *American Journal of Sociology* LXI (1956).

Inns of Court Conservative and Unionist Society, *A Giant's Strength* (London, 1958).

Institute of Office Management, *Clerical Salaries Analysis, 1962*.

International Labour Organization (ILO), 'Dismissal Procedures—V: United Kingdom', *International Labour Review* LXXX (1959).

JACKSON, BRIAN, and MARSDEN, DENNIS, *Education and the Working Class* (London, 1962).

JACKSON, ELTON F., 'Status Inconsistency and Symptoms of Stress', *American Sociological Review* XXVII (1962).

JENNINGS, HILDA, *Bryn Mawr* (London, 1934).

JEVONS, R., and MADGE, J., *Housing Estates* (Bristol, 1946).

JONES, D. CARADOG, ed., *A Social Survey of Merseyside* (Liverpool, 1934).

KAPLAN, NORMAN, 'Reference Group Theory and Voting Behavior' (abstract of Ph.D. thesis, Columbia University, 1955), *Dissertation Abstracts* XV (1955).

KELLER, SUZANNE, and ZAVALLONI, M., 'Classe Sociale, Ambition et Réussite', *Sociologie du Travail* IV (1962).

KELLY, H. H., 'Two Functions of Reference Groups', in G. H. Swanson *et al.*, *Readings in Social Psychology* (2nd edn.; New York, 1952).

KERR, M., *The People of Ship Street* (London, 1958).

KEYNES, J. M., *The Economic Consequences of the Peace* (London, 1919).

KIRKWOOD, DAVID, *My Life of Revolt* (London, 1935).

KLEIN, L. R., *et al.*, 'Savings and Finance of the Upper Income Classes', *Bulletin of the Oxford University Institute of Statistics* XVIII (1956).

KLINGENDER, F. D., *The Condition of Clerical Labour in Britain* (London, 1935).

KNIGHT, R. E. L., 'Unionism among Retail Clerks in Post-War Britain', *Industrial and Labour Relations Review* XIV (1961).

KNOWLES, K. G. J. C., *Strikes* (Oxford, 1952).

——, and ROBERTSON, D. J., 'Differences between the Wages of Skilled and Unskilled Workers, 1880-1950', *Bulletin of the Oxford University Institute of Statistics* XIII (1951).

References

KORNHAUSER, A., *et al.*, *How Labour Votes* (New York, 1956).

KUPER, L., ed., *Living in Towns* (London, 1953).

Labour Party Conference, *Annual Reports*.

LANE, ROBERT E., 'The Fear of Equality', *American Political Science Review* LIII (1959).

LAZARSFELD, P. F., *et al.*, *The People's Choice* (New York, 1944).

LENSKI, GERHARD E., 'Status Crystallisation: a Non-Vertical Dimension of Social Status', *American Sociological Review* XIX (1954).

LEWIS, R. and MAUDE, A., *The English Middle Classes* (London, 1949).

LINDSAY, KENNETH, *Social Progress and Educational Waste* (London, 1926).

LIPSET, S. M., 'Must Tories Always Triumph?', *Socialist Commentary* (November, 1960).

——, and BENDIX, R., *Social Mobility in Industrial Society* (Berkeley, Calif., 1959).

Liverpool University, *Neighbourhood and Community* (Liverpool, 1954).

——, *The Dockworker* (Liverpool, 1954).

LOCKWOOD, DAVID, *The Blackcoated Worker* (London, 1958).

——, 'The New Working Class', *Archives Européennes de Sociologie* I (1960).

LOWNDES, G. A. N., *The Silent Social Revolution: an Account of the Expansion of Public Education in England and Wales, 1895-1935* (London, 1937).

LYDALL, H. F., 'The Long-Term Trend in the Size Distribution of Income', *Journal of the Royal Statistical Society* CXXII (1959) I.

——, and TIPPING, G. D., 'The Distribution of Personal Wealth in Britain', *Bulletin of the Oxford University Institute of Statistics* XXIII (1961).

LYMAN, R. W., *The First Labour Government, 1924* (London, 1958).

MCALLISTER, G., *James Maxton* (London, 1935).

MCCALLUM, R. B., and READMAN, A., *The British General Election of 1945* (London, 1947).

MCCARTHY, W., 'The Future of the Unions', *Fabian Tract No. 339* (1962).

MACDONALD, J. R., *A Policy for the Labour Party* (London, 1920).

MCKENZIE, R. T., *British Political Parties* (London, 1955).

——, 'Bagehot and "The Rule of Mere Numbers" ', *Listener* (November, 1959).

——, and SILVER, A., 'Conservatism, Industrialism and the Working-Class Tory in England' (paper read at the Fifth World Congress of the International Sociological Association; Washington, D.C., 1962).

MACMILLAN, H., *The Middle Way* (London, 1938).

Manchester University, *Readjustment in Lancashire* (Manchester, 1936).

MANIS, J. G., and MELTZER, B. N., 'Attitudes of Textile Workers to Class Structure', *American Journal of Sociology* LX (1954).

MARSHALL, T. H., *Citizenship and Social Class* (Cambridge, 1950).

MARTIN, F. M., 'Some Subjective Aspects of Social Stratification', in D. V. Glass, ed., *Social Mobility in Britain* (London, 1954).

MARX, KARL, *Economic and Philosophic Manuscripts of 1844* (London, 1961).

——, and ENGELS, FREDERICK, *Communist Manifesto* (London, 1930).

326

References

MASTERMAN, C. F. G., *The Condition of England* (London, 1909).
——, *England After War* (London, 1922).
MERTON, R. K., *Social Theory and Social Structure* (rev. edn.; Glencoe, Ill., 1957).
MILL, J. S., *Essays on Politics and Culture* (ed. Gertrude Himmelfarb; New York, 1963).
MILLIBAND, R., *Parliamentary Socialism* (London, 1961).
MILNE, R. S., and MACKENZIE, H. C., *Straight Fight* (London, 1954).
——, and MACKENZIE, H. C., *Marginal Seat* (London, 1958).
Ministry of Education, *Early Leaving* (1954).
——, *15-18: A Report of the Central Advisory Council for Education (England), 1962* (Crowther Report).
Ministry of Labour, *Annual Reports*.
——, *Gazette*.
——, *Report on National Unemployment Insurance to July, 1923* (1923).
MOGEY, J. M., *Family and Neighbourhood* (Oxford, 1956).
MOWAT, C. L., *Britain Between the Wars* (London, 1955).
MULLALLY, FREDERIC, *Fascism Inside England* (London, 1946).
New Survey of London Life and Labour (London, 1930-35).
New Town Committee, *Final Report* (1946).
NEWCOMB, THEODORE M., *Social Psychology* (New York, 1950).
NICHOLAS, H. G., *The British General Election of 1950* (London, 1951).
NICHOLSON, J. H., *New Communities in Britain* (London, 1961).
NORWOOD, C., *The English Tradition of Education* (London, 1929).
OESER, O. A., and HAMMOND, S. B., *Social Structure and Personality in a City* (London, 1954).
ORLANS, H., *Stevenage: a Sociological Study of a New Town* (London, 1952).
ORWELL, GEORGE, *Inside the Whale* (London, 1940).
——, *England Your England and Other Essays* (London, 1954).
OSBORN, F. J., *Green-Belt Cities* (London, 1946).
PARETO, V., *The Mind and Society* (ed. Livingston; London, 1935).
Parliamentary Debates (Hansard).
PATON, J., *Left Turn* (London, 1936).
PELLING, HENRY, *The Origins of the Labour Party 1880-1900* (London, 1953).
——, *The British Communist Party* (London, 1958).
PERELMAN, CH., *The Idea of Justice and the Problem of Argument* (London, 1963).
Pilgrim Trust, *Men Without Work* (Cambridge, 1938).
Political and Economic Planning (PEP), 'Poverty: Ten Years after Beveridge', *Planning* XIX (1952-3).
——, 'Trade Union Membership', *Planning* XXVIII (1962).
POLLOCK, J. K., *et al.*, *British Election Studies, 1950* (Ann Arbor, 1951).
POPITZ, H., *et al.*, *Das Gesellschaftsbild des Arbeiters* (2nd edn.; Tübingen, 1961).
PREST, A. R., 'National Income of the United Kingdom 1870-1946', *Economic Journal* LVIII (1948).
PRIESTLEY, J. B., *English Journey* (London, 1934).

References

Punch.

RAMSBOTTOM, E. C., 'The Course of Wage Rates in the United Kingdom, 1921-1934', *Journal of the Royal Statistical Society* XCVIII (1935).

RAPHAEL, D. D., 'Conservative and Prosthetic Justice', *Political Studies* XII (1964).

RAWLS, JOHN, 'Two Concepts of Rules', *Philosophical Review* LXIV (1955).

——, 'Justice as Fairness', *Philosophical Review* LXVII (1958).

——, 'Constitutional Liberty and the Concept of Justice', *Nomos* VI (1963).

——, 'The Sense of Justice', *Philosophical Review* LXXII (1963).

——, 'Distributive Justice' (unpublished).

The Record.

Red Tape.

REISSMANN, LEONARD, 'Levels of Aspiration and Social Class', *American Sociological Review* XVIII (1953).

Report of the Consultative Committee on Secondary Education, 1938 (Spens Report).

Report of Provisional Joint Committee Presented to Meeting of Industrial Conference, 1919 (1920).

Report of the Transport Workers' Court of Enquiry, 1920 (Shaw Enquiry).

Report on the Post-War Organization of Private Domestic Service (1945).

Report on Social Insurance and the Allied Services, 1942 (Beveridge Report).

ROWNTREE, B. SEEBOHM, *Poverty* (London, 1901).

——, *Poverty* (rev. edn.; London, 1922).

——, *Poverty and Progress* (London, 1941).

Royal Commission on the Civil Service, 1929-31, *Report.*

——, 1953-5, *Minutes of Evidence.*

Royal Commission on the Taxation of Profits and Income, *Second Report* (1954).

——, *Final Report* (1955).

——, *Minutes of Evidence.*

RUBNER, A., *Fringe Benefits: the Golden Chains* (London, 1962).

RUNCIMAN, W. G., '*Embourgoisement*, Self-rated Class and Party Preference', *Sociological Review* n.s. XII (1964).

——, and SEN, A. K., 'Games, Justice and the General Will', *Mind* n.s. LXXIV (1965).

SARTORI, GIOVANNI, *Democratic Theory* (Detroit, 1962).

SAVILLE, J., 'Trade Unions and Free Labour; the Background to the Taff Vale Decision', in A. Briggs and J. Saville, eds., *Essays in Labour History* (London, 1960).

SCHUMPETER, JOSEPH, *Imperialism and Social Classes* (New York, 1955).

SHIBUTANI, T.. 'Reference Groups as Perspectives', *American Journal of Sociology* LX (1955).

SNOWDEN, P. *Autobiography* (London, 1934).

Socialist Review.

STACEY, MARGARET *Tradition and Change: a Study of Banbury* (London, 1960).

Statistical Abstract for the U.K., 1924-38.

STERN, ERIC and KELLER, SUZANNE, 'Spontaneous Group References in France', *Public Opinion Quarterly* XVII (1953).

STOUFFER, SAMUEL A., *et al.*, *The American Soldier, I: Adjustment During Army Life* (Princeton, 1949).

References

STRAW, K. H., 'Consumers' Net Worth: the 1953 Savings Survey', *Bulletin of the Oxford University Institute of Statistics* XVIII (1956).

TAWNEY, R. H., 'The Abolition of Economic Controls, 1918-1921', *Economic History Review* XIII (1943).

——, *Equality* (rev. edn.; London, 1952).

——, *The Radical Tradition* (ed. Rita Hinden; London, 1964).

Third Winter of Unemployment (London, 1923).

THOMAS, J. H., *When Labour Rules* (London, 1920).

The Times.

TISSET, P., 'Les Notions de Droit et de Justice', *Revue de Métaphysique et de Morale* XXXVII (1930).

TITMUSS, RICHARD M., *Problems of Social Policy* (London, 1950).

——, *Essays on The Welfare State* (London, 1958).

——, *Income Distribution and Social Change* (London, 1962).

TOCQUEVILLE, A. de, *The Old Regime and the French Revolution* (Garden City N.Y., 1955).

TOUT, H., *The Standard of Living in Bristol* (Bristol, 1938).

TOWNSEND, PETER, 'The Meaning of Poverty', *British Journal of Sociology* XIII (1962).

Trades Union Congress, *Annual Reports.*

TURNER, RALPH H., 'Role-taking, Role Standpoint and Reference Group Behavior', *American Journal of Sociology* LXI (1956).

VLASTOS, G., 'Justice and Equality', in R. B. Brandt, ed., *Social Justice* (Englewood Cliffs, N.J., 1962).

WASON, C. R., *Busman's View* (London, 1958).

WEBB, BEATRICE, *Diaries, 1912-24* (ed. M. I. Cole; London, 1952).

——, *Diaries, 1924-32* (ed. M. I. Cole; London, 1956).

WEBER, MAX, *From Max Weber* (ed. H. H. Gerth and C. Wright Mills; New York, 1947).

WEDDERBURN, DOROTHY COLE, 'Poverty in Britain Today—the Evidence', *Sociological Review* n.s. X (1962).

WERTHEIMER, E., *Portrait of the Labour Party* (2nd edn.; London, 1930).

WHEELER-BENNET, J. W., *George VI* (London, 1958).

WILLCOCKS, A. J., 'The Means Test', *Sociological Review* n.s. V (1957).

WILLENER, A., *Images de la Société et Classes Sociales* (Berne, 1957).

WILLIAMS, W. M., *Gosforth: The Sociology of an English Village* (London, 1956).

WILLMOTT, PETER, *The Evolution of a Community* (London, 1963).

——, and YOUNG, MICHAEL, *Family and Class in a London Suburb* (London, 1960).

WITTGENSTEIN, LUDWIG, *Philosophical Investigations* (2nd edn.; Oxford, 1958).

WOLLHEIM, RICHARD, 'Equality and Equal Rights', *Proceedings of the Aristotelian Society* LVI (1955-56).

WOODCOCK, GEORGE, 'The Trade Unions and Public Opinion', *Listener* (July, 1959).

WOOTTON, BARBARA, *The Social Foundations of Wage Policy* (London, 1955).

References

Young, G. M., *Stanley Baldwin* (London, 1952).

Young, Michael, *The Rise of the Meritocracy 1870-2033* (London, 1958).

——, and Willmott, Peter, 'Social Grading by Manual Workers', *British Journal of Sociology* VII (1956).

——, and Willmott, Peter, *Family and Kinship in East London* (London, 1957).

Zweig, F., *Labour, Life and Poverty* (London, 1948).

——, *The British Worker* (London, 1952).

——, *The Worker in an Affluent Society* (London, 1961).

INDEX

Abrams, Mark, 49n, 76n, 91n, 164n
acquiesence, in inequality, 3, 25; and Conservatism in politics, 144
age: and aspiration, 28f; and class, self-assigned, 167; and political preference, 172, 178; and poverty, 190
Agricultural Wages (Regulation) Act (1924), 92
agricultural workers, and insurance, 71
Allen, V. L., 128n; and Williams, S., 133n
ambitions, deviant, 27f
amenities at work, manual/non-manual, 83
America, *see* United States
anarchy, and social justice, 258f
Anderson, Sir John, 78
anomie, 22
Aristotle, 36, 37, 203, 258n
Arrow, K. J., 250n, 253n
Askwith, Sir George [Lord], 57
aspiration: and age, 28f; and inequality; 25ff; of Labour and employers in 1919, 58
Asquith, H. H. [Earl of Oxford and Asquith], 56, 104
assets, personal and class, 88
Assistance, National, extent of, 89
Attlee, C. R. [Earl], 90, 100f, 106, 133, 138n

Babeuf, F. N., 266
Bacon Industry Act (1938), 92
Bagehot, Walter, 144, 147
Bakke, E. Wight, 64
Baldwin, Stanley [Earl], 99, 123, 124, 141, 279
Banbury, 143
Bank Officer, 115, 116n, 130n
Banks, O., 110n
Barna, T., 72n, 108n
Barnes, George, 105
Barton, A. H., 23
Baumol, W. J., 249n
Bedwellty, 66
Benney, M., *et al.*, 172n, 173n
Berger, B. M., 51n
Berlin, Isaiah, 292n
Bethnal Green, 114

Beveridge Report, 61, 73n, 78, 79, 131
Bevin, Ernest, 25, 57, 63, 98, 104, 106, 122, 128
Birch, A. H., 143, 170n, 172n, 173n
Birch *v*. National Union of Railwaymen, 132
Birmingham, 143
Braithwaite, R. B., 253n
Black Friday, 122, 125
Blanc, Louis, 266
Bonham, John, 138n, 139n
Bonsor *v*. Musicans' Union, 132
Bott, Elizabeth, 43n
Bourricaud, François, 288n
Bowley, A. L., 73; and Burnett-Hurst, A. R., 74n
Bowley, Marian, 76n
Briggs, Asa, 60n, 77f
Bristol, 114
British Broadcasting Corporation, 103
British Institute of Public Opinion, 139
British Sugar (Subsidy) Act (1925), 92
Brockway, Fenner [Lord], 62
Bryce, Lord, 37n, 39, 275n, 289
Buchanan, J. M., and Tullock, G., 253n
Bullock, Alan, 62n
Burke, Edmund, 287
busmen, London, 64, 65n
Butler, D. E., 127n, 139, 141n; and Rose, R., 139, 140n

Carr-Saunders, A. M., *et al.*, 83n, 108n; and Jones, D. C., 109·
Castle, Barbara, 87n
Centers, R., 43n
Central Advisory Council for Education, Report (1962), *see* Crowther Report
Chamberlain, Neville, 65, 66, 68, 106
change: economic, and reference groups, 25; in political allegiance, 179, 182ff
Chapman, D. W., and Volkmann, J., 16n, 17
Chapman, J. W., 254n
Chapman, S. J., and Marquis, F. J., 84n